EXCESS AND TRANSGRESSION IN SIMONE DE BEAUVOIR'S FICTION

For Cairine

Excess and Transgression in Simone de Beauvoir's Fiction

The Discourse of Madness

ALISON HOLLAND
Northumbria University, UK

ASHGATE

Published by
Ashgate Publishing Limited
Wey Court East
Union Road
Farnham
Surrey, GU9 7PT
England

Ashgate Publishing Company
Suite 420
101 Cherry Street
Burlington
VT 05401-4405
USA

www.ashgate.com

British Library Cataloguing in Publication Data
Holland, Alison
Excess and transgression in Simone de Beauvoir's fiction: the discourse of madness
    1. Beauvoir, Simone de, 1908–1986 – Fictional works 2. Mental illness in literature
    3. Emotions in literature
    I. Title
    843.9'12

Library of Congress Cataloging-in-Publication Data
Holland, Alison.
    Excess and transgression in Simone de Beauvoir's fiction: the discourse of madness / by Alison Holland.
      p. cm.
    Includes bibliographical references and index.
    ISBN 978-0-7546-5152-9 (alk. paper)
    1. Beauvoir, Simone de, 1908–1986—Fictional works. I. Title.

PQ2603.E362Z719 2009
843'.914—dc22

    2008042591

ISBN: 978-0-7546-5152-9

Mixed Sources
Product group from well-managed forests and other controlled sources
www.fsc.org Cert no. SGS-COC-2482
© 1996 Forest Stewardship Council

Printed and bound in Great Britain by
TJ International Ltd, Padstow, Cornwall

Contents

Acknowledgements

I thank Northumbria University and especially my colleagues in the School of Arts and Social Sciences for their generous support during the writing of this book. In particular, I have greatly appreciated the insights into French grammar that Ariane Bogain has shared with me.

Special thanks are also due to Elizabeth Fallaize, Sarah Fishwick, and Ursula Tidd. I am very grateful to them for their valuable comments on earlier drafts of individual chapters. Since I first started writing on Simone de Beauvoir, Elizabeth Fallaize has been consistently supportive of my work, and I have benefitted enormously from her encouragement and generosity.

Several sections of this book have been previously published. Sections of Chapter 1 appeared in 'Mirrored Characters in Simone de Beauvoir's *L'Invitée*: Françoise and Élisabeth' in *Simone de Beauvoir Studies*, 17 (2000–2001), 89–97, and in 'Identity in Crisis: The Gothic Textual Space in *L'Invitée*,' *Modern Language Review*, Vol. 98 (April 2003), 327–34. My contribution to the international conference held in Paris in January 2008 to celebrate the centenary of Simone de Beauvoir's birth is a version in French of part of Chapter 2 and appeared as 'La Voix chancelante dans le monologue intérieur de Anne dans *Les Mandarins* de Simone de Beauvoir' in *(Re)découvrir L'Oeuvre de Simone de Beauvoir: Du 'Deuxième Sexe' à 'La cérémonie des adieux,'* Sous la direction de Julia Kristeva, Paris: éditions Le Bord de L'eau, 2008. In Chapters 3 and 4, I have used material from 'The Quest for Identity in the Later Fiction of Simone de Beauvoir' in *Women in Contemporary Culture: Roles and Identities in France and Spain*, ed. Lesley Twomey (Bristol: Intellect, 2000), pp. 151–70. Chapter 3 also includes material from 'Simone de Beauvoir's Writing Practice: Madness, Enumeration and Repetition in *Les Belles Images*' in: *Simone de Beauvoir Studies*, 15 (1998–1999), 113–25. I gratefully acknowledge permission to republish this material.

The cover image, Jean Dubuffet, *Conjugaison*, 1949, is reproduced courtesy of Centre Georges Pompidou, Paris.

Finally, I thank my family and friends for the interest they have shown in this project and for their unfailing patience when it took me away from them; without their loving support this book would not have been possible.

Key to Abbreviations

Page references to frequently quoted texts by Beauvoir appear in brackets in the text preceded by the abbreviations below. 'ta' means translation ammended. The editions used are those listed in the Bibilography.

AD	'L'Age de discrétion'
AMM	*All Men are Mortal*
ASD	*All Said and Done*
BI	*Les Belles Images* (French)
BO	*The Blood of Others*
DSi	*Le Deuxième Sexe*, vol. 1
DSii	*Le Deuxième Sexe*, vol. 2
FA	*La Force de l'âge*
FCi	*La Force des choses*, vol. 1
FCii	*La Force des choses*, vol. 2
FOC	*Force of Circumstance*
FR	*La Femme rompue*
I	*L'Invitée*
LBI	*Les Belles Images* (English)
LFR	'La Femme rompue'
LMi	*Les Mandarins*, vol. 1
LMii	*Les Mandarins*, vol. 2
M	*The Mandarins*
MDD	*Memoirs of a Dutiful Daughter*
MJF	*Mémoires d'une jeune fille rangée*

MO   'Monologue'

PL   *The Prime of Life*

QPS   *Quand Prime le Spirituel*

SA   *Le Sang des autres*

SCS   *She Came to Stay*

SS   *The Second Sex*

TAD   'The Age of Discretion'

TCF   *Tout Compte fait*

TH   *Tous les Hommes sont mortels*

TMO   'The Monologue'

TWD   'The Woman Destroyed'

WD   *The Woman Destroyed*

WTS   *When Things of the Spirit Come First*

Introduction

This study of Beauvoir's fiction focuses on her writing practice, on her textual strategies. I examine *how* she tells the stories she tells and intend to demonstrate that madness is an intrinsic quality of the text, of the very telling of the stories. I use the term *madness* metaphorically to designate those qualities that unsettle meaning. Madness is a useful conceit that encompasses interalia excess, transgression, instability, disruption, and incoherence.[1] My centre of interest is not the theme of madness in the fiction. What interests me is the way textual strategies duplicate madness in the text, the way the text structures an experience of madness (for readers) that is not locatable in any one character but is an effect of the text as a whole. I read madness metaphorically as an intrinsic quality of the texts. This is not to say that the texts per se are 'mad.'[2]

I must also underline, given the historical connection between women and madness in our patriarchal culture, that I do not wish to suggest that Beauvoir was 'mad' or to seek to devalue her work by doing so. I do not believe that my locating signs of madness in the text need be interpreted in this way. It is widely recognised that throughout history, women who have resisted patriarchal authority have been defined as mad and silenced.[3] This is pointed out by Alice Jardine, who argues that women writers are less willing to experiment in a radical way with existing literary conventions and relates women's 'respect for form' precisely to women's having been 'closer to all possible transgressions.' As she puts it, 'one fatal step

---

[1]   Madness is one of a number of possible ways of approaching this cluster of qualities in Beauvoir's fiction. They have also been associated with the feminine and the avant garde.

[2]   I do not intend to psychoanalyse the texts or Beauvoir or, for that matter, her characters.

[3]   See Phyllis Chesler, *Women and Madness*, New York: Avon, 1972. She describes the relationship between the female condition and madness, showing how both women who fully act out the conditioned female role and those who reject or are ambivalent about the female role are defined as mad (p. 56). 'The ethic of mental health is masculine in our culture,'she argues (p. 69). See also Elaine Showalter, *The Female Malady: Women, Madness and English Culture, 1830–1980*, London: Virago, 1987; and Martha Noel Evans, *Fits and Starts: A Genealogy of Hysteria in Modern France*, New York: Cornell University Press, 1991. During a discussion about the antipsychiatry movement in an interview with Alice Jardine, Beauvoir said: 'Given masculine norms, it is clear that women are more likely to be considered crazy – I'm not saying to be crazy. [...] It's terrible this tendency to consider women something dangerous to society ... but, truthfully speaking they are dangerous, even those who aren't feminists, because there has always been a women's revolt.' Jardine, Alice, 'Interview with Beauvoir,' *Signs*, Winter, 1979, 224–36, p. 229.

outside of symbolic pre-scriptions and [they are] designated as mad.'[4] In a sense, in reading transgression and resistance in Beauvoir's fiction as signs of madness, I am reappropriating madness as a positive force within the text.[5]

On the whole, Beauvoir's fiction in general and her writing practice in particular have been neglected, a fact that has not gone unnoticed. The position has changed little since 1987, when Elaine Marks edited a collection of critical essays on Beauvoir's work. In the introduction to the collection, she tells us that 'during the forty-five years in which Beauvoir has been written about in newspapers, literary magazines, women's magazines, scholarly journals, and specifically feminist journals and books, the major emphasis has been on her autobiographical writings and on her substantial essays on women and old age.'[6] She identifies a need for more work on close textual analyses (p. 11). Elizabeth Fallaize points out that 'the majority of the studies dealing with the fictional work have given at least as much attention to her essays and/or autobiographical writings.'[7] She adds that studies that deal with the fiction tend to focus on theme and content, rather to the exclusion of a consideration of form (p. 3). Likewise, Toril Moi regrets that little attention has been paid to the style of Beauvoir's writing.[8]

This present study of Beauvoir is positioned precisely in this 'gap' where fiction and form intersect. My own readings, however, have not emerged in a vacuum. They are intended not to silence other interpretations but to exist in dialogue with them, for Beauvoir's complex and ambiguous texts generate multiple readings, none of which is definitive or exclusive. With this in mind, it will be useful to consider the current state of Beauvoir criticism before going on to examine the relationship between madness and the text in detail.

Toril Moi provides a useful overview of full-length studies on Beauvoir published in French and English from 1958 to 1992.[9] She divides the studies into

---

[4]   Alice Jardine, 'Pre-texts for the Transatlantic Feminist,' *Yale French Studies*, 62, 1981, 220–36 (pp. 232–3).

[5]   In so doing, I do not wish to glamorise madness itself. As Elaine Showalter says, interpreting madness as a form of feminist protest comes 'dangerously close to romanticizing and endorsing madness as a desirable form of rebellion rather than seeing it as the desperate communication of the powerless' (*The Female Malady*, p. 5). Moreover, whilst my study does not specifically interrogate gender as a factor of the production of Beauvoir's texts, this nevertheless forms the context of the discussion.

[6]   Elaine Marks, 'Introduction,' in *Critical Essays on Simone de Beauvoir*, ed. by Elaine Marks, Boston, Massachusetts: G.K. Hall, 1987, p. 8. This book is a case in point. Only two of the contributions deal with the fiction. In 'Metaphysics and the Novel,' Maurice Merleau-Ponty offers a reading of *L'Invitée* (pp. 31–44) and in 'Psychiatry in the Postwar Fiction of Beauvoir,' Terry Keefe examines *Les Mandarins*, *La Femme rompue* and *Les Belles Images* (pp. 131–44).

[7]   Elizabeth Fallaize, *The Novels of Simone de Beauvoir*, London: Routledge, 1988, p. 2.

[8]   Toril Moi, *Simone de Beauvoir: The Making of an Intellectual Woman*, Oxford: Blackwell, 1994. See, for example, footnote 16, p. 269.

[9]   Moi, *Simone de Beauvoir*, footnote 8, pp. 267–8.

'impressionistic' categories: catholic, existentialist/socialist, scholarly, popular, and feminist. Between 1980 (when Beauvoir studies shifted away from France) and 1992, twenty-one studies were published. Five of these were 'scholarly,' six were 'popular,' and ten were 'feminist.' Of these studies, only two were dedicated to Beauvoir's fiction, one 'scholarly' and one 'feminist.'[10] Five books look at the fiction in the context of Beauvoir's writings as a whole.[11] Jane Heath's feminist study reads *L'Invitée, Les Mandarins,* and *Les Belles Images* together with the autobiographies, according to Toril Moi, in an attempt to 'rescue Beauvoir for poststructuralist feminism'(p. 77).[12] Other studies whose concerns are political or philosophical examine the fiction to a much lesser extent.[13]

Since 1992, just three of the major studies of Beauvoir that have been published focus exclusively on the fiction. Terry Keefe's book, *Simone de Beauvoir*, examines each of Beauvoir's novels and short stories in turn.[14] Genevieve Shepherd rereads the whole of Beauvoir's fictional output using Freudian and Lacanian psychoanalysis as critical lenses.[15] In *Simone de Beauvoir's Fiction: Women and Language*, each of the essays addresses the form of Beauvoir's fiction.[16] The writers examine Beauvoir's use of language in her texts, especially the relationship between women and language. A number of other recent studies, written by philosophy specialists rather than by literary specialists, look at the fiction – to a greater or lesser extent – in the context of Beauvoir's philosophy. *Philosophy as Passion: The Thinking of Simone de Beauvoir*, focuses on Beauvoir's ethics and includes an analysis of *Les Mandarins* as well as an overview of the philosophical ideas in Beauvoir's fiction as a whole.[17] Edward and Kate Fullbrook explore what they refer to as Beauvoir's

---

[10] They are Françoise Arnaud Hibbs, *L'Espace dans les romans de Simone de Beauvoir: son expression et sa fonction*, Stanford French and Italian Studies 59, Saratoga, California: Anma Libri, 1989 ('scholarly'); Fallaize, *The Novels* ('feminist').

[11] They are Carol Ascher, *Simone de Beauvoir: A Life of Freedom,* Boston: Beacon Press, 1981, a feminist study described by Toril Moi as verging on the adulatory; Terry Keefe, *Simone de Beauvoir: A Study of her Writings*, London: Harrap, 1983; Elaine Marks, ed., *Critical Essays on Simone de Beauvoir*; Catherine Savage Brosman, *Simone de Beauvoir Revisited*, Twayne's World Authors Series 820, Boston: Twayne, 1991. Moi classifies these three studies as 'scholarly.' The fifth study, this one in Moi's 'popular'category, is Renée Winegarten, *Simone de Beauvoir: A Critical View*, Oxford: Berg, 1988.

[12] Jane Heath, *Simone de Beauvoir*, London: Harvester Wheatsheaf, 1989.

[13] For example, Mary Evans, *Simone de Beauvoir: A Feminist Mandarin*, London: Tavistock, 1985; Judith Okely, *Simone de Beauvoir*, London: Virago, 1986. See also Margaret A. Simons, ed., *Feminist Interpretations of Simone de Beauvoir*, Pennsylvania: The Pennsylvania State University Press, 1995.

[14] Terry Keefe, *Simone de Beauvoir*, Basingstoke: Macmillan, 1998.

[15] Genevieve Shepherd, *Simone de Beauvoir's Fiction: A Psychoanalytic Rereading*, Oxford: Peter Lang, 2003.

[16] Alison T. Holland and Louise Renée, eds., *Simone de Beauvoir's Fiction: Women and Language*, New York: Peter Lang, 2005.

[17] Karen Vintges, *Philosophy as Passion: The Thinking of Simone de Beauvoir*, Bloomington and Indiapolis: Indiana University Press, 1996. Vintges mistakenly asserts that there are two first-person narrators in *Les Mandarins* (p. 77).

literary-philosophical method in *Simone de Beauvoir: A Critical Introduction*.[18] Eleanore Holveck's study, *Simone de Beauvoir's Philosophy of Lived Experience*, examines Beauvoir's philosophical thinking in her fiction, in particular in *Quand Prime le Spirituel*, *L'Invitée*, *Le Sang des autres*, and *Les Mandarins*.[19] *The Bonds of Freedom: Simone de Beauvoir's Existentialist Ethics* by Kristana Arp includes readings of *Le Sang des autres* and *Tous les Hommes sont mortels*.[20] A number of other studies examine Beauvoir's fiction in the context of her other work: Toril Moi's 'personal genealogy' of Beauvoir, *Simone de Beauvoir: The Making of an Intellectual Woman*, provides an exciting reading of *L'Invitée* and certainly underlines the importance of her rhetorical strategies. The second part of Sarah Fishwick's study, *The Body in the Work of Simone de Beauvoir*, offers readings of Beauvoir's fictional representations of bodily being, in the light of theoretical accounts of corporeality elaborated by Beauvoir in *Le Deuxième Sexe*, by Luce Irigaray and by Judith Butler.[21]

A number of critics comment on the disappointed, not to say hostile, tone of much Beauvoir criticism. Elaine Marks notes that at least half of the critical essays included in the collection she edited are 'sarcastic' to some degree. She asserts: 'They present Beauvoir as a slightly ridiculous figure, naive in her passions, sloppy in her scholarship, inaccurate in her documentation, generally out of her depth and inferior as a writer' (p. 2). She is criticised for being 'too feminist' and, paradoxically, for being 'not feminist enough.' Elaine Marks argues that theoretical divergence between Beauvoir and contemporary feminists results in hostility and debate becoming conflated. Elizabeth Fallaize also comments on the disappointment of readers who seek in the fiction a confirmation of *Le Deuxième Sexe* or a reflection of contemporary feminist thought (p. 3). Toril Moi investigates the perception that Beauvoir is an undistinguished writer and devotes a chapter of her book to a close examination of recurring themes in hostile responses to Beauvoir's work, responses that are surprisingly common even among critics who profess to be well-intentioned and unbiased.[22] She asserts that 'the hostile critics' favourite strategy is to personalize the issues, to reduce the book to the woman: their aim is clearly to discredit her as a speaker not to enter into debate with her' (p. 75). Certainly, it is not the case that Beauvoir should be above criticism. However, appraisal must be based on careful reading. When it comes to the fiction, dismissive comments as to the literary merits of Beauvoir's writing by critics who have barely engaged with the text are regrettable to say the least.

---

[18]   Edward Fullbrook and Kate Fullbrook, *Simone de Beauvoir: A Critical Introduction*, Cambridge: Polity, 1998

[19]   Eleanore Holveck, *Simone de Beauvoir's Philosophy of Lived Experience*, Oxford: Rowman & Littlefield, 2002.

[20]   Kristana Arp, *The Bonds of Freedom: Simone de Beauvoir's Existentialist Ethics*, Chicago: Open Court, 2001.

[21]   Sarah Fishwick, *The Body in the Work of Simone de Beauvoir*, Oxford: Peter Lang, 2002.

[22]   Moi, *Simone de Beauvoir*, Chapter 3, 'Politics and the Intellectual Woman: Clichés and Commonplaces in the reception of Simone de Beauvoir,' pp. 73–92.

In *Simone de Beauvoir: A Study of her Writings*, Terry Keefe regrets the fact that much of the work done on Beauvoir has centered on her feminism or her association with Jean-Paul Sartre, thus producing a distorted view of her as a writer.[23] He intends his study to be a balanced study of all her books, although his readings of the fiction centre on an interpretation of content, and character and little space is given to form. When form is addressed, it is generally narrative techniques that merit a brief mention. For example, he comments on shifting narrative viewpoints in *L'Invitée* but neglects other aspects of Beauvoir's writing. His relative neglect of form leads him to consider that the novel is somewhat long and repetitive and to find that this is justified only in so far as it reflects the shapelessness and texture of life itself (pp. 157–8). He does not consider the effect that recurring events may have (apart from inferring that it is boring) and neglects symbolic significance that accrues as the text gathers momentum. Just more than one page is allotted to a discussion of what Keefe refers to as the 'small scale stylistic devices' that Beauvoir uses in *Les Belles Images* to convey Laurence's state of mind (p. 211). His analysis leaves much room for development; for example, he alludes to the single viewpoint in the novel but fails to point out that there are in fact two narrative voices, a split between 'je' and 'elle' at the heart of the narrative. Likewise, Terry Keefe links the state of mind of Murielle, the narrator in 'Monologue,' the middle story in *La Femme rompue*, to the use of language in the story but does not develop the connection thoroughly, commenting only that erratic punctuation conveys the idea that words are whirling round in Murielle's head and that the intensity of her feelings is straining language to its limits (p. 216). There is no other mention of form in *La Femme rompue*. Despite this relative lack of analysis of form, Terry Keefe levels severe criticisms at Beauvoir's fiction and concludes that its aesthetic defects might make us 'disinclined even to consider whether they are accomplished works of art' (p. 229). Whilst acknowledging that *Les Belles Images* and 'Monologue' reveal her to be capable 'of the highest achievements on the artistic level,' he nevertheless attacks her fiction for its narrow range, for failure to make more use of conflicting perspectives, for lack of inventiveness, for Beauvoir's over-identification with its heroines, and for being limited and conventional (pp. 227–8). His praise can seem patronising and begrudging:

> Whatever the flaws in her books, we can only be grateful for stories that not only entertain us, but project us so firmly into the mentalities of imaginary figures that our awareness of people and the real world is permanently enriched, over however narrow a range.[24] (*Simone de Beauvoir: A Study of her Writings*, p. 228)

---

[23] Keefe, *Simone de Beauvoir: A Study of her Writings*, Preface.

[24] Keefe appears to associate the lack of a broader perspective and more balanced treatment with the absence of male focalizers in the shorter fiction (p. 221). He also makes the following strange comment: 'There has been a tendency, perhaps because of her relationship with Sartre, to expect too much of Beauvoir's works [...]' (p. 228).

Terry Keefe's introductory guide to *Les Belles Images* and *La Femme rompue*, published in 1991, provides a more thoughtful appreciation of Beauvoir's later fiction.[25] A whole section is devoted to narrative technique and style in *Les Belles Images*. He touches on a whole range of stylistic devices (focalization, reliability, use of pronouns and tense, repetition, questioning, use of parentheses and suspension points, and ambiguity), concluding that 'the style of the novel would undoubtedly repay closer study' (p. 36). Less attention is paid to the form of the three stories in *La Femme rompue*. The 'broadly literary orientation of 'L'Age de discrétion' is noted, and Terry Keefe comments that 'the style itself has certain minor poetic qualities not entirely common in Beauvoir's fiction' (p. 44). These are not explored. The remainder of the paragraph dealing with style is given over to a brief consideration of the use of the 'diary' form in the story. The form of 'Monologue' is treated somewhat more thoroughly and is related to the mental illness of Murielle, the narrator, although his argument appears to be somewhat contradictory in that, whilst the story is considered to be 'a successful attempt to project us into the strange mentality of a tortured woman,' the monologue form is seen to hamper our efforts to judge Murielle (p. 52). Likewise, the diary form in 'La Femme rompue' is acknowledged to be well suited to the depiction of a character undergoing change but it, too, is perceived as a barrier to making 'a sound judgement' (p. 61). No other aspect of the form of 'La Femme rompue' is examined.[26]

Terry Keefe's full-length study of Beauvoir's fiction published in 1998 is as dismissive of the formal qualities of Beauvoir's fiction as his study of 15 years earlier.[27] He concludes:

> Approaching the works from a different angle, many readers will undoubtedly believe that Beauvoir paid far too little attention to the technical, stylistic, artistic aspects of novel-writing. [...] In general there is – except in *Les Belles Images* – relatively little that is genuinely innovative in her fictional techniques as such. (*Simone de Beauvoir*, p. 172)

He concedes that Beauvoir 'mostly reworked her drafts very carefully' and 'produced some memorably written sequences in her novels' but asserts that it

---

[25]   Terry Keefe, *Simone de Beauvoir: Les Belles Images*, *La Femme rompue*, Glasgow Introductory Guides to French Literature 12, Glasgow: University of Glasgow French and German Publications, 1991.

[26]   In 1991 Keefe continues to regret the fact that Beauvoir's stories are narrated exclusively from the woman's point of view. As regards the upbringing of children in *Les Belles Images* and *La Femme rompue*, he argues, we are prevented from 'seeing things through the father's eyes, and therefore from making a balanced judgement on the father's contribution to the upbringing process' (p. 72). (This seems especially to concern Keefe in light of the fact that the stories in *La Femme rompue* 'are cautionary tales, warning against the unreliability of certain women's testimony.')

[27]   *Simone de Beauvoir*, Macmillan Modern Novelists, Basingstoke: Macmillan, 1998.

is ultimately the dominance of conversation or dialogue in her stories and her use of spoken language that preclude her from being considered as a (great) stylist (p. 172).

Renee Winegarten's declared aim is to 'assess the value of Beauvoir's activity and writings in the spheres of feminism, politics and literature.'[28] Her starting point is that 'basically, [Beauvoir] was not an inventive or highly imaginative writer' (p. 3). There is no careful evaluation of Beauvoir's writing in her book; instead, she concentrates on philosophical and autobiographical aspects of the fiction, concluding that Beauvoir's lack of inventive powers led her to write *romans à clef* and *romans à thèse* (p. 105). Her comments are consistently dismissive and unfounded. One page is allotted to *Les Belles Images*; she considers this to be Beauvoir's 'most accomplished work of fiction in the formal sense' (p. 114) but restricts herself to summarising the plot. Her verdict is that 'skilfully and smoothly constructed as it is, the novel seems thin and the plot mechanism artificial' (p. 115).[29] *La Femme rompue* is summed up and dismissed in 10 lines (p. 115). My argument here is that if critics claim to evaluate Beauvoir's fiction and her contribution to literature, then the least they owe is a careful reading of the texts.[30]

Catherine Savage Brosman looks at Beauvoir's fiction in the context of her work as a whole in *Simone de Beauvoir Revisited*. One chapter deals with the early fiction and drama and another with the later fiction. The Publisher's Note promises 'an objective consideration of Beauvoir's lasting contribution to literature and philosophy.' Indeed, Catherine Brosman's study is intended to fill the gap left by studies she considers to be overspecialised or 'unbalanced,' arguing that 'this is the case particularly with the numerous studies done from the feminist viewpoint.'[31] Although she claims to treat Beauvoir's fictional technique in detail, little space is actually given over to it. For instance, barely more than one page is devoted to the form of *L'Invitée*, and one paragraph of this is concerned with showing that autobiographical considerations weigh more heavily than questions of style (p. 55). Likewise, just one page deals with the form of *Les Belles Images* (p. 88), and there is one paragraph given over to the consideration of form in each of the stories in *La Femme rompue* (pp. 94, 95, 98). When technique is dealt with, concentration is on focalization. The tone of Catherine Brosman's study is hostile, begrudging, and dismissive. Her estimate of the portrait of Xavière in *L'Invitée,* for example, is that 'she may be the book's most successful portrait, and credit is due to Beauvoir, even though she had a live model' (p. 52). As for Beauvoir's technique, Catherine Brosman writes: 'The progress the author had made in storytelling since her early

---

[28] Winegarten, p. 6.

[29] She adds the following, rather odd remark: 'All is weighted against the majority of Laurence's circle, and the battle seems won in advance' (p. 115).

[30] I have not included Carol Ascher's book in this review. Her aim is 'to render the character, preoccupations, and main themes of de Beauvoir's life – as [she] see[s] them' (p. 3).

[31] Brosman, *Simone de Beauvoir Revisited*, Preface, p. ix.

attempts is visible in *L'Invitée*. Thanks perhaps to Sartre's influence, Beauvoir had a sense of what technique could contribute to her fiction. [...] The fact that two initial chapters had to be excised, on an editor's advice, suggests that the craftsmanship in the manuscript was not perfect' (p. 55).[32] Such comments recur throughout the study, which, though it can provide insights, also contains curious, unsubstantiated readings and misreadings of the texts.[33] Some of these will be dealt with during the course of my study. In particular, I want to show that her assertion that the tone of *Les Belles Images* is detached is untenable.[34]

It is not true to imply that all Beauvoir criticism is antagonistic or dismissive. A number of more balanced, well-founded studies have been published in the last 20 years. My study builds on the insights of a number of writers in particular. In her study of Beauvoir's fiction, Elizabeth Fallaize concentrates on Beauvoir as a writer and intends to make up for the relative lack of attention that has been paid to the formal literary qualities of her work until now.[35] She is especially interested in the narrative strategies Beauvoir uses in her novels and short stories and wishes to relate these both to the meaning of her texts and to the sexual politics of her writing (p. 1). She points out in the introduction to her book that narrative strategies will figure much more prominently in her discussion of certain texts where language is foregrounded than in others where philosophical, political, and personal concerns are dominant (p. 4).

In Beauvoir's fiction as a whole, Elizabeth Fallaize identifies an overall reduction in plurality and a loss of authority conceded to the female voice, which, however, becomes the dominant voice. She notes that gradually the narrative voice is taken over by negative, mad women and asks the crucial question as to how the connection between women and folly and the abuse of words can be accounted for (p. 179). Interesting autobiographical and historical points are advanced to explain developments in Beauvoir's narrative strategies. My readings

---

[32]   Brosman neglects to mention that these chapters were 'excised' from an early draft of the first hundred pages of what would be *L'Invitée*. Beauvoir discusses the genesis of her novel in *La Force de l'âge*, p. 346. (The two chapters appear in *Les Écrits*, pp. 275–316.)

[33]   For example, Brosman writes that in *L'Invitée* Françoise and Pierre bring Xavière to Paris to pursue her philosophical studies (p. 51). In fact, Pierre's first idea is that she should learn shorthand (I, p. 27). Brosman offers a strange interpretation of the ending of *Les Belles Images*: 'Laurence's task is enormous: to bring all her intimates to a common recognition of freedom and creation of an authentic self. There is some hope that she can do so for and with Catherine' (p. 92). It is hard to reconcile this with the tentative, personal 'resolution' reached in the final sentences of the novel: 'Mais les enfants auront leur chance. Quelle chance? elle ne le sait même pas' (BI, p. 183); 'But the children will have their chance. What chance? she doesn't even know' (LBI p. 222 ta). Brosman does not provide textual evidence that Monique in 'La Femme rompue' 'was indeed an oppressive mother' (p. 99). Certainly Monique expresses doubts about the way she brought up her children in the light of Maurice's criticism (pp. 186 and 219) but for conflicting evidence see pp. 188 and 250.

[34]   Brosman, p. 86.

[35]   Fallaize, *The Novels*, p. 3.

of Beauvoir develop Fallaize's insights into Beauvoir's narrative strategies by addressing the connections between madness and language in the text. I explore the textual strategies that call into question the meaningfulness of language and the nature of truth.

Jane Heath's study of three of Beauvoir's fictional works and her autobiographies focuses 'on textuality not personality.'[36] By placing emphasis on the process of the fictional texts, she seeks to examine the way in which the feminine in the texts, defined as a site of resistance, represents a challenge to the patriarchal order (pp. 8, 13, 14). She argues that Beauvoir is inscribed on the side of the masculine, speaking 'predominantly the discourse of repression' and allowing the man in her to speak (p. 9). However, in spite of repression of the feminine, Jane Heath tells us, the feminine returns in the texts. She offers interesting psychoanalytical readings of the fiction, but I share Toril Moi's disquiet at her use of the notions femininity and masculinity.[37] Many of the qualities she reads as the feminine my readings will identify as excess and transgression and reinterpret as madness in the text.

Toril Moi's book *Simone de Beauvoir: The Making of an Intellectual Woman* offers a close reading of 'the textual Beauvoir.' She makes no methodological distinction between 'life' and 'text'; 'Beauvoir' is a construction, the effect of the fictional, philosophical, autobiographical, and epistolary texts that she herself wrote and of all the texts that have been written about her (p. 4). For Toril Moi, all these texts participate in the same discursive network, and she aims 'to read them all with and against each other in order to bring out their points of tension, contradictions, and similarities' (p. 5).[38] She focuses on *L'Invitée, Le Deuxième Sexe*, and the memoirs, and her book is a dazzling combination not only of biography and literary criticism but also 'reception studies, sociology of culture, philosophical analysis, psychoanalytic inquiry and feminist theory' (p. 7). Attention is paid to Beauvoir's rhetorical strategies; *L'Invitée* is read as an existential melodrama, and its powerful imagery is analysed; the use of metaphor and metonymy in Beauvoir's account of subjectivity and sexuality in *Le Deuxième Sexe* is investigated; shifts in tone and style in the memoirs are read as effects of anxiety and depression. On balance, the emphasis in Toril Moi's study falls on psychoanalytic and philosophical readings of the texts.

This review of major critical studies of Beauvoir's fiction reveals that there is a place for further analysis. It confirms that the form of her novels and short stories remains a relatively neglected area of study. Attention here therefore centres on

---

[36] Heath, *Simone de Beauvoir*, p. 3.

[37] See Moi, *Simone de Beauvoir*, footnote 27, pp. 272–3.

[38] Moi acknowledges what she call the 'ethical integrity' of 'purely aesthetic' approaches to Beauvoir but regrets that they tend to miss the 'real cultural significance' of her work by concentrating on her as a writer of fiction (p. 5). However, given the dearth of studies that deal with the form of the fiction in any depth, it seems appropriate that, within the context of recognised cultural significance, effort should be devoted to an evaluation of Beauvoir's writing in the fiction, to the appraisal of *how* she writes. This is not to preclude comparable studies of nonfictional works.

text as opposed to *story* and *narration*. These are the terms used by Shlomith Rimmon-Kenan for the basic aspects of narrative fiction.[39] They correspond to Genette's distinction between *histoire, récit,* and *narration*.[40] 'Story' denotes the narrated events and the participants in these events, 'le contenu narrative,' however minimal. 'Text' denotes the discourse, spoken or written, that tells the story. 'Narration' denotes the act or process of production, the communication of the narrative by a fictional narrator within the text. All three aspects are essential and interrelated. To base an evaluation of narrative fiction on an appreciation of story only, that is an examination of events and characters, is evidently partial. To a great extent, the how of the telling *is* the meaning of the story.

Indeed, Beauvoir attached a great deal of importance to the artistic reworking of lived experience, to the creative process. She did not simply transcribe lived experience in her fiction. In a lecture she gave in Japan in 1966, when the bulk of her fiction was already written, she told her listeners: 'Écrire un roman, c'est en quelque sorte pulvériser le monde réel et n'en retenir que les éléments qu'on pourra introduire dans une re-création d'un monde imaginaire [...]. Un roman c'est une espèce de machine qu'on fabrique pour éclairer le sens de notre être dans le monde'; 'Writing a novel is like pulverising the real world and only keeping the elements you'll be able to introduce in a re-creation of an imaginary world [...]. A novel is a kind of machine that is designed to reveal the sense of our being in the world' (my translation).[41] Beauvoir believed that the transposition of experience into fiction, the creation of a work of literature required attention to be paid to form.[42] Elsewhere in *La Force des choses* she describes the exacting process of reworking the drafts of her books; the initial writing, 'un labeur pénible'; the second draft, '[le] brouillon'; and then the final rewriting:

> M'aidant de mon brouillon, je rédige à grands traits un chapitre. Je reprends la première page et arrivée en bas, je la refais phrase par phrase; ensuite je corrige chaque phrase d'après l'ensemble de la page, chaque page d'après le chapitre entier; plus tard, chaque chapitre, chaque page, chaque phrase d'après la totalité du livre. (FCi, p. 372)[43]

> With the help of my rough draft, I sketch the broad outlines of a chapter. I begin again at page one, read it through and rewrite it sentence by sentence; then I correct each sentence so that it will fit into the page as a whole, then each page so that it has its place in the whole chapter; later on, each chapter, each page, each sentence, is revised in relation to the work as a whole. (FOC, p. 285)

---

[39]   Shlomith Rimmon-Kenan, *Narrative Fiction: Contemporary Poetics*, London: Methuen, 1983, pp. 3–4.

[40]   Gérard Genette, 'Discours du récit,' in *Figures III*, Paris: Editions du Seuil, 1972, p. 72.

[41]   Beauvoir, 'Mon expérience d'écrivain,' Lecture given in Japan, 11 October 1966, in Claude Francis and Fernande Gontier, *Les Écrits de Simone de Beauvoir: La vie – L'écriture*, Paris: Gallimard, 1979, p. 443.

[42]   FCi, p. 119.

[43]   The whole process is described in 'Intermède,' FCi, pp. 371–4.

In her contribution to the 1964 debate, *Que peut la littérature?*, Beauvoir is categorical that in literature, which is essentially an exploration/a search ('une recherche'), 'la distinction entre le fond et la forme est périmée; et les deux sont inséparables'; 'the distinction between content and form is obsolete; the two are inseparable' (my translation).[44] She goes on to say: 'On ne peut pas séparer la manière de raconter et ce qui est raconté, parce que la manière de raconter c'est le rythme même de la recherche, c'est la manière de la définir, c'est la manère de la vivre'; 'How a story is told cannot be separated from what is told because how a story is told is the rhythm of the exploration, the way to define it, the way to experience it' (my translation).[45] Given the importance Beauvoir attached to form, given the care she took with the writing of her fiction, with the craft of writing, this aspect of her work deserves close examination.[46]

Consideration of Beauvoir's writing practice is amply rewarded. Not only does it reveal the richness of her texts, it can also afford alternative readings of her fiction. These may be deconstructive readings that undermine authorial readings of the texts.

Before going further, it is useful at this point to examine some of Beauvoir's own views with regard to her fiction. Beauvoir knew (thought she knew) what her texts meant. Her intentions are, in each case, clearly spelt out in her memoirs.[47] Toril Moi has pointed out how 'the autobiography becomes a repertoire of *authorized*

---

[44]   In *Que peut la littérature*, ed. by Yves Buin, Paris: Union Générale d'Éditions, 1965, pp. 73–92 (p. 84).

[45]   *Que peut la littérature*, p. 85. See also Beauvoir's comments in the interview with Catherine David, 'Beauvoir elle-même,' *Le Nouvel Observateur*, 22 January 1979, pp. 82–90 (pp. 88–9). She denies that style is of no great importance to her: 'Au contraire, j'y attache une grande importance. Je travaille énormément tout ce que j'écris. Vous savez, pour émouvoir, il faut que les choses soient dites d'une certaine façon, avec un certain ton, des ellipses, des images, des développements. Ça a toujours beaucoup compté pour moi. [...] Dans mes romans et mes Mémoires, je fais toujours très attention à la manière dont je dis les choses. On ne peut évidemment pas séparer la manière du contenu'; 'On the contrary, I attach a great deal of importance to it. I spend a long time working on everything I write. You know, to move people, things have to be said in a certain way, in a certain tone, with ellipses, images, developments. Style has always been very important to me. [...] In my novels and Memoires, I am always very careful about the way I say things. Obviously, style cannot be separated from content' (my translation).

[46]   Beauvoir states that some essays can also be described as works of literature to the extent that 'dans l'essai même il y a un style, une écriture, une construction; on communique aussi à travers ce qu'il y a de commun et de désinformatif dans le langage' ('even in essays there is a style, a way of writing, a construction; meaning is also communicated through what is ordinary and what is misleading in language') (my translation). 'Mon expérience,' p. 441.

[47]   *L'Invitée* in *La Force de l'âge*, pp. 384–93; *Le Sang des autres* in *La Force de l'âge*, pp. 618–25; *Tous les Hommes sont mortels* in *La Force des choses*, vol. 1, pp. 92–8; *Les Mandarins* in *La Force des choses*, vol. 1, pp. 358–70; *Les Belles Images*, in *Tout Compte fait*, pp. 172–5; *La Femme rompue*, in *Tout Compte fait*, pp. 175–81.

readings' as Beauvoir attempts to control the meaning of her books.[48] Martha Noel Evans also discusses the way in which Beauvoir's fiction is 'documented and shadowed' by her memoirs.[49] She sees the autobiography as 'a second writing that explains, completes, and justifies the first' (p. 77). Beauvoir's memoirs reveal a tension between her desire to control the meaning of her texts, particularly her fictional texts, and her wish to leave room for a certain ambiguity she intended to guarantee *vraisemblance* (in life there is no closure, no certainty, no Truth).

About *L'Invitée* she writes: 'Dans les passages réussis du roman, on arrive à une ambiguïté de significations qui correspond à celle qu'on rencontre dans la réalité' (FA, p. 391); 'In the novel's more successful sequences I achieved an ambiguity of meanings corresponding to the kind of thing one meets in real life' (PL, p. 344, ta). She quotes with approval what Blanchot says about existence in his essay on *le roman à thèse*: 'Le but de l'écrivain c'est de *la donner à voir* en la recréant avec des mots: il la trahit, il l'appauvrit, s'il n'en respecte pas l'ambiguité' (FA, p. 622); 'The writer's aim is to *make people see* the world, by re-creating it in words; he betrays and impoverishes it if he does not respect its essential ambiguity' (PL, p. 544). This is Beauvoir's declared reason for preferring *L'Invitée* to *Le Sang des autres*, because 'la fin en demeure ouverte; on ne saurait en tirer aucune leçon' ('it has an open ending, and no lesson could be drawn from it'), whereas *Le Sang des autres* 'aboutit à une conclusion univoque, réductible en maximes et en concepts' ('reaches a clear-cut, definite conclusion, which can be reduced to terms of maxims and concepts') (FA, p. 622; PL, p. 544).[50] Beauvoir is even more critical of her text than Blanchot, writing: 'Le défaut qu'il dénonce n'entache pas seulement les dernières pages du roman: d'un bout à l'autre, il lui est inhérent (FA, p. 622); 'The fault that he criticizes does not only mar the novel's final pages: it is inherent in the text from beginning to end' (PL, pp. 544–5). Ambiguity is what Beauvoir values in *Tous les Hommes sont mortels*:

> En le relisant je me suis demandé: mais qu'est-ce que j'ai voulu dire? Je n'ai voulu dire rien d'autre que l'aventure que j'inventai. Le récit se conteste sans répit; si on prétendait en tirer des allégations, elles se contrediraient; aucun point de vue ne prévaut définitivement; celui de Fosca, celui d'Armand sont vrais ensemble. J'aurais dit dans mon précédent essai que la dimension des entreprises humaines n'est ni le fini ni l'infini, mais l'indéfini: ce mot ne se laisse enfermer dans aucune limite fixe, la meilleure manière de l'approcher, c'est de divaguer

---

[48]   Toril Moi, 'Intentions and Effects: Rhetoric and Identification in Beauvoir's "The Woman Destroyed,"' in *Feminist Theory and Simone de Beauvoir*, Oxford: Blackwell, 1990, p. 67.

[49]   Martha Noel Evans, *Masks of Tradition: Women and the Politics of Writing in Twentieth-Century France*, Ithaca: Cornell University Press, 1987, p. 76. She contends that Beauvoir establishes a hierarchy in which the (masculine) commentary takes precedence over the (feminine) fiction and relates this to what she defines as Beauvoir's ambivalent views of fiction that are, in turn, linked with her ambivalence toward her gender.

[50]   Beauvoir was extremely critical of the ending of *L'Invitée* for aesthetic reasons. In *La Force de l'âge* she describes it as clumsy, abrupt, and implausible. See pp. 387–8.

sur ses possibles variations. *Tous les Hommes sont mortels*, c'est cette divagation organisée; les thèmes n'y sont pas des thèses mais des départs vers d'incertains vagabondages. (FCi, pp. 97–8)

Rereading it, I asked myself: But what was I trying to say? I was trying to say nothing more than the story I invented. The conflict is presented throughout within the narrative itself; an attempt to isolate specific assertions from it would only produce a set of contradictions; no one point of view finally prevails; Fosca's point of view and Armand's are true together. In my earlier essay I had said that the dimension of human enterprise is neither the finite nor the infinite but the indefinite: this word cannot be fixed within any given limits, the best way of approaching it is to explore its possible variations. *All Men are Mortal* is an organised version of such an exploration; its themes are not theses, but points of departure for uncharted wanderings. (FOC, p. 75)

Indeed, for Beauvoir, ambiguity is at the heart of the literary enterprise.[51] This is what she writes in *La Force des choses*: 'J'ai dit déjà quel est pour moi un des rôles essentiels de la littérature: manifester des vérités ambiguës, séparées, contradictoires, qu'aucun moment ne totalise ni hors de moi, ni en moi; en certains cas on ne réussit à les rassembler qu'en les inscrivant dans l'unité d'un objet imaginaire' (FCi, p. 358); 'I have already explained what is for me one of the essential purposes of literature: to make manifest the equivocal, separate, contradictory truths that no one moment represents in their totality, either inside or outside myself; in certain cases one can only succeed in grouping them all together by inscribing them within the unity of an imaginary object' (FOC, p. 275). Rejecting the idea that *Les Mandarins* is un *roman à thèse*, she writes:

La confrontation – existence, néant – ébauchée à vingt ans dans mon journal intime, poursuivie à travers tous mes livres et jamais achevée, n'aboutit ici non plus à aucune réponse sûre. J'ai montré des gens en proie à des espoirs et à des doutes, cherchant à tâtons leur chemin. Je me demande bien ce que j'ai démontré. (FCi, pp. 368–6)

The basic confrontation of being and nothingness that I sketched at the age of twenty in my private diary, pursued through all my books and never resolved, is even here given no certain reply. I showed some people, at grips with doubts and hopes, groping in the dark to find their way; I cannot think I proved anything. (FOC, p. 283)

Beauvoir's comments here are in line with the conception of fiction as a process of discovery for author and readers alike, a conception developed in 'Littérature et métaphysique,' where she writes:

---

[51] This is underpinned by Beauvoir's philosophy; ambiguity is a key element of her existential-phenomenology. For an exploration of what ambiguity means for Beauvoir see Monika Langer, 'Beauvoir and Merleau-Ponty on Ambiguity' in Claudia Card, ed., *The Cambridge Companion to Simone de Beauvoir*, Cambridge: Cambridge University Press, 2003, pp. 87–106.

Or ceci exige que le romancier participe lui-même à cette recherche à laquelle il convie son lecteur: s'il prévoit d'avance les conclusions auxquelles celui-ci doit aboutir, s'il fait pression sur lui pour lui arracher son adhésion à des thèses préétablies, s'il ne lui accorde qu'une illusion de liberté, alors l'oeuvre romanesque n'est qu'une mystification incongrue; le roman ne revêt sa valeur et sa dignité que s'il constitue pour l'auteur comme pour le lecteur une découverte vivante. ('Littérature et métaphysique,' p. 109)[52]

This expectation demands that the novelist himself participate in the same search he has invited his readers on; if in advance he predicts the conclusions to which his readers must come, if he indiscreetly pressures the reader into adhereing to preestablished theses, if he allows him only an illusion of freedom, then the work of fiction is only an incongruous mystification. The novel is endowed with value and dignity only if it constitutes a living discovery for the author as for the reader. ('Literature and Metaphysics,' p. 271)

Like the pursuit of ambiguity, Beauvoir's acknowledgement that readers play a role in the creation of meaning can also appear to stand in contradiction to her desire to control the meaning of her books. In view of the severity with which she criticises her readers (I shall come back to this shortly), it is somewhat surprising to find her writing, 'un livre est un objet collectif: les lecteurs contribuent autant que l'auteur à le créer [...]' ('A book is a collective object. Readers contribute as much as the author to its creation [...]') (FCi, p. 60; FOC, p. 45).[53] It is an idea echoed in her preface to Anne Ophir's book, *Regards féminins: condition féminine et création littéraire*, when she acknowledges with gratitude that, although she set out to reveal the *mauvaise foi* (bad faith) of her heroines in *La Femme rompue*, she had been shown how her texts ('récits') could be viewed from completely different angles. She tells us that Anne Ophir enabled her to discover new things in her book and asserts: 'Qu'une étude critique apporte à son écrivain des lumières inattendues sur son travail, je pense que c'est le plus grand éloge qu'on puisse faire'; 'When a critical study allows a writer to see their work in unexpected ways, I think that's the greatest praise it can be given' (my translation).[54] In fact, this is an attitude that appears early in Beauvoir's career. Comments she makes about the reception of *L'Invitée* are revealing; Beauvoir recognised that her book was now beyond her control, yet was happy with this state of affairs only insofar as it was interpreted in line with her intentions:

---

[52]   'Littérature et métaphysique' in *Existentialisme et la sagesse des nations*, Paris: Nagel, 1948, pp. 87–105; 'Literature and Metaphysics,' trans. Veronique Zaytzeff and Frederick M. Morrison in *Simone de Beauvoir: Philosophical Writings*, ed. Margaret A. Simons, Urbana and Chicago: University of Illinois Press, 2004, pp. 269–77.

[53]   Sartre echoes these sentiments in his contribution to the debate on literature published in *Que peut la littérature?*. He argues that an author depends on his readers to find out what he has actually written (p. 119).

[54]   Preface to Anne Ophir, *Regards féminins: condition féminine et création littéraire*, Paris: Denoël/ Gontier, 1976. [Pages not numbered.] Reprinted in Francis and Gontier, *Écrits*, pp. 577–9.

> Je lus avec un agréable étonnement les remarques que fit Thierry Maulnier [...]:
> je les trouvai justes et elles me prenaient au dépourvu; mon livre possédait donc
> l'épaisseur d'un objet: dans une certaine mesure, il m'échappait. Cependant
> j'eus plaisir aussi à constater qu'il n'avait pas trahi mes intentions. (FA, p. 637)

> I was pleasantly astonished by Thierry Maulnier's observations [...]. I felt that
> they were justified, but they caught me off my guard. So my book existed in
> depth; it was an object, and to a certain extent had passed beyond my control.
> Yet I was pleased, too, to see that it had not betrayed my original purpose. (PL,
> p. 557)

It is already clear from these comments that the freedom accorded to readers was
to be strictly limited.

Beauvoir was confident that she had said what she meant to say. In the light of
this, the extent to which her texts are read differently than she intended, 'misread'
and 'misunderstood' in her terms, is striking. In her memoirs she repeatedly deplores
the fact that her readers have, once again, failed to understand her message. She
sets out to correct misconceptions and is careful to tell us exactly what we would
have understood if only we had read more carefully. This is what she writes in *La
Force des choses* about the reception of her second novel:

> *Le Sang des autres* parut en septembre; le thème principal en était, je l'ai dit, le
> paradoxe de cette existence vécue par moi comme ma liberté et saisie comme
> objet par ceux qui m'approchent. Ces intentions échappèrent au public; le livre
> fut catalogué 'un roman sur la résistance.'

> Par moment, ce malentendu m'agaça [...]. (FCi, p. 59)

> *Blood of Others* was published in September; its main theme, as I have said, was
> the paradox of this existence experienced by me as my freedom and by those
> who came in contact with me as an object. Thios intention was not apparent to
> the public; the book was labelled a 'Resistance novel.'

> Sometimes this misunderstanding irritated me [...]. (FOC, pp. 44–5)

Unfortunately, Beauvoir was equally disappointed by the reception of *Les
Mandarins*. She rejects the idea that it is a *roman à clé* and goes on to write:
'J'aurais souhaité qu'on prenne ce livre pour ce qu'il est; ni une autobiographie,
ni un reportage: une évocation' (FCi, p. 367); 'I would have liked people to
take this book for what it is; neither autobiography, nor reportage: an evocation'
(FOC, p. 282). In her memoirs Beauvoir appears extremely defensive as regards
Le Deuxième Sexe, justifiably so, perhaps, in the light of the bitter reactions
it provoked.[55] She was convinced that her book had been misunderstood:
'Je souhaite que *Le Deuxième Sexe* soit compris tel que je l'ai écrit' ('I
would like *The Second Sex* to be understood in the spirit in which I wrote it')
(Note 1, FCi, p. 263; FOC, p. 199); 'Mes adversaires créèrent et entretinrent

---

[55] See FCi, pp. 257–68.

autour du *Deuxième Sexe* de nombreux malentendus' ('My adversaries created and maintained numerous misunderstandings on the subject of my book') (FCi, p. 265; FOC, p. 201); 'Mal lu, mal compris, il agitait les esprits' ('Misread and misunderstood, it got people worked up') (FCi, p. 266; FOC, p. 202, ta).

Beauvoir was aware of the risks involved in the new textual strategies she adopted in her later fiction: 'Demander au public de lire entre les lignes, c'est dangereux' ('It is dangerous to ask the public to read between the lines') (TCF, p. 175; ASD, p.140), she says. The technique in *Les Belles Images* is contrasted with what she had done previously:

> Dans mes précédents romans, le point de vue de chaque personnage était nettement explicité et le sens de l'ouvrage se dégageait de leur confrontation. Dans celui-ci, il s'agissait de faire parler le silence. Le problème était neuf pour moi. (TCF, p. 172)

> In my earlier novels each character's point of view was perfectly clear and the book's meaning arose from the opposition of these views. In this, it was a question of making the silence speak – a new problem for me. (ASD, p. 138)

Although the book was generally well received, a section of her public did not appreciate her intentions and, in particular, Beauvoir regretted that the character of Laurence's father was frequently misunderstood (TCF, p. 174). Even so, she went on to use the same strategy in *La Femme rompue*. 'La Femme rompue' and 'Monologue' are also constructed 'through silences' (TCF, p. 177).[56] It is with regard to 'La Femme rompue' that Beauvoir is most prescriptive. Her sympathies clearly lie with Maurice, and Beauvoir sets out to expose Monique's *mauvaise foi*:

> J'aurais voulu que le lecteur lût ce récit comme un roman policier; j'ai semé de-ci de-là des indices qui permettent de trouver la clé du mystère; mais à condition qu'on dépiste Monique comme on dépiste *un coupable*. (TCF, pp.175–6, emphasis added)

> I hoped that people would read the book as a detective-story; here and there I scattered clues that would allow the reader to find the key to the mystery – but only if he tracked down Monique as one tracks down the guilty character. (ASD, p. 140)

Beauvoir writes that sadly the book was even more misunderstood than *Les Belles Images* had been and that this time she was slated by most of the critics (TCF, p. 177). She regrets that her women readers shared Monique's blindness, and she believed their response rested on a serious misinterpretation (TCF, p. 178).

---

[56]   I am reminded of Kristeva's comments about women's writing and one of the ways women tend to deal with the art of composition: 'silence, and the unspoken, riddled with repetition, weave an evanescent canvas.' Julia Kristeva, 'Talking about *Polylogue*' in *French Feminist Thought*, ed. by Toril Moi, Oxford: Blackwell, 1987, pp. 110–17 (p. 113).

Beauvoir is severe: 'La plupart des critiques ont prouvé par leurs comptes rendus qu'ils l'avaient très mal lu' (TCF, p. 178); 'By their reviews, most of the critics proved that they had read it very imperfectly' (ASD, p. 142).[57]

In summary, there is an evident tension in Beauvoir's fiction between control and ambiguity. The desire to control the reading of her texts exists alongside Beauvoir's desire to enhance ambiguity in her texts. The freedom she professedly accords readers to participate in the creation of meaning coexists with the severe criticism she directs at readers whose interpretation differs from her own. These contradictions are revealing.

Why is Beauvoir so defensive? As Toril Moi says, 'the very intensity of Beauvoir's efforts to enforce the true meaning of her texts may make the sceptical reader wonder why she protests so much.'[58] Toril Moi wonders whether 'there is something in these texts that threatens to escape even Beauvoir?'[59]

Speaking of her intentions in her later fiction, Beauvoir uses phrases such as 'donner à voir' and 'faire transparaître' (reveal).[60] This is not a new way of looking at literature for Beauvoir; ambiguity and readers' participation in the creation of meaning were always crucial to her enterprise. She speaks of her earlier fiction in analogous terms.[61] What is new are the textual strategies used to put these intentions

---

[57] Critics have analysed why Beauvoir fails to achieve what she wished to do in 'La Femme rompue.' In 'Resisting Romance: Beauvoir, "The Woman Destroyed" and the Romance Script,' (in *Contemporary French Fiction by Women: Feminist Perspectives*, ed. by Margaret Atack, and Phil Powrie, Manchester: Manchester University Press, 1990, pp. 15–25), Elizabeth Fallaize looks at the ideology of romance in connection with Beauvoir's fiction. She shows how impossible a task Beauvoir set herself when she set out to undermine/ demystify the romance script in 'La Femme rompue.' No wonder Beauvoir's readers 'misunderstood' her story – it met almost all their expectations, notwithstanding the unhappy ending from Monique's point of view. Fallaize shows how structures and readership work against Beauvoir's subversive enterprise; it was published in serial form in *Elle* magazine and focused on the complications of love for an individual woman. Although Monique's strategies are implicated in her failure to win her man, the battle itself is not challenged; Maurice, vindicated by the narrative, is clearly identified as the prize. Readers are inclined to identify with Monique, not only because of the personal, intimate tone of the first person narrative, but also because of the lifestyle they generally shared with her.

In her analysis of the rhetorical strategies used in 'La Femme rompue,' Toril Moi has shown how they provoke the misreadings identified by Beauvoir and confirmed by her own experience of teaching the text ('Intentions and Effects,' pp. 61–93). She makes a useful distinction between the author's declared intentions which may not have any discernible textual effects and the intentionality of the text itself, that is, the logic of the text as produced by the reader, whether the writer knows it or not.

[58] Moi, 'Intentions and Effects,' p. 67.

[59] Moi, 'Intentions and Effects,' p. 67.

[60] See TCF, p. 172. These expressions are used with reference to *Les Belles Images*.

[61] See 'Littérature et métaphysique,' *Existentialisme et la sagesse des nations*, pp. 90 and 92; 'Literature and Metaphysics,' *Philosophical Writings*, pp. 270 and 271; 'Mon expérience,' *Les Écrits*, p. 447.

into effect and the changed emphasis to which this approach gives rise. Noteworthy in this connection is the explicit absence of Beauvoir from her later texts. Of course, the implied author is never completely absent (after all, it is she who in 'La Femme rompue' plants the clues[62]), but there is a definite shift from using multiple narrative viewpoints where the narrators' points of view coincide with Beauvoir's, to some extent at least, to the use of narrators that are placed at a distance from her. Speaking of *Les Belles Images*, she writes: 'Personne, dans cet univers auquel je suis hostile, ne pouvait parler en mon nom; cependant pour le donner à voir il me fallait prendre à son égard un certain recul' (TCF, p. 172); 'In this world that I dislike, no character could speak in my name: in order to reveal it I had to stand back and view it from a certain distance' (ASD, p. 137, ta). This can be contrasted with what Beauvoir says about *L'Invitée*: 'A chaque chapitre, je coïncidais avec un de mes héros [...]. J'adoptai d'ordinaire le point de vue de Françoise à qui je prêtai, à travers d'importantes transpositions, ma propre expérience' (FA, p. 385); 'In each successive chapter I identified myself with one of my characters [...]. Most often the viewpoint I adopted was that of Françoise, whom I endowed with my experiences, though making various important changes and transpositions (PL, p. 338). She tells us: 'Dans ce roman, je me livrais, je me risquais [...]' ('In this novel I exposed myself so dangerously') (FA, p. 388; PL, p. 340) and 'je m'y étais risquée tout entière' ('I had exposed myself completely') (FA, p. 636; PL, p. 556, ta). Beauvoir's fate is bound up with her character's fate in this text:

> Surtout, en déliant Françoise, par un crime, de la dépendance où la tenait son amour pour Pierre, je retrouvai ma propre autonomie. [...] Il me fallait aller au bout de mon fantasme, lui donner corps sans en rien atténuer, si je voulais conquérir pour mon compte la solitude où je précipitai Françoise. En effet, l'identification s'opéra. (FA, pp. 387–8)

> Above all, by releasing Françoise, through a murder, from the dependent position in which her love for Pierre kept her, I regained my own autonomy. [...] In order to surmount on my own account the solitude into which I had flung Françoise, I must work my fantasy through to the end, bring it to life (embody it) without diluting it in any way. And indeed, the process of identification took place. (PL, p. 340, ta)

In *Les Mandarins*, Beauvoir wished to put all of herself – 'je voulais y mettre tout de moi' (FCi, p. 268) – and divides her experience between Anne and Henri.[63]

It may seem paradoxical that the further Beauvoir ostensibly withdrew from her texts, the more prescriptive she became about what they truly meant. Heightened anxiety of control goes some way toward making sense of and explaining this. The more 'freedom' she gave readers, the less she trusted them. And the fact that they did misunderstand, of course, proved that she had been right. Beauvoir, who was disappointed in her readers, was very conscious of the fact that she

---

62   TCF, p. 176.
63   See FCi, p. 365.

had disappointed them. It is a recurring theme in her memoirs. She repeats her attempts to find understanding and approval, in her search for a positive closure, only to recreate the familiar sense of having failed, of having been misunderstood, a disappointment. She repeatedly (re)created the gap between intention and outcome where this pattern could be relived. It is the feeling of disappointment that predominates despite the evident success of her fiction, especially of her later books.

Beauvoir gives readers freedom to read between the lines, but their freedom is strictly limited. Authorial control is not renounced. Beauvoir seeks to retain power over the reader by imposing a true reading of her texts.[64] In Beauvoir's mind, there is a correct reading that readers are free to choose. Directed to find this reading, to read meaning between the lines, in the space which is empty, readers cannot but fail. Beauvoir's 'trust' in her readers is disappointed again and again. Inevitably, by failing to use their freedom correctly, they fall into the *mauvaise foi* trap that Beauvoir has set up. Her autobiography condemns her women readers as she invites her readers to condemn her characters.

Beauvoir, we have seen, valued ambiguity in literature in the name of realism, *vraisemblance*. Although she intended the ambiguity she sought to be controlled and contained between the lines, she also found it in language itself, in the madness in the text, that is to say, in those qualities that destabilise meaning and identity, that represent chaos. I see the 'second writing' in the memoirs as a bid to restore control, to contain the madness in the text, as a defence against chaos. In this, my understanding accords with the views expressed by Martha Noel Evans. During the course of her discussion on gender and the 'hidden complex of vulnerabilities and defenses' that Beauvoir's ambivalence gives rise to, she makes the following comment:

> While [Beauvoir's] ample commentary on her fiction betrays some uneasiness, some attempt to domesticate her fiction's wildness, the net effect of these commentaries is to cover the confusion, to shield or prevent the reader from facing the trouble that is there. (*Masks of Tradition*, p. 80)

Beauvoir's anxiety at the excess and ambiguity inscribed in her fiction seems to me to be a key factor underlying her efforts to prescribe how her texts should be read, her attempt to retrench in her memoirs. Her exegeses can be seen to

---

[64] Furthermore, the fact that readers encounter a slippery and unstable text increases the likelihood that they will have recourse to authorial comments beyond the text for confirmation of the 'correct' reading. Martha Noel Evans develops this point in relation to the use of the *style indirect libre* in *L'Invitée*: 'By maintaining the reader in a confused and confusing relation to her discourse, flipping in and out between emotional fusion and moral judgement, Beauvoir as author finally displaces the text as object of desire. The text is so undependable and contradictory that in order to take up a well-defined relation to it we must seek help, guidance, approval from *outside* the text, in the mind and will of its creator.' *Masks of Tradition*, p. 90.

mask other possible readings.[65] The 'second writing' in the memoirs also reveals Beauvoir's compulsion to complete. Fictional texts that replicate the openness and inconclusiveness of existence are defined (explained and circumscribed) in the memoirs.

Having examined some of Beauvoir's views on fiction and ambiguity, I now turn to the notion of madness. One of the most influential studies on madness to date was undertaken by Foucault in his *Histoire de la folie à l'âge classique.*[66] Much of what he argues there can be related to Beauvoir's textual practice. What interests Foucault is the way individuals and the social body are regulated through the articulation of discourses, through the application of knowledge or power. For Foucault, discourses are 'historically variable ways of specifying knowledge and truth.'[67] Discourses produce 'reality.' Discursive practices produce the categories in which we think ourselves and our society. Truth claims of knowledges are not verifiable outside the discourses in which they are produced. Foucault rejects conventional histories of psychiatry that interpret the emergence of psychiatric medicine as a series of humanitarian advances. For Foucault, the modern conception of mental illness and the asylum have been unknowingly constructed out of elements of the classical (seventeenth-century) experience of madness.[68]

A recurring idea in Foucault's study is that madness cannot be silenced, that it will find a voice. Although a critical awareness of madness has dominated since the Renaissance, the tragic consciousness of madness has never quite disappeared, and Foucault finds evidence of this in the work of Nietzsche, Van Gogh, Freud, and Artaud (*Histoire de la folie*, p. 40). The tragic experience of madness cannot be contained; it is dangerously masked by rational analysis of madness as mental illness but will inevitably manifest itself (*Histoire de la folie*, p. 40). Foucault argues that since the tragic experience of madness 'disappeared' with the Renaissance, interpretations of madness have combined, to differing degrees, four synchronous perceptions of madness: dialectical, ritual, lyrical, and analytical (*Histoire de la folie*, p. 187).[69] None of these elements ever disappears completely, though, at

---

[65]   I also relate this to the way that Beauvoir seems to have happily seized upon the debate about the 'bad' ending in *L'Invitée* and to have acquiesced in the criticism in order to elude the more threatening questions that a defence of its excess would have raised. Thus, the madness of the text was defined, curtailed, and dismissed. See Moi, *Simone de Beauvoir*, pp. 95–6 for a discussion of Beauvoir's attitude to the ending of *L'Invitée*.

[66]   Michel Foucault, *Histoire de la folie à l'âge classique*, Paris: Gallimard, 1972 (first published in 1961). Translated by Richard Howard, *Madness and Civilisation*, London and New York: Routledge, 1989. The translation is based on the abridged edition published in 1964 by Union générale d'éditions. Further references to this study in French and the published English translation (when possible) are included in the text.

[67]   This definition of Foucault's notion of discourses is given by Caroline Ramazanolu in the Introduction to *Up Against Foucault: Exploration of Some Tensions between Foucault and Feminism*, London: Routledge, 1993, p. 19.

[68]   For example, see *Histoire de la folie*, p. 177.

[69]   'A chaque instant, se fait et se défait l'équilibre de ce qui dans l'expérience de la folie relève d'une conscience dialectique, d'un partage rituel, d'une reconnaissance lyrique et enfin du savoir.'

any one time, one or other of them may predominate, leaving the others in virtual obscurity, giving rise to tensions and conflict 'au-dessous du niveau du langage' (beneath the level of language) (*Histoire de la folie*, p. 187). The nineteenth and twentieth centuries have favoured an analytical approach to madness, an approach that seeks an objective knowledge of madness. However, Foucault argues, all the other ways of apprehending madness continue to exist in the heart of our culture (*Histoire de la folie*, p. 188).

Foucault's notion of madness clearly converges at times with Beauvoir's writing practice. In spite of attempts to silence, confine, and ignore madness, madness finds a voice in her writing. In spite of repression, it forces its way into the text. Beauvoir's text gets away. It gets messy. The voice of the madness in Beauvoir's text is, in many ways, the voice that madness had in Western culture before 'The Great Confinement,' before it was silenced in the seventeenth century.[70] Characteristics of the tragic and critical experiences of madness, as depicted by Foucault, coincide with the experience of madness at a discursive level in the text of Beauvoir's fiction. Reading madness in the text is reading these qualities.

The tragic experience of madness informs Beauvoir's fiction. The first quality of madness I read for in her writing is excess. Madness was excess. Foucault tells us that, with the Renaissance, art becomes dominated by the imagination, liberated as Gothic forms disintegrate, no longer tied to strict, straightforward representations of scripture and spiritual significations, and 'l'image commence à graviter autour de sa propre folie' (*Histoire de la folie*, p. 29); 'the image begins to gravitate about its own madness' (*Madness and Civilisation*, p. 16). In Beauvoir, as in the tragic experience of madness, we find a multiplication of significances and meanings. And in her writing, too, 'le rêve, l'insensée, le déraisonable peuvent se glisser dans cet excès de sens' (*Histoire de la folie*, p. 29); 'dreams, madness, the unreasonable can also slip into this excess of meaning' (*Madness and Civilisation*, p. 16).

I also read Beauvoir's fiction for ambiguity. Madness was ambiguity: 'Tant de significations diverses s'insèrent sous la surface de l'image, qu'elle ne présente plus qu'une face énigmatique' (*Histoire de la folie*, p. 30); 'So many diverse meanings are established beneath the surface of the image that it presents only an enigmatic face' (*Madness and Civilisation*, p. 17). Madness exerted a powerful fascination and was represented as a temptation: 'La liberté, même effrayante, de ses rêves, les fantasmes de sa folie, ont pour l'homme du XVe siècle, plus de pouvoirs d'attraction que la réalité désirable de la chair' (*Histoire de la folie*, pp. 30–31); 'The freedom, however frightening, of his dreams, the hallucinations of his madness, have more power of attraction for fifteenth century man than the desirable reality of the flesh' (*Madness and Civilisation*, p. 18). If the fantastic and wild disorder of animality revealed the anger and madness at the heart of

---

[70] Internment, literally and symbolically, placed unreason at a distance. The mad were interned along with the poor, libertines, profaners, debauchees, spendthrifts, and so on. Chapter 2, 'Le Grand Renfermement,' *Histoire de la folie*, pp. 56–91; 'The Great Confinement,' *Madness and Civilisation*, pp. 35–60.

human beings, madness was also knowledge. In their foolish innocence, the mad had access to secret, forbidden knowledge. Madness is discernible in images that are the fruit of unrestrained imagination. I read Beauvoir's fiction for traces of the attraction of excess and disorder that, beyond the expression of anger and madness, convey a sense of elusive meaning. Madness in the text is excess, multivalence, and ambiguity.

The characteristics of the critical consciousness of madness, the second strand of the experience of madness in the Renaissance, and which came to dominate classical conceptions and thereafter modern conceptions of madness (*Histoire de la folie*, p. 39), also find echoes in Beauvoir's writing . In the critical consciousness of madness, madness and reason are seen as inextricably related (*Histoire de la folie*, p. 41). The human condition is madness when measured by the infinite wisdom ('raison démesurée') of God. Human madness is experienced as contradiction as everything is the opposite of what it appears and truth is never attained: 'tout l'ordre humain n'est que folie' (all human order is nothing but madness) (*Histoire de la folie*, p. 42). In its inexpressibility, the wisdom of God is also madness, 'un abîme de déraison'(an abyss of madness), where reason is silenced (*Histoire de la folie*, p. 43). So reason and madness cancel each other out at the same time as they construct and affirm each other in a perpetual dialectic. In the text, madness informs the rational and throws light on it. The rational is undermined. Signs of madness will be read where opposites are asserted as equivalents in a text where contradiction and paradox are familiar. Likewise, I shall read madness in Beauvoir's fiction at points where objective truth becomes elusive and when language is brought up against inexpressibility.

The madness that manifests itself in Beauvoir's texts is also inflected by classical conceptions of madness. By the end of the sixteenth century, madness is no longer at the margins, the threat on the horizon, 'cette fuyante et absolue limite' (*Histoire de la folie*, p. 53); 'that fugitive and absolute limit' (*Madness and Civilisation*, p. 31). Madness now plays on the ambiguous boundary between the real and the illusory, truth and appearance; it is the embodiment of contradiction: 'Elle cache et manifeste, elle dit le vrai et le mensonge, elle est ombre et lumière' (*Histoire de la folie*, p. 54); 'It hides and manifests, it utters truth and falsehood, it is light and shadow' (*Madness and Civilisation*, p. 32). In the 'Hospital of Madmen,' the 'Madhouse' that has replaced 'la Nef des fous' in the collective imagination at the end of the seventeenth century, the mad speak 'la contradiction et l'ironie, le langage dédoublé de la Sagesse' (*Histoire de la folie*, p. 53); 'contradiction and irony, the double language of Wisdom' (*Madness and Civilisation*, p. 32). Madness is 'le signe ironique qui brouille les repères du vrai et du chimérique' (*Histoire de la folie*, p. 55); 'an ironic sign that misplaces the guideposts between the real and the chimerical' (*Madness and Civilisation*, p. 33). Beauvoir's textual strategies that blur boundaries in an analogous way will be deemed to introduce madness in the text. Irony and contradiction can be read as madness in the text.

For Foucault, one word conveys what the experience of madness was in the asylums of the classical age: 'furieux' (furious). It designated 'une sorte de région indifférenciée du désordre' (an undifferentiated region of disorder) (*Histoire de la folie*, p. 125). Madness disturbs and disrupts. Who (what) is mad is recognised, determined by reference to reason and the sense of logic and coherence and continuity of their discourse. Madness is instantly recognisable in its negativity: 'Elle est de l'ordre de la rupture. Elle surgit tout d'un coup comme discordance' (It is in the nature of a rupture. It erupts suddenly as discordance) (*Histoire de la folie*, p. 198). Reading for madness in Beauvoir's text means reading for disruption, incoherence, discordance, and fragmentation.

In this nexus, the meaningfulness of language is cast into doubt. Indeed, Foucault argues that the obvious signs of madness are error, fantasy, illusion, and meaningless language deprived of content – '[Elle] ne se présente dans ses signes les plus manifestes que comme erreur, fantasme, illusion, *langage vain et privé de contenu*' (*Histoire de la folie*, p. 191, emphasis added). On a textual level, madness is apparent wherever the capacity of language to be meaningful is undermined.

To summarise, I read the characteristics of madness outlined by Foucault as madness in the text. The tragic experience of madness in the Renaissance figures on a discursive level as excess, disorder, multiplicity, ambiguity, and fascination and elusoriness. The critical experience of madness of that era is enacted in the text as contradiction and paradox and in inexpressability and the unattainability of truth. Finally, the classical experience of madness is duplicated in the text when boundaries are obscured and in irony, disruption, incoherence, discordance, and fragmentation. Madness is discernible at a discursive level whenever the text puts meaningfulness of language into question.

My reading of madness in the text is also indebted to Julia Kristeva's theoretical writing on language. The object of attention in my study of Beauvoir's writing practice is language itself, what Kristeva calls poetic language, the language of materiality as opposed to transparency where meaning is assumed to lie behind or beyond language. Kristeva has identified two types of signifying processes at work within the production of meaning: the 'semiotic' and the 'symbolic.' The semiotic process relates to the *chora*, which is pre-symbolic. As Toril Moi puts it, 'the semiotic is linked to the pre-Oedipal primary processes, the basic pulsions of which Kristeva sees as predominantly anal and oral, and as simultaneously dichotomous (life v. death, expulsion v. interjection) and heterogeneous. The endless flow of pulsions is gathered up in the *chora* [...].'[71] The symbolic process relates to the imposition of symbolic law, what Leon S. Roudiez refers to as 'the establishment of sign and syntax, paternal function, grammatical and social constraints.'[72] Poetic language is the outcome of a specific connection between the semiotic and the symbolic and hence undoes that binary. Toril Moi explains that once the subject has entered into the symbolic order, the *chora* is repressed to a

---

[71] Toril Moi, *Sexual Textual Politics: Feminist Literary Theory*, London: Methuen, 1985, p. 161.

[72] Leon S. Roudiez, 'Introduction' in Julia Kristeva, *Desire in Language: A Semiotic Approach to Literature and Art*, ed. by Leon S. Roudiez, New York: Columbia University Press, 1980, p. 7.

greater or lesser extent and is identifiable only 'as pulsional *pressure* on symbolic language: as contradictions, meaninglessness, disruption, silences and absences in the symbolic language.'[73] Traditionally, fiction has been dominated by the symbolic. Recently, it has been more affected by the semiotic.[74] For Kristeva, poetic language is revolutionary. She believes that writing disrupted by the semiotic, the 'spasmodic force' of the unconscious, undermines conventional meaning, which is the structure that upholds the patriarchal symbolic order, that is to say, all human social and cultural institutions. This disruption is related to madness. Toril Moi explains:

> If unconscious pulsations of the *chora* were to take over the subject entirely, the subject would fall back into pre-Oedipal or imaginary chaos and develop some form of mental illness. The subject whose language lets such forces disrupt the symbolic order, in other words, is also the subject who runs the greater risk of lapsing into madness. (*Sexual Textual Politics*, p. 11)

I read marks of disruption metaphorically as signs of madness in the text.

My study of the madness that finds concrete expression in Beauvoir's writing practice dovetails with Shoshana Felman's work on literature and madness. Her exploration of madness in Stendhal's novels is based on close textual analysis, which allows her to advance a classification of the instances of madness and of the experiences of madness found in them.[75] She goes on to trace the evolution of Stendhal's treatment of madness over time. In the concluding chapter to her study, 'Écriture et folie,' Shoshana Felman raises an important question about madness and language: 'Comment la folie pourrait-elle accéder au language, puisqu'elle est, par essence, ce qui se tait, ce qui boulverse le registre du sens et qui, par là même s'exclut du domaine de l'intelligible?' (p. 242); 'How can madness accede to language since it is, in essence, that which does not speak, that which disrupts the register of meaning and which, for that very reason is excluded from the domain of the intelligible?' (my translation). Madness is opposed to reasonableness and reason: 'La folie désire l'hyperbole; la raison impose la litote, pose les bornes même du discours – et du sens: conditions de la rencontre de l'Autre. L'hyperbole est violence, folie du désir; la litote – barrage, discipline du langage' (pp. 242–3); 'Madness seeks hyperbole; reason imposes understatement, places limits on discourse itself – and on meaning; these are the conditions of meeting the Other. Hyperbole is violence, the madness of desire; understatement – a barrier, the discipline of language' (my translation). Felman identifies a permanent tension in Stendhal between reason and madness. I want to investigate the extent to which this tension obtains in Beauvoir's fiction, the way in which the excess of madness upsets lucid, measured prose.

---

73   Moi, *Sexual Textual Politics*, p. 162.

74   Roudiez, p. 7.

75   Shoshana Felman, *La «Folie» dans l'oeuvre romanesque de Stendhal*, Paris: Librairie José Corti, 1971. (It is interesting to note that Stendhal was one of Beauvoir's favourite writers. See 'Stendhal ou le romanesque du vrai,' DSi, pp. 375–89.)

The question raised in the conclusion to Felman's study of Stendhal is one of the starting points of her book, *La Folie et la chose littéraire*.[76] In the introductory chapter entitled 'Écriture et folie: pourquoi ce livre,' she states her aim to explore the connection between literature and madness. Her study seeks to determine not only how texts speak of madness but also how madness is repressed in texts (pp. 15–16). Her analyses cut across my own readings of Beauvoir. Shoshana Felman examines the rhetorical strategies of different writers in relation to madness.[77] She distinguishes between 'la rhétorique de la folie' (that is, discourse about madness which, she argues, is always 'une rhétorique de la dénégation'), and 'la folie de la rhétorique':

> Mais si le discours sur la folie n'est pas un discours *de* la folie, n'est pas, proprement, un discours fou, il n'est pas moins, dans ces textes, une *folie qui parle*, une folie qui se joue toute seule à travers le langage mais sans que personne ne puisse devenir le sujet parlant de ce qui se joue. C'est ce mouvement de jeu qui déjoue le sens et par lequel l'*énoncé* s'aliène à la *performance* textuelle, que je dénomme, dans ce livre, 'folie de la rhétorique.' (*La Folie et la chose littéraire*, pp. 347–8)

> But even though the discourse *on* madness is not a discourse *of* madness (is not strictly speaking a mad discourse), nevertheless there still exists in these texts a *madness that speaks*, a madness that is acted out in language, but whose role no speaking subject can assume. It is this movement of non-totalizable, ungovernable linguistic play, through which meaning misfires and the text's *statement* is estranged from its *performance*, that I call in this book the 'madness of rhetoric.' (*Writing and Madness*, p. 252)

She argues that discourse about madness is subverted by 'la folie de la rhétorique,' for me, the madness in the text. My exploration of Beauvoir's writing practice centres on 'la folie de la rhétorique' and this process of subversion.

Another influential study on madness and literature is *The Madwoman in the Attic* by Sandra M. Gilbert and Susan Gubar.[78] It deals with the character of the madwoman in nineteenth century fiction by women. Mad women characters are read as an expression of women authors' rage against patriarchy and their

---

[76] Shoshana Felman, *La Folie et la Chose Littéraire*, Paris: Seuil, 1978. Eight chapters of this book have been translated into English by Martha Noel Evans and the author, with the assistance of Brian Massumi in *Writing and Madness* (*Literature/ Philosophy/ Psychoanalysis*), Palo Alto, California: Stanford University Press, 2003.

[77] The writers whose work she explores are Gérard de Nerval, Arthur Rimbaud, Honoré de Balzac, Gustave Flaubert, and Henry James. The rhetorical strategies she considers include the destabilising of identity and repetition, irony and parody.

[78] Sandra M. Gilbert and Susan Gubar, *The Madwoman in the Attic: The Woman Writer and the Nineteenth-Century Literary Imagination*, New Haven, Connecticut: Yale University Press, 1979.

anxiety of authorship.[79] The argument is that nineteenth century women authors tell the truth but 'tell it slant,' concealing deeper, less acceptable levels of meaning, thus 'simultaneously conforming to and subverting patriarchal literary standards.'[80] This impressive study is ultimately flawed as author and character are conflated, the madwoman taken to be 'the *author's* double, an image of her own anxiety and rage.'[81] Yet, in spite of this and in spite of Gilbert and Gubar's focusing on identifying hidden plots in the works they study, *The Madwoman in the Attic* pinpoints textual strategies related to the expression of women's revolt against patriarchy in nineteenth century fiction that can also be traced in Beauvoir's fiction. I shall read textual strategies such as the use of parody and irony and the subversion of the conventions of language, as the stamp of madness on a textual level.

This study is not intended to provide readings of all Beauvoir's fiction. The following four chapters explore the nature and extent of textual excess and transgression in the novels and short stories published at paradigmatic moments in the evolution of Beauvoir's fiction between 1943 and 1967. The novels *L'Invitée*, *Les Mandarins*, and *Les Belles Images* and the short story collection *La Femme rompue* are among Beauvoir's most interesting and most challenging books.

My readings of Beauvoir are based on close textual analysis to show how madness is enacted in the text. Autobiographical and philosophical matters, whilst they form the context of my analyses, will not, in the main, be directly addressed here. My study interrogates the text itself and seeks to be as little distracted from that examination as possible.

My starting point is Beauvoir's first published novel and the symbolic universe she creates there.

---

[79]   Gilbert and Gubar's ideas on women's creativity and the use of images of enclosure are related to 'La Femme rompue' by Phil Powrie in 'Rereading Between the Lines: A Postscript on *La Femme rompue*,' *Modern Language Review*, 87, 1992, 320–29.

[80]   Gilbert and Gubar, p. 73.

[81]   Gilbert and Gubar, p. 78. For a detailed evaluation of *The Madwoman in the Attic*, see Moi, *Sexual Textual Politics*, pp. 57–69. *The Madwoman in the Attic* is discussed in relation to Beauvoir in Fallaize, *The Novels*, p. 179.

Chapter 1
L'Invitée

L'Invitée is a highly figurative text. In this chapter I examine the symbolic universe that Beauvoir creates in her first published novel. The term *symbolic universe* refers to more than the sum of the images in the text; it is also the network of repeated key images, words, and motifs that accumulate in the text, contributing to the atmosphere of the text.

The symbolic universe of *L'Invitée* is Gothic. This may be a surprising assertion considering that this text has been read, for the most part, as a realist, philosophical, autobiographical novel. Indeed, this reading has authorial authority. In *La Force de l'âge*, Beauvoir discusses her first novel at length, describing how the real life trio, Jean-Paul Sartre, Olga Kosakievicz (to whom the novel is dedicated), and herself, was transposed into fiction (FA, pp. 384–93). Beauvoir placed herself at the heart of her novel in the character of Françoise (FA, p. 347). She also writes about the form of *L'Invitée* and acknowledges a debt to certain American writers of that time, notably to Dashiell Hammett and to Hemingway, as well as to Dostoyevsky and Agatha Christie.[1] She places emphasis on the realism she set out to achieve:

> Dans les passages réussis du roman, on arrive à une ambiguïté de significations qui correspond à celle qu'on rencontre dans la réalité. Je voulais aussi que les faits ne s'enchaînent pas selon les rapports univoques de causalité, mais qu'ils soient à la fois, comme dans la vie même, compréhensibles et contingents. (FA, p. 391)

> In the novel's more successful sequences I achieved an ambiguity of meanings corresponding to the kind of thing one meets in real life. I also tried to ensure that events I described should not develop in terms of some cut-and-dried causal pattern, but should be, just as in real life, simultaneously comprehensible and contingent. (PL, p. 344, ta)

This is not to suggest that Beauvoir belonged to the nineteenth-century realist tradition. In an interview with Jill M. Wharfe, Beauvoir clarified her approach to realism/reality: 'Je ne dis pas que je suis un écrivain réaliste. Je suis un écrivain qui a essayé de rendre compte un peu de la réalité'; 'I am not saying that I am a realist writer. I am a writer who has tried in a small way to give an account of reality' (my translation).[2] Her notion of reality was, of course, quite different from nineteenth-century notions of reality. As Françoise Arnaud Hibbs expresses it, Beauvoir's was

---

[1]   The influence that American writers had on Beauvoir is discussed in Anne-Marie Celeux, *Jean-Paul Sartre, Beauvoir: Une expérience commune, deux écritures*, Paris: Librairie Nizet, 1976. Toril Moi explores the contradictions inherent in Beauvoir's use of the thriller and detective story models in *Simone de Beauvoir*, p. 100.

[2]   Wharfe, Jill M., 'Perfect Interlocutors: Intertextuality and Divergence in the Fiction of Beauvoir and Sartre' (unpublished doctoral thesis, University of Birmingham, 1988).

a 'subjective realism.'[3] Lorna Sage describes her as a writer of 'realist novels that put reality in quotation marks.'[4]

Judith Okely's reading of *L'Invitée* is autobiographical and psychoanalytical, exploring the transposition of Beauvoir's life into the novel and providing psychoanalytical interpretations of both.[5] Elizabeth Fallaize highlights the autobiographical nature of the psychological crisis in *L'Invitée* and also directs our attention to the way Beauvoir seems to advocate a philosophical reading of the novel by placing a quotation from Hegel as its epigraph: 'Chaque conscience poursuit la mort de l'autre' ('Each consciousness seeks the death of the other').[6] Emphasis in Renée Winegarten's reading of *L'Invitée* also falls on autobiographical and philosophical aspects of the work.[7] Toril Moi's reading of *L'Invitée* as a modern melodrama is closer to my own.[8] Indeed, melodrama and the Gothic share a number of characteristics, notably, excess. Although the emphasis in her reading remains philosophical and psychoanalytical, Toril Moi examines the imagery associated with Xavière and the threat she represents and she identifies what she refers to as 'a kind of luridly gothic imagination.'[9] It is this area that my reading explores and develops. It is my contention that this realist, philosophical novel is embedded in a Gothic universe that Beauvoir created in order to confront pain and madness, to express that darker side of herself. A close reading of the text reveals the extent to which she had recourse to Gothic conventions and figures, which makes it justifiable to speak of the Gothic economy of the text.[10]

Interview with Beauvoir: Paris, 6 July 1985, Appendix 1, p. 344. I gratefully acknowledge permission to quote from this interview.

[3]   Hibbs, p. 10.

[4]   Lorna Sage, *Women in the House of Fiction: Post-War Women Novelists*, London: Macmillan, 1992, p. viii.

[5]   Okely, pp. 139–40.

[6]   Fallaize, *The Novels*, p. 26. Unfortunately, the epigraph is missing from the English teanslation.

[7]   Winegarten, pp. 101–6.

[8]   Moi, *Simone de Beauvoir*, pp. 95–124.

[9]   Moi, *Simone de Beauvoir*, p. 97. Note Moi's use of a small 'g' rather than a capital for the term *gothic*.

[10]   Beauvoir's correspondence with Jean-Paul Sartre reveals that she was reading M.G. Lewis's *The Monk* (1795), a quintessential Gothic novel, at the time she was writing *L'Invitée*. Letter of Saturday, 16 December 1939 in *Beauvoir: Lettres à Sartre*, 1930–1939, ed. Sylvie le Bon de Beauvoir, 2 vols (Paris: Gallimard, 1990) I, 356 (no. 125). Beauvoir notes in this letter that she is reading Antonin Artaud's version of *The Monk*. This is neither a translation nor an adaptation but 'une sorte de "copie" en français du texte anglais original.' Antonin Artaud, *"Le Moine" de Lewis raconté par Antonin Artaud* (1931), in Artaud, *Oeuvres complètes*, 18 vols (Paris: Gallimard, 1956–), vol. VI (1966), 'Avertissement', p. 13. Artaud cut the original and intensified 'la violence et l'atrocité du récit' (Notes, p. 417). Interesting echoes link *L'Invitée* and *The Monk/Le Moine*. For example, in the first chapter of *The Monk*, an ageless gypsy woman who sings and dances tells the fortune of the

The object here is to explore the insights to be gained from looking again at *L'Invitée* through the lens that the Gothic provides.[11] In the introduction to his book on the Gothic, Fred Botting tells us that it is impossible to define a fixed set of Gothic conventions; for him the Gothic is a hybrid form incorporating and transforming other literary forms and developing and changing its own conventions in relation to newer modes of writing (p. 14). The aim Eve Kosofsky Sedgwick sets out in the introduction to *The Coherence of Gothic Conventions* is instructive. She writes:

> I want to make it easier for the reader of 'respectable' nineteenth-century [we might add 'and twentieth-century'] novels to write 'Gothic' in the margin next to certain especially interesting passages, and to make that notation with a sense of linking specific elements in the passage with specific elements in the constellation of Gothic conventions. (*The Coherence of Gothic Conventions*, p. 2)

What then does the term Gothic mean? What elements might go to make up 'the constellation of Gothic conventions,' albeit unfixed, that can be identified in *L'Invitée*? In the Gothic mode, feeling and emotion exceed reason. Ambivalence and ambiguity prevail, and suspense and uncertainty are fostered. Typically, Gothic texts are concerned with the nature of language, its limits and its power, and they are characterised by a concomitant fear of representation.[12] Gothic texts tend to be preoccupied with madness, identity, and the dissolution of the self. In Gothic novels images of enclosure and weight coexist with images of space and vertigo, and this is also true of *L'Invitée*. Magic and the supernatural also figure prominently in Gothic texts. The cruel passions and supernatural terror of the first Gothic novels and the characteristically obsessive, gloomy, violent, doom-laden, and terrifying atmosphere of later Gothic works find an echo in *L'Invitée*, where a corresponding threat of irrational and evil forces looms over everything. The bestial within the human is a characteristic Gothic theme and sexuality a central concern. In Gothic texts sexuality tends to be distorted, and emphasis is commonly lain on incest and eroticism. Uncertainties about sexuality are regularly linked to wider

---

heroine (*The Monk*, pp. 34–9, *Le Moine*, pp. 48–52). Throughout the novel, details call to mind *L'Invitée*. In terms of tone, the two texts are congruous. It is interesting to recall that Foucault considered that Artaud's writing exemplified the tragic consciousness of madness. See Michel Foucault, *Histoire de la folie à l'âge classique*, Paris: Gallimard, 1972, p. 40. (Section omitted from the English translation.)

[11]   Three main sources have been referred to: Fred Botting, *Gothic*, London: Routledge, 1996; Elizabeth MacAndrew, *The Gothic Tradition in Fiction*, New York: Columbia University Press, 1979; Eve Kosofsky Sedgwick, *The Coherence of Gothic Conventions*, Revised Edition, New York: Arno Press, 1980.

[12]   The unspeakable is quintessential Gothic; sometimes the term is used simply to mean awesome, whilst sometimes, according to Eve Kosofsky Sedgwick, it implies 'a range of reflections on language,' whilst at other times it may be enacted in text as characters contend with the despair of the uncommunicable. Sedgwick, p. 3.

threats of disintegration.[13] Some of the figures that populate Gothic landscapes as the embodiment of real or imagined threats are also found in the pages of Beauvoir's novel: demons, corpses, fainting heroines, monks and nuns, the mad.[14] The favourite Gothic themes of live burial and tombs are prominent too, as are mirrors, a stock Gothic device, generally signifying alienation.

The uncanny is one of the essential ingredients of the Gothic. At the beginning of his essay on the uncanny, Freud tells us that 'the uncanny is that class of the frightening which leads back to what is known of old and long familiar.'[15] He refines this definition and determines that the uncanny is 'something repressed which recurs' (p. 241). As we shall see, this notion can help elucidate the nature of the danger that threatens Françoise.

An 'over-abundance of imaginative frenzy, untamed by reason' and a style characterised by boundlessness and over-ornamentation have been interpreted as signs of transgression in the Gothic.[16] It is precisely in the expression of the inexpressible and the excesses of the Gothic mode that I locate the madness in the text of *L'Invitée*. Insofar as it is Gothic and thus transgressive, the text of *L'Invitée* is mad; it enacts madness.[17]

'Gothic signifies a writing of excess.'[18] These are the first words in Fred Botting's book, signaling how central this notion is to the Gothic. Much of the writing in *L'Invitée* is, as we shall see, excessive, hyperbolic, extravagant; it is Gothic writing to the extent that it is more likely to evoke emotion and work on readers' feelings than it is to prompt an intellectual response or rational argument. It is useful to begin this exploration of the Gothic in *L'Invitée* with a number of key passages that, in particular, epitomise Gothic writing, a writing of excess. A close reading of these passages highlights a dense network of words and motifs that are found throughout the text and that go to make up what I have referred to as the Gothic economy of the text. These words and motifs are analysed in detail subsequently.[19] What is of interest here is the quality of the writing that makes it justifiable to speak of its excess.

---

[13]   Botting, p. 5.

[14]   In *L'Invitée* there is a whole cast of other minor Gothic figures including ghosts (pp. 147, 179, 359) and puppets, also associated with death (pp. 153, 179, 335). Françoise is described as 'une vieille machine déréglée,' I, p. 434 ('an old, broken down machine,' SCS, p. 351). Paule dances 'la danse des machines,' I, pp. 182–3 ('the dance of the machines', SCS, p. 145).

[15]   'The Uncanny,' *The Complete Psychological Works of Sigmund Freud*, Vol XVII (1917–1919), ed. James Strachey, London: The Hogarth Press, 1955, pp. 218–52 (p. 220).

[16]   Botting, pp. 5–6.

[17]   Foucault discusses the links between unreason, internment and what he terms 'la littérature fantastique de folie et d'horreur' that appeared in the nineteenth century. See *Histoire de la folie*, 'La Grande Peur', pp. 375–82; *Madness and Civilisation*, 'The Great Fear', pp. 191–200.

[18]   Botting, p. 1.

[19]   The first key passage can be found on pp. 354–5 of *L'Invitée*. The second key passage is on pp. 362–4. The third key passage is on pp. 499–501.

These highly coloured, extravagant passages occur at climactic points in the narrative. The first passage relates the incident in the nightclub when Xavière deliberately and repeatedly burns herself with a cigarette during a dance performance:

> Xavière ne regardait plus, elle avait baissé la tête, elle tenait dans sa main droite une cigarette à demi consumée et elle l'approchait lentement de sa main gauche. Françoise eut peine à réprimer un cri; Xavière appliquait le tison rouge contre sa peau et un sourire aigu retroussait ses lèvres. (I, p. 354)

> Xavière was no longer watching, her head was lowered. In her right hand she held a half-smoked cigarette which she was slowly moving towards her left hand. Françoise barely repressed a scream. Xavière was pressing the glowing brand against her skin with a bitter smile curling her lips. (SCS, p. 284)

Françoise then watches in horror as Xavière burns herself again: '[...] Xavière soufflait délicatement sur les cendres qui recouvraient sa brûlure; quand elle eut dispersé ce petit matelas protecteur, elle colla de nouveau contre la plaie mise à nu le bout embrasé de sa cigarette' (I, p. 354); '[...] Xavière was gently blowing the ash which covered her burn. When she had blown away this little protective layer, she once more pressed the glowing end of her cigarette against the exposed wound' (SCS, p. 284, ta). Françoise's crisis, which is a metaphysical one,[20] is related not in cool, rational prose but rather in hyperbolic terms: 'Françoise eut un haut-le-corps; ce n'était pas seulement sa chair qui se révoltait; elle se sentait atteinte d'une façon plus profonde et plus irrémédiable, jusqu'au coeur de son être. Derrière ce rictus maniaque, un danger menaçait, plus définitif que tous ceux qu'elle avait jamais imaginés' (I, p. 354); 'Françoise flinched; not only did her flesh rise up in revolt; she was affected more deeply and more irrevocably to the very core of her being. Behind that maniacal grin, was the threat of a danger more positive than any she had ever imagined' (SCS, pp. 284–5, ta). Ambiguity is fostered. The danger is at once the most absolute and indeterminate.

The second key passage that exemplifies excess is, in many ways, a continuation of the previous one that had been interrupted.[21] During the rendering of a Spanish poem, Xavière is as if in a trance and Françoise suffers another access of panic:

> Xavière ne regardait plus la femme, elle fixait le vide; une cigarette se consumait entre ses doigts et la braise commençait à atteindre sa chair sans qu'elle parût s'en apercevoir; elle semblait plongée dans une extase hystérique. Françoise

---

[20]   See pp. 375–6, where Françoise discusses her crisis with Pierre. In her relationship with Xavière, Françoise has been confronted with the reality that other consciousnesses exist in the world besides her own.

[21]   Moi suggests that Xavière deliberately burns herself on two occasions and that it is 'when Xavière tries to burn herself for the second time' that Françoise reacts vehemently (*Simone de Beauvoir*, p. 115). In fact, during the rendering of the Spanish poem, Xavière seems to be in a kind of hysterical trance, and a lit cigarette between her fingers has burnt down and begins to scorch her flesh. Françoise's reaction is due to her recollection of the previous incident in a charged atmosphere. See I, p. 363.

passa la main sur son front; elle était en sueur, l'atmosphère était étouffante et au-dedans d'elle-même, ses pensées brûlaient comme des flammes. Cette présence ennemie qui s'était révélée tout à l'heure dans un sourire de folle devenait de plus en plus proche, il n'y avait plus moyen d'en éviter le dévoilement terrifiant; jour après jour, minute après minute, Françoise avait fui le danger, mais c'en était fait, elle l'avait enfin rencontré cet infranchissable obstacle qu'elle avait pressenti sous des formes incertaines depuis sa plus petite enfance; à travers la jouissance maniaque de Xavière, à travers sa haine et sa jalousie, le scandale éclatait, aussi monstrueux, aussi définitif que la mort; en face de Françoise, et cependant sans elle, quelque chose existait comme une condamnation sans recours: libre, absolu, irréductible, une conscience étrangère se dressait. (I, pp. 363–4)

Xavière was no longer watching the woman, she was staring into space; a cigarette was alight between her fingers and the glowing end was beginning to touch her flesh without her seeming to be aware of it; she seemed to be in the grip of hysterical ecstasy. Françoise passed her hand across her forehead; she was dripping with perspiration, the atmosphere was stifling and deep down her thoughts were burning like flames. The hostile presence, which earlier had betrayed itself in a lunatic's smile, was getting closer and closer, there was now no way of avoiding its terrifying disclosure; day after day, minute after minute, Françoise had fled the danger, but now it had happened, she had at last come face to face with the insurmountable obstacle which she had sensed in a shadowy form since her earliest childhood; through Xavière's maniacal pleasure, through her hatred and her jealousy, the abomination was being revealed, as monstrous, as definitive as death; facing Françoise, and yet without her, something existed like a sentence without an appeal: free, absolute, implacable, there stood an alien consciousness. (SCS, pp. 291–2, ta)

Again, one is struck by the heightened and intense tone of the text. Readers of *L'Invitée*, like readers of Gothic romance, are placed in a state of suspense and uncertainty.[22] The text builds to a crescendo; words are piled on words, clause upon clause in a long sentence (nine lines, 113 words) that seems to draw readers into the text, enacting the weight of language and reproducing Françoise's feelings of suffocation. Together, these passages represent one of the climaxes in the novel. It is at this point that Françoise realises that Xavière is a threat, not only to her happiness but to her very existence.

The final key passage I consider is the culmination of the text that is reached as Françoise comes to the decision that Xavière must die. This passage, too, is characterised by hyperbole:

[Françoise] traversa le couloir, elle titubait comme une aveugle, les larmes brûlaient ses yeux: 'J'ai été jalouse d'elle. Je lui ai pris Gerbert.' Les larmes brûlaient, les mots brûlaient comme un fer rouge. Elle s'assit au bord du divan et répéta hébétée: 'J'ai fait cela. C'est moi.' Dans les ténèbres, le visage de Gerbert brûlait d'un feu noir, et les lettres sur le tapis étaient noires comme un pacte infernal. Elle porta son mouchoir à ses lèvres. Une lave noire et torride coulait dans ses veines. Elle aurait voulu mourir. (I, p. 499)

---

22   See Maggie Kilgour, *The Rise of the Gothic Novel*, London: Routledge, 1995, p. 6.

[Françoise] crossed the passage, she was staggering as though blind, tears burned her eyes: 'I was jealous of her. I took Gerbert from her.' The tears burned, the words burned like a red hot iron. She sat on the edge of the bed and stupified repeated: 'I did that. It's me.' In the shadows, black flames flickered round Gerbert's face, and the letters scattered on the carpet were as black as an infernal pact. She put her handkerchief to her mouth. A black, torrid lava was coursing in her veins. She wanted to die. (SCS, p. 406, ta)

A succession of short and asyntactic sentences convey Françoise's distress; their rhythm could almost be the rhythm of broken sobs. Repetition adds to the intensity of the text: 'brûler,' 'larmes,' 'noir.' The same motifs are found again a few lines later: 'Elle ferma les yeux. Les larmes coulaient, la lave brûlante coulait et consumait le coeur' (I, p. 500); 'She closed her eyes. Her tears were flowing, the burning lava was flowing and consuming her heart' (SCS, p. 406, ta). Françoise has finally come face to face with the threat to her being: 'Elle était tombée dans le piège, elle était à la merci de cette conscience vorace qui avait attendu dans l'ombre le moment de l'engloutir' (I, p. 500); 'She had fallen into the trap, she was at the mercy of this voracious consciousness that had been waiting in the shadows for the moment to swallow her up' (SCS, p. 406, ta). This writing relies on hyperbole for its impact.

In each case, the relating of these three incidents gives rise to a meta-commentary on language. Excess results from language coming up against the inexpressable. What is threatening Françoise is beyond language, beyond thought even: 'On ne pouvait pas s'en approcher même en pensée, au moment où elle touchait au but, la pensée se dissolvait; ce n'était aucun objet saisissable, c'était un incessant jaillissement et une fuite incessante, transparente pour soi seule et à jamais impénétrable' (I, pp. 354–5); 'Approach to it was impossible even in thought, just when she seemed to be getting near it, the thought dissolved; it was not a tangible object, it was an incessant flux and an incessant flight, transparent only to itself and forever impenetrable' (SCS, p. 285, ta). Only contradiction, language pushed to the limit of meaningfulness, can begin to express the nature of the threat:

C'était comme la mort, une totale négation, une éternelle absence, et cependant par une contradiction boulversante, ce gouffre de néant pouvait se rendre présent à soi-même et se faire exister pour soi avec plénitude; l'univers tout entier s'engloutissait en lui, et Françoise, à jamais dépossédée du monde, se dissolvait elle-même dans ce vide dont aucun mot, aucune image ne pouvait cerner le contour infini. (I, p. 364)[23]

---

[23]   See earlier, too, where Françoise realises: 'Les mots ne pouvaient que vous rapprocher du mystère mais sans le rendre moins impénétrable' (I, p. 162); 'Words could only bring you nearer the mystery but without making it any less impenetrable' (SCS, p. 128, ta).

> It was like death, a total negation, an eternal absence, and yet through a
> staggering contradiction, this abyss of nothingness could make itself present
> to itself and make itself fully exist for itself; the entire universe was engulfed
> in it, and Françoise, for ever excluded from the world, was herself dissolved in
> the void, whose infinite contour no word, no image could encompass. (SCS,
> p. 292, ta)

The threat is like death and not like it, excessive and immeasurable. Language
cannot remove the threats to Françoise's existence, 'on ne pouvait pas se
défendre avec des mots timides' ('she could not defend herself with timid words')
(I, pp. 500-501; SCS, p. 407).

This is an important realisation for Françoise who, before this crisis, had used
language to ward off the unthinkable. Language guarantees our existence and
identity; we must be able to say 'I am' (I, p. 146). Language confers reality. For
Françoise, 'tant qu'elle ne l'avait raconté à Pierre, aucun événement n'était tout
à fait vrai: il flottait, immobile, incertain, dans des espèces de limbes' ('nothing
that happened was completely real until she had told Pierre about it; it remained
poised, motionless and uncertain, in a kind of limbo') (I, p. 30; SCS, p. 17).[24] This
attitude is discussed by Elizabeth Fallaize in relation to the concept of Françoise
and Pierre's indivisibility.[25] I should like to modulate slightly her argument that
Françoise 'has an unshakable belief in the power of words.' This is true in the
sense that Françoise, a writer, never loses her fear of the power of narrative or
representation (see below); however, as Françoise's crisis deepens, language lets
her down. Her belief that as soon as she had explained things to Pierre, everything
would be alright is disappointed (I, p. 195). Likewise, her hope that if she managed
to encapsulate her anguish in words, she would be able to escape it; her words did
not relieve her (I, p. 369). As language becomes problematical, Françoise comes
to see it as part of her predicament rather than as a solution. Language itself is
inherently mysterious and ambiguous. Emblematic of this and a Gothic moment in
the text is the illegible note, written on a torn piece of paper, that Xavière slipped
under Françoise's door ('les dernières phrases étaient tout à fait illisibles') and
the illegible notice she pinned to her door ('un gribouillage illisible'): ' – C'est
illisible, dit Pierre. Il considéra un moment les signes mystérieux' (I, pp. 387-8);
'"It's illegible," said Pierre, as he studied the mysterious marks for a moment'
(SCS, p. 313). Françoise loses her trust in words (I, p. 145). She wonders: '[...]
Avec Pierre, on se sert tant de mots; mais qu'y a-t-il au juste dessous?' (I, p. 159);
'[...] With Pierre, we use so many words, but what exactly lies behind them?'
(SCS, p. 126, ta). Language – which amounts to ambiguous symbols (I, p.160,
SCS, p. 177) – is duplicitous. And Françoise is forced into a position where she
never knows what anything means: 'Derrière les mots et les gestes, qu'y avait-
il?' ('What was there beneath the phrases and the gestures?') (I, p. 166; SCS,
p. 131); 'Les phrases de Xavière étaient toujours à double sens' ('Xavière's words

---

24   Xavière accuses Françoise and Pierre of substituting language for life. 'Vous aviez
l'air de vivre les choses pour une fois, et pas seulement de les parler' (I, p. 253).

25   Fallaize, *The Novels*, p. 37.

always held a double meaning') (I, p. 294; SCS, p. 233). She is reduced to guessing (I, p. 314).

Excess that is manifest in Beauvoir's writing is present on a thematic level too. In *L'Invitée*, the confrontation between consciousnesses, signalled in the epigraph, is related in terms of Gothic excess. It is a fight to the death. Literally. This confrontation is overlain by the mortal battle for narrative authority;[26] Françoise will kill Xavière, who wishes to 'se saisir de Françoise et la faire entrer de force dans son histoire' ('batten on Françoise and force her to become part of her story') (I, p. 491; SCS, p. 399). Her fear is a Gothic fear of the power of representation.[27] Françoise's sense of identity is intimately threatened by Xavière. It is as if she were reduced to a character in Xavière's fiction, as if her identity were nothing more than an effect of Xavière's narrative. She will kill Xavière in order to be able to tell her own story, to impose her version of the truth. Françoise destroys the flesh and blood Xavière so as to destroy Xavière's narrative: 'Jalouse, traîtresse, criminelle. On ne pouvait pas se défendre avec des mots timides et des actes furtifs. Xavière existait, la trahison existait. Elle existe en chair et en os, ma criminelle figure. Elle n'existera plus' (I, pp. 500–501); 'Jealous, traitorous, guilty. She could not defend herself with timid words and furtive deeds. Xavière existed, the betrayal existed. My criminal face exists in the flesh. It will exist no more' (SCS, pp. 406–7, ta). As Elizabeth Fallaize argues, 'she crushes the claim of another to narrate her story.'[28]

L'Invitée is Gothic in its violence. The novel celebrates Françoise's criminal behaviour. Eve Kosofsky Sedgwick tells us that the most characteristic energies of the Gothic novel concern the impossibility of restoring to their original oneness characters divided from themselves.[29] A Gothic preoccupation with the dissolution of the self runs through *L'Invitée* as a whole. Françoise's identity progressively disintegrates in her encounter with Xavière; as we read at one of the crisis points in the novel, 'Françoise, à jamais dépossédée du monde, se dissolvait elle-même dans ce vide' ('Françoise, for ever excluded from the world, was herself dissolved in the void') (I, p. 364; SCS, p. 292, ta). She is divided from herself: 'séparée d'elle-même' (I, p. 301) and we read: 'Françoise considéra avec horreur cette femme que contemplaient les yeux fulgurants de Xavière, cette femme qui était elle' (I, p. 499); 'Françoise considered with horror the woman that Xavière looked

---

[26]   There is a third struggle taking place, too. This struggle is an allegorical battle: 'A la longue, le caprice, l'intransigeance, l'égoïsme superbe, toutes ces valeurs truquées, avaient dévoilé leur faiblesse et c'était les vieilles vertus dédaignées qui remportaient la victoire. J'ai gagné, pensa Françoise avec triomphe' (I, p. 467); 'In the long run, capriciousness, intransigence, arrogant selfishness, all these artificial values had revealed their weakness, and it was the old disdained virtues which had triumphed' (SCS, pp. 378–9). Françoise's satisfaction is clearly premature. In any case, readers may find it difficult to concur with her, asking themselves exactly which virtues she has in mind. Françoise has made much of jettisoning her 'pure soul,' and this 'victory' seems to reside in deceiving and lying to Xavière. A signal example of *mauvaise foi*?

[27]   This aspect of Gothic fiction is discussed by Botting. See pp. 14, 157, 171.

[28]   Fallaize, *The Novels*, p. 36.

[29]   Sedgwick, pp. 12–13.

at with blazing eyes, the woman that she was' (SCS, p. 405, ta). She can only reintegrate her personality through sacrificial violence. As Xavière is dying, the the final words of the text assert: 'C'était sa volonté qui était en train de s'accomplir, plus rien ne la séparait d'elle-même. Elle avait enfin choisi. Elle s'était choisie' (I, p. 503); 'It was her own will which was being accomplished, now nothing at all separated her from herself. She had at last made a choice. She had chosen herself' (SCS, p. 409). On another level Xavière comes between Françoise and Pierre, who assert their unity: 'Toi et moi, on ne fait qu'un; c'est vrai, tu sais, on ne peut pas nous définir l'un sans l'autre' (I, p. 29); 'You and I are simply one. That's the truth, you know. Neither of us can be defined without the other' (SCS, p. 17, ta). When Françoise disagrees with Pierre over Xavière, Françoise 'avait l'impression pénible d'être divisée contre elle-même' ('she had the painful impression of being divided against herself') (I, p. 133; SCS, p. 104). Violence is Françoise's only chance to reintegrate the sundered elements. The text vindicates Françoise, but she is also depicted as a monster.[30] *L'Invitée* undermines villain/victim and villain/heroine dichotomies and ultimately subverts the Gothic convention itself; our villain/heroine triumphs, and readers are deprived of the expected Gothic closure advancing moral resolutions.[31]

Xavière, whose very existence is conceived as a threat to Françoise's sense of identity, the embodiment of the threat to Françoise, is constructed by the text as a demoniacal, nonhuman figure. The mystery and threat that Xavière represents are accentuated by the fact that she appears in the text with no introduction. Her relationship with Françoise before the point when they are sitting in the Moorish café together (I, p. 21) is not elucidated. Like other Gothic characters, Xavière, an orphan, appears as it were out of nowhere, with almost no history, like a mysterious foundling. She is the mysterious 'X.' As Beauvoir writes in *La Force de l'âge*, the novel begins when a stranger enters Françoise and Pierre's life (FA, p. 337).

A number of details contribute to the construction of Xavière as a menacing figure. When she burns herself, she is portrayed as crazy and dangerous. Xavière's smile encapsulates her madness: 'Un sourire aigu retroussait ses lèvres; c'était un sourire intime et solitaire comme un sourire de folle, un sourire voluptueux et torturé de femme en proie au plaisir' (I, p. 354); 'A bitter smile [was] curling her lips. It was an intimate, solitary smile, like the smile of a half-wit; the voluptuous, tortured smile of a woman possessed by sexual pleasure' (SCS, p. 284, ta). Xavière's madness is not foregrounded but is all the more 'threatening' in the way it is hinted at. During the Christmas Eve party, Xavière's response to Paule's dance reveals her susceptibility and foreshadows the incidents in the nightclub: 'La bouche entreouverte, les yeux embués, Xavière respirait avec peine; elle ne savait plus où elle était, elle semblait hors d'elle-même; Françoise détourna les yeux avec gêne, l'insistance de Pierre était indiscrète et presque obscène; ce

---

[30]   Beauvoir refers to her as such (albeit to regret the aesthetic mistake she made) in FA, p. 387.

[31]   See Botting, pp. 7–8. He points out that some moral endings were, in any case, no more than 'perfunctory tokens.'

visage de possédée n'était pas fait pour être vu' (I, p. 184); 'With lips parted, and lack-lustre eyes, Xavière scarcely breathed; she no longer knew where she was; she seemed out of her body. Françoise looked away, embarrassed: Pierre's insistence was indiscreet and almost obscene, this rapt face was not for public view' (SCS, p. 146). Xavière's reaction to Pierre's telling Françoise that Xavière and he are in love is suggestive of madness: 'Xavière se débattait sans secours parmi ces menaces écrasantes qu'elle apercevait tout autour d'elle, seule comme une hallucinée' (I, p. 255); 'Xavière was struggling all alone with the crushing threats she saw around her, alone like someone suffering from hallucinations.' (SCS, p. 204, ta). Xavière's room is described as the cell of a lunatic ('un cachot d'hallucinée', I, p. 342). Françoise wonders about Xavière's sanity because of her violent reaction to having had sex with Gerbert: 'Et si Xavière était devenue brusquement folle?' (I, p. 387); 'What if Xavière had suddenly become insane?' (SCS, p. 312). There is only one other reference to Xavière's madness: during a quarrel with Pierre, Xavière looks at him 'with the sly and triumphant look of a lunatic' (I, p. 414, SCS, p. 335), and after the quarrel it is as if she were possessed by an enraged demon (I, p. 416, SCS, p. 336).

Repeated references to Xavière's smile, which is not a smile but a maniacal rictus or grin, accumulate in the text and contribute to the creation of a threatening, demoniacal persona. [32] For the most part, her smiles are connoted negatively, connected with scorn, malice, and cruelty. Her first smile is 'curious', expressing scorn and even spite, and Xavière's 'jugement malveillant,' her 'malicious reaction,' gives Françoise an unpleasant shock (I, p. 36, SCS, p. 22). The term 'rictus,' commonly used to denote Xavière's smiles, suggests an unnatural, twisted smile, and the image of an animal baring its teeth is often conveyed. Her smiles are frequently secretive and mysterious, expressing connivance with herself. Examples are plentiful. One of the most striking is when Xavière smiles to herself, imagining sadistic sexual pleasure:

> Les lèvres de Xavière se retroussèrent sur ses dents blanches.
> 'Je le ferais souffrir,' dit-elle d'un air voluptueux.
> Françoise la regarda avec un peu de malaise [...]. A quelle image d'elle-même cachée aux yeux de tous souriait-elle avec une mystérieuse connivence? [...]
> Le rictus s'effaça [...]. (I, pp. 228–9)

> Xavière's lip curled back over her white teeth.
> 'I'd make him suffer,' she said voluptuously.
> Françoise looked at her a little uneasily [...]. What picture of herself, concealed from the eyes of the world, was she smiling at with mysterious complicity? [...]
> The strange smile left her face [...]. (SCS, p. 183, ta)

At one point, her smile is clearly described in terms of vaginal imagery. It is depicted as dangerous, a wound infected by jealousy: 'Une passion de haine et de souffrance

---

[32] Moi notes how Xavière's mouth is repeatedly emphasised and discusses references to her smile, *Simone de Beauvoir*, p. 116.

gonflait sa face, où la bouche s'entrouvrait dans un rictus semblable à la blessure d'un fruit trop mûr; par cette plaie béante, éclatait au soleil une pulpe secrète et vénéneuse' (I, p. 407); 'A wave of violent hatred and suffering swelled her face where her mouth was partly open in a rictus, like a cut on an over-ripe fruit; and this open wound exposed to the sun a secret, venomous pulp' (SCS, pp. 328–9, ta). This is a vivid, horrific Gothic image.[33] To a great extent it is the accumulation of the motif of the mouth in the text that accounts for its symbolical power.[34]

Animal imagery associated with Xavière reinforces the impression that she is demoniacal. The bestial within the human is, as already noted, a characteristically Gothic theme. These powerful images can suggest slaughter and cannibalism. The word 'proie' reappears over and over in the text.[35] Françoise becomes aware that Xavière is 'charnelle' (animal, sensual) when they are out dancing and when, once again, Xavière's sexual fantasies are under discussion:

> Les yeux avides, les mains, les dents aiguës que découvraient les lèvres entrouvertes cherchaient quelque chose à saisir, quelque chose qui se touche. Xavière ne savait pas encore quoi: les sons, les couleurs, les parfums, les corps, tout lui était une proie. (I, pp. 311–12)

> Her avid eyes, her hands, her sharp teeth visible between her partly opened lips were in search of something to sieze, something tangible. Xavière did not yet know what; sounds, colours, perfumes, bodies, everything was her prey. (SCS, p. 247)

Pierre, who has been surreptitiously watching Xavière, whom he suspects of falling in love with Gerbert, tells Françoise that it is as if Xavière wants to eat up Gerbert. Françoise remembers noticing Xavière's avid look during the Christmas Eve party (I, p. 243, SCS, p. 195). Shortly after the episode in the nightclub, Françoise realises she has been powerless against Xavière's hatred, against her affection, and against her thoughts: Elle les avait laissées mordre sur elle, elle avait fait d'elle-même une proie' (I, p. 364); 'She had let them bite into her; she had turned herself into a prey' (SCS, p. 293). She feels impelled to run away from Xavière and her 'tentacules avides qui voulaient la dévorer toute vive' ('avid tentacles which wanted to eat her alive') (I, p. 367; SCS, p. 295, ta). In her room Xavière is like an animal in her den; the terms 'se terrer' (to go to earth) and 'ruminer' (to ruminate) are used (disturbingly discordant with the term 'cloîtrée' [cloistered] used in the same sentence).[36] According to Pierre, Xavière 'se terre dans son coin comme une bête malade' ('buries herself in her lair like a sick animal') (I, p.163; SCS, p.129). To Françoise, listening behind Xavière's door, it is as if Xavière's thoughts are alive, as if they are 'animal': 'On aurait cru entendre

---

[33]   The word 'plaie' recalls Xavière's self inflicted wound, I, p. 354.

[34]   References to Xavière's smile can be found on I, pp. 68, 72, 75, 124, 190, 253, 308, 366, 395, 416, 495, and twice on p. 498.

[35]   Examples: I, pp. 312, 354, 364, 365.

[36]   Conventual imagery is typically Gothic.

palpiter les secrètes pensées que Xavière caressait dans sa solitude' (I, p. 341); 'It was like listening to the heartbeat of the secret thoughts that Xavière caressed when alone' (SCS, p. 274, ta). Xavière's sobbing is described as plaintive animal cries ('plainte animale', I, p. 386), and Françoise imagines her 'huddled wild-eyed in a corner' ('traquée dans un coin') (I, p.387; SCS, p. 312). The sexual associations of the powerful animal image of Xavière that opens the final episode of *L'Invitée* are unmistakable: 'Une femelle, pensa [Françoise] avec passion. [...] Elle était là, tapie derrière la porte, dans son nid de mensonges [...]' (I, p. 491); '"A bitch," she thought, enraged. [...] She was there, crouching behind the door, in her nest of lies [...]' (SCS, p. 399). The animalisation of Xavière combined with the sense of hidden danger make this a supremely Gothic image, full of dread.[37]

This animal imagery is in sharp contrast to the religious overtones of other images. For example, Françoise hesitates before going into Xavière's room:

> C'était vraiment un lieu sacré; il s'y célébrait plus d'un culte, mais la divinité suprême vers qui montaient la fumée des cigarettes blondes et les parfums de thé et de lavande, c'était Xavière elle-même, telle que ses propres yeux la contemplaient. (I, p. 166)

> It really was a holy place. Here more than one form of worship was celebrated, but the supreme deity towards whom there rose the smoke of Virginian cigarettes, the scent of tea and of lavender, was Xavière herself, as she imagined herself to be. (SCS, p.132, ta)

(This is consistent with Xavière's manner when attending to herself; 'there was always something mysterious and ritualistic in her gestures' (I, p. 226; SCS, p. 181).) Xavière is divine then, as well as animal. The resulting discordance adds to readers' uneasiness. However, religion here is distorted; the worship taking place is suggestive of idolatry and narcissism; cigarette smoke and perfume replace incense, and the blood-red light in the room is redolent of sacrifice ('lueur sanglante' I, p. 167). Another memorable religious image occurs in the final lines of Part One of *L'Invitée*; Françoise refers to Xavière as a miracle in her life:

> Elle était en train de se déssécher à l'abri des constructions patientes et des lourdes pensées de plomb, lorsque soudain, dans un éclatement de pureté et de liberté, tout ce monde trop humain était tombé en poussière; il avait suffi du regard naïf de Xavière pour détuire cette prison et maintenant, sur cette terre délivrée, mille merveilles allaient naître par la grâce de ce jeune ange exigeant. Un ange sombre avec de douces mains de femme, rouges comme des mains paysannes, avec des lèvres à l'odeur de miel, de tabac blond et de thé vert. (I, pp. 264–5)

> She had been slowly withering away under the protection of painstakingly constructed ideas and leaden-heavy thoughts when suddenly, in a burst of purity and freedom, all this too-human world had crumbled away. One open childlike look from Xavière had sufficed to destroy that prison, and now, on this

---

[37] This is not the first mention of a nest in connection with Xavière. See I, p. 152.

delivered earth a thousand marvels would come into being, through the grace of
this exacting young angel. A dark angel with gentle feminine hands, as red as
those of a peasant woman, with lips perfumed with honey, Virginian tobacco and
green tea. (SCS, pp. 211–12, ta)

This dramatic metaphor is Gothic in its emphasis on weight and imprisonment,
and it is perfectly integrated in the dense symbolic network of *L'Invitée*. What is of
particular interest here is the religious diction employed, 'terre délivrée,' 'grâce,'
'jeune ange,' and the discordances set up; the angel is 'exigeant' and 'sombre.'
Paradoxically, it is this dark, destructive angel bringing light into Françoise's life.
The sexual overtones of the image are unmistakable. Xavière is surely a fallen
angel. According to Xavière herself, her soul is black; it is the bond she claims
with Pierre in opposition to Françoise's pure soul. She says to Pierre: 'Vous et moi,
nous ne sommes pas des créatures morales [...]. [...] Au fond vous êtes aussi traître
que moi et vous avez l'âme aussi noire' (I, p. 443); 'You and I are not moral beings
[...]. [...] Deep down you're as treacherous as I am and your soul is just as black'
(SCS, p. 359). Xavière's divinity is diabolical. Discordance is set up and resolved.
Brought together, the two groups of images, animal and religious, ultimately
reinforce each other and the impression of uneasiness conveyed is accentuated.[38]
    The notion that Xavière casts a shadow on Françoise's life is recurrent. In this
example Xavière is defined as a mystery beyond language: 'Les mots ne pouvaient
que vous rapprocher du mystère mais sans le rendre moins impénétrable: il ne
faisait qu'étendre sur le coeur une ombre plus froide' (I, p. 162); 'Words could
only bring you nearer the mystery, but without making it any less impenetrable;
it only masked the heart in a more chilling shadow (SCS, p. 128, ta). As the
narrative enters its final stages, we read: 'Xavière s'obstinait à demeurer cette
étrangère dont la présence refusée étendait sur Françoise une ombre menaçante'
(I, p. 420); 'Xavière stubbornly remained a stranger whose rejecting presence cast
a threatening shadow over Françoise' (SCS, p. 340, ta). And on the evening before
Françoise will kill Xavière, Françoise again refers to Xavière as 'cette présence
ennemie qui étendait sur elle, sur le monde entier, une ombre pernicieuse' ('this
alien presence which cast a pernicious shadow over her and over the whole world')
(I, p. 484; SCS, p. 393).
    One of the recurring motifs associated with Xavière is her smell. References
to her smell are disquieting and add to her malignant aspect. They underline her
mysteriousness and hint of the supernatural. It is a motif closely linked to the
religious imagery and becomes a condensed reminder of Xavière's 'divinity/
fiendishness.' From the beginning, Françoise is tempted by Xavière's 'faint scent
of risk and mystery' (I, p. 39; SCS, p. 25). Smells associated with Xavière were
important elements of the religious images already quoted: 'la fumée des cigarettes
blondes et les parfums de thé et de lavande' (I, p. 166); 'lèvres à l'odeur de miel,

---

[38]   Religious diction is frequently used in connection with the trio and their relationships.
Xavière venerates Françoise (I, pp. 137, 312, 397) and Pierre (I, p. 227). Françoise reveres
Xavière (I, pp. 228, 262) and Pierre (I, 374). An explicit religious image casts Pierre as a
Christ figure and Françoise and Xavière as Marthe and Marie (I, p. 493).

de tabac blond et de thé vert' (I, p. 265). Xavière's smell becomes an obsession for Françoise; as she tries and fails to imagine Pierre and Xavière together in Xavière's room, it is one of the things she focuses on (I, p. 162). When Françoise herself is invited to spend the evening in Xavière's room, she enjoys 'cette lumière funèbre, et cette odeur de fleurs mortes et de chair vivante qui flottait toujours autour de Xavière' ('the funereal light, and the scent of dead flowers and living flesh that always emanated from Xavière') (I, p. 168; SCS, p. 133, ta). Somehow death and living flesh are conflated here; the effect is sinister. The gap between Françoise's pleasure and readers' response produces disquiet.[39] When they dance together, Françoise appreciates Xavière's smell: 'avec tendresse, elle respira l'odeur de thé, de miel et de chair qui était l'odeur de Xavière' (I, p. 186); 'with a certain tenderness, she inhaled the odour of tea, honey and flesh – Xavière's odour' (SCS, p. 148). The repetition of 'chair' in particular recalls the menacing associations that have been built up in the text until now, associations that again clash with Françoise's positive experience. Her disquiet is not aroused until she smells a new, mysterious odour: 'mêlée au parfum de tabac blond et de thé qui flottait toujours autour de Xavière, une étrange odeur d'hôpital' (I, pp. 418–19); 'in addition to the usual whiff of Virginia tobacco and tea peculiar to Xavière, a strange new medicinal smell' (SCS, p. 339). Suspense concerning the unusual smell ('l'odeur insolite', I, p. 422) is built up until Françoise realises that Xavière has been smelling ether (I, p. 423). This, too, has Gothic resonances.

Xavière's facial expressions are frequently referred to as a grimace.[40] Of course, a grimace is a facial expression closely related to a rictus. A grimace is not an attractive look. Paradoxically, Xavière is both ugly and beautiful. Her face is transformed almost miraculously from one to the other. Her physical changeability is highlighted when the two women leave the Moorish café at the beginning of the novel; one moment her face is puffy under the eyes and she looks liverish (I, p. 24); a few moments later her eyes are shining and her skin is pearly again (I, p. 25). Xavière's beauty is diabolical; when Xavière confronts Françoise over her affair with Gerbert, emphasis is placed on fire and burning, motifs that have gathered momentum in the text and are emblematic of hell: 'Elle fixait sur Françoise des yeux brûlants, ses joues étaient en feu, elle était belle' (I, p. 498); 'She was staring at Françoise with burning eyes, her cheeks were on fire, she was beautiful' (SCS, p. 404). Her face exemplifies her duplicity, being at once expressive and indecipherable and full of contradictions, inhuman almost. We read:

> Elle avait un séduisant visage, si nuancé, si changeant qu'il ne semblait pas fait
> de chair; il était fait d'extases, de rancunes, de tristesses, rendues magiquement

---

[39] This disparity pervades the whole episode. Xavière, 'her eyes shining with satisfaction,' appears to take sadistic pleasure in seeing Françoise, who hates tomatoes, swallow a thick tomato purée sandwich. It is impossible to concur with Françoise's indulgent reaction that you would have to have had a heart of stone not to be touched by her joy (I, pp. 168–9, SCS, p. 133).

[40] See 'grimace' (I, p. 22), 'grimace tragique' I, p. 41), 'grimace de dégoût' (I, p. 42), 'affreuse grimace' (I, p. 53), 'grimace' (I, p. 120).

sensibles aux yeux; pourtant malgré cette transparence éthérée, le dessin du nez, de la bouche était lourdement sensuel. (I, p. 75)[41]

Her face ws extremely attractive with such subtly variable shadings that it seemed not to be composed of flesh, but rather of extasy, of bitterness, of sorrow, to which the eye became magically sensitive. Yet, despite this ethereal transparency, the outlines of her nose and mouth were extremely sensual. (SCS, p. 55)

The same idea is repeated later in the book: 'Son visage décomposé par la fatigue et par l'angoisse semblait plus impalpable encore que coutume' (I, p. 263); 'Her face, drawn with fatigue and anguish, seemed even more impalpable than usual' (SCS, p. 210). Françoise feels that there is always something new to be discovered in Xavière's face: 'Xavière était une incessante nouveauté' (I, p. 284); 'Xavière had something fresh every time she looked at her' (SCS, p. 226). She has the uncanny feeling that a stranger is hidden behind Xavière's familiar features (I, p. 229). Xavière's face is a mask. Discordant language reproduces the contradictions on a textual level:

Ce visage parfumé, tout bruissant de tendresse, quelles pensées vénéneuses l'avaient soudain altéré? Elles s'épanouissaient avec malignité sous ce petit front têtu, à l'abri des cheveux de soie, et Françoise était sans défense contre elles [...]. (I, p. 293)[42]

What venomous thoughts had suddenly transformed this fragrant face which was lately redolent with tenderness? Malignantly they blossomed beneath her stubborn little forehead, under the shelter of her silky locks, and Françoise was defenceless against them. (SCS, p. 233)

Xavière's treacherous face and her 'features devoid of mystery' are asserted as equivalents and in her dependence, Françoise would like to collude with the mirage, with the 'illusions charmantes,' which hide untold venom (I, p. 404, SCS, pp. 326–7). Françoise is repelled by Xavière's fresh cruel face ('frais visage cruel', I, p. 482). In a typically Gothic fashion, the text fosters ambiguity. Xavière's innocent, childlike face is asserted as equivalent to her evil face. She is demoniacal and animal and she is also 'une petite fille aimante et désarmée dont on aurait voulu couvrir de baisers les joues nacrées' ('a fond ingenuous little girl, and one almost wanted to cover her pearly cheeks with kisses') (I, p. 48; SCS, p. 33). When she opens wide her 'pure' eyes and smiles charmingly (I, p. 79), Françoise wants to believe that Xavière's 'traits charmants composaient une honnête figure d'enfant et non un masque inquiétant de magicienne' ('these charming features went to make up the honest face of a child, and not the disquieting mask of a witch'), but this denial only tends to confirm that the latter is the case (I, p. 168; SCS, p. 133).

---

[41]   This is the second mention of Xavière's 'nez sensual.' See I, p. 32.
[42]   The original title of *L'Invitée* was 'Légitime defense.'

Is Xavière an instance of the Gothic split personality? This reading is supported by the text to some extent. She does display the self hatred of the Gothic (anti)heroine: 'Elle fixa dans le vide un regard farouche et dit à voix basse: "Je me dégoûte, j'ai horreur de moi"' (I, p. 131); 'She stared fiercely into space and said quietly: "I'm disgusted with myself. I loathe myself"' (SCS, p. 102, ta). Pierre tells Françoise about one of Xavière's crises of self-disgust (I, p. 162); he believes that everything in Xavière is pure and violent and recognises in her a perverse need to harm others and herself and to make herself hated (I, p. 164). Nevertheless the ambiguity remains, residing in our dependence on a narrator who is far from impartial, not to say unreliable. Xavière is denied the opportunity to tell her own story.

Xavière is not the only demoniacal character in *L'Invitée*. Françoise, we have noted, can be read as a monster. Élisabeth is also an evil figure. Élisabeth is clearly demoniacal in her madness and delirium as she fantasises about harming the trio:

> Est-ce un jour ils n'allaient pas descendre eux aussi au fond de cet enfer sordide? Attendre en tremblant, appeler au secours en vain, supplier, rester seul dans les regrets, l'angoisse et un dégoût de soi sans fin. Si sûrs d'eux, si orgueilleux, si invulnérables. Ne trouverait-on pas un moyen de leur faire du mal, en guettant bien? (I, p. 104)

> Would not they, too, some day drop into the the depths of this sordid hell? to wait in fear and trembling, to call vainly for help, to implore, to stand alone in the midst of regrets, anguish and an endless disgust of self. So sure of themselves, so proud, so invulnerable. By keeping careful watch, could not some way be found to hurt them? (SCS, p. 79)

Her jealousy sustains her desire to make them suffer: 'Quelque chose à faire; un acte authentique qui ferait couler de vraies larmes' (I, p. 283); 'Something that could be done; an authentic act that would make genuine tears flow' (SCS, p. 224). She sees it as a way of feeling truly alive. Her evilness is underlined. In the scene where she manipulates Gerbert, using him to upset what she takes to be the harmony of the trio, her evil machinations make her an Iago figure (I, pp. 333–5). She bears the burden of Françoise's darker side. She is the negative mirror image of Françoise, constructed in opposition to her, as Françoise's evil opposite. Evil doubles are stock Gothic characters. However, at the same time as Françoise and Élisabeth are opposed, they are intimately connected on a textual level by shared imagery and lexis, and the attempt to separate the two characters fails. In constructing Françoise and Élisabeth as character doubles, the text undermines the demoniac/benign dichotomy. For if Élisabeth is constructed as demoniac, textual inter-references and interferences make it impossible to sustain the image of Françoise as blameless victim. Interestingly, Élisabeth progressively 'disappears' from the text as Françoise jettisons her fine moral scruples.[43]

---

[43] For a full discussion of the connection between Françoise and Élisabeth, see my article 'Mirrored Characters in Beauvoir's *L'Invitée*: Françoise and Élisabeth' in *Beauvoir Studies*, 17 (2000–2001), 89–97.

The fear and horror evoked in the climactic moments and elsewhere in *L'Invitée* are characteristic of the Gothic. The effects produced, Françoise's dread and her feelings of revulsion, are best understood in the light of Freud's notion of the uncanny. What happens in the nightclub is a good illustration of this; what is horrible and dangerous is hidden behind Xavière's smile: 'Il recélait quelque chose d'horrible. [...] Derrière ce rictus maniaque, un danger menaçait, plus définitif que tous ceux qu'elle avait jamais imaginés' (I, p. 354); 'It concealed something horrible. [...] Behind that maniacal grin, was the threat of a danger more positive than any she had ever imagined' (SCS, pp. 284–5). Françoise is horrified that something that she has known and feared since she was a small child is now going to be revealed:

> Il n'y avait plus moyen d'en éviter le dévoilement terrifiant; jour après jour, minute après minute, Françoise avait fui le danger, mais c'en était fait, elle l'avait enfin rencontré cet infranchissable obstacle qu'elle avait pressenti sous des formes incertaines depuis sa plus petite enfance. (I, p. 363)

> There was now no way of avoiding its terrifying disclosure. Day after day, minute after minute, Françoise had fled the danger; but the worst had happened, and she had at last come face to face with this insurmountable obstacle which she had sensed, behind a shadowy outline, since her earliest childhood. (SCS, p. 292)

What should have remained hidden is about to be exposed, the repressed to return. The fact that the danger is undetermined heightens the sense of mystery and fear. These episodes epitomise what Botting finds to be one of the defining characteristics of Gothic texts, namely, 'a sense of a grotesque, irrational and menacing presence pervading the everyday and causing its decomposition.'[44] The sense of something strange and threatening hidden behind everydayness is something that recurs throughout *L'Invitée* where the banal and the sinister are juxtaposed.[45]

As the novel reaches its climax, Françoise's distress is heightened as 'derrière chacun de ces meubles familiers, quelque chose d'horrible guettait' ('behind each familiar piece of furniture something horrible was lying in wait') (I, p. 498; SCS, p. 404). This recalls Élisabeth's experience during her quarrel with Claude when she was aware that 'dans l'ombre quelque chose d'horrible menaçait' ('in the shadows something horrible was threatening her') (I, p. 100; SCS, p. 76). This, in turn, recalls Françoise's memory of an incident during her chidhood when she had found herself alone in her grandmother's house:

> C'était drôle et ça faisait peur; les meubles avaient l'air de tous les jours, mais en même temps ils étaient tous changés: tout épais, tout lourds, tout secrets; sous la bibliothèque et sous la console de marbre stagnait une ombre épaisse. (I, p. 146)

---

44   Botting, p. 160.
45   The cigarette ash deposited on Xavière's burn is a small protective matress – 'le petit matelas protecteur' (I, p. 354). The benign everydayness of the object jars with sinister role it is playing here.

> It was funny and frightening; the furniture looked just as it always did, but at
> the same time it was completely changed: thick and heavy and secret; under
> the book-stand and under the marble console there lurked an ominous shadow.
> (SCS, p. 115)

The idea of someone or something lurking in the shadows recurs as the novel
reaches its culmination when we read: 'cette conscience vorace qui avait
attendu dans l'ombre le moment de l'engloutir' (I, p. 500); 'this voracious
consciousness that had been waiting in the shadows for the moment to swallow
her up' (SCS, p. 406, ta).

An atmosphere of mystery and secrecy pervades the narrative and fosters
ambiguity. Words, sentences, events have multiple or uncertain meanings.
Questions are a distinguishing feature of the text. The words 'mystère' (mystery),
'mystérieux' (mysterious), and 'secret' (secret) constantly reappear, particularly
associated with Xavière. There is 'mysterious agitation' when Françoise knocks
at Xavière's door (I, p. 45; SCS, p. 31). When Françoise imagines the café where
Xavière and Pierre are meeting, a sense of mystery surrounds everything, and
Françoise will never know 'the secret of their tête-à-tête' (I, p. 153; SCS, p. 120).
Françoise surprises Xavière looking at Gerbert, and it is as if she is secretly and
imperiously taking possession of him (I, p. 186; SCS, p. 148). Xavière enfolds
Pierre's image in 'a mysterious caress' (I, p. 493; SCS, p. 400). It is only natural
that in this atmosphere, whispering should be a recurring motif.[46]

There are repeated references to magic and the supernatural in L'Invitée.
Françoise, Pierre and Xavière, and Élisabeth are all portrayed as victims of spells
that have been cast over them. After the incident in the nightclub, it is as if the trio
has been turned to stone by a magic spell (I, pp. 365 and 366). Earlier, '[Françoise]
avait envie de briser ce cercle magique où elle se trouvait retenue avec Pierre et
Xavière et qui la séparait de tout le reste du monde' ('[Françoise] wanted to smash
this magic circle in which she found herself confined with Pierre and Xavière
and which cut her off from the rest of the world') (I, p. 345; SCS, p. 277). After a
pleasant evening spent alone with Pierre, Françoise believes that 'enfin ce cercle
de passion et de souci où la sorcellerie de Xavière les retenait s'était rompu et ils
se trouvaient tout mêlés l'un à l'autre au coeur du monde immense' ('at last the
circle of passion and anxiety, in which Xavière's sorcery imprisoned them, had
been broken, and they found themselves completely at one with each other again
at the heart of the vast world') (I, p. 377; SCS, p. 303, ta). (Note the sense of
space and the contrast with images of enclosure that generally predominate.) But
minutes later her hopes are dashed; Pierre sees a light under Xavière's door and
his obsession takes over again. Françoise is overcome by despair as 'il lui semblait
s'être laissée leurrer par la précaire lucidité d'un fou qu'un souffle suffisait à
rejeter dans le délire' ('she felt that she had allowed herself to be deluded by the
precarious lucidity of a lunatic who could be toppled back into madness by a
breath of wind') (I, p. 378; SCS, p. 304, ta). In these examples, emphasis is lain

---

46   For examples, see I, pp. 215, 255, 378.

on enforced immobility, an idea linked with weight and enclosure. In Élisabeth's case, she believes that a spell has been cast on her that makes her incapable of authentic existence: 'Elle changeait tout ce qu'elle touchait en carton-pâte' (I, p. 272); 'She turned everything she touched into cardboard' (SCS, p. 215, ta). Xavière blames magic for making her destructive: 'Oh! Il y a un malheur sur moi, gémit-elle passionnément' (I, p. 130); 'Oh! there's a curse on me,' she wailed passionately' (SCS, 102).[47] She feels she is beyond help because she is marked out ('marquée') (I, p. 132). Thus Xavière is portrayed as a victim of magic, but, as we have seen, she is constructed as a demoniacal figure in the text, and she is also portrayed as a witch and magical powers are attributed to her. There are multiple references to her as a witch ('une sorcière') (I, pp. 190, 192, 298), a bewitcher ('l'ensorceleuse') (I, p. 491), and Françoise is afraid of her powers: 'Ce masque attirant, c'était une ruse, elle ne céderait pas à cette sorcellerie; [...] elle savait seulement qu'un danger la menaçait' (I, p. 164); 'That alluring mask was a trap, she would not give in to such witchcraft. [...] All she knew was that some danger was threatening her' (SCS, p. 130, ta). Xavière's malevolence is reiterated in the text; as *L'Invitée* reaches its climax, Françoise imagines Xavière 'dans la lumière mortuaire de sa chambre, [...] assise, enveloppée de son peignoir brun, maussade et maléfique' ('there in the sepulchral light of her room, [...] sitting wrapped in her brown dressing gown, sullen and maleficent') (I, p. 490; SCS, p. 398). The detail of the brown dressing gown is telling, as evocative perhaps of a witch's robe as it is of a monk's habit.[48]

In a central series of images, Xavière's hatred and, metonymically Xavière herself, become an embodiment of magic, an evil spell. Françoise is depicted as imagining, containing, and controlling this spell with magic of her own. It is worth quoting a key passage in full as it contains a rich web of resonances.

> Est-ce qu'on ne pouvait pas contempler la haine de Xavière en face, tout juste comme les gâteaux au fromage qui reposaient sur un plateau? Ils étaient d'un beau jaune clair, décorés d'astragales roses, on aurait presque eu envie d'en manger si on eût ignoré leur goût aigre de nouveau-né. Cette petite tête ronde n'occupait pas beaucoup plus de place dans le monde, on l'enfermait dans un seul regard; et ces brumes de haine qui s'en échappaient en tourbillon, si on les faisait rentrer dans leur boîte, on les tiendrait aussi à sa merci. Il n'y avait qu'un mot à dire: dans un écroulement plein de fracas la haine se résoudrait en une fumée exactement contenue dans le corps de Xavière et aussi inoffensive que le goût sur caché sous la crème jaune des gâteaux; elle se sentait exister, mais ça ne faisait guère de différence, en vain se tordait elle en volutes rageuses: on verrait tout juste passer sur le visage désarmé quelques remous imprévus et réglés comme des nuages au ciel. (I, p. 301)

---

[47]   This is echoed in the dramatic scene in Françoise's hospital room that follows Pierre's declaration that Xavière and he love each other when Xavière exclaims: 'C'est un malheur, j'en suis sûre, je ne suis pas de force' (I, p. 255); 'It's a curse, I know it is, I'm not up to it' (SCS, p. 204, ta).

[48]   The monk is a Gothic figure connected with mystery and evil. See I, p. 481.

Wasn't it possible to look Xavière's hatred in the face, exactly as she did the cheese-cakes laid out on a tray? They were a beautiful pale yellow, decorated with pink swirls; you might almost have been tempted to eat one if you didn't know they tasted sour like a new-born baby. Xavière's small round head didn't occupy much more space in the world, it could be held in a single glance; and if the mists of hatred whirling from it could only be forced back into their container, then they too, could be at your mercy. Only one word was needed: the hatred would collapse in a mighty din, reduced to fumes perfectly contained in Xavière's body and as harmless as the sour taste hidden under the yellow cream of the cakes; it felt it existed, but that made very little difference, it writhed in vain in whorls of rage: a few eddies would be glimpsed passing almost imperceptibly over Xavière's defenceless face, unforseen and regulated like clouds in the sky. (SCS, p. 239, ta)[49]

Xavière's pernicious spell might be shut up in a box, reduced to vapour/fumes. There are strong echoes of genies here. Once contained, Xavière's spell would be as harmful, that is, harmless, as the pale yellow cheesecakes. Xavière's head is conflated with the cakes; they are on a tray and there are clear suggestions of beheading. (The mention of the pink decorations adds to the sinister overtones.) There are numerous other Gothic features in this passage. Like Xavière, the cakes are not what they seem; their true nature is hidden. They may look appetizing, but their taste is sour. The 'goût aigre de nouveau-né' is a repellant, disgusting image with overtones of cannibalism and evil.[50] The image of a collapsing building is typically Gothic and ties up with other images of glossy exteriors that hide rotting interiors and risk sudden collapse. Françoise's power to contain and control Xavière's 'spell' resides in her own gaze and in her use of language. For one moment Françoise imagines she has succeeded, that her words have worked. The text is interrupted by Pierre taking his leave. Sixteen lines later, Françoise has to acknowledge that she is powerless to resist Xavière's evil magic, she does not believe her own words. The text goes on as if there had been no interruption: 'Le mot magique, il aurait fallu qu'il jaillît du fond de son âme, mais son âme était tout engourdie. Le brouillard maléfique restait suspendu à travers le monde, il empoisonnait les bruits et les lumières, il pénétrait Françoise jusqu'aux moelles' (I, p. 302); 'The magic word would have had to spring from the depths of her soul, but her soul was completely numb. The maleficent fog still hung over the world,

---

[49]   The published translation of this passage is particularly misleading.

[50]   The adjective 'aigre' recalls the description of the morning when Françoise asked Xavière to come to live in Paris (I, p. 252). See also I, p. 192: 'toutes ses pensées avaient un goût aigre.' The cakes have already acquired symbolic significance; earlier Françoise's thoughts about 'an enormous white cake decorated with fruit and swirls of icing' ('un énorme gâteau blanc, garni de fruits et d'astragales') interrupt a story she is telling that no one is listening to (I, p. 73, SCS, p. 53, ta). The sickly cake comes to stand for her alienation, her sickness at heart. The same image recurs later, this time connected directly with Xavière, who fills her thoughts 'as heavily as the huge cake at the Pôle Nord': 'elle remplissait la pensée aussi lourdement que le gros gâteau du Pôle Nord' (I, p. 83; SCS, p. 61).

distorting sounds and lights, penetrating Françoise to the very marrow of her bones' (SCS, p. 240, ta). This image is akin to those images relating Xavière to a shadow that looms over Françoise's life. It is reiterated later, after the climactic moments in the nightclub: 'Ça faisait des semaines que Françoise n'était plus capable de réduire en inoffensives fumées la haine, la tendresse, les pensées de Xavière' (I, p. 364); 'For many weeks Françoise had no longer been able to reduce Xavière's hatred, her affection, her thoughts, to harmless vapors' (SCS, p. 293, ta).

Poison is a recurrent Gothic motif in *L'Invitée* and one frequently linked with Xavière.[51] In one related image, Xavière's hatred is compared to an acid producing noxious fumes. It occurs after Xavière has harmed herself and before Françoise suffers her second crisis in the nightclub: 'Ça reprenait: à nouveau corrosive comme un acide, la haine s'échappait de Xavière en lourdes volutes; c'était inutile de se défendre contre cette morsure déchirante [...]' (I, p. 361); 'It was beginning all over again. Dense vapors of hatred, as corrosive as an acid, were once more emanating from Xavière, and there was no defence against its excruciating bite' (SCS, p. 290).[52]

Françoise's experience with the fortune teller adds to the strange and Gothic atmosphere in the novel. The gypsy appears to know all about Françoise's life. She takes her to one side and, in secret, tells Françoise that she knows about the unhappiness that Xavière has brought into her relationship with Pierre and offers to sell her a charm that will make her happy again (I, pp. 158–9; SCS, p. 125). The whole episode is redolent of the Gothic; note the pathetic fallacy of the drizzle ('cette bruine poisseuse avait pénétré jusqu'au fond de son âme'), 'the presence on stage of a big doll that seemed almost alive' (I, p. 153; SCS, p. 121), Françoise's trembling and holding out her hand 'machinalement' (mechanically/

---

[51]   See earlier quotations: 'mille venins cachés' (I, p. 404), 'pulpe secrète et vénéneuse' (I, p. 407).

[52]   Interestingly, these images are akin to images of unreason that, according to Foucault, inspired such fear in the middle of the eighteenth century: 'Tout d'abord le mal entre en fermentation dans les espaces clos de l'internement. Il a toutes les vertus qu'on prête à l'acide [...]. Le mélange aussitôt bouillonne, dégageant vapeurs nocives et liquides corrosifs [...]. Ces vapeurs brûlantes s'élèvent ensuite, se répandent dans l'air et finissent par retomber sur le voisinage, imprégnant les corps, contaminant les âmes. [...] Par cette atmosphère chargée de vapeurs maléfiques, des ville entières sont menacées [...]' (*Histoire de la folie*, p. 376); 'First the evil began to ferment in the closed spaces of confinement. It had all the virtues attributed to acid [...]. The mixture boiled immediately, releasing harmful vapors and corrosive liquids [...]. These burning vapors then rise, spread through the air, and finally fall upon the neighborhood, impregnating bodies and contaminating souls. [...] By this atmosphere laden with maleficent vapors, entire cities were threatened [...]' (*Madness and Civilisation*, p. 193). Poison is mentioned in *L'Invitée* at other moments too. In her suffering, Françoise has the impression that the blood running in her veins is poisoned: 'le sang qui courait dans ses veines était empoisonné' (I, p. 261). As the novel culminates, Françoise feels she cannot go on living in the poisoned air: 'cet air empoisonné' (I, p. 491).

without thinking), and the secrecy and magic. There is also the strange, unsettling suggestion that the future is already mapped out and can be known.

The text enacts this strangeness. Prefiguration is disturbing and unsettling. The dance that takes place just before Xavière harms herself prefigures the text and what Xavière is about to do. The dancer mimes a seduction scene where the woman appears to encourage then reject her suitor before falling into his arms. Xavière's behaviour with Pierre is brought to mind. In miming a sorceress whose every movement suggests dangerous mystery – 'une sorcière aux gestes pleins de dangereux mystère' – and a peasant woman spinning wildly ('la tête folle'), the dancer seems to presage Xavière's crazy gesture that has such dangerous and mysterious connotations (I, p. 354; SCS, p. 284).[53] In a similar way, the Spanish poem which triggers Françoise's crisis and which is intensely symbolic, prefigures the narrative:

> Même si l'on ne comprenait pas le sens des mots, on était pris aux entrailles par cet accent passionné, par ce visage que défigurait une ardeur pathétique; le poème parlait de haine et de mort, peut-être aussi d'espoir, et à travers ses sursauts et ses plaintes, c'était l'Espagne déchirée qui se faisait présente à tous les coeurs. Le feu et le sang avaient chassé des rues les guitares, les chansons, les châles éclatantes, les fleurs de nard; les maisons de danse s'étaient éffondrées et les bombes avaient crevé les outres gonflées de vin; dans la chaude douceur des soirs rôdaient la peur et la faim. Les chants flamencos, la saveur des vins dont on se grisait, ce n'était plus que l'évocation funèbre d'un passé défunt. Pendant un moment, les yeux fixés sur la bouche rouge et tragique, Françoise s'abandonna aux images désolées que suscitait l'âpre incantation; elle aurait voulu se perdre corps et âme dans ces appels, dans ces regrets qui tressaillaient sous les mystérieuses sonorités. (I, pp. 362–3)

> Even if you didn't understand the words, you were gripped by her impassioned accent, by her moving face distorted with passion; the poem was about hatred and death, about hope too perhaps, and through its leaps and plaintive cries, the fate of ravaged Spain was there in everyone's hearts. Fire and blood had driven the guitars from the streeets, gone were the songs, the dazzling shawls, and the spikenard blossoms; the cabarets had been razed and the bombs had ripped open the goatskins full of wine; in the warm gentle evenings, fear and hunger stalked. The flamenco songs and the taste of intoxicating wines were now no more than funereal evocations of a dead past. For a little while, her eyes fixed on the red and tragic mouth, Françoise gave herself up to the desolate pictures evoked by this rasping incantation; she longed to lose herself, body and soul, in these lamentations, in the regrets trembling beneath the mysterious sounds. (SCS, p. 291, ta)

---

[53]   Xavière is associated with the notion 'paysanne.' When she is introduced, one of the details that is highlighted is her red peasant woman's hands, her 'doigts rouges de paysanne' (I, p. 21) and, although since she came to Paris, Xavière is no longer 'paysanne' (I, p. 227), her hands remain 'rouges comme des mains paysannes' (I, p. 265).

The poem and the narrative share a significant number of motifs: hatred and death, fire and blood, regrets. Fear is prowling around, though the evening is apparently mild and pleasant. Note the terms 'âpre incantation' and mystérieuses sonorités' suggestive of magic spells. A comparable effect is recreated later in the novel; Françoise has just recalled Xavière's maniacal smile when 'un long chant sanglotant perça l'épaisseur brûlante de l'air' ('a long sobbing chant pierced the dense burning air') (I, p. 420; SCS, p. 340, ta). For Françoise, 'cette musique veule dans cette solitude torride lui paraissait l'image même de son coeur. [...] [Elle] eut envie de s'asseoir au bord du trottoir et de n'en plus bouger' ('the listless music in this scorching solitude seemed to her the very reflection of her heart. [...] Françoise longed to sit down on the edge of the pavement and never move again') (I, pp. 420–21; SCS, p. 340, ta).[54]

The prefiguration that occurs in *L'Invitée* is all the more disturbing in that it recurs. Freud points to the sense of helplessness that is aroused by the unintended recurrence of the same situation, the impression of 'something fateful and inescapable' ('The Uncanny', p. 237). He relates recurrence to the uncanny, classing it as an instance of the phenomenon of the double. Françoise is imprisoned in her obsession, and the text underlines how the same things recur time and time again:

> Depuis combien de temps durait-elle cette discussion indéfinie et toujours neuve? Qu'a fait Xavière? Que fera-t-elle? Que pense-t-elle? Pourquoi? Soir après soir, l'obsession renaissait aussi harassante, aussi vaine, avec ce goût de fièvre dans la bouche, et cette désolation au coeur, et cette fatigue du corps sommeilleux. Quand les questions auraient enfin trouvé une réponse, d'autres questions, toutes pareilles, reprendraient la ronde implacable: Que veut Xavière? Que dira-t-elle? Comment? Pourquoi? Il n'y avait aucun moyen de les arrêter. (I, p. 379)

> How long was this unending and perpetually new discussion to last? What has Xavière done? What would she do? What was she thinking? Why? Evening after evening, the obsession was revived, always as exhausting, always as futile, and with the same feverish taste in her mouth, the same desolation in her heart, the same weariness in her sleepy body. When these questions had finally been

---

[54]   It is interesting to note that the dances that Paule Berger performs at the Christmas Eve party also prompt painful thoughts in Françoise (I, pp. 182–4 and 193–4). At one point, Paule is wearing a mask, a Gothic motif associated with Xavière, and mimes a storm: 'elle était à elle seule tout un ouragan déchaîné' (I, p. 193); 'alone she became a raging hurricane personified' (SCS, p. 154, ta). There are strong echoes here of the image of a natural disaster applied to Xavière: 'Avec un peu d'effroi, Françoise considéra cette vivante catastrophe qui envahissait sournoisement sa vie; c'était Pierre qui par son respect, son estime avait brisé les digues où Françoise la contenait. Maintenant qu'elle était déchaînée, jusqu'où ça irait-il?' (I, p. 128); 'A little terror-stricken, Françoise looked at this living catastrophe that had surreptitiously invaded her life. It was Pierre who, by his respect, by his esteem, had broken the dykes within which Françoise had confined her. Now that she was let loose, how far would it all go?' (SCS, p. 100, ta). See also 'ce fut une tournade qui secoua Françoise' (I, p. 210); 'a tournado shook Françoise' (SCS, p. 168, ta).

answered, a new series of identical questions would take up their relentless
round. What does Xavière want? What will she say? How? Why? There was no
way of putting a stop to them. (SCS, p. 305, ta)

The archetypal symbol of the circle expresses the never-ending nature of the trap.
It is a recurring motif; Françoise hoped she had finished with all the interpretations
and detailed analyses of Xavière's behaviour where Pierre could go round in circles
for hours on end (I, p. 244; SCS, pp. 195–6); reference has already been made to
'le cercle de passion et de souci' ('circle of passion and anxiety') where Xavière's
spell holds Françoise and Pierre (I, p. 377; SCS, p. 303, ta); Françoise, shortly
after this, will compare the busy 'lucid' street outside with her anguish-ridden
room ('engluée d'angoisse'), where her obsessive thoughts go round and round
without respite (I, p. 388; SCS, p. 313). She can see no way out: 'Des attentes, des
fuites, toute l'année s'était passée ainsi. [...] Il ne restait aucun salut. On pouvait
fuir, mais il faudrait bien revenir, et ce seraient d'autres attentes, et d'autres fuites,
sans fin' (I, p. 438); 'Waiting, fleeing, the whole year had been spent like that. [...]
There was no salvation. She could flee but she would have to return, and there
would be more waiting and more fleeing, endlessly' (SCS, p. 355, ta).

Textual parallels also produce an uncanny effect whilst adding to the intensity
of the text. The text duplicates the trap where Françoise is caught, reproducing her
never-ending nightmare. If we take the climatic moments in the book discussed
earlier, the parallels are conspicuous: the use of the verb 'consume'; the motif of
burning flesh; Xavière's insensibility; her ecstatic response; the sexual overtones,
which are connoted negatively – 'un sourire voluptueux et torturé de femme en
proie au plaisir' ('the voluptuous, tortured smile of a woman possessed by secret
pleasure') (I, p. 354); 'la jouissance maniaque' ('maniacal pleasure') (I, p. 363;
SCS, p. 292) – and the repetition of 'lunatic's smile' and the word 'maniacal.' In the
final pages of the novel, the words that burn like a branding iron recall Xavière's
'branding' of herself with the 'glowing end of her cigarette', and it is Françoise's
heart that is consumed by 'the burning lava' (I, p. 500; SCS, p. 406), recalling how
her thoughts had been 'burning like flames' (I, p. 363; SCS, p. 292, ta).[55]

Reflections in mirrors are also connected with the idea of the double. Freud
discusses the figure of the double in general and the way in which meeting one's
own image unexpectedly may be perceived as uncanny; but he is, he admits,
unable to explain this (Freud, pp. 236 and 238). In L'Invitée, the three motifs, gaze,
image/ reflection, and mirror, are interwined. These quintessential Gothic motifs
acquire their power in the book by force of their recurrence.

One of the sinister features of the concluding pages of L'Invitée, is the street
light that is lent the human capacity to look: 'On avait caché le globe du réverbère
sous un masque de fer noir et dentelé comme un loup vénitien. Sa lumière jaune
ressemblait à un regard' (I, p. 500); 'The globe of the street-lamp had been
disguised with a black metal shield scolloped like a venetian mask. Its yellow

---

[55] Eve Kosofsky Sedgwick considers repetition as the temporal metaphor of
doubleness, p. 139.

light resembled a glance' (SCS, p. 406). In this symbolic space, to be seen is to give others power.[56] Remember how Xavière bewitched Françoise: 'Cette sorcière s'était emparé de son image et lui faisait subir à son gré les pires envoûtements' (I, p. 298); 'The witch had had taken possession of her image and was casting the worst kinds of spells over it just as she wished' (SCS, p. 237, ta). Fear of being gazed upon and having her self stolen from her might explain why, faced with Xavière's version of events, Françoise would have liked to hide her face (I, p. 490; SCS, p. 398). Françoise is clear that she must defend her 'image' against those who have been trying to rob her of it (I, p. 500; SCS, p. 406). Her 'image' is far more than simply her reflection. It is her self/who she is. The idea that others can reduce us to an image is introduced very early in the text. Françoise tells Gerbert she is terrified when she is forced to realise that others also have consciousness: 'On a l'impression de ne plus être qu'une image dans la tête de quelqu'un d'autre' (I, p. 18); 'We feel as though we're nothing but an image in someone else's mind' (SCS, p. 7, ta). Others act as our mirror, showing us reflections of ourselves that threaten our sense of identity. In destroying Xavière, Françoise destroys her 'criminelle figure' that Xavière reflects back to her.

Françoise turns away from the gaze of the street light to be met by her reflection that springs up in the mirror. ('Son image jaillit soudain au fond du mirroir' (I, p. 500); 'Her image suddenly sprang from from the depth of her looking-glass' (SCS, p. 406).) This is a Gothic moment. As Françoise's identity disintegrated, we read: '[elle] n'avait plus que la pâle consistance d'une image' ('she now possessed no more than the pale substance of an image') (I, p. 364; SCS, p. 292, ta), and she was reduced to a ghostly presence: 'une vague phosphorescence qui traînait à la surface des choses, parmi des milliers et des milliers de vains feux follets' ('a faint phosphorescence hovering over the surface of things, amongst thousands and thousands of illusory will-o'-the-wisps') (I, p. 365; SCS, p. 293, ta). Thus 'image' also denotes Françoise's loss of self, loss of identity. When Françoise looks hard at her reflection ('Elle fixa l'image', p. 500) she claims back her self. It is a moment of reintegration. Significantly, Françoise's earlier moment of triumph had also been marked by her looking in the mirror (I, p. 467).

Françoise's defiant gesture, when she stares at herself in the mirror in the culminating moments of the novel, is all the more potent in view of her noted reluctance to look at herself at all, although, it must be said, this reluctance is not completely borne out by the text, where numerous examples of Françoise looking in mirrors can be found. Xavière says that Françoise never looks at herself (I, p. 179, repeated p. 183) and Françoise agrees that she treats her face like an 'objet étranger' (an unfamiliar object). What is important is that when Françoise does look at herself, she sees a blank, an absence. Her lack of a face is her lack

---

[56]   In his discussion of the ending of *L'Invitée*, Maurice Merleau-Ponty points out that 'once we are aware of the existence of others, we commit ourselves to being, among other things, what they think of us, since we recognize in them the exorbitant power to *see us.*' 'Metaphysics and the Novel', in *Critical Essays on Beauvoir*, ed. by Elaine Marks, Boston: Hall, 1987, pp. 31–44 (p. 41).

of self, of identity: 'Je ne suis personne, pensa Françoise. [...] Elle toucha son visage: ce n'était pour elle qu'un masque blanc' (I, p. 184); '"I am no one," thought Françoise. [...] She touched her face: to her it was no more than a white mask' (SCS, p. 146). Pierre's gaze could have given Françoise a shape, an identity, but he is looking at Xavière, not at her; she is part of him and invisible to him. Françoise blames herself for her loss of identity: 'Il n'y avait personne. [...] Elle avait cessé d'être quelqu'un; elle n'avait même plus de figure' (I, p. 216); 'There was no one. [...] She had ceased to be someone; she no longer even possessed a face' (SCS, p. 173, ta).[57] It is revealing to compare Françoise's attitude about mirrors with Xavière's. Just before Françoise is taken seriously ill and decides to go for a walk, she glances at her face in the mirror: 'C'était un visage qui ne disait rien; il était collé sur le devant de la tête comme une étiquette: Françoise Miquel. Le visage de Xavière, au contraire, c'était un intarissable chuchotement, c'était sans doute pour cela qu'elle se souriait si mystérieusement dans les miroirs' (I, p. 215); 'It was a face which conveyed no meaning; it was stuck on the front of her head like a label: Françoise Miquel. Xavière's face, on the contrary, was the source of inexhaustible conjecture: that was probably why she smiled at herself so mysteriously in mirrors' (SCS, p. 172, ta). However, note how Françoise, too, smiles at her reflection as she resigns herself to defeat (I, p. 417).

Reflections in mirrors suggest a sense of alienation and unreality. As she leaves her hospital room after weeks of confinement, Françoise's experience is compared to going through a mirror ('pénétrer à travers une glace') and a journey in the beyond ('un voyage dans l'au-delà') (I, pp. 239–40). Once she is well again, Françoise's alienation is captured when instead of living her life, she watches what is happening in a mirror behind the bar in the café (I, pp. 300–301). Élisabeth had a similar experience, watching the trio living their apparently happy lives in the mirror whilst she suffers in a sordid hell ('au fond d'[un] enfer sordide') (I, p. 104; SCS, p. 104).

Hell is a recurring motif in *L'Invitée* and is a further manifestation of the Gothic. The incident when Xavière harms herself terminates with an evocation of hell. It is suggestive of Dante's 'Inferno': 'On ne pourrait que tourner en rond tout autour dans une exclusion éternelle' (I, p. 355); 'Shut out for all eternity, she could only continue to circle round and round it' (SCS, p. 285, ta). Xavière's assessment of the episode that takes place shortly afterwards, when the trio are listening to the Spanish poem and when Xavière herself is in a trance like state, is ominous: 'On était au fond de l'enfer, je croyais qu'on n'en sortirait plus jamais' (I, p. 366); 'We were in the depths of hell. I began to think we'd neve get out again' (SCS, p. 294). Françoise is afraid that for the trio, 'c'était un noir enfer qui les attendait' ('a black hell lay in wait for them') (I, p. 397; SCS, p. 320). The depiction of Françoise's life is reminiscent of a vision of hell: 'Elle se laissait flotter passivement comme une épave, mais il y avait de noirs écueils à l'horizon; elle flottait sur un océan gris,

---

[57] See also I, p. 348: 'Françoise se sentait par contraste lisse et nue comme ces têtes sans visage des tableaux de Chirico.' ('Françoise, by contrast, felt as smooth and naked as the faceless heads in a picture by Chirico' (SCS, p. 280).)

tout autour d'elle s'étendaient des eaux bitumeuses et soufrées [...]' (I, p. 236); 'She was drifting passively like a bit of wreckage, but there were dark reefs on the horizon; she was drifting on a grey ocean, all round her stretched bituminous, sulherous waters [...]' (SCS, pp. 188–9, ta). Black ('noirs' and 'bitumeuses') and sulpher suggest hell. Grey is also a motif here, suggestive of depression. This is reiterated later; in Françoise's heart, it was always grey (I, p. 418).

Françoise's living hell is reproduced in the text. One feature of this symbolic space is fire, and fire and burning are motifs that appear time and time again. In the passages quoted, the poem speaks of fire, and there is not only Xavière's burning flesh in the episodes in the nightclub, Françoise's thoughts also burned like flames (I, p. 363). As the novel culminates, the burning motif that has accumulated throughout the text reaches its crescendo: 'Les larmes brûlaient ses yeux [...]. Les larmes brûlaient, les mots brûlaient comme un fer rouge. [...] Dans les ténèbres, le visage de Gerbert brûlait d'un feu noir, et les lettres sur le tapis étaient noires comme un pacte infernal. [...] Une lave noire et torride coulait dans ses veines' (I, p. 499); 'Tears burned her eyes [...]. The tears burned, the words burned like a red hot iron. [...] In the shadows, black flames flickered round Gerbert's face, and the letters scattered on the carpet were as black as an infernal pact. [...] A black, torrid lava was coursing in her veins.' (SCS, p. 406, ta). The effect is intensified even further with the repetition a few lines later: 'Les larmes coulaient, la lave brûlante coulait et consumait le coeur' (I, p. 500); 'Her tears were flowing, the burning lava was flowing and consuming her heart' (SCS, p. 406, ta). Françoise's experience has a hallucinatory quality. There are distinct echoes of Marlowe's *The Tragical History of Dr. Faustus*, reinforced by mention of a 'pacte infernal.'[58] Françoise's ordeal is almost Faustian, Faustian in the sense that Françoise is now to pay the price for her black soul. She had welcomed the black and bitter hatred she felt for Xavière almost as a release (p. 445, 'délivrance' in French, which is a word with religious overtones), and when she learns that Pierre no longer values his relationship with Xavière, 'Françoise accueillit sans scandale la joie mauvaise qui envahissait son coeur; ça lui avait coûté trop cher naguère de vouloir se garder l'âme pure' ('Unashamedly, Françoise welcomed the evil joy pouring into her heart. Not so very long ago, it had cost her dearly to try to keep her soul pure') (I, p. 466; SCS, p. 378).

Pierre speaks of Xavière's self-inflicted burns as sacred and interprets her gesture as a holy, penitential burn: 'une brûlure sacrée,' 'une brûlure expiatoire' (I, p. 357; SCS, p. 286). This is another instance of distorted religion, the blasphemous substitution of an idolatrous diabolical creed for genuine faith.

L'Invitée is a dark book. In the final pages the predominance of the colours red and black is clear ('red hot iron', 'black flames', 'black as an infernal pact', 'black lava'). These colours also appear in the black hair and red comb and shawl of the Spanish dancer (I, p. 353) and 'the red and tragic mouth' of the Spanish woman

---

[58]   Christopher Marlowe, *The Tragical History of Dr. Faustus*, ed. by R.G. Lunt. London: Blackie & Son, [n.d.].

declaiming the poem (I, p. 363) at the other climactic moments in the book. Because of their repeated appearances throughout *L'Invitée*, the colours red and black gather symbolic weight, adding to the doom laden, Gothic atmosphere in the text. Black is associated with hell and evil. Black and red and fire are inextricably linked. And red is also related to blood, another recurring motif. These colours recur so very frequently they are almost a constant. Often they figure in the detail of the text. Black has been mentioned in a significant number of the quotations previously made, and there are many other examples: Xavière is described as 'a black pearl' (I, pp. 164 and 491; SCS, pp. 129 and 399); the future is 'a black tunnel' (I, p. 291; SCS, p. 231); Pierre's silences are black (I, p. 402; SCS, p. 325); the water of the Seine is shining black (I, p. 490; SCS, p. 398); when Françoise knows Xavière has found Gerbert's letters, her love for him is 'black as treason' (I, p. 497; SCS, p. 403), and her life is akin to the 'coal-black night' ('devant elle et en elle cette nuit de bitume') (I, p. 497; SCS, p. 404).

There are splashes of red throughout the book, often with sinister overtones: Élisabeth's red nail varnish leaves 'a kind of bloody deposit' around the edges and she has 'butcher's fingers' (I, p. 85; SCS, p. 63); in the café where Françoise goes with Gerbert, the singer dressed up as a soldier has his face 'daubed with rouge' (I, p. 153; SCS, p. 121), and the musicians and the life-size doll are dressed in crimson and red and black (I, p. 158; SCS, p. 125); in Xavière's bedroom a red lampshade filled the room with blood-coloured light ('une lueur sanglante' (I, p. 167; SCS, p. 132); Françoise's head is filled with a painful reddish whirling: 'un grand tournoiement rougeâtre et piquant' (I, p. 192; SCS, p. 153).[59]

Two antithetical series of distinctively Gothic images related to the evocation of hellishness, the threat of the abyss, inform the text as a whole. There is one series of images to do with weight, immobilisation, engulfment, enclosure, and suffocation and another to do with the void and emptiness. These two series are brought together as the text underlines the paradox of being engulfed by nothingness:

> C'était comme la mort, une totale négation, une éternelle absence, et cependant par une contradiction bouleversante, ce gouffre de néant pouvait se rendre présent à soi-même et se faire exister pour soi avec plénitude; l'univers tout entier s'engloutissait en lui, et Françoise, à jamais dépossédée du monde, se dissolvait elle-même dans ce vide dont aucun mot, aucune image ne pouvait cerner le contour infini. (I, p. 364)

> It was like death, a total negation, an eternal absence, and yet through a staggering contradiction, this abyss of nothingness could make itself present to itself and make itself fully exist for itself; the entire universe was engulfed

---

[59]   In the dark theatre in the opening pages of the novel, the red carpet and seats stand out. The setting of the novel (many scenes take place in Parisian cafés and hotel rooms) is not at first sight Gothic (Gothic tales typically take place in medieval castles, monasteries, or ruined houses), and yet readers may feel there is something Gothic in the description of Françoise walking through the dark, mysterious and seemingly labyrinthine theatre. See I, pp. 12–13.

in it, and Françoise, for ever excluded from the world, was herself dissolved in the void, whose infinite contour no word, no image could encompass. (SCS, p. 292, ta)

Space has become palpable, a mass that will swallow up Françoise. The cluster of images that have to do with weight that characterise the text bring together favourite Gothic motifs. The words 'écraser' (crush) and 'lourd' (heavy) are repeated many times. To give just a few examples, Françoise experiences Xavière as a weight in her life: 'Tout prenait un tel poids quand elle était là, c'en était accablant' (I, p. 187); 'In her presence everything became so heavy, it was overwhelming' (SCS, p. 149, ta). Yet Françoise hopes that Xavière will release her from the prison of her 'leaden-heavy thoughts' (I, p. 264; SCS, p. 212). The idea that her future will be committed to the trio fills Françoise with dread: '[Elle] sentit comme une lourde chape qui s'abattait sur ses épaules [...]' (I, p. 290); 'She felt as if a heavy cape had fallen on her shoulders' (SCS, p. 230). Unsurprisingly, the words that seal their pact, 'cinq ans' (five years), are heavy. The same motif figures when Françoise realises that Xavière knows about her relationship with Gerbert; she falls back into an armchair, 'crushed by a deadly weight' (I, p. 497; SCS, p. 403). As for Xavière, she is distressed by the 'weight' of her relationship with Pierre once it has been put into words: 'C'est tellement lourd maintenant; c'est comme une gangue autour de moi; elle tremblait de la tête aux pieds. C'est tellement lourd' (I, p. 255); '"Everything's so heavy now. It's like being encased in rock." She was trembling from head to foot. "It's so heavy"' (SCS, p. 204, ta). She too struggles against crushing threats ('menaces écrasantes') she sees all around her (I, p. 255).

Beneath this weight it is difficult to move; a group of complementary images related to immobilisation are to be found throughout *L'Invitée*. At the climactic moments in the nightclub, the trio is captured, as if frozen in a tableau. Xavière comes round from her trance-like state 'as if waking from a nightmare' (I, p. 364; SCS, p. 292) only to take hold of Françoise and Pierre to take them with her 'au fond de l'enfer' (to 'the depths of hell') (I, p. 366; SCS, p. 294):

> Brusquement, elle leur prit à chacun une main, ses paumes étaient brûlantes. Françoise frissonna au contact des doigts fiévreux qui se crispaient sur les siens; elle aurait voulu retirer sa main, détourner la tête, parler à Pierre, mais elle ne pouvait plus faire un mouvement; rivée à Xavière [...].
>
> [...] Les mains de Xavière n'avaient pas lâché leur proie, son visage figé n'exprimait rien. Pierre non plus n'avait pas bougé; on aurait cru qu'un même enchantement les avait tous trois changés en marbre. (I, pp. 364–5)
>
> Abruptly she took them each by the hand. The palms of her hands were burning. Françoise shuddered when she came into contact with these feverish fingers which tightened on hers; she wanted to withdraw her hand, look away, speak to Pierre, but she was now unable to move; riveted to Xavière [...].
>
> [...] Xavière's hands had not let go their prey, her set face bore no expression. Pierre had not moved either. It was as if the same spell had changed all three of them into marble. (SCS, pp. 292–93, ta)

When she is ill, Françoise is 'paralysed between the sheets' (I, p. 255; SCS, p. 204). In the trio, she feels as if she is 'bound hand and foot' (I, p. 29; SCS, p. 230). Being bogged down is an idea that is found repeatedly. The weight of Xavière makes it hard for Françoise to move forward: 'Avec Xavière les choses s'alourdissaient tout de suite: on avait l'impression de marcher dans la vie avec des kilos de terre glaise sous ses semelles' (I, pp. 119–20); 'With Xavière everything became immediately burdonsome; it made one feel like one was walking through life with clods of clay on the soles of one's shoes' (SCS, p. 93, ta). There are echoes of this when the nightmare quality of Françoise's life is evoked in a strange, contradictory image:

> Sa vie avait perdu toute consistence, c'était une substance molle dans laquelle on croyait s'enliser à chaque pas; et puis on rebondissait, juste assez pour aller s'engluer un peu plus loin, avec à chaque seconde l'espoir d'un engloutissement définitif, à chaque seconde l'espoir d'un sol soudain raffermi. (I, pp. 481–2)

> Her life had lost all consistency of late, it had become a flacid substance into which she expected to sink at every step, and then she would get free again just enough to get stuck a little further along, with at every moment the hope of being engulfed once and for all and at every moment the hope of finding the ground suddenly solid once more. (SCS, p. 391, ta)

Her life is like a sticky trap. This recalls an earlier evocation of an oppressive afternoon when the tar on the road melted in the heat and stuck to Françoise's feet and Françoise felt she had become a dull mass like cotton-wool ('une masse fade et cotonneuse') (I, p. 420; SCS, p. 340).[60]

The atmosphere of *L'Invitée* is claustrophobic. The characters' world shrinks, and they are shut in with their obsession; the real world is elsewhere.[61] Indeed, their obsession becomes their world; it is their prison. Images of enclosure and suffocation recur, for example: 'Elle commençait à étouffer dans ce trio qui se refermait de plus en plus hermétiquement sur lui même' ('she was beginning to feel stifled in this trio, which was in danger of becoming hermetically sealed') (I, p. 296; SCS, p. 235) and 'l'atmosphère tendue, passionnée, étouffante dans laquelle Pierre et Xavière l'enfermaient' ('the tense, pasionate, suffocating atmosphere in which Pierre and Xavière had imprisoned her') (I, p. 340; SCS, p. 273). There is the sense of a rich, vast world that exists outside the confines

---

[60]   Beauvoir's depictions that underline stickiness, soft yielding substances, cloying sweetness, and so on clearly echo the existentialist imagery of the threat of *mauvaise foi* in Sartre's *Being and Nothingness*. To quote Moi, 'according to Sartre, stickiness, unlike wetness or dryness, represents the attempt of the in-itself to swallow up, engulf or immobilize the for-itself. The sticky, he writes, represents the "sugary death of the For-itself."' Moi, *Simone de Beauvoir*, p. 102.

[61]   For readers, the text is rendered more claustrophobic by the absence of historical context from the greater part of the novel. As Fallaize points out, the historical situation of the characters assumes importance only in the final chapter when the war, which formed the context of the actual writing of the book, becomes a reality. *The Novels*, p. 28.

of the trio and that is evoked when Françoise remembers her past with Pierre (I, p. 377), or when it is a matter of the holiday with Gerbert (I, pp. 437 and 445–6), or even when Françoise simply looks out of the window and sees the busy, lucid street where everything looks reasonable, before turning back to her room, which is sunk in anguish ('engluée d'angoisse') (I, p. 388; SCS, p. 313).

Xavière's hotel room is the epitome of a Gothic space. The gaudy walls, suggestive of delerium ('bariolés comme une vision de fièvre'), enclose unsatisfied desires, boredom, and resentment that make the air unbreathable (I, p. 342; SCS, p. 274). In an extended metaphor, these feelings become the rank and poisonous vegetation in a hothouse, where the air is thick with moisture and sticks to the body. It inspires fear in Françoise:

> Ce n'était pas seulement un sanctuaire où Xavière célébrait son propre culte: c'était une serre chaude où s'épanouissait une végétation luxuriante et vénéneuse, c'était un cachot d'hallucinée dont l'atmosphère moite collait au corps.
> (I, p. 342)

> It was not only a sanctuary where Xavière celebrated her own worship; it was a hothouse in which flourished a luxuriant and poisonous vegetation; it was the cell of a bedlamite, in which the dank atmosphere adhered to the body.
> (SCS, p. 274)

The word 'cell' linked with dankness could be suggestive of a Gothic dungeon. Be that as it may, the Gothic emphasis on suffocation and enclosure is clear.

Weight threatens to drag characters down into the abyss, into nothingness. Witness Élisabeth: 'Sa tête était toute gonflée d'eau et de nuit; elle devenait énorme et si lourde qu'elle l'entraînait vers l'abîme: le sommeil ou la mort, ou la folie, un gouffre sans fond où elle allait se perdre à jamais' (I, p. 106); 'Her head was swollen with water and the night, it was getting enormous and so heavy that it was dragging her towards the abyss: sleep, or death or madness, a bottomless pit where she would be lost forever' (SCS, p. 81, ta). And Françoise: 'Des pieds à la tête elle se sentait changée en bloc de plomb; la séparation de [Pierre] était cruelle, mais rien ne saurait la faire glisser sur cette pente de mirage au bout de laquelle s'ouvrait elle ne savait quel abîme' (I, p. 131); 'She felt herself turning into a block of lead from head to foot; her separateness from him was cruel, but nothing would induce her to slide down the illusory slope at the bottom of which yawned she knew not what abyss' (SCS, p. 102, ta).

The motif of the pit or the abyss is one that is repeated time and time again. On the verge of being ill, Françoise is overwhelmed by a sense of space as the abyss at her feet expands to encompass the stars above ('à ses pieds ce gouffre qui se creusait jusqu'aux étoiles') (I, p. 216; SCS, p. 173). Quite paradoxically, given the impression of weight and enclosure that prevails, a sense of infinity and emptiness also pervades *L'Invitée*. This is created by an accumulation of references in the text: 'infini' (infinite), 'sans fin' (endless), 'vide' (empty). As we have seen, these motifs figure large in the evocation of the danger threatening Françoise: 'Ce n'était aucun objet saisissable, c'était un incessant jaillissement et une fuite incessante, transparente pour soi seule et à jamais impénétrable' (I, p. 355); 'It was not a tangible object, it was an incessant flux and an incessant flight, transparent only to itself and forever impenetrable' (SCS, p. 285, ta). The words 'un incessant jaillissement et une fuite incessante' contribute to the evocation of emptiness and infinity. The effect is reinforced a little later: 'Françoise, à jamais dépossédée du monde, se dissolvait elle-même dans ce vide dont aucun mot, aucune image ne pouvait cerner le contour infini' (I, p. 364); 'Françoise, for ever excluded from the world, was herself dissolved in the void, whose infinite contour no word, no image could encompass' (SCS, p. 292, ta). Space suggests expansion and disintegration. As Françoise chooses between her own survival and Xavière's, space and emptiness is evoked by Françoise's being alone in an icy sky (I, p. 501). It is on this immense stage that Françoise fights Xavière for her existence in the final pages of *L'Invitée*. And Xavière herself embodies contradiction; she excludes and encloses, is infinite expansion and pure interiority: 'Elle était là, n'existant que pour soi, tout entière réfléchie en elle-même, réduisant au néant tout ce qu'elle excluait; elle enfermait le monde entier dans sa propre solitude triomphante, elle s'épanouissait sans limites, infinie, unique' (I, pp. 502–3); 'There she was, existing only for herself, entirely self-referential, reducing to nothingness everything she excluded; she encompassed the whole world within her own triumphant aloneness, flourishing without bounds, infinite, unique' (SCS, p. 408).

White and the light associated with it play a particular role in the dark symbolic landscape in *L'Invitée*. White is the colour of emptiness. Light is painful. These elements are brought together in the text: 'Avec un éblouissement douloureux, Françoise se sentit transpercée d'une lumière aride et blanche qui ne laissait en elle aucun recoin d'espoir; un moment elle resta immobile à regarder briller dans la nuit le bout rouge de sa cigarette' (I, p. 180); 'Painfully dazzled, Françoise felt herself pierced by a barren, white light that left her with no recess of hope. She stood motionless for a moment watching the red tip of her cigarette glowing in the darkness' (SCS, p. 143, ta). (Note the reappearance of black and red.) A few pages later we read: 'La lumière qui l'avait pénétrée tout à l'heure ne lui avait découvert que du vide' (I, p. 183); 'The light that had penetrated her a short while before had revealed nothing but emptiness' (SCS, p. 146, ta). Indeed, white is repeatedly the colour of the pain of self-knowledge: 'Ce bloc de blancheur translucide et nue, aux arêtes râpeuses, c'était elle, en dépit d'elle-même, irrémédiablement (I, p. 312); 'This block of bare and transluscent whiteness with its jagged edges was her, in spite of herself, irrevocably' (SCS, p. 248). Paradoxically, it is Françoise's emptiness that brings relief to her during her long illness. It is a light/white/silent space in the book. Françoise is calm in this vast space out of time. (See I, pp. 222–3.)[62]

---

[62]   The motifs of silence, emptiness, timelessness, and calm underlined there are picked up and foregrounded again in the final pages of the book: 'Soudain un grand calme descendit en Françoise. Le temps venait de s'arrêter. Françoise était seule dans un ciel glacé. C'était une solitude si solonnelle et si définitive qu'elle ressemblait à la mort' (I, p. 501). Freud mentions but does not explicate the uncanny effect of dark, silence, and solitude. (Freud, 'The Uncanny', p. 246.) I am content here simply to point out the extent to which these motifs predominate in the final pages of *L'Invitée*.

In *L'Invitée* there is a Gothic emphasis on death, tombs, mummies, and ghosts, all motifs related to the uncanny (Freud, p. 241). There is a constant stream of explicit references to death. For example, during the climactic moments in the nightclub, death is mentioned four times in the space of 25 lines: 'le poème parlait de haine et de mort' ('the poem was about hatred and death'); 'l'évocation funèbre d'un passé défunt' ('no more than funereal evocations of a dead past', ta); 'le scandale éclatait, aussi monstrueux, aussi définitif que la mort' ('the abomination was being revealed, as monstrous, as definitive as death', ta); 'c'était comme la mort' ('it was like death') (I, pp. 363–4; SCS, 291–2). Tombs also feature prominently, and they are, of course, an archetypal instance of enclosure. Françoise says Pierre's love for her is like the beautiful whited sepulchres of the Gospels that can even be given a new covering now and again with fine words, but which contain nothing but ash and dust (I, p. 199).[63] She describes his feelings as mummies, which are completely embalmed (I, p. 200). Combining the motifs of death and weight, we find the image of their love as an old corpse that they drag around with them ('un vieux cadavre que nous traînons avec nous', I, p. 202). The light in Xavière's hotel room is funereal ('funèbre') (I, p. 168). As Xavière's death approaches, the flat that Françoise shares with her is repeatedly compared to a tomb: it was as if the blue window panes were screening the interior of a tomb (I, p. 484); the light there is funereal ('mortuaire') (I, p. 490); and Françoise says the flat itself is like a catafalque (I, p. 491). And in a nice Gothic touch, as Françoise runs to her secret rendez-vous with Gerbert, an owl hoots behind the wall of the cemetery (I, p. 484).

A related series of images focuses on hidden decay. Shiny surfaces hide inner decomposition/corruption/disintegration. The image is first introduced in connection with actresses whom Françoise and Élisabeth are discussing:

> Les corps étaient jeunes [...] mais cette jeunesse n'avait pas la fraîcheur des choses vivantes, c'était une jeunesse embaumée; ni ride, ni patte d'oie ne marquait les chairs bien massées; cet air usé autour des yeux n'en était que plus inquiétant. Ça vieillissait par en dessous; ça pourrait vieillir encore longtemps sans que craquât la carapace bien lustrée et puis,un jour, d'un seul coup, cette coque brillante devenue mince comme un papier de soie tomberait en poussière; alors on verrait apparaître une vieillarde parfaitement achevée [...]. (I, pp. 175–6)

> The bodies were young [...] but this youthfullness had none of the freshness of living things, it was embalmed youthfulness; not a wrinkle, not a crow's-foot marred this carefully assembled flesh; this made the worn-down look round the eyes only more disturbing. They were ageing underneath, they could go on ageing for a long time before the well-polished carapace cracked and then,

---

[63] 'Ye are like unto whited sepulchres, which indeed appear beautiful outward, but are within full of dead men's bones, and of all uncleanliness.' Matthew 23.27. There are echoes of this image in Xavière's outburst after the outbreak of war: 'Ça ne me suffit pas de contempler les événements du fond d'un sépulcre!' (I, p. 483); 'I'm not content to contemplate events from the bottom of a tomb!' (SCS, p. 393).

one day, suddenly, this shiny shell worn as thin as tissue paper would crumble into dust; then an old woman would appear, complete in every detail [...]. (SCS, p. 139, ta)

This image has a number of affinities with the Gothic; the intimation of the living dead, the fact that the decay is hidden, the animal associations, the idea that the shell will one day crumble into dust without warning. It is an uncomfortable image.[64] Parallel images are applied to Françoise and Pierre's relationship:

Ils avaient édifié de belles constructions impeccables et ils s'abritaient à leur ombre, sans plus s'inquiéter de ce qu'elles pourraient bien contenir. [...] Sans perdre sa forme parfaite, leur amour, leur vie se vidait lentement de sa substance; comme ces grandes chenilles à la coque invulnérable mais qui portent dans leur chair molle de minuscules vermisseaux qui les récurent avec soin. (I, pp. 193–4)

They had built beautiful, faultless structures in whose shadow they were sheltering, without giving any further thought to what they contained. [...] Without losing their perfect form, their love, their life, was slowly being emptied of substance; like huge caterpillars with invulnerable shells, but who carry in their soft flesh microscopic worms that painstakingly consume them. (SCS, p. 154, ta)

Again, there is the disturbing allusion to hidden decomposition combined with the repellent image of worms eating away at living flesh.

The text inscribes the body. The body in this symbolic landscape is a site of pain rather than pleasure. Françoise conforms to the role of Gothic heroine and is taken ill and takes to her bed. Her illness is described in terms of Gothic excess. Françoise's mental pain is translated into physical suffering. This is true during her illness, of course, but it is also the case before and after her illness. Images that evoke her illness are echoed elsewhere in the text, showing the extent to which Françoise's mental and physical suffering become conflated. The images are violent ones of tearing, burning, biting and stabbing. They are Gothic in their hyperbole.[65]

---

[64]   An explicit connection is made with tinned lobster ('des conserves de homard'), and readers' unease increases when textual echoes establish a link between this image and Françoise's eating shellfish. It is another telling detail reinforcing suggestions of cannibalism, I, p. 292; SCS, pp. 231–2).

[65]   Illness:

'Elle frisonna; elle devait avoir la fièvre, ses mains étaient moites et tout son corps brûlait' (I, p. 211). (After the rendition of the poem in the nightclub,when Xavière takes hold of Françoise's hand 'ses paumes étaient brûlantes' and Françoise 'frissonna au contact des doigts fiévreux' (I, p. 364).)

'Une douleur lancinante lui coupa le souffle; elle s'arrêta et porta les mains à ses côtes [...] Un grand frisson la secoua de la tête aux pieds; elle était en sueur, sa tête bourdonnait [...]' (I, p. 217).

'Une bouffée de sang lui brûla le visage et son coeur se mit à battre avec violence' [...]' (I, p. 218).

References to the throat and heart reverberate in the text. Commonly these references are to do with tightness and express Françoise's deep upset. To give just two examples: 'Son coeur restait serré de souffrances et de colère' (I, p. 295); 'Her heart was constricted by suffering and anger' (SCS, p. 234); 'Elle ne voulait pas sentir à nouveau un étau lui serrer la gorge' (I, p. 437); She did not want to feel a vice grip her throat once again' (SCS, p. 354). These dead metaphors, 'le coeur serré' and 'la gorge serrée' (the heart wrung and the throat constricted), recur throughout *L'Invitée* at least 15 and 12 times each, respectively, almost like a refrain.[66] The text returns almost obsessively to these motifs, which gain symbolic weight. They are consonant with images of enclosure. Furthermore, they form only part of the dense web of references to the heart and throat, which become veritable leitmotifs in the text.

We have already noted the importance of blood in Beauvoir's symbolic landscape. It is mentioned directly more than 13 times, generally in connection with upset, draining from or rushing to Françoise's face. Sweat is also a natural feature when emphasis is placed on burning and airlessness. Tears are shed with almost monotonous regularity; sobbing intersperses the text. The body is messy, a leaky vessel.

'des ondes brûlantes la parcoururent' (I, p. 218).

'une douleur aiguë lui déchira la poitrine' (I, p. 219).

'le sol fuyait en tourbillon sous ses pieds, ça lui donnait la nausée. [...] la sueur perlait à grosses gouttes sur son front' (I, p. 240).

'sa tête était vide et lourde' (I, p. 240).

'elle gisait paralysée entre les draps' (I, p. 255).

'Françoise avait l'impression que tout son corps allait se dissoudre en sueur' (I, p. 246).

Elsewhere:

'une souffrance aiguë la déchira' (I, p. 166).

'Sa tête bourdonnait; il lui semblait que quelque chose en elle, une artère ou ses côtes ou son coeur, allait éclater' (I, p. 196).

'mille images douloureuses tourbillonnaient dans sa tête et lui déchiraient le coeur' (I, p. 261).

After witnessing Xavière's self-harm, Françoise is paralysed by 'l'angoisse' (I, p. 356).

'ce goût de fièvre dans la bouche' (I, p. 379).

'sa gorge brûlait' (I, p. 383).

'Il se fit en Françoise un déchirement si aigu qu'un cri lui monta aux lèvres, elle serra les dents mais les larmes jaillirent (I, p. 433).

'le remords la déchira [...] Elle avait mal à la tête et ses yeux brûlaient' (I, p. 435).

'une morsure au coeur' (I, p. 488.) (I, pp. 260, 373, et al.).

'Son visage brûlait (I, p. 494).

'Tout son corps bourdonnait. Elle sentait son coeur entre ses côtes, sous son crâne, au bout de ses doigts. (I, p. 496)

[66]   Examples: 'le coeur serré,' I, pp. 13, 20, 31, 36, 146, 156, 178, 295, 335, 339, 343, 427, 470; 'la gorge serrée,' I, pp. 37, 54, 78, 126, 143, 161, 173, 260, 316, 430, 437, 472.

Sexuality in *L'Invitée* is distorted in true Gothic fashion. Sex is generally connoted negatively. Distaste is evinced even in small details in the text; when she is comforting Éloy, Françoise feels 'slight revulsion for her plump little body, so often pawed and still intact' (I, p. 197; SCS, p. 157, ta). As Elizabeth Fallaize demonstrates, Xavière's sexuality is foregrounded in the text.[67] Xavière's behaviour in the nightclub, when she deliberately harms herself, suggests an aberrant, masochistic sexuality; her smile is 'the voluptuous, tortured smile of a woman possessed by sexual pleasure,' and she pouts her lips coquettishly as she blows away the ash to burn herself a second time (I, p. 354; SCS, p. 284, ta); Xavière is 'in the grip of hysterical ecstasy' and her 'jouissance' (pleasure and orgasm in French) is maniacal (I, p. 363; SCS, p. 292).[68] The act of burning itself is described in sexual terms, according to a heterosexual image of desire, as the open wound is exposed to receive the burning end of the cigarette.[69] In a more minor key, Élisabeth's sexuality is also linked with self harm. She relives the sexual arousal that in the past had led her to take back her lover Claude and to stop herself repeating this pattern. 'Élisabeth quickly put her hand to her mouth and bit her wrist' (I, p. 85; SCS, p. 63). Sex is depicted as animal, as opposed to human. Élisabeth will not be 'had' in the same way this time, she is not 'a bitch on heat,' 'une femelle.' Her sexual liaison with Guimot is depicted negatively; during their lovemaking 'a scorching humiliation swept over her' and she simply wants it to end (I, p. 110; SCS, p. 84). Françoise is horrified to think she may be a woman like Élisabeth, 'a woman who takes' (I, p. 454; SCS, p. 368). In relation to Xavière, Françoise is horrified at the idea that Pierre will make love with her, make her swoon with pleasure ('Pierre en ferait une femme pâmée'), feeling that to think of Xavière as a sexual woman is sacrilegious (I, p. 260; SCS, p. 208). The language used to describe Françoise's feelings is laden with depreciatory overtones: 'Elle apercevait clairement chaque étape de ce chemin fatal qui mène des baisers aux caresses, des caresses aux derniers abandons; par la faute de Pierre, Xavière allait y rouler comme n'importe qui' (I, p. 260); 'She could envisage every step along the fatal path that leads from kisses to caresses, from caresses to complete surrender; because of Pierre, Xavière would end up there like anyone else' (SCS, pp. 208–9, ta).[70]

The erotic and incestuous tendencies of Gothic texts have been well documented. Françoise has clear maternal feelings toward Xavière, and Xavière is repeatedly referred to as a child. For example, early in the narrative, Françoise responds tenderly to Xavière, who is 'simply an affectionate and helpless

---

[67] Fallaize, *The Novels*, pp. 30–33. Xavière's ambivalence to sexuality is related to the portrait of adolescent sexuality in *Le Deuxième Sexe*. See also Moi, *Simone de Beauvoir*, p. 113.

[68] Xavière inflicts pain on herself. In her dissociated state she feels no pain: 'Xavière ne semblait pas souffrir de sa brûlure' (I, p. 356). Later she says: 'Jamais je n'aurais cru que ça puisse faire si mal' (I, p. 399).

[69] This is one more example of Xavière's revealing something that should have remained hidden. A point made but not developed by Moi, *Simone de Beauvoir*, p. 116.

[70] In French the word 'faute' also means 'sin.'

little girl'(I, p. 48; SCS, p. 33, ta). Françoise calls her moods 'childish whims' (I, p. 66; SCS, p. 48), and she loses her adoptive 'silky, golden little girl' to Pierre (I, p. 252; SCS, p. 201, ta).[71] These maternal feelings are overlain with sexual, and thus quasi-incestuous desire.[72] The ambiguity about their relationship that Xavière promotes, and with which Françoise willingly colludes, is also fostered by the text. Xavière likes Françoise and herself to be taken for a couple, and Françoise enjoys being linked with Xavière in this way as it feels as though 'they have been cut off together from the rest of the world and imprisoned in a passionate tête-à-tête' (I, p. 309; SCS, p. 246, ta).[73] When they dance together on this occasion, Xavière holds Françoise closer than usual, and Françoise's response is far from maternal:

> Elle sentait contre sa poitrine les beaux seins tièdes de Xavière, elle respirait son haleine charmante; était-ce du désir? Mais que désirait-elle? Ses lèvres contre ses lèvres? Ce corps abandonné entre ses bras? Elle ne pouvait rien imaginer, ce n'était qu'un besoin confus de garder tourné vers elle à jamais ce visage d'amoureuse et de pouvoir dire passionnément: elle est à moi. (I, p. 310)

> She felt Xavière's beautiful warm breasts against her, she inhaled her sweet breath; was this desire? But what did she desire? Her lips against hers? Her body surrendered in her arms? She couldn't imagine anything. She only felt a confused need to keep for ever this lover's face turned towards hers, and to be able to say with passion: 'She's mine.' (SCS, p. 246, ta)

Françoise's physical response to Xavière and her desire to possess her have unmistakable lesbian overtones. Back in Xavière's room, Françoise continues to be unsettled by the physical closeness of Xavière. She is afraid that Xavière is out of reach, and although she wants to break into Xavière's solitude ('forcer l'accès'), she is 'paralysed by the intimidating grace of the beautiful body she didn't know how to desire' ('la grâce intimidant de ce beau corps qu'elle ne savait pas désirer') (I, p. 315; SCS, p. 251, ta). On impulse, as she is leaving, Françoise takes Xavière into her arms: 'Xavière s'abandonna, un instant elle resta contre son épaule, immobile et souple' (I, p. 316); 'Xavière sank into her arms, for a moment she lay relaxed against her shoulder without moving' (SCS, p. 251, ta). Again Françoise wonders what Xavière expects of her: to let her go or to hold her more tightly?[74] Françoise lets Xavière go and goes back to her own room, ashamed of her

---

[71]   Fallaize's reading of the trio as a 'pseudo-oedipal triangle' is pertinent here. *The Novels*, pp. 29–30.

[72]   Jane Heath examines the relationship between Pierre and Xavière as both paternal and sexual, pp. 36–7. She also identifies maternal and lesbian feelings in Françoise's relationship with Xavière, pp. 37–41. Sarah Fishwick offers a detailed and perceptive analysis of Françoise's desire for Xavière: pp. 197–9, 203–4, 206–9.

[73]   I in no way wish to suggest that lesbianism is a distorted form of sexuality. It is only in relation to the heterosexual norms of the text that it should be viewed as such.

[74]   Before they go into the bar, Françoise wonders whether Xavière had been referring to her lack of physical tenderness when she said she hated purity. The sexual diction is clear: 'ne savait-elle [Françoise] donc être tendre qu'avec des mots alors qu'il y avait cette

'futile gesture of tenderness' ('tendresse inutile'). I have examined this incident at length as it is of central importance in considering the sexual nature of Françoise's feelings for Xavière; here her desire is explicit. However, it is not a lone incidence of Françoise's sexual response to Xavière. It fits into a matrix of more ambiguous allusions, allusions that occur from very early on in the text. Lesbian overtones gather momentum in Part One, Chapter 2. References to Xavière's boyish head ('tête de garçonnet') and the face of a young woman that had enchanted Françoise (I, p. 24), at first seemingly neutral, accrue resonances. As the chapter proceeds, the text dwells on the number of times Françoise touches Xavière (touching is rather rare in *L'Invitée*), each gesture bolder than the last: on the wrist – 'elle effleura le poignet de Xavière' (I, p. 39); on the shoulder – 'elle posa la main sur l'épaule de Xavière' (I, p. 44); along her arm – 'sa main quitta l'épaule de Xavière et glissa le long de son bras' (I, p. 44); finally stroking Xavière's hand in hers – 'elle caressa la main chaude qui reposait avec confiance dans sa main' (I, p. 45). The chapter culminates in a scene redolent of romantic, physical love:

> [Xavière] se laissa aller de tout son poids contre l'épaule de Françoise; un long moment elles demeurèrent immobiles, appuyées l'une contre l'autre; les cheveux de Xavière frôlaient la joue de Françoise; leurs doigts restaient emmêlés.
> 'Je suis triste de vous quitter,' dit Françoise.
> 'Moi aussi,' dit Xavière tout bas.
> 'Ma petite Xavière,' murmura Françoise; Xavière la regardait, les yeux brillants, les lèvres entrouvertes; fondante, abandonnée, elle lui était tout entière livrée.
> C'était Françoise désormais qui l'emporterait à travers la vie.
> 'Je la rendrai heureuse,' décida-t-elle avec conviction. (I, p. 45)[75]

> She sank with all her weight against Françoise's shoulder; for some time they remained motionless, leaning against each other. Xavière's hair brushed against Françoise's cheek. Their fingers remained entwined.
> 'It makes me sad to leave you,' said Françoise.
> 'Me too,' said Xavière softly.
> 'My darling Xavière,' murmured Françoise. Xavière looked at her, her eyes shining, her lips parted; yielding, abandoned, she had given herself completely to her. From now on, it would be Françoise who would lead her through life.
> 'I'll make her happy,' she decided with conviction. (SCS, p. 30, ta)

Françoise's desire to possess Xavière completely, expressed in this early chapter for the first time (I, pp. 23, 40), becomes a constant in the book. Françoise wants

---

main veloutée dans sa main et ces cheveux parfumés qui frôlaient sa joue? Était-ce cela, sa maladroite pureté?' (I, p. 309). See also I, p. 303, where Françoise and Xavière hold hands.

[75] See also I, pp. 219, 263–5, 398, for romantic, sexual love scenes. Sexual and maternal feelings are blended on I, p. 263. See also I, p. 79. Françoise's physical/sexual response to Xavière is condensed into her awareness of her hands; in addition to quotations already given, see I, p. 260: 'ses mains caressantes d'homme', and I, p. 265: 'douces mains de femme, rouges comme des mains de paysanne.'

'a complete union' with Xavière (I, p. 398; SCS, p. 321).[76] A close reading of the text supports the view that Françoise's jealousy is more directed at Pierre for his relationship with Xavière than it is directed at Xavière for taking Pierre from her. Françoise's jealousy is physical: 'Elle n'avait aucune prise sur cette petite âme butée ni même sur le beau corps de chair qui la défendait; un corps tiède et souple, accessible à des mains d'homme mais qui se dressait devant Françoise comme une armure rigide' (I, p. 300); 'She had no real hold on this stubborn little soul, not even on the beautiful living body protecting it; a warm, lithe body, accessible to a man's hands, but which now confronted Françoise like a rigid suit of armour' (SCS, pp. 238–9, ta). The suggestion is that physical domination would be a means to the emotional domination that Françoise desires. When Pierre tells Françoise that Xavière has spent the early hours of the morning in his arms, Françoise's reaction is telling: 'Ça lui était toujours douloureux que Pierre pût étreindre ce corps dont elle n'eût même su accueillir le don' (I, p. 373); 'It was always painful for her that Pierre could embrace the body that she would not even have known how how to receive were it offered to her' (SCS, p. 300, ta).

In many ways, Françoise's relationship with Gerbert stands out in the narrative as something quite exceptional, something innocent and pure and healthy, 'light and tender as the morning wind on the dewy meadows', although even this relationship can be reread as a 'sordid betrayal' (I, p. 500; SCS, p. 406, ta). Moreover, the diction of the seduction scene is remarkably similar to that used in connection with Françoise's pain and suffering in the trio: Françoise feels 'a sickening emptiness within her' (I, p. 446; SCS, p. 361); her desire for Gerbert is overwhelming ('étouffant') (I, p. 446; SCS, p. 362); she fears she is going to 'dream, regret and suffer in vain' (I, p. 447; SCS, p. 362, ta); when she realises that Gerbert is not as fond of Xavière as she had thought, her 'indecent joy' is like a burst of light (I, p. 451; SCS, p. 366, ta); and as they get ready to go to sleep, she can think of nothing but the 'gripping constriction in her stomach' ('cette dure consigne qui lui barrait l'estomac'), and her only desire is to rid herself of her obsession (I, p. 456; SCS, pp. 369–70). Interestingly, Françoise's feelings for Gerbert are tinged with incest too: 'C'était indéniable, elle avait des sentiments maternels pour Gerbert; maternels, avec une discrète nuance incestueuse' (I, p. 51–2); 'There was no denying it, she had a maternal feeling toward Gerbert – maternal, with a faintly incestuous touch (SCS, p. 36).[77]

Just as in the Gothic tradition, uncertainties to do with sexuality are linked to wider threats of disintegration, so in *L'Invitée*, the turmoil in the trio's lives is

---

[76] See also I, p. 186: 'Si je pouvais l'avoir à moi, je l'aimerais.' ('If I could have her to myself, I would love her') (SCS, p. 148).

[77] Moi's discussion of Françoise and Gerbert's first kiss is pertinent here. She argues that Françoise is unintentionally cast as a maternal figure in relation to Gerbert when she offers her lips for a kiss and tells him: 'Eh bien, faites-le, stupide petit Gerbert' (I, p. 460); 'Well, kiss me, you silly little Gerbert' (SCS, p. 373). *Simone de Beauvoir*, p. 141. Whether or not this is unintentional, it reinforces the incestuous undercurrent.

related to the turmoil in the wider context, to the Second World War.[78] Françoise's feelings are explicitly placed on a par with international tensions: 'Tout était devenu si compliqué maintenant, les sentiments, la vie, l'Europe' (I, p. 236); Everything had now become so complicated – feelings, life, Europe' (SCS, p. 188). In a metaphor reminiscent of war, Françoise is drifting like a wreck at sea and on the horizon are black reefs/dangers ('de noirs écueils') (I, p. 236). At an earlier point in the narrative, Françoise equated the effect Xavière would have on her future with the outbreak of war, taking advantage of ambiguity/Pierre's misunderstanding ('cette équivoque') to seemingly talk about one whilst actually talking about the other (I, pp. 291–2). The most powerful images of war occur in Part Two, Chapter 3, where Gerbert is the focalizer. These images have much in common with imagery attached to Françoise's emotional distress. In the following example, the animalisation of a hidden danger echoes imagery linked with Xavière and other motifs – funeral, engulfment, black, sticky, weight, exploding light – are ones that resonate throughout the text:

> [La guerre] était là, en effet, tapie entre le poêle ronflant et le comptoir de zinc aux reflets jaunes, et ce repas était une agape mortuaire. Des casques, des tanks, des uniformes, des camions vert-de-gris, une immense marée boueuse déferlaient sur le monde; la terre était submergée par cette glu noirâtre où l'on s'enlisait, avec sur les épaules des vêtements de plomb à l'odeur de chien mouillé, tandis que des lueurs sinistres éclataient au ciel. (I, pp. 324–25)

> [The war] was actually already there, crouching between the roaring stove and the zinc-topped bar, glinting yellow, and this meal was a wake. Helmets, tanks, uniforms, blue-green trucks – a vast muddy tide was breaking over the world; the earth was being submerged in this blackish quagmire, that sucked down everyone, the leaden garments on their shoulders reeking like a wet dog, while ominous lights burst in the sky. (SCS, pp. 258–9, ta)

War is 'a rain of grey dust descending on Europe,' drowning everything, including the bright rainbow lights of Montparnasse (I, p. 335; SCS, p. 268), matching the way Xavière casts Françoise's life in shadow. When Françoise discovers that Xavière knows about her relationship with Gerbert, the metaphor expressing her reaction could so easily be a depiction of the the war that frames these final scenes. The affinities are conspicuous: 'Une nuit âcre et brûlante venait de s'abattre sur le monde' (I, p. 497); 'A bitter buning night had just descended on the world (SCS, p. 403, ta).

It is not unusual for Gothic tales to parody the convention they embody. In *L'Invitée* the Gothic economy of the text is undermined by parody of the Gothic.

---

[78]   The poem that prefigures the text evokes Spain torn apart by war (I, p. 363). Fallaize offers an interesting reading of the history of the trio and Françoise's growing frustration, which ends in murder, as an expression of the gathering sense of doom of 1937–1939, and the imminent destruction. *The Novels*, p. 28. In 'War and Alterity in *L'Invitée*,' Christine Everley argues that 'war is an experience of alterity and a determining factor in the awareness of alterity in personal relations.' *Simone de Beauvoir Studies*, 13, 1996, 137–50 (p. 137).

This parody increases readers' discomfort. They accept the values of the text and the frame it provides, only to find these thrown into question. Parody places an ambiguity at the heart of the text. Beauvoir was well aware of the ambiguity produced by the shift in narrative focus/focalization, from Françoise to Élisabeth and the way in which what Françoise experiences as tragic can also be comical (FA, p. 388).[79] I suggest that shifts in focalization are not the only way in which ambiguity and humour are generated in *L'Invitée*. Specifically, parody of Gothic conventions introduces a comic element with its concomitant ambiguity. The point at which the text tips over into parody is sometimes difficult to gauge; it can be no more than a slight shift in tone or nuance that makes the difference between what is expected within a Gothic economy and exaggeration. For example, Élisabeth's murderous fantasy slips into parody, partly because of the skull and crossbones on the bottle of poison and partly because of the dramatic syntax and the use of enumeration: 'La nuit se fit dans la salle; une image traversa Élisabeth, un revolver, un poignard, un flacon avec une tête de mort; tuer. Claude? Suzanne? Moi-même? Peu importait, ce sombre désir de meurtre gonflait puissamment le coeur' (I, p. 94); 'The auditorium grew dark. A picture flashed through Élisabeth's mind – a revolver – a dagger – a phial with a death's head on it – to kill someone ... Claude? Suzanne? Myself? – it didn't matter. This dark murderous desire violently took possession of her heart' (SCS, pp. 70–71). The discrepancy between heightened tone and mundane subject pushes the description of Xavière's room over the dividing line. We can only smile at Françoise and Pierre's hyperbolical reaction to Xavière's packing:

> Ils restèrent cloués sur place.
> – Qu'est-ce que vous faites là dit Pierre.
> La gorge de Xavière se gonfla.
> – Je déménage, dit-elle d'un ton tragique. Le spectacle était atterrant. [...] Tout semblait futile au prix du cataclysme qui dévastait la chambre et le visage de Xavière. Trois valises béaient au milieu de la pièce; les placards avaient dégorgé sur le sol des monceaux de vêtements fripés, de papiers, d'objets de toilette.
> – Et vous comptez avoir fini bientôt? dit Pierre qui regardait avec sévérité le sanctuaire saccagé.
> – Je n'en viendrai jamais à bout! dit Xavière; elle se laissa tomber sur un fauteuil et serra ses tempes entre ses doigts. Cette sorcière. (I, pp. 117–18)

> Françoise and Pierre stood rooted to the spot.
> 'What are you doing?,' said Pierre.
> Xavière's throat swelled.
> 'I'm moving,' she said in a tragic voice. The scene was stupefying. [...] Everything seemed trivial in comparison with the cataclysm that was ravaging the room as well as Xavière's face. Three suitcases lay gaping in the middle of the room; the cupboards had disgorged on to the floor piles of crumpled clothing, papers, and toilet articles.

---

[79] In fact, despite a number of humorous remarks, the chapters focalized through Élizabeth do not generally provide a comical vision of the trio. This is more the case as regards the chapter focalized through Gerbert.

'And do you expect to be finished soon?' asked Pierre who was looking sternly at the havoc-stricken sanctuary.

'I'll never manage it!' said Xavière. She sank into an armchair and pressed her fingers against her forehead. 'That old witch.' (SCS, pp. 91–2)

As in the first example, there are a striking number of Gothic elements in these lines, too many perhaps. Elements that elsewhere contribute to the impression of awfulness, in the full Gothic sense of the word, conveyed by the text, are here used to comic effect. A similar effect is produced when a 'choucroute' is termed 'a mystical communion' (I, p. 228; SCS, p. 182). Also at this point in the text, suspense is built up only to end in bathos. It is to Gerbert's focalization that we owe the parodic vision of Pierre and Françoise 'leaning towards Pagès like two tempting devils' (I, p. 320; SCS, p. 255). The notion of demoniacal presence that is treated as sinister and threatening elsewhere in L'Invitée is comical here and Gerbert had to make an 'heroic' effort not to burst out laughing. Does the text also drift into parody when Françoise wards off misfortune ('le malheur') by taking off her nail varnish (I, p. 381)?

Clearly, the Gothic informs L'Invitée to a great extent. A dense web of images, words, and motifs build to the final crescendo when Françoise decides to take Xavière's life. Beauvoir had recourse to the Gothic in order to express what Jung refers to as 'the shadow side of our personalities.'[80] Beauvoir tells us in La Force de l'âge that writing the final scenes of L'Invitée was a truly cathartic experience for her:

> Il m'était indispensable de m'arrêter à ce dénouement: il a eu pour moi une valeur cathartique. [...] Il me fallait aller au bout de mon fantasme, lui donner corps sans en rien atténuer, si je voulais conquérir pour mon compte la solitude où je précipitai Françoise. Et en effet, l'identification s'opéra. Relisant les pages finales, aujourd'hui figées, inertes, j'ai peine à croire qu'en les rédigeant j'avais la gorge nouée comme j'avais vraiment chargé mes épaules d'un assassinat. Pourtant c'est ainsi. Stylo en main, je fis avec une sorte de terreur l'expérience de la séparation. Le meurtre de Xavière peut paraître la résolution hâtive et maladroite d'un drame que je ne savais pas terminer. Il a été au contraire le moteur et la raison d'être du roman tout entier. (FA, pp. 387–8)

> It was essential that I should end with this denouement, which possessed a cathartic quality for me personally. [...] In order to overcome on my own account the solitude into which I had pushed Françoise, I must work my fantasy through to the end, bring it to life (embody it) without diluting it in any way. And indeed, the process of identification took place. Rereading the final pages, today so contrived and dead, I can hardly believe that when I wrote them my throat was as tight as though I had the burden of a real murder on my shoulders. Yet so it

---

[80] Jung, Carl G., 'Approaching the Unconscious', in *Man and His Symbols* by Jung, Carl G., and M.-L. von Franz, Joseph L. Henderson et al., New York: Dell Publishing, repr. 1979, p. 51.

was; and sitting there, pen in hand, it was with a sort of terror that I experienced separation. Xavière's murder may look like the abrupt and clumsy conclusion of a drama I had no idea how to finish; but in fact it was the motive force and *raison d'être* behind the whole novel. (PL, p. 340, ta)

The Gothic diction Beauvoir uses here is striking. The Gothic symbolic universe she created provided her with the ideal location for her confrontation with madness and pain. Her writing invites readers to feel, prompting empathy and identification as opposed to analysis. As Elizabeth MacAndrew puts it, the Gothic makes readers experience ideas.[81] In *L'Invitée* the philosophical veneer is no more than that, a veneer placed there in an attempt to justify the unjustifiable. Beauvoir (our implied author), together with her *alter ego*, Françoise, can be read as a perfect nineteenth-century Gothic subject, an embodiment of Botting's definition: 'Gothic subjects were [...] no longer in control of [their] passions, desires and fantasies [...]. Excess emanated from within, from hidden, pathological motivations that rationality was powerless to control.'[82] *L'Invitée* functions as a Gothic text, providing a structure to contain the threats to rational and humanist values that it explores.

---

[81]   MacAndrew, p. ix.
[82]   Botting, p. 12.

Chapter 2
Les Mandarins

Les Mandarins, begun around 1949 and published in 1954, is Beauvoir's longest and, for some, her richest and most complex novel. The aim of this chapter is to examine Beauvoir's writing practice in *Les Mandarins*, investigating the nature and extent of textual excess and transgression. Is it possible to locate madness, metaphorically speaking, in the text of *Les Mandarins*? Can it be argued that madness – defined as excess and transgression – finds a voice in this novel, that, in spite of any repression, it forces its way into her text? I also examine how far what I identified as the Gothic economy of *L'Invitée* can be seen to persist in *Les Mandarins*, a text of a quite different tone.

Les Mandarins has a dual narrative structure. There is an external narrator whose third-person narrative is focalised through Henri Perron. The second narrator, who speaks in first person, is Anne Dubreuilh. The narratives of Henri and Anne, which are of equal length and importance, alternate throughout the book.[1] They each have a different quality. Beauvoir writes in her memoirs that she split her experience between the two characters:

> Ce sont surtout les aspects négatifs de mon expérience que j'ai exprimés à travers [Anne]: la peur de mourir et le vertige du néant, la vanité du divertissement terrestre, la honte d'oublier, le scandale de vivre. La joie d'exister, la gaieté d'entreprendre, le plaisir d'écrire, j'en ai doté Henri. (FCi, p. 365)

> It was mainly the negative aspects of my experience that I expressed through [Anne]: the fear of dying and the panic of nothingness, the vanity of earthly diversions, the shame of forgetting, the scandal of living. The joy of existence, the gaiety of activity, the pleasure of writing, all those I bestowed on Henri. (FOC, p. 280)

The characteristics of madness for which I am reading are to be found mainly in Anne's narrative.

The early part of this chapter focuses on Anne's interior monologue in the first and final chapters of the novel. After an initial consideration of Anne's psychological instability, it explores how this is reproduced in the text. My analysis then addresses transgression and instability in Anne's narrative as a whole, first considering Beauvoir's use of tense and then looking at character function in the novel as a whole, specifically at the parallels that are drawn between Anne

---

[1]   Beauvoir describes the narrative techniques she employs in *Les Mandarins* in FCi, pp. 360–61. Elizabeth Fallaize has written a detailed and compelling analysis of the narrative structure in *Les Mandarins* in 'Narrative Structure in *Les Mandarins*,' in *Literature and Society: Studies in Nineteenth and Twentieth Century French Literature*, ed. C.A. Burns, Birmingham: Goodman, 1980, pp. 221–32. See also Heath, Chapter 3, pp. 89–91.

and Paule. The final part of this chapter deals directly with the Gothic in Anne's narrative. It discusses Gothic excess and shows how this inflects language. It also traces some of the Gothic motifs that contribute to the sombre and, at times, menacing atmosphere in the novel.

Les Mandarins includes the account of Anne's sense of loss of identity. I begin my analysis of the novel by looking briefly at the nature of Anne's fragile subjectivity before going on to explore how this is reproduced in the text. Anne is not the only character in the novel to face a crisis of subjectivity. Henri and Paule are also in search of who they are.[2] But, as Jane Heath argues, 'of all the protagonists, Anne is the most acutely anxious (to the brink of suicide) about her sense of identity [...].'[3] Anne concludes what Jane Heath refers to as her 'psychobiography'[4], saying: 'Me voilà donc clairement cataloguée et acceptant de l'être, adaptée à mon mari, à mon métier, à la vie, à la mort, au monde, à ses horreurs. C'est moi, tout juste moi, c'est-à-dire personne' (LMi, p. 46); 'There I am then, clearly catalogued and willing to be so, adjusted to my husband, to my profession, to life, to death, to the world and all its horrors; precisely me, that is to say, no one' (M, p. 39). Anne's words have been taken to be an assertion of her lack of identity.[5] However, her following comments suggest a more restricted meaning for her words at this point in the text; she is a nobody; that is, she is not a well-known public figure (LMi, p. 46). She is congratulating herself on not being exposed to the public gaze. Anne's crisis of subjectivity is actually made explicit a few pages later; she realises that she cannot only define herself negatively as a nobody, as not a public figure: 'Je ne suis personne, c'est facile à dire: je suis moi. Qui est-ce? où me rencontrer?' (LMi, p. 57); 'I'm no one, its easy to say: "I am me." Who is that? where can I find myself?' (M, p. 48, ta). In fact, she grants inordinate power to others to define her, to the gaze of others which she calls a 'dizzying pit' ('un gouffre vertigineux') (LMi, p. 57; M, p. 48).[6] It is as if she would know who she is only if she knew what others thought of her: 'Il faudrait être de l'autre côté de toutes les portes, mais si

---

[2]   Susan Bainbrigge has written about the way in which Henri's sense of self is shaken: 'The Case of Henri Perron: Writing and Language in Crisis' in Holland and Renée, pp. 97–112. In the same volume, Elizabeth Viti has examined how the language in Anne's narrative is inflected by her tenuous sense of self: 'A Questionable Balance: Anne Dubreuilh and the Language of Identity Crisis',' pp. 113–35.

[3]   Heath, p. 98.

[4]   Heath, p. 94.

[5]   See Heath, p. 96; Viti, p. 114. It is also interesting to note in passing the striking gap between Anne's confident assertions about being adjusted to life, death, the world and its horrors, and the evidence of her fear of death and her anguish in the face of the horrors of the Second World War. Jean-Raymond Audet discusses this denial of Anne's obsession with death in *Simone de Beauvoir face à la mort*, Paris: L'Age d'homme, 1979, p. 54.

[6]   See also: 'Quand je devine au fond d'une conscience étrangère ma propre image, j'ai toujours un moment de panique' (LMi, p. 58); 'When I make out my own image in the depths of someone elses's consciousness, I always experience a moment of panic' (M, p. 49, ta).

c'est moi qui frappe, ils se tairont' (LMi, p. 57); 'I would have to be on the other side of every door, but if it's me who knocks, they'll stop talking' (M, p. 48, ta). This image of forever unknowable secrets being whispered behind closed doors echoes images/ incidents in *L'Invitée* and links Anne with Françoise. It has definite Gothic overtones.

Anne lives in a symbiotic relation to Robert.[7] Anne's opening interior monologue reveals the nature of their relationship. He has given Anne her world: 'C'est une grande chance à vingt ans de recevoir le monde de la main qu'on aime! c'est une grande chance d'y occuper exactement sa place!' (LMi, pp. 73–4); 'It's an incredible stroke of luck, when you're twenty years old, to be given the world by the hand you love! it's an incredible stroke of luck to occupy your exact place there!' (M, p. 61, ta). Yet Anne's certainty has been shaken. The exclamation marks here and the nostalgia they evoke suggest that the situation may now have changed. Anne is no longer even sure of the past she shares with Robert (LMi, p. 75).[8] And, in fact, her uncertainty is more profound: 'Jusqu'ici j'ai toujours fait confiance à son destin; jamais je n'ai essayé de prendre sa mesure: la mesure de toutes choses, c'était lui; j'ai vécu avec lui comme en moi-même, sans distance. Mais soudain, je n'ai plus confiance, en rien' (LMi, p. 68); 'Up to now I've always trusted his destiny; I have never tried to take his measure. For me the measure of all things was Robert. I have lived with him as in myself, no distance between us. But suddenly, I no longer have any trust, in anything' (M, p. 57, ta). Robert has been an extension of herself, and Anne is distressed at the sudden realisation that she and Robert are separate, distressed and frightened by an interruption to confluence:

> Soudain je me suis mise à pleurer. J'ai pensé: "Ce sont mes yeux à moi qui pleurent; il voit tout, mais pas avec mes yeux." Je pleurais, et pour la première fois depuis vingt ans j'étais seule: seule avec mes remords, avec ma peur. (LMi, p. 67)

> Suddenly I began to weep. 'These are my eyes that are weeping,' I thought. 'He sees everything but not through my eyes.' I was weeping, and for the first time in twenty years I was alone, alone with my remorse, my fear. (M, p. 57)

Anne is so afraid of the ultimate separation that death represents that she is brought to the brink of commiting suicide. The analogy she draws is with a prisoner facing the death penalty who hangs himself a few days before his execution (LMi, p. 493). The interior monologue, which forms the final chapter of the novel, reveals Anne's preoccupation with Robert's death. She has a hyper-awareness of Robert's physical degradation to the extent that it is as if he is (in a way redolent of the Gothic tradition) already decomposing before her eyes. The words 'il mourra avant moi' ('he'll die before me') are repeated in the text (LMii, p. 494; M, p. 758). Anne is now certain that she is separate and alone:

---

[7]   Heath describes Anne's relation to Robert as narcissistic (p. 103).

[8]   There are distinct echoes here of 'L'Age de discrétion.' See especially AD, pp. 65–6.

> On peut bien mélanger nos cendres: on ne confondra pas nos morts. J'ai cru pendant vingt ans que nous vivions ensemble; mais non; chacun est seul, enfermé dans son corps, [...] avec sa mort qui mûrit sourdement en lui et qui le sépare de tous les autres. (LMii, pp. 494–95)

> They may well mix our ashes: they won't unite our deaths. For twenty years I believed we were living together; but no; everyone is alone, imprisoned in their body, [...] with their death maturing noiselessly inside them and which separates them from everyone else. (M, p. 758, ta)

The idea is intolerable to her.

Anne's fragile sense of self is further undermined when Lewis no longer loves her. In the first days of their relationship Anne can say: 'Je ne me demandai jamais qui Lewis aimait en moi: j'étais sûre que c'était moi' (LMii, p. 56); 'I [...] never wondered who it was that Lewis loved in me. I was certain it was myself' (M, p. 435). This confidence contrasts starkly with her pain and distress during her third trip.On an outing at the fair, Anne realises: 'Pour lui je n'avais plus de corps, et à peine un visage. Si du moins j'avais pu penser qu'un cataclysme m'avait défigurée! Mais c'est moi telle qu'il m'avait aimée qu'il n'aimait plus; [...] je fondais, je m'effondrais' (LMii, p. 398); 'For him I no longer had a body, I barely had a face. If only I could have felt that a catacysm had disfigured me! But it was the same me whom he had loved whom he no longer loved; [...] I was crumbling, I would collapse' (M, pp. 686–87, ta). Shortly afterwards, Anne is knocked off balance by a waxwork exhibition depicting alongside famous murders, the death camps at Buchenwald and Dachau:

> Quand je me suis retrouvée dehors, dans l'étourdissement du soleil, l'Europe tout entière avait filé aux confins de l'espace. Je regardais les femmes aux épaules nues, les hommes en chemises fleuries qui croquaient des hot-dogs ou qui léchaient des glaces: personne ne parlait ma langue, moi-même je l'avais oubliée; j'avais perdu tous mes souvenirs, et jusqu'à mon image: il n'y avait pas un miroir chez Lewis qui fût à hauteur de mes yeux, [...] c'est à peine si je me rappelais qui j'étais, et je me demandais si Paris existait encore. (LMii, pp. 399–400)

> When I found myself outside again in the sun's dazzling light, the whole of Europe had vanished somewhere in the outer limits of space. I looked at the women with their bare shoulders, at the men in their bright sports shirts, biting into hot dogs or licking ice-cream cones. No one spoke my language, and I myself had forgotten it. I had lost all my memories, even the memory of my own face: there was no mirror in Lewis's house which I could look into at eye level [...]. I hardly remebered who I was, and I wondered if Paris still existed. (M, p. 687)

When Lewis leaves her to spend a day in Chicago, Anne is utterly bereft. She appears to be without any inner resources. She panics: 'Être paralysée, aveugle, sourde, avec une conscience qui veille, je me suis dit souvent qu'il n'y a pas de pire sort: c'était le mien' (LMii, p. 407); 'I had often told myself that there could be no worse fate than to be paralysed, blind and deaf, with a mind that was alive. And that was my fate' (M, p. 693).[9] Lewis's absence is a 'vide dévorant,' 'un vide qui engloutissait tout' ('a 'gaping, all-devouring emptiness') (LMii, p. 409; M, p. 694). Anne's sense of abandonment is so intense that only Gothic excess can articulate it. She waits for Lewis to return without knowing who he is or who she is.

I now look at how Anne's sense of loss of identity and her instability are duplicated in the text of Les Mandarins. To begin to do this, I examine Anne's interior monologue, focusing on those characteristics that might be interpreted as transgressive.

Before doing so, it is helpful to look briefly at the way Anne's narrative is structured. As Elizabeth Fallaize notes, Anne's narrative is made up of two elements: an interior monologue, in which the two selves that make up the first-person narrator, the experiencing and narrating selves, coincide; and a first-person narrative of past events – a 'récit' – in which the experiencing and narrating selves are disassociated.[10] The 'récit' dominates in terms of length, but it is the interior monologue that frames this 'récit' in the first and last sections of Anne's narrative and forms the final chapter of the novel as a whole. It is partly for this reason that Elizabeth Fallaize argues that the interior monologue holds a privileged place in Anne's discourse even though Beauvoir, in her memoirs, tells us 'le récit d'Anne est sous-tendu par un monologue qui se déroule au présent, ce qui m'a permis de le briser, de le racourcir, de le commenter librement' ('underlying Anne's narrative is a monologue occuring in the present, which allowed me to break up the narrative, elide it and comment on it freely') (FCi, p. 369; FOC, p. 283), clearly indicating that she considers the narrative of past events to be the most important narrative mode. Elizabeth Fallaize suggests that another reason for the privileged place the interior monologue holds is the impression it gives readers that they have direct access to Anne's consciousness. It is this that makes Anne's interior monologue particularly relevant to my reading.

I now turn to the characteristics of Anne's interior monologue that mirror her instability and constitute a discourse of madness. For those familiar with Les Mandarins, it can be difficult to imagine reading the novel again for the very

---

9   This is reminiscent of the fate Anne had feared for Robert: 'Une créature vivante qui se change en écume, c'est affreux, mais il y a un sort pire: celui du paralytique à la langue nouée' (LMi, p. 76); 'It's awful to think of a living creature turning into foam, but there's an even worse fate: that of a paralysed man who can't move his tongue' (M, p. 64). Note the reference to the little mermaid with whom Anne has identified up to this point: 'un peu d' écume blanche sans souvenir, sans voix' (LMi, p. 38); 'a bit of white foam without memory, with no voice' (M, p. 33, ta).

10   Fallaize, 'Narrative Structure,' pp. 226–7. According to Emery Snyder, Anne's retrospective narration is problematic – I would say transgressive – because it is literally impossible; it is neither written nor spoken to anyone and whilst such unanchored and unaddressed discourse is characteristic of interior monologue, this is not the case in retrospective first-person narration. Unpublished paper quoted by Susan Rubin Suleiman in 'Simone de Beauvoir and the Writing Self,' L'Esprit créateur, 29 (4), 1989, 42–51 (p. 46).

first time and to remember the sense of disorientation experienced in the middle of the first chapter when the narrative focus shifts from Henri to Anne and as the retrospective third-person narrative is replaced by a first-person narrative in the present tense: 'Non, ce n'est pas aujourd'hui que je connaîtrai ma mort; ni aujourd'hui, ni aucun jour. Je serai morte pour les autres sans jamais m'être vue mourir' (LMi, p. 38); 'No, I shan't experience my death today; not today or any other day. I'll be dead for others without ever having seen myself die' (M, p. 33, ta). It is almost with a sense of shock that readers encounter the force of this negativity, hammered home by four negatives in the first sentence. Readers are momentarily confused; who can be the source of these morbid, anxious thoughts? Only gradually does it emerge that it is Anne and that she is lying awake in bed after the Christmas party at Paule's.[11] This shift in narrative focus knocks readers off balance; it forces them to question their expectations and introduces instability in the text.

Time and chronology are also sources of instability in the text. Jane Heath's study highlights how the linear chronology of Henri's narrative is suspended in the second half of Chapter 1. She argues that there are two chronologies in *Les Mandarins*, masculine/chronic time in Henri's narrative and feminine/linguistic time in Anne's interior monologue, and that at this point in the text, it is 'almost impossible to establish even a chronology of linguistic time.'[12] She suggests that atypically, in this opening chapter, Anne is unconstrained by time and observes no chronology as her thoughts range over events in the past, present, and future in an apparently random way. To develop this point further, although narrative time is clearly indicated as four o'clock in the morning (LMi, p. 39), the chronology of Anne's interior monologue is confused and even reversed. The narrative opens with Anne's reflections on death. She then notes that she closed her eyes but could not fall asleep again (LMi, p. 38). The earlier moment when she woke with a start is recorded only after intervening accounts of her childhood awareness of death, the little mermaid, her loss of faith in God, the role Robert plays in her life, and her current fears: 'Je me suis redressée en sursaut, j'ai ouvert les yeux' (LMi, p. 39); 'Suddenly I sat bolt upright, opened my eyes' (M, p. 33). One hour later, Anne's narrative returns to the same moment that opened it: 'Je me suis réveillée en sursaut et la peur était toujours là' (LMi, p. 68); 'I woke up with a start, and the fear was still there' (M, p. 57). Furthermore, Anne repeats the gesture of reaching out to the light: 'Je tends la main vers la poire électrique, je la laisse retomber' ('I stretch out my hand towards the light switch, I let it go')

---

[11] Heath also makes the point that readers must be confused when the narrative switches from Henri to Anne and that she can be identified only by reference to Henri's narrative (pp. 91–2).

[12] Heath, p. 92. She adopts Benveniste's definitions. Chronic time is objective; it is the time of events situated on a fixed scale. Linguistic time is a function of discourse, and past and future are located as points behind or ahead of the present of the discourse, the 'now' of the utterance. See Heath, p. 52.

(LMi, p. 41; M, p. 35, ta); 'J'allume, j'éteins' ('I switch on the lights, turn them off') (LMi, p. 68; M, p. 57). An hour has passed, but this repetition and recurrence create a sense of a space out of time, of time not moving on.

Also linked to reversed chronology, a sense of strangeness (disorientation) is created when fragments of narrative are 'repeated' before the episodes in which they 'first' appear are actually narrated. For instance, Anne uses the expression 'c'est fête' ('tonight's a celebration') about the Christmas party that has just taken place (associated in her mind with the absence of Diégo), echoing Nadine and Diégo's invitation to her shortly before Diégo was arrested: 'Venez dîner avec nous, viens, ce soir c'est fête' ('Come and have diner with us, come on, tonight's a celebration') (LMi, pp. 40 and 42; M, pp. 34 and 36, ta). Similarly, Anne remembers the words of Félix, the German soldier bribed to help Diégo and his father, and the words 'on les a abattus' ('they killed them') erupt in her monologue (between speech marks) before the the circumstances of their death are ever narrated (LMi, pp. 40 and 44; M, pp. 35 and 37, ta).[13]

Anne's interior monologue is also transgressive to the extent that it is marked by extravagance and excess. Extravagance and excess are apparent in a number of the quotations already made. One of the most striking characteristics of the monologue is the diction used to describe Robert, which is extravagant with strong religious overtones. Aged 15, Anne understood that having lost her faith in God, she was condemned to die. Her ensuing fear of death was banished by Robert: 'Du moment où j'ai aimé Robert, je n'ai plus jamais eu peur, de rien. Je n'avais qu'à prononcer son nom et j'étais en sécurité' (p. 39); 'From the moment I fell in love with Robert, I never again felt fear, of anything. I had only to speak his name and I would feel safe and secure' (M, p. 33). Robert has become a substitute for God; Anne repeats his name as those with religious faith might call on God. At the party, Anne looks at the guests and asks how they could be arrogant or stupid enough to want to be well-known public figures; for her, Robert is different from all the others – she sees him as predestined ('prédestiné') – for greatness, we understand (LMi, p. 46). His fate has been closely bound to the fate of the world: 'Autrefois, les crises les plus inquiétantes, j'étais sûre qu'on en sortirait; Robert devait s'en sortir, forcément; son destin me garantissait celui du monde, et réciproquement' (LMi, p. 74); 'Up to now, I always knew in my heart that we would somehow pull out of the gravest crises. Certainly Robert *had* to pull out of them; his destiny guaranteed that of the world, and vice versa' (M, p. 62). Robert has incarnated order, meaning and coherence for Anne, not through his theories but through his actions, even his very being (LMi, p. 72).[14]

---

[13] Repeated again, LMi, p. 66.

[14] Mussett discusses how Robert replaces God and embodies the absolute for Anne in 'Personal Choice and the Seduction of the Absolute' in *The Contradictions of Freedom: Philosophical Essays on Simone de Beauvoir's 'Les Mandarins,'* Sally J. Scholz and Shannon M. Mussett, eds, New York: State University of New York Press, 2005, pp. 135–56.

The portrayal of Robert as godlike is reinforced by the biblical overtones in Anne's account of the impact Robert has had on her life. For Anne, Robert brought the world out of darkness, nothingness, and chaos: 'Robert avait tiré du chaos un monde plein, ordonné, purifié par cet avenir qu'il produisait' (pp. 72–3); 'From chaos, Robert had drawn a full, orderly world, cleansed by the future he was producing (M, p. 61, ta). Thanks to Robert 'les idées sont descendues sur terre et la terre est devenue cohérente comme un livre [...]; le mal était déjà vaincu, le scandale balayé' ('ideas came down to earth and the earth became coherent like a book [...]; evil had already been conquered, death swept away') (LMi, p. 72; M, p. 60, ta).[15] Robert freed her (delivered her) – the verb used is 'délivrer' (LMi, p. 72; M, p. 60). The biblical imagery and diction, the use of the phrase 'come down to earth' combined with the biblical rhythms and the repetition of 'the earth' all contribute to the extravagant tone.[16]

The terms in which Anne describes the threat now facing Robert and herself are cataclysmic: 'La terre craque sous nos pieds; au-dessus de nos têtes il y a un abîme, et je ne sais plus qui nous sommes, ni ce qui nous attend' (LMi, p. 39); 'The earth is splitting open under our feet, and above our heads there is an infinite abyss. I no longer know who we are, nor what awaits us' (M, p. 33, ta). Robert had rid the world of horror and death ('le scandale') (LMi, p. 72) and saved Anne from the vast emptiness of the universe: 'le ciel s'est refermé au-dessus de ma tête et les vieilles peurs m'ont quittée' (LMi, p. 72); 'The sky closed above my head and the old fears left me' (M, p. 60). But Anne is losing confidence that Robert will be able to continue to play this role. Now she feels surrounded by horror and death ('le scandale') and chaos again: 'Diégo est mort, il y a eu trop de morts, le scandale est revenu sur terre, le mot de bonheur n'a plus de sens: autour de moi, c'est de nouveau le chaos' (LMi, p. 74); 'Diégo is dead, too many others have died, death has returned to the earth, the word happiness has lost its meaning. All around me, nothing but chaos again' (M, p. 62, ta). Anne is wholly invested in Robert's continuing to write and in his writings' having meaning. The language used is grandiose. Her fear is that Robert stops writing and that his work will be swallowed up into nothingness ('que toute son oeuvre passée s'engloutisse dans le

---

[15]   This is a further connection with *L'Invitée* where Pierre – named after the disciple whose name, of course, means rock of the Church – is portrayed in a similar way.

[16]   The echoes are many. I am thinking in particular of the Old Testament, Genesis 1, especially verse 2: La terre était informe et vide: il y avait des ténèbres à la surface de l'abîme, et l'esprit de Dieu se mouvait au-dessus des eaux. And in the New Testament, Jean 1:1: Au commencement était la Parole, et la Parole était avec Dieu, et la Parole était Dieu; Jean 1:14: Et la parole était faite chair, et elle a habité parmi nous, pleine de grâce et de vérité; et nous avons contemplé sa gloire, une gloire comme la gloire du fils unique venu du Père; Jean 3:13: personne n'est monté au ciel, si ce n'est celui qui est descendu du ciel, le Fils de l'homme qui est dans le ciel; Jean 3:16: Car Dieu a tant aimé le monde qu'il a donné son Fils unique, afin que quiconque croit en lui ne périsse point, mais qu'il ait la vie éternelle; Jean 3:17: Dieu, en effet, n'a pas envoyé son Fils dans le monde pour qu'il juge le monde, mais pour que le monde soit sauvé par lui. La Bible (Louis Segund).

vide,' LMi, p. 65). Writing is linked with life. Should Robert not write or should his work not survive, then he and Anne would also perish and the future become a tomb (LMi, pp. 77 and 78), a living death ('mourir tout vif,' LMi, p. 78). These motifs have clear Gothic resonances.[17] They encapsulate the excess at the heart of Anne's interior monologue.

Anne's interior monologue also dominates the final chapter of the novel, and the characteristics of Anne's interior monologue in the opening chapter of the novel are mirrored here. In it, Anne's narrative comes full circle, echoing and repeating the opening chapter, creating a sense of stangeness. Once again, Robert is working nearby; Anne recognises that she could reach out to him but does not do so (LMi, p. 39; LMii, p. 497). The same action of sitting up in bed recurs (LMi, p. 39; LMii, p. 499). As she did in the opening chapter, Anne is continuing to wake with a start during the night (LMi, p. 68; LMii, p. 494). Again, Anne is preoccupied by Robert's vulnerability (LMi, p. 68 and LMii, p. 494).[18] Again, Anne recalls her first awareness of death and has the same sense that death is stalking her: 'Mais de nouveau, comme en ce jour de mes quinze ans, où j'ai crié de peur, la mort me traque' (LMii, p. 493); 'But once more, as on that day when I was fifteen, when I cried out in fear, death is stalking me' (M, p. 757). During this final chapter, Anne reneacts the childhood memory recalled in the opening chapter, lying on her bed, eyes closed, waiting for death, a death she now holds in her hands in the shape of the vial of poison (LMi, p. 38; LMii, p. 497).[19] The link is made explicit in the text as Anne describes the silence surrounding her as 'un grand silence religieux comme au temps où je me couchais sur mon édredon en attendant qu'un ange m'enlève' ('a great religious silence, the same silence I knew when I used to lie on my eiderdown, waiting for an angel to carry me off') (LMii, p. 498; M, p. 761, ta). The words Anne spoke as a child – 'je suis morte' ('I'm dead') (LMi, p. 38; M, p. 33) – are recalled as Anne whispers the words 'je veux mourir' ('I want to die') (LMii, p. 493; M, p. 757). Some of the very first words of Anne's interior monologue ('Je serai morte pour les autres sans jamais m'être vue mourir' ('I'll be dead for others without ever having seen myself die'), LMi, p. 38; M, p. 33, ta) are echoed in her realisation that her suicide does not only concern herself: 'Je ne verrai rien, mais ils me verront. [...] Je mourrai seule; pourtant ce sont les autres qui la vivront' (LMii, p. 499); 'I won't see anything but they'll see me. [...] I'll die alone, yet it's others who will live my death' (M, p. 761, ta). Such repetition and recurrence create a sense of timelessness, reproducing for readers something like the feeling Anne has when visiting Paule after her second trip to the United States:

---

[17]   These motifs will be analysed in more detail later.

[18]   See also LMi, pp. 286–7. Anne's awareness of Robert's vulnerability will culminate in her hyper-awareness of Robert's physical degradation in the final chapter of the novel.

[19]   It is perhaps worth highlighting that Anne withdraws into her room like an archetypal Gothic heroine who lies on her bed holding a phial of poison to her breast.

Pendant qu'elle déballait les tissus brodés, je m'approchai de la fenêtre; on apercevait, comme d'habitude, Notre-Dame et ses jardins: à travers un rideau de soie jaunissante et caduque le lourd entêtement des pierres; au long du parapet, les boîtes à surprises étaient cadenassées, une musique arabe montait du café d'en face, un chien aboyait et Paule était guérie; c'était un très ancien soir, je n'avais jamais rencontré Lewis; il ne pouvait pas me manquer. (LMii, p. 349)

While she was unpacking the embroidered fabrics, I went over to the window; as always, you could see Notre Dame and its gardens: through a yellowing, old-fashioned silk curtain the stubborn weight of stones; along the parapet. the bookstalls were padlocked, Arab music was drifting up from the across the street, a dog was barking and Paule was better; it was an evening out of the distant past, I had never met Lewis; I couldn't miss him. (M, p. 650, ta)

Furthermore, in Anne's interior monologue in the final chapter, a sense of disorientation results from shifting narrative moments and breaks in the text, breaks that are not marked typographically. Anne is at first lying on the grass in the garden: 'J'appuie ma joue contre l'herbe chaude, je dis à voix basse: "Je veux mourrir"' (LMii, p. 493); 'I press my cheek against the warm grass; I say softly "I want to die"' (M, p. 757).[20] A few pages on, she props herself up on her elbow (LMii, p. 495). The narrative moment then shifts. Anne's sitting up and looking at her granddaughter; Maria is recounted in the perfect tense ('Je me suis redressée, j'ai regardé Maria.'). Then, as she looks at Maria sleeping (in the present), Anne projects herself into a future from which she will be absent and remembers how sleep has sometimes been 'tendre comme un sourire' ('as tender as a smile') (LMii, p. 496; M, p. 759).[21] In the present again, she is distressed by the past selves, the dead selves she carries with her, that have no grave and that are desperate to be able to sleep ('elles appellent en gémissant le sommeil,' LMii, p. 497). The narrative moment shifts again, and Anne is now lying on her bed (LMii, p. 497). Her leaving the garden, walking by Robert's window, going upstairs, finding the vial of poison in her glove drawer, and lying down are recounted in the perfect tense. This account in the perfect tense is interrupted. Anne's consciousness shifts briefly to the moment she walks past Robert's window and decides not to call out to him (LMii, p. 497). It is interrupted, too, as Anne's consciousness shifts to the moment she picks up the vial of poison and experiences a sense of satisfaction that death is in her control (LMii, p. 497). As Anne lies on her bed struggling to reach a decision, the past, future, and present converge in the text:

---

[20]   This is a tender, intimate moment with maternal overtones. Anne's laying her cheek against the warm earth contrasts with the vast cold emptiness of the universe. This moment recalls the moment when Anne is reborn as she makes love with Lewis when she becomes 'odorante comme la terre' ('fragrant as earth') (LMii, p. 39; M, p. 423).

[21]   The text achieves a lyrical intensity as Anne recalls the different places and different types of bed she has slept in. This is not the first time she painfully relives these lost moments. See also LMii, p. 394.

J'avais froid et pourtant j'étais en sueur; j'avais peur. Quelqu'un allait m'empoisonner. C'était moi, ce n'était plus moi, il faisait nuit noire, tout était très loin. Je serrai la fiole. J'avais peur. Mais de toute mon âme, je voulais vaincre la peur. Je la vaincrai. Je boirai. Sinon tout recommencera. Je ne veux pas. (LMii, p. 497)

I was cold, and yet I was bathed in sweat. I was afraid. Someone was going to poison me. It was me, it was no longer me, it was pitch black, everything was very far away. My fingers tightened around the vial. I was afraid. But with all my soul, I wanted to conquer the fear. I will conquer it. I will drink. If not, everything will begin again. I don't want it to. (M, p. 760, ta)

Anne's struggle is reflected in the jerky rhythm, the repetition, the contradiction, the series of short sentences. The use of the imperfect tense evokes a sense of time enduring. The use of the past historic tense is wholly unexpected and its force hits readers as narrative perspective suddenly shifts, placing that action at a distance, fixed in time and making that moment self-contained and pivotal. The narrative moment continues in the present as Anne states her determination to end her life:

Non! J'ai assez renié, assez oublié, assez fui, assez menti; une fois, une seule fois et à jamais, je veux faire triompher la vérité. La mort a vaincu: à présent, c'est elle qui est vraie. Il suffit d'un geste et cette vérité deviendra éternelle. (LMii, p. 498)

No! I've denied enough, forotten enough, fled enough, lied enugh. Once, one single time and forever, I want to make truth triumph. Death has won; death is now the only truth. A single move and that truth will become eternal. (M, pp. 760–61)

At this point there is another break in the text. The narrative moment shifts; Anne is now sitting at her dressing table in front of the mirror, speaking to Nadine: 'Nadine a frappé, elle est entrée, elle est debout à côté de moi' (LMii, p. 499): 'Nadine has knocked, has come in; she is standing beside me' (M, p. 762). The intervening account of Anne's reaching the decision to kill herself and of her changing her mind, getting up and staggering to sit at her dressing table is given in the perfect and imperfect tenses. The present tense intrudes, unsettling the narrative: 'Mon coeur ne bat plus pour personne' ('My heart is no longer beating for anyone') (LMii, p. 498; M, p. 761); 'Je ne peux pas' ('I can't') (LMii, p. 499; M, p. 761). The past historic is used just once: 'L'echo répéta: "Je n'aurais pas dû"' (LMii, p. 499); 'The echo repeated, "I shouldn't have done it"' (M, p. 761). The use of the past historic tense underlines the pivotal status of this key moment when Anne once more projects herself into the future and Nadine's words overheard in the garden (in relation to Maria) take on a new meaning (in relation to Anne's suicide). There is another break in the text at the point when Anne goes back out into the garden with her daughter. The narrative moment shifts. Anne's reaching the garden and being offered a drink are recounted in the past (in the perfect and past-historic tenses), and then story time and narrative moment reconverge;

Anne is sitting talking with the others, looking for a title for the new magazine Henri and Robert are going to publish. Shifting narrative moments and sudden shifts in tense, combined with Anne's projecting herself into a future from which she will be absent, on a textual level, reinforce the sense that Anne is 'lost in time' and reproduce the dizzyness she feels:

> Je me suis redressée, j'ai regardé Maria. Sur son petit visage fermé, c'est encore ma mort que j'apperçois. Un jour, elle aura mon âge et je ne serai plus là. [...] Mon absence sera si parfaite que tout le monde l'ignorera. Ce vide me donne le vertige. (LMii, p. 496)

> I sat up. I looked at Maria. On her inscrutable little face I again see my death. One day she'll be as old as I am, and I'll no longer be here. [...] My absence will be so complete that no one will be aware of it. The thought of that emptiness makes be dizzy. (M, p. 759)

In the final chapter, Anne's Gothic sensibility is underlined. Gothic themes and motifs that have been present throughout her narrative reach a climax. The text is marked by extravagance. Anne's hyperawareness of death and decomposition is foregrounded. Her awareness is physical. She sees the bone beneath the skin; Robert's teeth are his skeleton exposed (LMii, p. 494). The horror (and disgust) produced by the exposure of something that should remain hidden is typically Gothic. So, too, is the sense of decomposition and degradation happening out of sight:

> Chacun est seul, enfermé dans son corps, avec ses artères qui durcissesnt sous la peau qui déssèche, avec son foie, ses reins qui s'usent et son sang qui pâlit, avec sa mort qui mûrit sourdement en lui et qui le sépare de tous les autres. (LMii, pp. 494–5)

> Everyone is alone, imprisoned in their body, with their arteries hardening under their withering skin, with their liver, their kidneys, wearing out and their blood turning pale, with their death maturing noiselessly inside them and which separates them from everyone else. (M, p. 758, ta)

Death, which has been stalking Anne, is now there with her: 'La mort est là; elle masque le bleu du ciel, elle a englouti le passé et dévore l'avenir; la terre est glacée, le néant l'a reprise. Un mauvais rêve flotte encore à travers l'éternité: une bulle, que je vais crever' (LMii, p. 495); 'Death is here. It's masking the blue of the sky, it has swallowed the past and devoured the future. The earth is frozen over; nothingness has reclaimed it. A bad dream is still floating through eternity, a bubble which I shall burst' (M, p. 758). The diction is Gothic: 'engloutir' (swallow up), 'dévorer' (devour), 'le néant' (nothingness). Anne is lost (weightless and without substance) in the infinitely vast emptiness of time. The scale of events is cosmic.

Already, Anne is no longer 'une vivante,' one of the living. The Gothic motif of the living dead culminates here. Anne's past selves are so many dead selves she carries with her. It is a lurid, pitiful vision. Their death throes are reawakened by a memory. Like the undead, the peace of the grave (the peace of forgetting) is denied them, and they implore Anne to be able to sleep at last (LMii, p. 497): 'Elles n'ont pas de tombe: c'est pour ça qu'on leur interdit la paix des enfers; elles se souviennent encore, faiblement, et elles appellent en gémissant le sommeil' (LMii, p. 497).[22] It is zombie like that Anne walks from the garden to her room. The effect is reinforced by the sequence of simple clauses reporting her actions. She sees Robert as if from an unbridgable distance ('une distance infranchissable') (LMii, p. 497). There can be no communication ('pas de passage') between his life and her death.[23]

To sum up, my reading of the passages of Anne's interior monologue in the opening and closing chapters of *Les Mandarins* has explored how they duplicate Anne's instability and revealed the extent to which they are transgressive. I have shown that Anne's interior monologue creates a sense of disorientation and strangeness. I have also argued that the text is transgressive to the extent that it is marked by excess and extravagance and that Beauvoir's treatment of time and chronology destabilises the text.

I now address transgression and instability in Anne's narrative as a whole and begin this by considering the use of tense. Throughout the novel, Anne is clearly preoccupied by the passing of time.[24] In relation to the past, she struggles to come to terms with the failure to remember the dead, although she knows the process of forgetting is inevitable and even necessary; 'Que faire d'un cadavre?' ('What can you do with a corpse?'), she asks, accepting that Nadine could not go on living with the memory of Diégo, her dead lover, always with her (LMi, p. 44). In relation to the future, it is her fear of ageing and death that are marked. In a sense, Anne is 'lost in time'; situating herself in time is problematical for her. This is reflected in the text.

Sustained use of the imperfect tense suggests Anne is very much anchored in and drawn to the past.[25] This tense underlines the enduring nature of the past and

---

[22]   See also LMii, p. 375: 'Sous ma chair défraîchie j'affirme la survivance d'une jeune femme aux exigences intactes, rebelle à toutes les concessions, et qui dédaigne les tristes peaux de quarante ans; mais elle n'existe plus, elle ne renaîtra jamais, même sous les baisers de Lewis.' ('Under my wilting skin, I affirm the survival of a young woman with her demands still intact, a rebel against all concessions, and disdainful of those sad forty-year-old hags. But she doesn't exist any more, that young woman; she'll never be born again, even under Lewis's kisses) (M, p. 668).

[23]   This moment recalls the episode when Anne's flight from the States lands two hours early and she arrives home before she is expected. She finds it hard to breathe when Robert appears to be so very far away from her as he works ('suffoquée au moment où dans l'entrebâillement de la porte je l'avais aperçu tête baissée, en train d'écrire, très loin de moi') (LMii, p. 346; M, p. 647). She is struck by Robert's self-sufficiency and plenitude, his separateness from her.

[24]   Fallaize also notes this in 'Narrative Structure in *Les Mandarins*,' p. 228.

[25]   Sonia Kruks has argued that, although Beauvoir's explicit pronouncements on the nature of time generally echo Sartre's in affirming that the present takes its meaning from one's future goals, 'from the late 1940s, she develops a more dialectical notion of time,

evokes melancholy and nostalgia. The imperfect – sometimes referred to as 'the present in the past' – makes the past more immediately present. The imperfect tense is used extensively in Anne's account of her early relationship with Robert (LMi, pp. 68–71). More unusually perhaps, the imperfect tense is used to relate events at the Christmas party: 'Nadine riait avec Lambert, un disque tournait, le plancher tremblait sous nos pieds, les flammèches vacillaient. Je regardais Sézenac qui était couché de tout son long sur un tapis: il rêvait sans doute aux jours glorieux où il se promenait dans Paris avec son fusil en bandoulière. Je regardais Chancel [...]' (LMi, p. 45); 'Nadine and Lambert were laughing together, a record was playing loudly, the floor was trembling beneath our feet, the blue flames of the candles were fickering. I looked at Sézenac who was lying on the rug, thinking no doubt of those glorious days when he strutted down the boulevards of Paris with a rifle slung over his shoulder. I looked at Chancel [...]' (M, p. 38). The imperfect tense is also used to relate the visit Anne and Robert made to Bruay, the town where Robert grew up:

> Nous nous promenions dans les rues de son enfance, il me montrait l'école où son père enseignait, et la sombre bâtisse où à neuf ans il avait entendu Jaurès; il me racontait ses premières rencontres avec le malheur quotidien, avec le travail sans espoir. (LMi, p. 76)

> We walked through the streets of his childhood and he showed me the school where his father taught, the sombre building in which, at the age of nine, he had heard Jaurès; he told me about his first encounters with daily misfortune and with work without hope. (M, p. 63, ta)

Here and in the following example it is as if Anne is reluctant to let go of the precious moments she is describing:

> Ils savaient être heureux avec tant de fugue! Près d'eux je retrouvais ma jeunesse. "Venez dîner avec nous, viens, ce soir c'est fête", disaient-ils en me tiraillant chacun par un bras. (LMi, p. 42)

> And they knew how to be happy with so much fire! When we were together, I would rediscover my youth. 'Come and have diner with us, come on, tonight's a celebration,' they said, each one pulling me by the arm. (M, p. 36, ta)

Anne would like the moment when Nadine and Diégo invite her to eat with them to never end, to be repeated over and over. As indeed it is in her mind. To give a further example, the use of the imperfect tense is striking in the account of Anne's life during Nadine's trip to Portugal. At this point, Anne's nostalgia is made explicit:

---

in which the weight of the past, as well as the openness of projects towards a future, shapes the meaning of the present.' 'Living on Rails: Freedom, Constraint, and Political Judgement in Beauvoir's "Moral" Essays and *Les Mandarins*' in Scholz and Mussett, pp. 67–86 (n. 6, p. 83).

Les portes de l'appartement ne claquaient plus, je pouvais causer avec Robert sans frustrer personne et veiller tard la nuit sans qu'on frappe à ma porte; j'en profitais. J'aimais surprendre le passé au fond de chaque instant. Il suffisait d'une minute d'insomnie: la fenêtre ouverte sur trois étoiles ressuscitait tous les hivers, les campagnes gelées, Noël; dans le bruit des poubelles remuées, tous les matins de Paris s'éveillaient depuis mon enfance. (LMi, p. 265)

The doors of the appartment no longer slammed, I could chat with Robert without frustrating anyone and stay up late at night without someone knocking at my door. I took advantage of it. I enjoyed recapturing the past in the depths of each instant. I needed only a brief moment of sleeplessness; a cluster of stars seen through the open window, and all the winters of my life, all the frozen fields, all the Christmases were brought to life again; the noise of clattering garbage bins made me relive every morning of Paris waking I had known since my childhood. (M, p. 216)

Throughout Anne's narrative as a whole, the predominance of the imperfect tense, translating the pull the past exerts on Anne, is striking.

Related to this, fairly lengthy passages narrated in the pluperfect tense clearly place the consciousness of the narrator in the past. There are numerous examples in Anne's interior monologue in Chapter 1. To give just two:

Nous dansions, nous nous embrassions autour de l'arbre scintillant de promesses, et ils étaient nombreux, ah! si nombreux à ne pas être là. Personne n'avait recueilli leurs dernières paroles et ils n'étaient enterrés nulle part: le vide les avait engloutis. Deux jours après la Libération Geneviève avait touché un cercueil: était-ce bien le bon? On n'avait pas retrouvé le corps de Jacques [...]. (LMi, p. 40)

We were dancing, we were kissing each other around the tree sparkling with promises, and there were many, oh, so many, who weren't there. No one had heard their last words; they were buried nowhere, swallowed up in emptiness. Two days after the liberation, Geneviève had placed her hand on a coffin. Was it the right one? Jacques' body had never been found [...]. (M, p. 34)

Il était venu un jour lui apporter ses poèmes et c'est ainsi que nous l'avions connu. Dès l'instant où il avait rencontré Nadine, il lui avait donné impétueuesement son amour: son premier, son unique amour; elle avait été bouleversée de se sentir enfin nécessaire. Elle avait installé Diégo à la maison. (LMi, p. 41)[26]

He had come one day to show Robert his poems, which was how we had first met him. The moment he had met Nadine, he had impetuously given her his love, his first, his only love. She had been overwhelmed to feel herself needed at last. She had moved Diégo in to live with us. (M, p. 35, ta)

---

[26] Readers of *Les Mandarins* in translation should note that ideas have been reordered chronologically in this section of the English text.

Similar examples are found in *Les Mandarins* as a whole.

Anne's narrative is sometimes in the perfect tense (passé composé) and sometimes in the past historic tense (passé simple). The past historic tense, the tense used throughout Henri's narrative, generally speaking, situates actions precisely in the past as completed and discrete, places actions at a distance, and is more authoritative. The perfect tense, on the other hand, suggests a greater degree of emotional involvement and is less precise in terms of situating actions in time. This is the tense that is normally used for actions in the past in the interior monologue form. The switching between these two tenses in Anne's narrative is a source of instability in the text. The switching is uncomfortable and unsettling for readers for whom it is difficult to fix or situate the narrative. They are provided with no steady perspective on events. The alternating of these tenses results in a kind of multilayering; to some extent, the narrative in the past historic frames the narrative in the perfect tense.

Shifts occur within Anne's interior monologue as well as in her narrative of past events. The first shift into the past historic tense occurs some four pages into Anne's interior monologue. Until this point, past events, that is, events in her remote past (her childhood) and recent past (the previous evening and waking up), have been related in the perfect tense, albeit with fairly extensive passages in the imperfect and pluperfect tenses. The shift into the past historic tense is unexpected; Anne is remembering an evening she spent with Nadine and Diégo: 'Quand je les rencontrai le soir dans la rue [...]' ('When I met them on the street that evening [...]'); 'Robert [...] refusa de quitter son travail [...]' ('[Robert] refused to leave his work [...]'); '[le maître d'hôtel] nous désigna une table [...]' ('[the maître d'hôtel] showed us to a table [...]') (LMi, p. 42), and so on. Readers are likely to be disconcerted. Why the shift? Is the shift related to the fact that this is one of the last happy times Anne spent with the couple before Diégo was arrested? The narrative continues: 'Ce fut à peu de temps de là qu'un matin les Allemands sonnèrent chez M. Serra' (LMi, p. 43); 'It wasn't long after this that the Germans one morning knocked at Mr. Serra's door' (M, p. 37). Are the sense of loss and the events themselves more bearable if they are placed at a distance and delimited in time? Possibly. And yet, the text reverts to the perfect tense to relate Anne's desperate hope and then despair at the even more painful events that follow. We learn that after some time in captivity, bribes save Diégo and his father from being deported with the other prisoners, but it becomes more and more difficult for Anne and Nadine to believe they are still alive. The perfect and past historic tenses collide in the text:

> Peu à peu leur absence a cessé de se situer en aucun lieu: ils furent absents, rien de plus. N'être nulle part, ne plus être, ça ne fait pas beaucoup de différence. Il n'y a rien eu de changé quand Félix dit enfin avec mauvaise humeur: 'Il y a longtemps qu'on les a abattus.' (LMi, p. 44)

> It became increasingly difficult to locate their absence in any particular place; they were gone, that was all. To be nowhere or not to be at all isn't very different. Nothing changed when at last Félix said irritably, 'They killed them a long time ago.' (M, p. 37, ta)

The narrative then continues in the perfect tense but shifts into the past historic are frequent and inexplicable. Readers might find themselves wondering, for instance, why the past historic is used intermittently in Anne's account of the Christmas party or the walk home with Robert (LMi, pp. 59–64).

The effect of the instability resulting from such shifts in tense is felt in later chapters, too. Here the balance has changed. Anne's narrative in the second part of Chapter 2 possibly shocks readers' expectations by begining in the past historic tense. After all, in Chapter 1, Anne's narrative begins and ends in the present tense and the impression of immediacy associated with the interior monologue form is generally sustained.[27] In Chapter 2, readers encounter a narrative in the first person ('récit'), where the past-historic tense is the predominant tense and where it is the present and perfect tenses that disrupt and destabilise the text.

The reflections (in the present tense) of the narrating character interrupt the narrative. Admittedly, the effect of these interruptions is, generally speaking, quite muted as the views of the narrating character and those of the experiencing character tend to coincide. This is the case in the following examples: 'Bien sûr, je me suis toujours posé un tas de questions; guérir c'est souvent mutiler [...]' ('It's true, I've always asked myself a lot of questions; healing often means mutilating [...]') (LMi, p. 92; M, p. 76, ta); 'Je ne voyais aucune raison d'être triste, non; ce qu'il y a c'est que ça me rend malheureuse de ne pas me sentir heureuse, j'ai sans doute été trop gâtée' ('I could see no reason for being sad. It's just that it makes me unhappy not to feel happy; I must have been badly spolied') (LMi, p. 104; M, p. 86). Such reflections continue to interrupt Anne's narrative in the past historic tense ('récit') throughout the novel. Early in the second volume, an account of her sadness and distress at being without Lewis is interrupted by Anne's observation: 'J'admire les gens qui enferment la vie en formules définitives' (LMii, p.62); 'I admire people who can contain life in definite formulas' (M, p. 439). As the narrative progresses, the enduring sadness of the narrating character and the unchanging painfulness of her separation from Lewis is clear. An account in the past of how Anne (the experiencing character) was missing Lewis one summer's evening is interrupted by the following reflections in the present tense:

> Je suis triste moi aussi et ça ne nous rapproche pas. Je murmure: 'Pourquoi êtes-vous si loin?' Il répond en echo: 'Pourquoi êtes-vous si loin?' et sa voix est chargée de reproche. Parce que nous sommes séparés, tout nous sépare et même nos efforts pour nous rejoindre. (LMii, p. 91)

> I, too, am sad and it's bringing us no closer together. I murmur, 'Why are you so far away?' Echoing my words, he answers, 'Why are you so far away?' and his voice is heavy with reproach. Because we're separated, everything separates us, even our efforts to join each other. (M, p. 460, ta)

---

[27] This is discussed in detail in Fallaize, 'Narrative Structure in *Les Mandarins*,' pp. 225–8.

Elsewhere, verbs in the perfect tense occur unexpectedly in stretches of narrative in the past historic tense. Tenses clash between and even within sentences. For example, in Chapter 2, verbs in the perfect tense erupt in lengthy passages written in the past historic tense: 'J'ai réussi à ne plus penser au petit Fernand, ni à mon métier, mais je n'y gagnai pas grand-chose; le disque a recommencé à tourner dans ma tête [...]' ('I did succeed in driving little Ferdinand, as well as all thoughts of my profession, from my mind. But I gained little by it – one more the record began turning insistently in my head [...]') (LMi, p. 93; M, p. 77); and 'Elle hésita et puis elle me regarda avec un peu de défi: "Henri m'emmène au Portugal." J'ai été prise au dépourvu [...]' ('She paused, gave me a rather defiant look, and added, "Henri is taking me to Portugal with him." I was taken by surprise [...]' (LMi, p.95; M, p. 79). The account of Nadine's behaviour after Diégo's death which follows, is in the perfect tense but it is framed by verbs in the past historic: 'Je me levai, j'allumai une cigarette' ('I stood up. I lit a cigarette') and 'Je restai longtemps debout à regarder les flammes' [...] (For a long while I stood there looking at the flames [...]' (LMi, p. 98; M, p. 81). This account is followed by an account of Nadine's childhood and adolescence, also in the perfect tense. Could this be a stategy to distinguish the reflections and later recollections of the narrating chartacter as opposed to those of the experiencing character? Possibly. Yet this does not explain why the past-historic reappears within these accounts, introducing instability in the text. For example: 'Je la grondai le moins possible, mais elle a senti mes réticences: je lui ai toujours été suspecte' (LMi, p. 99); 'I scolded her as little as possible, but she was well aware of my reticence; to her, I've always been suspect' (M, pp. 81–2). Such shifts in tense are disconcerting.

A similar effect is produced later in the same chapter. The account of Anne's evening and disastrous lovemaking with Scriassine is in the past historic tense. The tense shifts to the perfect tense to recount her feelings the following morning. The past historic and perfect tenses then alternate as Anne waits for Scriassine in the café at lunchtime before reverting to the past historic tense again once he has arrived (LMi, pp. 123–4). The account of their meeting ends in the perfect tense. Narrative time and story time now converge (Anne is sitting in front of the mirror in her bedroom), and a passage of interior monologue, reminiscent of Anne's narrative in Chapter 1, closes this chapter (LMi, pp. 126–7). The lack of balance in the text replicates Anne's lack of steadiness.

Thus, the text reflects how problematical it is for Anne to situate herself in time, and the use of tense in the text as a whole is a source of transgression and instability. Anne's attachment to the past and her will to make time stand still are revealed in the extensive use of the imperfect and pluperfect tenses. The instability introduced in the text as a result of the switching between the perfect and past historic tenses mirrors Anne's own instability.

In the novel as a whole, the uncomfortable effect of these shifting perspectives is heightened by the fact that for the most part, in Anne's narrative, narrative time is indeterminate. As Elizabeth Fallaize points out, whilst narrative time is made clear in Chapter 1 and whilst it is possible to surmise that narrative time in Chapter 2 corresponds to a period when Anne is sitting at the mirror of her dressing-table (LMi, p. 127), in Chapters 4, 6, 8, and 10, 'there is no real evidence of narrative time and in most cases even surmise is difficult.'[28]

I now turn to character function in *Les Mandarins*, which is a further source of transgression and instability in the text. Paule explicitly carries the burden of madness in the narrative, yet it is Anne who is brought to the point of suicide. Paule's insanity is foregrounded in the novel but, paradoxically, although Anne does not 'go mad,' she shares the same feelings and emotions as Paule, and it is actually Anne who comes close to acting out this madness by almost commiting suicide, whereas Paule betrays her feelings by getting well again. Beauvoir saw Paule as a foil for Anne. She tells us: 'Je remarque que dans la plupart de mes romans j'ai placé à côté des héroïnes centrales un repoussoir: Denise s'oppose à Hélène dans *Le Sang des autres*, Paule à Anne dans *Les Mandarins*' ('I may add here that in most of my novels there is a foil to the main heroine. Denise and Hélène are thus balanced in *Le Sang des autres* [*The Blood of Others*], as are Anne and Paula in *The Mandarins*).[29] In her account of *Les Mandarins* in *La Force des choses*, Beauvoir draws a distinction between Anne and Paule. For Beauvoir, Anne's dependence on her husband and daughter is compensated for by her engagement with the world and those around her, whereas Paule embodies the *amoureuse* – the woman who makes a cult of love: 'une femme radicalement aliénée à un homme et le tyrannisant au nom de cet esclavage' (FCi, p. 362); 'a woman radically alienated from herself by an exclusive attachment to one man, and tyrannizing him in the name of her slavery' (FOC, p. 278).[30] In line with this authorial view, Elizabeth Fallaize suggests that Paule functions as a warning, as an image of what Anne might become.[31] I should like to suggest an alternative reading. I want to explore the extent to which, far from highlighting the diffences between the two women, the text might actually also underline their essential affinity.

Generally speaking, the connections between Anne and Paule are recognised by critics, but their extent and significance have not been fully appreciated. Terry Keefe rightly argues that the similarities between the situations of Anne and Paule are deliberately and systematically drawn in the the novel, but he does not develop this point in any detail. He suggests that this parallelism may make readers uneasy as Anne is so stable and rational in other ways.[32] I find this suggestion surprising; as I have shown, Anne appears psychologically vulnerable and full of doubts and uncertainty from the very beginning of her monologue. Shannon M. Mussett's philosophical reading of *Les Mandarins* sees Paule as a mirror, which Anne uses to 'reflect upon her own dependency on foreign absolutes.'[33] She explores the

---

[28]   'Narrative Structure in *Les Mandarins*,' footnote 7, p. 232.

[29]   FA, footnote 1, p. 389; PL, p. 342.

[30]   DSii, pp. 546–81.

[31]   Fallaize, *The Novels*, p. 108.

[32]   Keefe, *Simone de Beauvoir*, p. 106.

[33]   'Personal Choice and the Seduction of the Absolute,' in Scholz and Mussett, p. 136.

parallels between the Paule's relationship with Henri and Anne's relationship with Lewis but neglects the parallels with Anne's relationship with Robert.[34]

To support my argument that the text tends to underline what unites rather than what separates Anne and Paule, I will trace the parallels drawn between them. Elizabeth Fallaize argues that Anne, unlike Paule, avoids mythmaking discourse. She cites the irritation Anne feels when Paule describes Henri's work as 'a mission' and their shared life as 'a kind of experience that's simply incommunicable,' yet it strikes me that the grandiose terms Anne uses to talk about her relationship with Robert and his work are not so very different.[35] Anne wholly identifies with Robert: 'J'ai vécu avec lui comme en moi-même, sans distance' ('I have lived with him as in myself, no distance between us') (LMi, p. 68; M, p. 57, tr. adap), she asserts. She firmly believes that when you are as close to someone as she is to Robert, then even judging them is a betrayal and feels guilty for questioning his actions (LMi, p. 351). Indeed, she uses the same argument with Paule, telling her that if she criticises Henri, then that is proof they are not one being (LMi, p. 295). (Her underlying assumption seems to be that she and Robert are.) Paule rejects Anne's argument and denies that she and Henri are two separate beings: 'fondamentalement, nous sommes un seul être' (LMi, p. 295); 'fundamentally, we're one single being' (M, p. 240). The religious overtones of her discourse are unmistakable: 'Je me rappelle même avec netteté ma première illumination: j'en ai été presque effrayée; c'est étrange, tu sais, de se perdre absolument en un autre. Mais quelle recompense quand on retrouve l'autre en soi! Elle fixait le plafond d'un regard inspiré' (LMi, p. 295); 'I clearly remember my first enlightenment. I was almost frightened; it's stange, you know, to lose yourself absolutely in another. But how rewarding it is when you find the other in yourself! With an inspired look, she gazed at the ceiling' (M, p.240, ta). This is reminiscent of the religious diction used to portray Robert as a godlike figure, predestined for greatness, already discussed.

The parallels drawn between the women's views of their relationships are replicated when it comes to their views of their partner's work. About Robert's writing Anne says: 'Ecrire, c'est ce qu'il aime le plus au monde, c'est sa joie, c'est son besoin, c'est lui-même. Y renoncer ça serait un suicide' (LMi, p. 78); 'Writing is the thing he loves most in the world; it's his joy, his necessity; it's he, himself. Renouncing writing would be suicide for him' (M, p. 65). Anne's concerns that Robert may be prevented from writng by his involvement in politics is mirrored in Paule's concerns over Henri (LMi, p. 293). Significantly, Anne tells Paule that she should trust Henri, something she is finding it hard to do in her own case with respect to Robert's plans. Admittedly, Anne makes no claims that it is she who has made Robert as Paule claims to have made Henri (Anne adopts a much more subservient stance), but fundamentally I see no difference between the two women's attitudes to their partner's work and role in life. Paule says Henri is not a

---

[34] 'Personal Choice and the Seduction of the Absolute,' in Scholz and Mussett, p. 146.

[35] Fallaize, *The Novels*, p. 109. The quotations can be found in LMi, pp. 293 and 295.

writer like any other: 'Ce que je lui ai appris c'est que sa vie et son oeuvre devaient être une seule réussite: une réusitte si pure, si absolue qu'elle servît d'exemple au monde' (LMi, p. 294); 'What I have taught him is that his life and his work should become a unit so completely realised, so pure, so absolute that it would serve as an example to all the world' (M, p. 39). And Anne describes Robert's books as unique (LMi, p. 62). Anne encourages Paule to allow Henri to change but, for herself, finds the idea that Robert may stop writing intolerable. She admits that Robert does not see things in exactly the same way that she does but asserts that 'il espère bien laisser un nom derrière lui, un nom qui signifie beaucoup, pour beaucoup de gens' ('he definitely hopes to leave a name behind him, a name that will mean a great deal to a great many people') (LMi, pp. 77–8; M, p. 65). Is she right? Is the difference between the two women only the fact that, in terms of the values of the text, readers are meant to accept unquestioningly that Anne is right and that Paule is wrong?

It has been suggested that one of the differences between the two characters is that Anne, unlike Paule, does not refuse the passage of time.[36] This is worthy of further analysis. It is the case that Anne overtly accepts that time passes, yet she is tempted to see her relationship with Lewis as timeless. Anne says of Paule: 'Elle était prête à nier l'espace et le temps avant d'admettre que l'amour pût n'être pas éternel' (LMi, p. 47); 'She was ready to deny the existence of space and time rather than admit that love might not be eternal' (M, p. 40). She is concerned for her friend, but at times her own attitude is similar. In the very first days of her relationship with Lewis, Anne enjoys feeling that time is standing still, that 'on aurait dit une soirée quotidienne qu'allaient suivre mille soirées toutes semblables' ('it was like an ordinary, everyday evening which would be followed by a thousand other evenings all alike') (LMii, p. 53; M, p. 433).[37] Visiting the States for the second time, Anne tells herself that it is impossible to go back, 'un an passe, des choses se passent, plus rien n'est pareil' ('a year passes, things happen, nothing is the same') (LMii, 222; M, p. 557), but once she is in Lewis's arms again, her attitude changes: 'C'était Lewis, il n'avait pas changé, ni moi, ni notre amour. J'étais partie mais j'étais revenue: j'avais retrouvé ma place et j'étais délivrée de moi' (LMii, p. 223); 'It was Lewis. No, he hadn't changed, nor had I, nor had our love. I had left, but I had come back; I had found my place again and I was released from myself' (M, p. 558). To Anne's mind, she and Lewis will never be separated again because, even when they are apart, they will be waiting together for their separation to end, they are 'united forever' ('réunis pour toujours') (LMii, p. 224; M, p. 559). With Lewis, travelling by boat down the Mississipi, Anne delights in a sense that they are in a space out of time: 'Nous aimions qu'un seul matin ressuscitât de matin en matin, un seul soir de soir en soir' (LMii, p. 225); 'We liked it that way – a single morning being reborn from morning to morning, a single evening from eveniing to evening' (M, p. 560). As Shannon M. Musset notes,

---

[36]   Fallaize, *The Novels*, p. 109.
[37]   For Anne, a sense of well-being is linked with such moments. See also LMi, p. 265.

'at its greatest intensity, Anne's love for Lewis places her squarely in the eternity of the present, rather than rushing her forward into her future death.'[38]

During her stay, Anne is brought up against the reality that things have in fact changed when Lewis lies to her over the need to cut short their trip to South America to be in New York and when he prefers to spend time in Rockport with the Murrays rather than be alone in Chicago with her. Even once the couple begin to enjoy being together again, despite her hope that she might save the relationship, Anne appears to realise that it would be an illusion to suppose that nothing has changed; she knows that if Lewis would only tell her that he loves her, she *could believe* everything was exactly the same (LMii, p. 271, my emphasis). She apparently accepts that their affair will end one day: 'Pour les serments d'éternité, j'habitais trop loin, j'étais trop âgée' (LMii, p. 273); 'I was too old for pledges of eternal love; I lived too far away' (M, p. 594). However, she hopes for lifelong friendship in its place. And when they go back to Chicago, Anne's express wish is to recapture what they had the previous year. Finally, when Lewis does tell her he loves her – 'J'ai essayé de moins vous aimer: je n'ai pas pu' ('I tried to love you less. I couldn't') – Anne readily believes that everything is back the way it was: 'Tout m'a été rendu' (LMii, p. 286); 'Everything was given back to me' (M, p. 603). She denies the reality of change.

When Lewis invites Anne to stay for the third time, it is as if time has no meaning, has not passed: 'Assise près de lui dans la chambre de New York, j'avais dit: "Nous reverrons-nous?" Il répondait: "Venez." Entre nos deux répliques, rien ne s'était passé, cette année fantôme était abolie et je retrouvais mon corps vivant. Quel miracle!' (LMii, p. 378); 'Sitting beside him last year in the hotel room in New York, I had asked, "Will we ever see each other again?" And now he replied, "Come." Between the question and the answer, nothing had happened; that phantom year had been obliterated, and I once more found my living body. What a miracle!' (M, p. 671).[39] When she arrives, at first she tries to persuade herself that what she knows – that things have changed – is not true: 'Évidemment, je délirais. Lewis m'avait dit un an plus tôt: "Je ne'essaierai plus de ne pas vous aimer. Jamais je ne vous ai tant aimée." Il me l'avait dit, c'était hier et c'était toujours moi, et c'était toujours lui' (LMii, p. 382); 'Obviously, I was going mad. A year earlier, Lewis had said to me, "I'll stop trying not to love you. I've never loved you as much as now." He'd said it to me, it was yesterday and it was still me, and it was still him' (M, p. 674, ta). The series of repetitions suggests Anne's sense of panic. Again, she denies the passage of time; one year ago is yesterday.

The pages that follow record the painful process of Anne's coming to terms with the fact that Lewis no longer loves her. One week before Anne is due to leave Lewis and Chicago for the last time, she spends some time with Myriam and Philippe, apart from Lewis. She glimpses the fact that her life might start

---

[38]   'Personal Choice and the Seduction of the Absolute,' in Scholz and Mussett, p. 144.

[39]   There is an echo here of 'le banquet fantôme,' the banquet with no food that Paule gives for guests she has forgotten to invite as she loses her grip on reality (LMii, pp. 207–8, 258).

again, that 'l'avenir n'était plus tout à fait impossible' ('the future was no longer completely impossible') (LMii, p. 424; M, p. 705). This is one of the few instances in the book when Anne momentarily associates the idea of starting again with hope rather than pain and despair.[40] Nevertheless, she cries for the love she has lost:

> Parce que je suis là, parce que je ne reviendrai pas, parce que le monde est trop riche, trop pauvre, le passé trop lourd, trop léger; parce que je ne peux pas fabriquer du bonheur avec cette heure trop belle, parce que mon amour est mort et que je lui survivrai. (LMii, p. 425)

> Because I am here, because I'll never return, because the world is too rich, too poor, the past too heavy, too light, because I can't turn this too-beautiful hour into hapiness, because my love has died and I wll survive it. (M, p. 706, ta)

Significantly, only paradox and contradiction can express the the anguish Anne feels.

I have been discussing Anne's relationship with Lewis in relation to time. There is, of course, an important distinction between Anne's attitude toward her relationships with Robert and Lewis. The relationship with Robert is presented as a love unaffected by time. Although Anne has a new sense of her own and Robert's mortality, she has lived and loved Robert as if forever: 'Nous nous aimions comme nous vivions, à travers l'éternité' (LMi, p. 286). Anne may question her shared past with Robert, but she never once doubts that their relationship will continue unchanging if she so wishes. Only death will bring an end to their relationship. Anne sees her relationship with Lewis differently. At the very beginning of this relationship, Anne is aware that it may end and end painfully and identifies with Paule (LMii, p. 54). In terms of the values of the text, Paule's mistake is to define her relationship with Henri in the same way that Anne defines her relationship with Robert instead of recognising that it is merely love on a human scale.[41]

Elizabeth Fallaize identifies aspects of Anne's behaviour that are echoes of Paule's and so represent danger signals in her relationship with Lewis. She finds echoes of Paule's bizarre interpretations of Henri's behaviour in Anne's misunderstandings of Lewis.[42] One instance occurs in Chichicastenango when Lewis asks Anne to stay with him always. Anne thinks Lewis has understood her refusal and accepts her reasoning and she cries for joy (LMii, p. 246). Later in New York, she learns that Lewis had wanted to say more but had been silenced by her tears and her fear of losing him (LMii, p. 266). Of course, an important difference between Paule and Anne remains; Anne is able immediately to acknowledge her mistake and admit that she had forced Lewis's hand:

---

[40]   See also LMi, p. 359: 'Survivre, après tout, c'est sans cesse recommencer à vivre.' ('To survive is, after all, perpetually to begin to live again') (M, p. 290).

[41]   This distinction recalls the distinction drawn by Beauvoir and Sartre between necessary and contingent loves. FA, p. 30.

[42]   Fallaize, The Novels, p. 109.

Je me revoyais pleurant sur son épaule, nous étions unis à jamais; mais j'étais unie toute seule. Il avait raison: j'aurais dû me soucier de ce qui se passait dans sa tête, au lieu de me contenter des mots que je lui arrachais. (LMii, p. 267)

I saw myself crying on his shoulder; we were united forever. But I was united alone. He was right: I should have tried to find out what was going on inside his head instead of contenting myself with words I forced out of him. (M, p. 589)

Anne makes the link between herself and Paule explicit at the point in the text where she realises that Lewis has lied to her about needing to cut short their trip to New York: 'Le soir où Paule avait donné son banquet fantôme j'avais senti le sol basculer sous mes pieds. Aujourd'hui c'était pire. Lewis n'était pas fou: il fallait que ce soit moi!' (LMii, p. 258); 'The night Paule gave her phantom banquet, I had felt the floor swaying under my feet. Now it was worse. Lewis wasn't crazy; it had to be me!' (M, p. 583, ta). She has completely misunderstood Lewis, and reality no longer makes sense.

Anne wants desperately to save their love. Like Paule before her, she tries to reason with her lover, to show him he has more to gain that to lose by remaining in their relationship. The echoes in the text are striking:

Anne: 'Je prendrai ce que vous me donnerez et je n'exigerai jamais rien' (LMii, p. 269); 'I'll take what you give me and I'll never demand anything.' (M, p. 591)

Paule: 'Maintenant je suis prête à t'aimer dans une totale générosité, pour toi, non pour moi' (LMi, p. 161); 'I'm now prepared to love you with complete generosity, for you, not for me'. (M, p. 131, ta)

Anne: 'Ne gâchez plus les choses pour le seul plaisir de les gâcher!' (LMii, p. 269); 'Stop spoiling things for the sake of spoiling them.' (M, p. 591)

Paule: 'Tu ne vas pas faire exprès d'abîmer notre amour?' (LMi, p. 135) 'You're not going to damage our love on purpose, are you?' (M, p. 109, ta)

Anne: 'Je n'ai jamais eu l'impression que je vous tyrannisais'; (LMii, p. 261) 'I've never had the feeling I was tyrannising you. (M, p. 585, ta)

Paule: 'Je ne veux pas que tu penses que je te tyrannise' (LMi, p. 136); 'I don't want you to think of me as a tyrant'. (M, p. 109)[43]

Love is as much an absolute for Anne as it is for Paule. Anne encourages Paule to get better, telling her that 'love isn't everything,' but she knows what she is saying is meaningless and that in Paule's place she would never want to get over her love:

---

[43]   In quite different circumstances, the vocabulary used by Anne and Paule is strikingly similar. Paule is convinced that Henri is hurting her out of revenge ('une vengeance'), LMii, p. 196; Anne interprets Lewis's behaviour as retaliation ('des représailles'), LMii, p. 265.

Je lui jetais des mots dépourvus de sens seulement pour entendre le ronron de
ma voix. "Tu guériras, il faut guérir. L'amour n'est pas tout." Sachant bien qu'à
sa place je ne voudrais jamais guérir et enterrer mon amour avec mes propres
mains. (LM ii, p. 207)

I began saying meaningless words to her, for no other reason than to hear the purr
of my own voice. 'You'll get well, you've got to get well. Love isn't everything.'
And I knew very well that in her place I would never want to get well and bury
my love with my own hands. (M, p. 546)

The association of lost love and death and the image of burying love like a corpse
chime with the Gothic in the text.[44] Later in the same chapter, Anne says the same
words to Lewis – 'l'amour n'est pas tout.' ('love isn't everything') – but her words
are immediately undercut: 'Qu'il comprenne! qu'il me garde cet amour qui n'était
pas tout mais sans lequel je ne serais plus rien' (LMii, p. 246); 'Let him understand!
let him go on loving me with that love which wasn't everything but without which
I would be nothing' (M, p. 574, ta). Once more, only paradox can express Anne's
reality; Lewis's love may not be everything, but without it Anne would be nothing.
Anne recognises that the life Paule is leading is not normal but knows she is in no
position to criticise:

Une existence normale: qu'y a-t-il de plus déraisonnable? C'est fou le nombre
de choses auxquelles on est obligé de ne pas penser pour aller sans dérailler d'un
bout de la journée à l'autre, c'est fou le nombre de souvenirs qu'il faut refuser,
de vérités qu'il faut éluder. (LMi, p. 296)[45]

A normal existence – what could be more irrational? It's fantastic the number of
things you're forced not to think about in order to go from one end of the day to
the other without jumping the track! And the number of memories that have to
be driven from your mind, the truths that have to be evaded! (M, pp. 240–41)

Anne questions the meaning of normality, the distinction between reason and
unreason. Anne identifies with Paule and projects her own pain on to her:

J'aime bien Paule, et en même temps elle me fait un peu horreur. Souvent le
matin, je sens sur moi l'ombre étouffante de tous les malheurs qui sont en train
de se réveiller, et c'est à elle d'abord que je pense; j'ouvre les yeux, elle les
ouvre et tout de suite il fait noir dans son coeur. (LMi, p. 288)

---

[44]   Subsequently, Anne laments that her love is dead, but there is no corpse to bury
(LMii, p. 410).
[45]   This is echoed by Laurence in *Les Belles Images*: 'On existe. Il s'agit de ne pas s'en
apercevoir, de prendre son élan, de filer d'un trait jusqu'à la mort' (BI, p. 44); 'We exist. The
thing to do is to take no notice but to go at it with a run and to keep on going right on until
you die' (LBI, p. 54, ta).

I'm fond of Paule but at the same time I'm a bit horrified by her. Often, in the morning, I feel a suffocating shadow spread over me, the shadow of all the misfortunes that are awakening, and my first thought is of her. I open my eyes, she opens hers, and immediately it's dark in her heart. (M, p. 234, ta)

It is as if Paule's eyes are Anne's eyes, as if Paule experiences the feelings Anne experiences when she wakes; the dark shadow that suffocates Anne is the blackness in Paule's heart. These Gothic motifs – horror, shadow, suffocation, blackness – are familiar to readers of *L'Invitée*.

Anne's love for Lewis is as all-consuming as Paule's love for Henri was before her breakdown. When she receives a hostile letter from Lewis, Anne can think of nothing else. Even in the face of the renewed threat of war, the only question that concerns her is whether she will see Lewis smile at her ever again. She knows that 'être aimée, ce n'est pas une fin ni une raison d'être, ça ne change rien à rien, ça n'avance à rien: même moi, ça ne m'avance à rien' ('being loved isn't an end in itself, or a *raison d'être*; it changes nothing, it doesn't lead anywhere: even me, it's not leading me anywhere') (LMii, pp. 376–7; M, p. 670, ta); she knows she must be mad to have made her fate dependent on one heart out of millions of others; but she has no choice (LMii, p. 377).

The portrayal of the relationship between Anne and Lewis when Lewis no longer loves her echoes the portrayal of the relationship between Paule and Henri early in the novel. The first night of Anne's final trip to the States, even before Lewis tells her he no longer loves her, the couple's lovemaking has changed. Anne does not really want to make love but wants to be sure that Lewis still desires her; before entering her, Lewis turns out the light and does not smile at Anne or say her name (LMii, pp. 379–80). Later, at the house by the lake in Parker, Anne convinces herself that she has given up too easily on Lewis's love and allows herself to hope that he may yet love her again. Their lovemaking is even more disastrous and Lewis (like Henri with Paule) takes the easy way out and makes love with Anne rather than rejecting her:

Je retrouvai sa bouche et mon corps fondait de désir tandis que ma main rampait sur le ventre tiède; il me désirait lui aussi et entre nous le désir avait toujours été de l'amour; quelque chose recommençait cette nuit, j'en été sûre. Soudain il fut couché sur moi, il entra en moi, et il me posséda sans un mot, sans un baiser. Ça se passa si vite que je restai interdite. [...] Une rage désespérée m'a prise à la gorge. 'Il n'a pas le droit', murmurai-je. Pas un instant il ne m'avait donné sa présence, il m'avait traitée en machine à plaisir. Même s'il ne m'aimait plus, il ne devait pas faire ça. (LMii, p. 393)

I found his mouth again, and as my hand crept over his warm belly my body burned with desire. He, too, desired me, and between us desire had always been love. Something was beginning again that night. I was sure of it. Suddenly he was lying on top of me, he penetrated me, and he possessed me without a word, without a kiss. It all happened so fast that I remained dumbfounded. [...] A desperate anger gripped my throat. 'He has no right to do this,' I murmured.

Not for an instant had he given me his presence; he had treated me as a pleasure machine. Even if he didn't love me any more, he shouldn't have done that. (M, p. 683, ta)[46]

Of course, Paule has no direct voice in the narrative, but this episode cannot fail to recall Henri's treatment of her, and it is hard not to project Anne's feelings onto Paule retrospectively. The links between the two women's situations are evident, too, when Lewis returns home after 24 hours in Chicago. Anne, in a manner reminiscent of Paule's, greets him 'avec la disgrâce habituelle aux femmes qui ne sont plus aimées: trop de chaleur, trop de questions, trop de zèle' ('with the customary ineptitude of women who are no longer loved – too much warmth, too much zeal, too many questions') (LMii, p. 410; M, p. 695). Lewis, for his part, is reluctant to share his trip in any detail. The words Anne says to Lewis during their quarrel might well have been said by Paule, admittedly, with less objective truth: 'Je ne suis ici que pour vous, je n'ai que vous! Quand je vous pèse, qu'est-ce que je peux devenir?' (LMii, p. 413); 'I'm here only for you; all I have is you! When I feel I'm being a burden on you, what can I do?' (M, p. 697).

The links between the two characters are nowhere more complex than in relation to Paule's breakdown and madness and Anne's contemplated suicide. Anne is extremely ambivalent about Paule's cure, which is linked with a sense of loss and defeat for her. Beauvoir saw Anne's decision not to commit suicide in the same way: 'Son retour au consentement quotidien ressemble plutôt à une défaite qu'à un triomphe. [...] Elle [...] trahit quelque chose' (FCi, p. 368); 'Her return to an acceptance of the everyday world seems more like a defeat than a triumph. [...] She is betraying something' (FOC, p. 283). This is in terms of the narrative. In terms of the narrative process, Beauvoir explains that Anne does not commit suicide because she, Beauvoir, did not wish to repeat what she saw as the error she had made in L'Invitée 'of attributing to [her] heroine an act motivated by purely metaphysical reasons' (FCi, p. 368; FOC, p. 283). Beauvoir also defends her decision in terms of characterisation, asserting that 'Anne is not made of the stuff of suicides' ('Anne n'a pas l'étoffe d'une suicidée'), yet it seems to me that Anne's suicide would have been wholly credible. Anne's preoccupation with death is long standing. Robert has tried to persuade her otherwise, but her old belief that death makes everything meaningless and any action derisory is back: 'La mort ronge tout' (LMii, p. 71); 'Death gnaws everything' (M, p. 446, ta). Anne's suicide is prefigured in the text. She lies down on the sofa, closes her eyes, and lets go of everything (the French term used is 'délivrée'); it is as if she were dead: 'Comme elle est égale et clémente, la lumière de la mort! Lewis, Robert, Nadine étaient devenus légers comme des ombres, ils ne pesaient plus sur mon coeur: j'aurai pu supporter le poids de quinze millions d'ombres, ou de quatre cents millions' (LMii, p. 71); 'How even and kind the light of death is! Lewis, Robert, Nadine

---

[46]   The text has been cut in English translation and the physical details of this sexual encounter are missing. It is worthy of note that this is not the only occasion on which Lewis's lovemaking is cold and hostile. See also LMii, p. 46.

had become as light as shadows, they no longer weighed on my heart. I could have borne the weight of fifteen million shadows, or four hundred million' (M, p. 446, ta). Anne is referring to the millions of prisoners in Soviet labour camps and the Chinese dying from famine and epidemics – they, too, have become no more than shadows. However, there is a bathetic break in mood: 'Au bout d'un moment, j'ai tout de même été chercher un roman policier; il faut bien tuer le temps: mais le temps aussi me tuera, violà bien la vraie harmonie préétablie' (LMii, p. 71); 'nevertheless, after a few moments, I went to get a detective story. You have to kill time. But time will kill me too – and there's the true, pre-established balance' (M, p. 446).[47] Significantly, when Robert comes home Anne imagines she sees him as she saw Diégo at Drancy, as a disincarnated image in the distance, as if through opera glasses.[48] At this point Anne is able, however provisional and mitigated her engagement is, to bring herself to reengage with life. In the immediate, she discusses suicide with Robert in terms of reality and indifference (LMii, pp. 72–3; M, pp. 446–7). During the discussion, Robert tells Anne that someone who 'honestly believes that death alone is real' should commit suicide. Anne replies that carrying on living is an easy way out and suggests people go on living as the result of being bewildered and cowardly ('étourdi et lâche'). Moreover, by the final chapter of the novel, the distance between Anne and Robert has become unbridgable ('infranchissable') (LMii, p. 497).[49]

To return to the question of Anne's ambivalence, having taken Paule to be admitted to the hospital, Anne wonders what exactly Paule is going to be cured of and who she will be afterwards. The answer – 'Elle serait comme moi, comme des millions d'autres: une femme qui attend de mourir sans plus savoir pourquoi elle vit' ('She'd be like myself, like millions of others: a woman waiting to die, no longer knowing why she's living') – suggests Anne's admiration for the old Paule (LMii, pp. 219–20; M, 556). Certainly, Anne felt closer to Paule before

---

47   The notion that life is a matter of killing time recurs. This was Anne's view when she was a young woman, before she met Robert: 'Et quelle absurdité, ces journées qui se répètent de semaine en semaine, de siècle en siècle, sans aller nulle part! Vivre c'était attendre la mort pendant quarante ou soixante ans en piétinant dans du néant' (LMi, p. 72); 'And how absurd, the days which repeat themselves from week to week, from century to century, without ever getting anywhere! Living is waiting for forty or sixty years for death whilst marking time in nothingness' (M, p. 60, ta). Anne's decision to go to bed with Scriassine toward the beginning of the novel is in part influenced by her views on time; she considers her life to be over but finds herself in the absurd position of still having many years to kill (LMi, p. 117). Anne's awareness of time is intensified as she waits for a letter from Lewis, which she has decided to allow to determine her future: 'Pour l'instant je n'étais ni ici ni là, ni moi-même ni une autre, rien qu'une machine à tuer le temps, le temps qui d'ordinaire meurt si vite et qui n'en finissait pas d'agoniser' (LMii, p. 359); 'For the moment, I was neither here nor there, neither myself nor another, nothing but a machine for killing time, time which usually dies so quickly, but whose death throes now seemed endless' (M, p. 657, ta).

48   See LMii, p. 71.

49   Anne also vaguely contemplates commiting suicide in LMii, p. 201.

her treatment. Afterwards, Anne regrets that: 'Paule [lui] semblait plus étrangère que lorsqu'elle était folle' (LMii, p. 352); 'Paule seemed more a stranger [to her] now than when she was mad' (M, p. 652, ta). She is sorry that everything is now back to normal.[50] It is hard not to apply her verdict about Paule – 'Elle jouerait probablement jusqu'à sa mort le rôle d'une femme normale' ('She would probably play the part of a normal woman until the day she died') – to Anne herself (LMii, p. 351; M, p. 651). Anne identifies with Paule. Paule's situation and Anne's (future) situation are conflated as Anne's thoughts slip from Paule's delerium to her own remorse within the same sentence: 'A quoi bon ces délires, ces grimaces, si tout était rentré dans l'ordre, si la raison et la routine avaient triomphé? à quoi bon mes remords passionnés si je devais un jour me réveiller dans l'indifférence? (LMii, p. 349); 'Of what use was all the delerium, the pain, if everything had returned to its place, if reason and routine had triumphed? of what use was my passionate remorse if one day I would have to wake up indifferent?' (M, p. 650, ta). She is scathing about the woman Paule has become:

> Oui, pour délivrer Paule il fallait ruiner son amour jusque dans le passé; mais je pensais à ces microbes qu'on ne peut exterminer qu'en détruisant l'organisme qu'ils dévorent. Henri était mort pour Paule, mais elle était morte elle aussi; je ne connaissais pas cette grosse femmme au visage mouillé de sueur, aux yeux bovins, qui lampait du whisky à côté de moi. (LMii, p. 353)

> Yes, to release Paule it was necessary to reach back into the past in order to destroy her love. But I thought of those microbes which can't be exterminated except by destroying the organism they are devouring; Henri was dead for Paule, but she, too, was dead. I didn't know that fat woman with the sweaty face and the bovine eyes who was swilling scotch beside me. (M, p. 653)

Cure is destruction.[51] Anne grieves for Paule's lost love: 'J'avais envie de pleurer avec elle sur cet amour qui avait été pendant dix ans le sens et l'orgeuil de sa vie et qui venait de se changer en un chancre honteux' (LMii, p. 356); 'I felt like weeping with her over that love which had for ten years been the meaning and the pride of her life and which had now become a shameful sore' (M, p. 654). Anne finds intolerable the idea that one day she, like Paule, will betray her love: 'Plutôt souffrir à en mourir, me disais-je, que de jamais éparpiller au vent en ricanant

---

[50]   Even the environment has lost its sinister aspect, and when Anne presses the button under the sign 'CHAMBRES MEUBLÉ' ('Furnished Room To Let') that had once seemed so sinister (LMii, p. 214; M, p. 552), the door opens normally, 'too normally,' thinks Anne (LMii, p. 349; M, p. 650).

[51]   This belief is at the heart of Anne's ambivalence about her profession, which is evident from early in the novel. She thinks 'guérir, c'est souvent mutiler' ('healing often means mutilating') (LMi, p. 92; M, p. 76, ta). The same sentiment will be expressed by Laurence in Les Belles Images: 'Sous prétexte de guérir Catherine [...] on allait la mutiler' (BI, p. 159); On the pretext of curing Catherine [...] they were going to maim her. (LBI, p. 193, ta).

les cendres de mon passé' (LMii, p. 356); "'I'd rather die of suffering," I said to myself, "than ever sneeringly scatter the ashes of my past to the winds"' (M, p. 655). But she realises that betrayal is inevitable. Anne puts her disillusionment with her profession down to sadness she feels at Paule's cure, finding it hard to resign herself to Paule's resignation (LMii, p. 375).

It is in order not to be like Paule that Anne is driven to commit suicide. The echoes are clear in the final chapter of the novel. Anne's indifference to the world is in no doubt: 'Mon coeur ne bat plus pour personne: c'est comme s'il ne battait plus du tout, c'est comme si tous les autres hommes étaient déjà retombés en poussière' (LMii, p. 498); 'My heart is no longer beating for anyone; it's as if it were no longer beating at all, it's as if everyone else in the world has already fallen to dust' (M, p. 761). Her decision to commit suicide is linked to her refusal to accept that life goes on, that everything begins again. The anguish Anne feels as she contemplates suicide is presaged when she is afraid of exposing herself to change by leaving her safe life in Paris to visit the United States for the first time:

> Quelles évidences vont soudain m'aveugler? Quels abîmes se découvrir? Les abîmes se cicatriseront, les évidences s'éteindront, c'est sûr et certain; j'en ai vu d'autres. Nous valons bien ces vers de terre qu'on coupe vainement en deux ou ces homards dont les pattes repoussent. Mais le moment de la fausse agonie, le moment où l'on souhaite mourir plutôt que de se raccommoder encore une fois, quand j'y pense le coeur me manque. (LMi, pp. 296–97)

> What obvious facts are suddenly going to blind me? What chasms open up before me? Chasms heal over, obvious facts fade, that's for definite; I've seen others. We're just as good as those earthworms that one vainly cuts in two or those lobsters whose claws grow back again. But the false death throes, the moment when you'd rather die than mend yourself once again, when I think of it, my courage fails me. (M, p. 241, ta)

It is important to note that it is not the idea of pain, but the idea of recovering from pain, that distresses Anne. She cannot bear the thought of once again suffering and surviving, of hurting so badly she thinks the pain will kill her, knowing she would rather die than get better and then getting better after all. As Anne struggles to find the courage to go through with her suicide, she is tormented by the idea that, if she fails, order will be restored: 'Tout recommencera; je retrouverai mes idées en ordre, toujours dans le même ordre, et aussi les choses, et les gens, [...]' (LMii, p. 497); 'Everything will begin again; once more, I'll find my thoughts in order, still in the same order, and things as well, and people, [...]' (M, p. 760, ta).[52]

---

[52]   In the very first chapter of the novel, Anne rejects reason and order in very similar terms. She does not want to wait until she is less tired and more sober to discuss the future: 'Demain matin les murs ne tangueraient plus, les meubles et le bibelots seraient bien en ordre, toujours dans le même ordre, mes idées aussi et je recommencerais à vivre au jour le jour, sans tourner la tête en arrière, en regardant devant moi à bonne distance, je ne m'occuperais plus de ces menus charivaris dans mon coeur. J'étais fatiguée de cette hygiène.' (LMi, p. 66); 'Tomorrow morning the walls would not be spinning, the furniture

That would mean forgetting Lewis, being reasonable. Anne rejects reason. She sees her suicide in cataclysmic terms as a triumph of truth over order, the truth of death – the truth that death has won (LMii, p. 498). The words 'everything will begin again' ('tout recommencera') are repeated three times in the final pages of the novel (LMii, pp. 497–8; M, p. 760); Anne finds this idea intolerable. Time is related to the reason and order that Anne rejects and that her suicide is intended to defeat:

> Le passé en arrière, l'avenir en avant, invisible, la lumière séparée des ténèbres, ce monde émergeant victorieusement du néant et mon coeur tout juste là où il bat, ni à Chicago, ni près du cadavre de Robert, mais dans sa cage, sous mes côtes. (LMii, p. 498)

> The past behind, the future ahead, invisible, light distinct from darkness, this world emerging victoriously from nothingness, and my heart precisely in the place where it's beating, neither in Chicago, nor beside Robert's corpse, but in its cage under my ribs. (M, p. 760)

Anne does not want to be confined by the present moment, unable either to live in the past or project herself into the future. By commiting suicide Anne would escape from time. The text echoes the creation myth already so evident in Anne's opening interior monologue.[53] Anne's suicide is a revolt against, almost a reversal of the story of creation; the world would return to chaos and light and dark, day and night, would no longer be separated.[54]

Anne fails. She lives to forget Lewis as Paule has forgotten Henri. As she says at the beginning of her final interior monologue, 'je guérirai, je ne pourrai pas m'en empêcher' ('I'll recover, I won't be able to stop myself recovering') (LMii, p. 493; M, p. 757, ta); she may not have sunk into indifference, but her apparently reasonable stance ('Puisque mon coeur continue à battre, il faudra bien qu'il batte pour quelque chose, pour quelqu'un'; 'Since my heart continues to beat, it will have to beat for something, for someone'), is in fact an act of faith that is undercut by the question that ends the book: 'Qui sait?'; 'Who knows?' (LMii, p. 501; M, p. 763).[55]

---

and the ornaments would be in order, still in the same order, my ideas too and I'd start to live day by day again, without looking back, looking just the right distance ahead of me, I'd stop paying attention to the minor clatter in my heart. I was tired of that hygiene' (M, p. 55, ta). Notice the same repetition: 'en ordre, toujours dans le même ordre.' See also LMii, p. 296, where Anne addresses the cost of being 'normal' in relation to Paule.

[53]   'Et Dieu sépara la lumière d'avec les ténèbres' (Genèse 1:4); 'And God divided the light from the darkness' (Genesis 1:4).

[54]   Even before she swallows the poison this process has begun: 'Il faisait jour; mais il n'y avait plus de différence entre la nuit et le jour' (LMii, p. 498); 'It was daytime. But there was no longer any difference between night and day' (M, p. 761).

[55]   In 'Personal Choice and the Seduction of the Absolute' (Scholz and Mussett), Mussett argues that Paule's break from Henri leads to madness and isolation but that Anne's break from her dependency on Robert and Lewis leads to 'reconnection, hope, and the opening of future action' (p. 136). To my mind, the contrast is less stark. Mussett's reading

In summary, I have been exploring how the text brings out the affinities between Anne and Paule. Parallels exist in the characters' relationships with their partners and their attitudes to their partners' work, in relation to time, in their approach to love and in the end of their relationships. Anne's ambivalence toward Paule's recovery following her breakdown at the end of her relationship with Henri foreshadows her own desire to end her life so as not to be like Paule. Anne valorises Paule's madness and comes very close to acting it out. Anne is almost more like Paule than Paule in the sense that she comes closer than Paule to not betraying the feelings they share.[56]

The final part of this chapter specifically examines the extent to which *Les Mandarins* is marked by Gothic excess and traces some of the Gothic motifs that are found in the novel. The Gothic is present in *Les Mandarins* in a much more muted way than in *L'Invitée*. Nevertheless, there is perhaps something excessive in the way the Gothic thread – the strange and extravagant – is integrated in the sober weft and weave of the text. The Gothic is the ideal mode to express Anne's melancholy and her experience of trauma in the aftermath of the Second World War, which is especially acute given the psychoanalytical work she does with survivors of the Holocaust.

Gothic excess inflects the language in Anne's narrative. At times, in *Les Mandarins*, as in *L'Invitée*, language is brought up against the inexpressible. At the point in the text where Anne is in Italy with Robert, waiting for a letter from Lewis we read:

> Autour de nous, il y avait une énorme odeur de plantes amoureuses, rien ne manquait, nulle part, sinon sur une feuille jaune des signes noirs, et ils auraient été les signes d'une absence; l'absence d'une absence: ce n'est vraiment rien; elle dévorait tout. (LMii, p. 361)

> All around us hung a powerful fragrance of amorous plants, nothing was missing, anywhere, except black marks on a yellow sheet of paper, and they would have been the signs of an absence; the absence of an absence: it's really nothing; it was devouring everything. (M, p. 659, ta)

The suggestion of an overpowering smell from possible rampant vegetation is vaguely sinister. Characteristically for the Gothic, language is reduced to black signs on a page. The use of the verb *devour* ('dévorer') also adds to the Gothic

---

suggests Paule remains sitting 'among the shattered glass of her identity' (p. 152), but Paule's experience of insanity is temporary and Anne, too, experiences a period of isolation and is brought to the brink of suicide. Anne is dismissive of the life Paule reconstructs for herself after her breakdown, but it is important to understand this in the light of Anne's view that recovery means failure. Significantly, Paule herself has no voice in the narrative. The final words of the novel are extremely tentative; yes, Anne chooses life over suicide, but it was to have been her suicide that separated her from Paule. Ultimately, of course, Beauvoir defined Anne's recovery as a failure, too.

[56]   This is not to suggest that Anne is contemplating suicide simply because of the end of her relationship with Lewis. See LMii, p. 493.

overtones of this quotation. As we have already seen in a number of quotations, only paradox and contradiction can begin to express Anne's experience of the world. The text of Anne's narrative as a whole is characterised by contradiction.[57] I have drawn attention to a number of examples already. Repeatedly, distinctions between opposites are undermined and their equivalence asserted: 'guérir' – 'mutiler' (cure – mutilate) (LMi, p. 92); 'unir' – 'séparer' (unite – separate) (LMi, p. 102); 'plein' – 'vide' (full – empty) (LMi, p. 281); 'normal'– 'déraisonnable' (normal – irrational/ insane) (LMi, p. 296); 'vieille' – 'jeune' (old – young) (LMii, p. 57); 'lentement' – 'vite' (slowly – quickly) (LMii, p. 179); 'folie' – 'sagesse' (madness – wisdom) (LMii, p. 269); 'tout dire' – 'ne rien signifier' (mean everything – mean nothing) (LMii, p. 362); 'être' – 'ne pas être' (to be – not to be) (LMii, p. 409); 'riche' – 'pauvre,' 'lourd'- 'leger' (rich – poor, heavy – light) (LMii, p. 425); and 'près' – 'loin' (near – far) (LMii, p. 497).

At times, language almost topples into meaninglessness. The following sentence occurs early in Anne's first interior monologue: 'C'est fête cette nuit; le premier Noël de paix; le dernier Noël à Buchenwald, le dernier Noël sur terre, le premier Noël que Diégo n'a pas vécu' (LMi, p. 40); 'Tonight's a celebration, the first Christmas of peace, the last Christmas at Buchenwald, the last Christmas on earth, the first Christmas Diégo hasn't lived through' (M, p. 34, ta). It is interesting for a number of reasons. The repetition and opposition 'premier' – 'dernier' – 'dernier' – 'premier' and the insistent rhythm are dizzifying, and the propositions almost seem to cancel each other out. Added to this, the proposition 'le dernier Noël sur terre' is ambiguous to the point of incomprehensibility. What can be meant? The last Christmas on earth? If so then for whom? If 'dernier' is used here to mean 'most recent,' then this, too, highlights the slipperiness of meaning. The use of litotes evokes a stronger sense of what the absence of Diégo means; there is no closure – Diégo will always never experience another Christmas.

A number of Gothic motifs contribute to the dark and, at times, excessive tone of *Les Mandarins*. Inevitably, my reading has already considered some of these motifs that accumulate in the text, and they have figured, sometimes unremarked, in quotations that have already been made. I now wish to draw closer attention to some of them, including the abyss, death, and the associated motifs of ghosts and tombs, magic spells, violence and torture, the horror of existence, the hidden, unknowable nature of reality, and secret decay.

The motif of the abyss, associated with nothingness and infinite space and dizzyness, recurs throughout the novel and has distinctly Gothic overtones. Typically, the abyss encapsulates contradiction and paradox. It is at once above and below; it holds the threat of falling and of being swallowed up as well as the threat of infinite expansion and dissipation. The motif is linked to Anne's fragile sense of self; it is as if Anne is threatened with disintegration in the vast emptiness of the universe, an emptiness emblematic of death. As we have seen, Anne's sense

---

[57]   This is consonant with Beauvoir's view of the nature of literature. See, for example, 'Mon expérience d'écrivain' in *Les Ecrits*, p. 447 and FCi, p. 358.

of self is bound up with the others' views of her, and their gaze is a 'dizzying pit' ('un gouffre vertigineux') (LMi, p. 57; M, p. 48). It is clear from the quotations already made that this motif is to be found at key moments. It is introduced early in the novel, in Anne's first interior monologue. As we have seen, until this point, Robert has played a key role, imposing a boundary and containing Anne's world: 'le ciel s'est refermé au-dessus de ma tête et les vieilles peurs m'ont quittée' (LMi, p. 72); 'The sky closed above my head and the old fears left me' (M, p. 60). But this safety is now under threat. We read: 'au-dessus de nos têtes il y a un abîme' (LMi, p. 39); 'above our heads there is an infinite abyss' (M, p. 33).

The threat of being swallowed up is ever present. Earlier quotations have contained a number of examples of this. Anne's thoughts continually turn to those who have died and who are absent and buried nowhere: 'le vide les avait engloutis' (LMi, p. 40); '[they had been] swallowed up in emptiness' (M, p. 34). The same words recur in relation to Lewis's brief absence in Chicago when Anne is apart from him in Parker: 'Comment son absence était-elle devenue ce vide dévorant? un vide qui engloutissait tout' (LMii, p. 409); 'How could his absence have become that gaping, all-devouring emptiness?' (M, p. 694). Also, as we have seen, in relation to Robert's writing, Anne is afraid that everything he has written 's'engloutisse dans le vide' ('be swallowed up into nothingness') (LMi, p. 65; M, p. 55).

The first sentence of Anne's interior monologue places death at the centre of her narrative. She is utterly preoccupied by death. The notion that death is prowling around recurs insistently, duplicating Anne's obsession: 'Pourquoi la mort a-t-elle de nouveau traversé mes rêves? elle rôde, je la sens qui rôde. Pourquoi?' ('Why has death entered my dreams again? it is on the prowl, I can sense it prowling. Why?') (LMi, p. 38; M, p. 33, ta); 'J'ai rêvé que j'étais morte. Je me suis réveillé en sursaut et la peur était toujours là. Depuis une heure, je me débats contre elle; elle est encore là, et la mort continue à rôder 'I dreamed I was dead. I woke up with a start, and the fear was still there. For an hour I have been fighting it; it is still there and death continues to prowl') (LMi, pp. 67–8; M, p. 57, ta); 'Pourquoi est-ce que la mort est revenue rôder? Elle continue à rôder: pourquoi? ('Why has death come back to prowl? It continues to prowl: why?') (LMi, p. 74; M, p. 62, ta). Death is so woven into the fabric of *Les Mandarins* that it appears ever present. Readers are constantly reminded of death.

Death is silence. The reality of death is not being able to say, 'I am dead.' Without a voice, without language, there is no consciousness, and it is imposible to possess eternity: 'Le silence de la mort, c'est avec horreur que je l'ai découvert' ('I was horrified when I first discovered the silence of death'), says Anne (LMi, p. 38; M, p. 33). She identifies with the little mermaid in the fairy story who gives up her immortal soul for love and who becomes only 'un peu d'écume blanche sans souvenir, sans voix' ('a bit of white foam without memory, with no voice') (LMi, p. 38; M, p. 33, ta). Anne asserts that it is not a fairytale; she is the mermaid. Later in her relationship with Lewis, there is a reversal of the fairy tale: 'Son désir me transfigurait. Moi qui depuis si longtemps n'avait plus de goût, plus de forme, je possédais de nouveau des seins, un ventre, un sexe, une chair; j'étais nourrissante comme le pain, odorante comme la terre' (LMii, p. 39); 'His desire transformed me. I who for so long a time had been without taste, without form, again possessed breasts, a belly, genitals, flesh; I was as nourishing as bread, as fragrant as earth' (M, p. 423, ta)[58]. There is a further echo of the fairytale when, during her second trip to see Lewis, Anne is suddenly afraid. She asks: 'Est-ce qu'un jour je serais punie d'avoir osé aimer sans donner toute ma vie?' (LMii, p. 229); 'Would I be punished some day for having dared to love without giving my whole life?' (M, p. 562).

Death is silence. The silence in the garden becomes the silence of death and overtakes Anne. 'Tout se tait' ('Everything is silent'), we read (LMii, p. 495; M, p. 758, ta). She listens for a sound to call her back from death but hears none (LMii, p. 496). In the future from which she will be absent, her silence will be lost in the silence of the universe (LMii, p. 496). In her room, as she waits for the moment when she will swallow the poison, it is as if Anne has already 'passed over.'[59] We read: 'J'ai ouvert les yeux. Il faisait jour; mais il n'y avait plus de différence entre la nuit et le jour. Je flottais sur du silence [...]' (LMii, p. 498); 'I opened my eyes; it was daytime. But there was no longer any difference between night and day. I was floating on silence [...]' (M, p. 761). The noises coming from the garden do not at first disturb this silence: 'Je voyais et j'étais aveugle, j'entendais et j'étais sourde. [...] Les mots ont passé au-dessus de ma tête sans m'effleurer, leurs mots ne pouvaient plus m'atteindre' (LMii, p. 498); 'I could see, and I was blind; I could hear and I was deaf. [...] The words passed over my head without touching me; their words could no longer reach me' (M, p. 761, ta). Again, paradox and contradiction communicate Anne's experience. Anne is ready to die when suddenly Nadine's words find an echo in her, faintly at first, then more insistently and 'le silence ne s'est pas refermé' ('the silence didn't close in again') (LMii, p. 499; M, p. 761). Words call Anne back from death, back from the other side. As Elizabeth Fallaize puts it, it is the sound of voices, the power of language, that stops Anne commiting suicide – 'the power of language again triumphs.'[60] If death is silence, then life is words and language. The link between life and language is made explicit: 'Je suis ici. Ils vivent, ils me parlent, je suis vivante. [...] Les mots entrent dans mes oreilles, peu à peu ils prennent un sens. [...] Puisque je ne suis pas sourde, je m'entendrai de nouveau appeler' (LMii, pp. 500–501); 'I am here. They are living, they speak to me, I'm alive. [...] Words are entering my ears; little by little, they take on meaning. [...] Since I'm not deaf, I'll once more hear people calling me (M, pp. 762–63).

---

[58]   The reference to genitals has been omitted from the English translation.

[59]   Later, Anne uses the term 'passé de l'autre côté' to describe what was happening, LMii, p. 500. 'Passed over to the other side' is an expression used by psychics. This echoes the words Anne uses earlier in the novel to describe her sense of being dead alive (LMi, p. 265).

[60]   Fallaize, *The Novels*, p. 110.

Death is absence and forgetting. In Anne's world, absence and death are conflated: 'J'accepte l'absence et je trahis mon amour, j'accepte de survivre aux morts, je les oublie, je les trahis' (LMii, p. 70); 'I accept absence and I betray my love; I accept surviving the dead and I forget them, betray them' (M, p. 445). For Anne, the Christmas party is part of the process of forgetting the dead: 'Nous dansions, nous nous embrassions autour de l'arbre scintillant de promesses, et ils étaient nombreux, ah! si nombreux à ne pas être là! Personne n'avait recueilli leurs dernières paroles et ils n'étaient enterrés nulle part: le vide les avait engloutis' (LMi, p. 40); 'We were dancing, we were kissing each other around the tree sparkling with promises, and there were many, oh, so many, who weren't there. No one had heard their last words; they were buried nowhere, swallowed up in emptiness' (M, p. 34). Later Anne shares her feelings with Robert: 'Eh bien, moi, j'ai trouvé que c'était une drôle de fête, ce soir, avec tous ces morts qui n'étaient pas là!' (LMi, p. 66); 'Well, in my opinion we went to a very peculiar party tonight, with all the dead who weren't there' (M, p. 56). Only Anne cannot let go of the past, let go of the dead whose absence is ever present. She sees living on without them, forgetting them as betraying them.[61] The text explores and undermines the distinction between presence and absence, being and non-being. She imagines a world from which she will be truely absent because her absence will not be present: 'Mon absence sera si parfaite que tout le monde l'ignorera. Ce vide me donne le vertige (LMii, p. 496); 'My absence will be so complete that no one will be aware of it. The thought of that emptiness makes me dizzy' (M, p. 759).

As we have seen, Anne portrays herself as dead in life, one of the living dead. When Nadine is away with Henri, Anne has the sense that she is living life from beyond her death. She discovers that 'survivre, habiter de l'autre côté de sa vie: après tout, c'est très confortable; on n'attend plus rien, on ne craint plus rien, et toutes les heures ressemblent à des souvenirs' ('surviving, living on the other side of your life, is very comfortable after all. You no longer expect anything, no longer fear anything, and every hour is like a memory') (LMi, p. 265; M, p. 216, ta). She has a sense that she is living out of time in a space unaffected by change. The past is there to be discovered in every moment, everything is familiar and unchanging, and Anne begins to think that death is perhaps kinder ('plus clémente') than she has thought (LMi, p. 265). But Anne's retreat from reality cannot last when she is confronted by the full horror of the war; 'il avait fallu me barricader dans ma tombe' ('I would have had to barricade myself in my tomb'), she realises (LMi, p. 266; M, p. 216).

The prospect of the trip to the States reawakens her memories and desires: 'Pourquoi venait-on déranger ma sage petite vie de morte?' (LMi, p. 288); 'Why were they disturbing my sensible little life of a dead woman?' (M, p. 234, ta). At the end of this chapter, she finally decides to accept the invitation, revising her view of herself; she is not really buried alive in the past, she says. She nevertheless depicts herself as a spirit venturing beyond the grave: 'C'était sans doute une folle

---

61   See also LMi, p. 66, pp. 185 and 266.

imprudence d'aller m'égarer au monde des vivants, moi qui m'étais fait un nid sous les myrtes' (LMi, p. 359); 'It was probably foolhardy for me to go wandering in the world of the living, I who had built myself a nest under the myrtles' (M, p. 290, ta). Anne's words – her commitment to life – at this point, contrast sharply with her weariness at the prospect of having to carry on at the end of the novel: 'Survivre, après tout, c'est sans cesse recommencer à vivre' (LMi, p. 359); 'To survive is, after all, perpetually to begin to live again' (M, p. 290). Anne's encounter with Lewis is like rising from the dead. As we have seen, it is a reversal of the story of the little mermaid. She explicitly compares herself to Lazarus (LMii, p. 37). Leaving Lewis is like dying again: 'Oui, quelqu'un était mort: une femme joyeuse qui se réveillait chaque matin, toute rose et chaude, en riant' (LMii, p. 59); 'Yes, someone had died; a happy woman, all rosiness and warmth, who woke up laughing every morning' (M, p. 437, ta).[62] Anne's separation from Lewis is represented in the same terms as death, in terms of silence. Lewis's first letter does not bring Lewis back. His signature is 'implacable comme une dalle mortuaire' ('implacable as a tombstone') (LMii, p. 76; M, p. 449). The letter changes nothing: 'Le même silence: mais il n'y avait plus d'espoir, ce serait toujours ce silence' (LMii, p. 76); 'The same silence: only there was no longer any hope in it; there would always be that same silence' (M, p. 449). Anne realises 'de lui à moi il n'existait aucun passage' ('there was no path between us') just as, in the final pages of the novel, she realises that between Robert's life and her death 'il n'y a pas de passage' ('there is no path') (LMii, p. 497; M, p. 760, ta). When she is apart from Lewis, Anne again occupies a space where time does not move on, a space that suggests the eternity of death: 'Pour moi cette journée froide et grise qui recommençait à chaque réveil recommencerait sans fin' (LMii, p. 192): 'For me that cold, grey day which commenced with every awakening would endlessly repeat itself' (M, pp. 535–6). After her second trip, waiting for Lewis's letter while she is in Italy, Anne describes herself as not alive (LMii, p. 361; M, p. 659), just as in the final chapter of the novel, she is no longer 'une vivante' (a living being) (LMii, p. 495).

The figure of Diégo haunts the novel. When Anne and Nadine caught a glimpse of him in the distance at the detention centre at Drancy, he was already like a ghost: 'son image flottait hors du monde' (LMi, p. 43); 'his image was floating in another world' (M, p. 37, ta). When Nadine first learnt of Diégo's death, her dreams were full of his ghost, but after a while even his ghost evaporated. Repeatedly Anne compares the death of Lewis's love to the death of Diégo. When she learns at the beginning of her last, three-month stay with him, that he no longer loves her, Anne is faced with the decision to stay or to go. 'A quoi bon trois mois d'agonie?' ('What was the use of going through death throes for three months?'), she asks. But she decides to stay: 'Non, je ne voulais pas qu'un jour Lewis fût pour moi aussi mort que Diégo' (LMii, p. 389); 'No, I didn't want Lewis to be as dead for me one day

---

[62]   This is one of the dead sleves that Anne laments in the final pages of the novel: 'l'amoureuse qui se réveillait en riant dans les bras de Lewis's (LMii, p. 497); 'the woman in love who who would wake up laughing in Lewis's arms' (M, p. 760).

as Diégo' (M, pp. 679–80, ta). After the disastrous episode where the couple makes love (LMii, pp. 393–4), the reality of the situation hits Anne: 'Le passé était bel et bien mort. Une mort sans cadavre, comme celle de Diégo: c'est ce qui rendait difficile d'y croire. Si seulement j'avais pu pleurer sur une tombe, ça m'aurait bien aidée' (LMii, p. 395); 'The past was unmistakably dead – a death without a corpse, like Diégo's. That's what made it so difficult to believe. If only I could have cried over a tombstone, that would have really helped' (M, p. 684, ta). Anne comes to realise that nothing can replace Lewis's love and that the end of their love is as final as a death. Again, Anne thinks: 'Si au moins il me restait dans les bras un cadavre!' (LMii, p. 410); 'If at least I held a corpse in my arms!' (M, p. 695).

Magic and spells, typically Gothic motifs, are found in *Les Mandarins*. The cumulative effect of small details is to create a sense of menace. I have in mind details such as the reference to a crystal ball ('boule de verre,' LMi, p. 47) and the description of the embroidery on Anne's blouse as evil ('maléfique,' LMii, p. 389). At times, a sense is created that Anne inhabits a dream world or an alternative reality. This sense is especially heightened when Anne actually travels between France and the States, leaving one world for another. For instance after her first trip:

> Dix-huit heures, c'est court pour sauter d'un monde dans un autre, d'un corps dans un autre. J'étais encore à Chicago, écrasant mon visage en feu contre une fleur, quand Robert soudain m'a souri; j'ai souri moi aussi, j'ai pris son bras, et je me suis mise à parler. [...] Dès que j'ai ouvert la bouche, j'ai senti que je déchaînais un monstrueux cataclysme: tout ces jours si vivants que je venais de vivre se sont brusquement pétrifiés; il ne restait plus derrière moi qu'un bloc de passé figé; le sourire de Lewis avait pris la fixité d'une grimace de bronze. Moi j'étais là, je me promenais dans des rues que je n'avais jamais quittées, serrée contre Robert dont je n'avais jamais été séparée et je dévidais une histoire qui n'était arrivée à personne. (LMii, p. 60)

> Eighteen hours: a short time in which to leap from one world to another, from one body to another. I was still in Chicago, crushing my burning face against a flower, when Robert suddenly smiled at me. I, too, smiled, took his arm and began speaking. [...] As soon as I opened my mouth I felt I was unleashing a monstrous cataclysm. All those days so full of life I had just lived, suddenly petrified; behind me there remained nothing but a frozen block of past, and Lewis's smile had taken on the rigidity of a grimace cast in bronze. I was there, walking through streets I had never left, clinging to Robert from whom I had never been separated, and unfolding a tale that had happened to no one. (M, pp. 437–38, ta)

Anne is the victim of a terrible spell; her world in Chicago is turned to stone the moment she speaks to Robert in Paris, where she has never left.[63] Paule imagines

---

[63]   Chicago is explicitly a dream world for Anne, a world created for her by Lewis that she has seen through his eyes (LMii, p. 423); when their relationship ends, she encounters the actual city but as a ghost shut outside (LMii, p. 425). There is a clear echo here of the way in which Robert also created the world for Anne at the beginning of their relationship.

she is the victim of a magic spell when, in the presence of her friends, she is unable to hold on to her suspicions that they intend to harm her (LMii, p. 210). There are overtones of magic and fairy tales when Paule breaks down: 'Elle tremblait, des larmes roulaient sur ses joues, elle était si fiévreuse et si moite qu'il me sembalit que d'ici un instant elle aurait tout entière fondu, laissant à sa place une flaque de poix, noire comme ses yeux' (LMii, p. 219); 'She was trembling, tears were streaming down her cheeks; she was so feverish and damp that I felt as if she were going to melt away completely at any moment, leaving behind only a puddle of pitch, black as her eyes' (M, p. 555). And, of course, there is the story of the little mermaid.[64]

There is evidence of lurid imagination and flashes of violence and torture in the novel. For instance, at Lucie Belhomme's Anne sees Paule as being burnt alive (LMii, p. 85). In Parker, waiting for Lewis to return from Chicago Anne is portrayed as a prisoner, a victim of torture. She is crushed by the weight of things, blinded by the letters on the page of her book which stick to her eyes, imprisoned in the present moment, with her hands tied and an iron collar around her neck, suffocated by her own weight and poisoned by her own breath (LMii, p. 411). When Henri meets Anne and Robert in a café, l'Isba, the decor has Gothic resonances:

Dehors la nuit était si déserte, si muette que le luxe de l'Isba semblait inquiétant: on aurait dit l'anti-chambre perverse d'une salle de tortures. Les murs capitonnés étaient badigeonnés de sang, du sang dégoulinait dans les plis des tentures et les chemises des musiciens tziganes étaient satinées de rouge. (LMi, p. 173)

Outside the night had been so empty, so quiet, that the Isba's luxury was disturbing; it made one think of a perverted ante-chamber to a torture dungeon. The quilted walls were painted with blood, the folds of the draperies dripped blood, and the gypsy musicians' shirts had a crimson sheen. (M, p. 141, ta)

The domininance of red linked with blood and torture and the presence of the gypsies, a familiar Gothic motif, combine to suggest the strangeness and the latent threat of violence at the heart of existence.

Red, one of the colours that was so prevalent in *L'Invitée*, recurs in *Les Mandarins* with similar overtones. Red is the colour of Paule's studio flat.[65] It is a womblike, suffocating space. During their lovemaking, when Henri penetrates Paule, he is repelled because 'en elle il faisait rouge comme dans le studio trop rouge' (it was red inside her like in the overly red studio flat) (LMi, p. 27; omitted in the translation, M, p. 32).[66] Paule's studio flat is out of keeping with everything

---

[64]   Magic spills over into Henri's narrative; the villagers he sees in Portugal seem to him like the victims of a curse (LMi, p. 156; M, pp. 126–7).

[65]   Her studio is reminiscent of Xavière's room in *L'Invitée*. Robert refers to Paule's studio as her brothel because of the big mirrors and red draperies (LMi, p. 15).

[66]   Fallaize also uses this quotation. She argues that 'the red room [...] re-emerges here as a figure of female sexuality viewed as an obscene phenomenon.' *The Novels*, p. 108.

around it – it is a splendid, dreamlike, unreal space in the middle of 'a village full of unfortunate people' ('un village de malchanceux'), where each detail adds to the impression of a menacing, insalubrious environment (LMi, p. 289; M, p. 234). Anne is aware of being shut in, or even trapped, in the red studio flat with Paule – 'enfermée avec elle entre ces murs rouges' – not knowing what she is thinking (LMi, p. 292; M, p. 237). She looks out of the window in a doomed attempt to see the world through Paule's eyes; the surreal scene she sees is Gothic in its strangeness: 'Le soir tombait, un homme déguenillé promenait au bout d'une laisse un luxueux danois; sous l'inscription mystérieuse "Spécialité d'oiseaux rares et saxons", un singe enchaîné à la barre d'une fenêtre semblait lui aussi interroger avec perplexité le crépuscule' (LMi, p. 292); 'Evening was falling, a man in a ragged coat was walking a magnificent Great Dane at the end of a leash, and under the mysterious inscription "Speciality: Rare and Saxon Birds" a monkey chained to the bars of a window seemed also to be perplexedly questionning the dusk' (M, p. 237). Note in particular the disturbing clash between the man dressed in rags and the well-groomed Great Dane and the characteristically Gothic reference to a mysterious inscription. And when Paule sinks into folly and confronts Anne at what she will later call the 'banquet fantôme,' Anne is afraid: 'Soudain tout était devenu possible. Ce studio rouge, quel beau décor pour un meurtre!' (LMii, p. 209); 'Suddenly everything had become possible. That red studio flat – what a beuatiful setting for a murder!' (M, p. 548, ta).

Magic, latent violence, torture, and a strange sense of menace all accord with the Gothic vision of existence that underpins Anne's narrative in *Les Mandarins*. This vision is exemplified when, listening to Robert explain that 'horror is everywhere,' Anne has the sense that 'tout le malheur du monde est venu s'abattre sur la campagne ensoleillée' ('all the wretchedness of the world descended on the sun-drenched countryside') (LMii, p. 68; M, p. 444, ta). Her vision of the world is bleak in the extreme. It is as if the horrific reality of the Second World War and the concentration camps and the social and political oppression of the postwar world have a literal, physical impact on Anne's world: 'Autour de nous des hommes mouraient par millions sans avoir jamais vécu, leur agonie obscurcissait le ciel et je me demandais comment nous osions encore respirer' (LMii, p. 68); 'All around us, men were dying by the millions without ever having lived; their death throes blackened the sky and I wondered how we still dared to breathe' (M, p. 444, ta). Horror in the world is a dark, physical presence blocking out the light.[67] Similarly, in Yucatan, the cityscape is redolent of death:

> Nous avons suivi des avenues luxueuses et délabrées; la pluie, la pauvreté avaient rongé les villas bâties dans un dur style castillan; les statues pourrissaient derrière les grilles rouilliées des jardins; des fleurs luxuriantes, rouges, violettes et bleues, agonisaient au pied des arbres à demi nus; alignés sur la crête des murs, de grands oiseaux noirs guettaient. Partout ça sentait la mort. (LMii, p. 227)

---

[67]   In the final pages of the novel, the image of the darkening sky recurs when death blocks out the blue of the sky (LMii, p. 495).

We went along avenues at once sumptuous and seedy. The rain, poverty had gnawed at the mansions built in a harsh Castilian style; the statues were rotting behind the rusty iron gates of the gardens; luxuriant flowers, red, violet, and blue, were dying at the foot of the half-bare trees; lined up along the tops of the walls, large, black birds were watching. Everywhere there was a smell of death. (M, p. 561, ta)

The same is true in Chichen Itza too: 'Nous avançions à tâtons sur un chemin fangeux; une eau lourde dégouttait des arbres qui nous cahchaient le ciel; on ne voyait rien et j'étais étourdie par une odeur pathétique d'humus, de feuilles pourries, de fleurs moribondes' (LMii, p. 230); 'We groped our way along the muddy road; heavy drops of water were dripping from the trees which hid the sky from us. It was pitch-black and the oppressive smell of mould, rotting leaves and dying flowers made me dizzy' (M, p. 563). Here the landscape is more menacing because of the fireflies, which are like so many invisble cats with shining eyes, lurking in the shadows.

In the Gothic tradition, physiognomy is sometimes taken to be an indication of character. That there are suggestions of this in *Les Mandarins* may strike readers as particularly strange given Anne's profession. Nevertheless, this is Anne's assessment of Lambert:

Je supposais aussi qu'il n'aurait été que trop enclin à se chercher une mère dans une femme plus âgée que lui et qu'il se raidissait contre cette tentation infantile. Son visage au nez retroussé, aux joues un peu molles, trahissait un coeur et une chair hantés par des rêves de soumission. (LMi, p. 271)

I thought, too, that he was only too inclined to seek a mother in a woman older than he, and that he fought that infantile temptation. His face with its upturned nose and soft cheeks, betrayed a heart and flesh haunted by dreams of submission. (M, p. 221)

In a similar vein, the representation of Vincent as a monster, physically speaking, may well, in terms of the Gothic, presage the role Vincent will play in the murder of Sézenac in the penultimate chapter of the novel. The description of him is shocking: 'Au milieu de son visage blême, ses yeux injectés de sang avaient l'air de deux plaies; et sa bouche ressemblait à une cicatrice' (LMi, p. 100); 'In his pallid face, his bloodshot eyes seemed like two gashes; his mouth looked like a scar (M, pp. 82–3, ta).

Typical of the Gothic is the dreadful (in the fullest sense of the word) presentiment that reality is simply a veneer, that there is an underside to existence beyond our ken. At the end of the public meeting to launch the SRL, despite its success, Anne experiences the same fear that kept her awake the night after the Christmas party in the opening chapter of the book. She is tormented by doubts about Robert, about how others will see him, about how he will see himself: 'Si seulement je pouvais décider: il n'y a pas de vérité! Mais il y en aura une. Notre vie est là, lourde comme une pierre, et elle a un revers que nous ne connaissons pas: c'est effrayant. J'étais sûre cette fois de ne pas délirer, je n'avais rien bu, il ne faisait pas nuit, et la peur m'etouffait' (LMi, p. 341); 'If only I could decide: there is no truth! But there will be one. Our life is there, heavy as a stone, and it has another side which we don't know. It's frightening. This time I was sure I wasn't going mad, I'd had nothing to drink, it wasn't night-time, and I was choked with fear (M, p. 276, ta). Related to this is a Gothic sense of decay occurrring, hidden from sight, preparing for sudden collapse and disintegration. Anne has an acute sense of her own body's decline:

> Je soulève mes cheveux: ces stries blanches, ce n'est plus une curiosité ni un signe: un commencement; ma tête va prendre, vivante, la couleur de mes os. Mon visage peut paraître lisse et dru, mais d'un instant à l'autre, le masque va s'effondrer, dénudant des yeux enrhumés de vieille femme. Les saisons se recommencent, les défaites se réparent: mais il n'y a aucun moyen d'arrêter ma décrépitude. (LMi, p. 127)[68]

> I run my fingers through my hair. These white streaks are no longer a curiosity, a sign; they're a beginning. My head is going to turn, still living, the colour of my bones. My face may appear smooth and firm, but from one moment to the next, the mask is going to crumble, laying bare the rheumy eyes of an old woman. Each year the seasons repeat themselves, defeats are overcome. But there's no way of stopping my decrepitude. (M, p. 103, ta)

Finally, a brief word about humour as a potential source of transgression in the text. In *Les Mandarins* humour results from bathos and a repeated sense of anti-climax. At the very beginning of Anne's relationship with Lewis, she explicitly finds herself ridiculous (LMii, p. 36), and the ridiculousness of the situation in which she has placed herself is foregrounded by the pantomime quality of the narrative. Having arranged to travel to Chicago to see Lewis, Anne fantasises happily about their reunion: 'Je me couchai, tout émue de penser qu'un homme m'attendait pour me serrer contre son coeur' (LMii, p. 25); 'I went to sleep, deeply stirred by the thought that a man was waiting to hold me tightly against his heart' (M, p. 413). The next words in the text (after a typographical break) are a ludicrous descent to the ordinary: 'Il ne m'attendait pas; il n'y avait personne dans le hall'; 'He wasn't waiting for me; there was no one in the arrivals lounge.' (M, p. 413, ta) The same bathetic effect is repeated when Anne's hopes that she is finally walking arm in arm with Lewis 'vers la paix, vers la joie' ('towards peace, towards happiness') are dashed when he bumps into Teddy, a writer and pickpocket he knows –

---

[68]   See also the description of Huguette, the wife of Louis Volange, through Henri's eyes: 'Elle n'avait pas changé non plus; elle était blonde, diaphane et élégante comme autrefois, et elle souriait du même sourire parfumé; elle ne changerait jamais; mais un jour on l'effleurerait du bout du doigt et elle tomberait en poussière' (LMi, p. 414); 'Neither had she changed. She was blonde, delicate, and as elegant as ever, and she still had the same perfumed smile. She would never change, but one day at the touch of a finger-tip she would fall to dust' (M, p. 332).

and immediately drops her arm (LMii, p. 35; M, p. 420).[69] A few days later, Anne's decision to tell Lewis about her life in Paris is delayed by an unexpected visitor waiting for them on Lewis's balcony when they return home. Anne is unaware for a long while that Maria, whom she immediately perceives as a rival for Lewis's affections, has in fact escaped from a mental hospital. Anne's incomprehension is comic and her fears ludicrous. The humour is intensified by anticlimax when Maria asks for a razor just after Lewis has told her that he and Anne are married; Maria uses the blade she finds on the draining board to shave her legs, not to slit her wrists, and her worst threat is to do the washing-up (LMii, p. 51–2)!

In conclusion, my reading of *Les Mandarins* has sought to highlight the excess and transgression that are woven in the text. I have shown how the Gothic sensibility, so evident in *L'Invitée*, persists in Anne's narrative. I have also argued that Anne's lack of a secure sense of self and instability are duplicated in the text, both in Anne's interior monologue and throughout her narrative. Anne's is a discourse of madness. In the final chapter, she comes close to acting out the madness explicitly associated with Paule, who is constructed in the text as her *semblable*. In Anne's narative, the odd, the extraordinary, and the extravagant are normalised, integrated in the everyday; it would be easy to overlook them, yet they contribute to the thread of strangeness and menace that runs through the novel, unquestioned.

---

[69] Anne's second reunion with Lewis is also delayed to comic effect when she forgets Lewis's address and his flat 'disappears' (LMii, pp. 221–2). Mussett suggests that Paule is a comic figure but I find no evidence for this. 'Personal Choice and the Seduction of the Absolute,' in Scholz and Mussett, p. 148.

Chapter 3
Les Belles Images

Les Belles Images is the story of Laurence, the portrait of a woman facing a nervous breakdown, on the brink of madness. Beauvoir's textual strategies duplicate this madness in the text, which structures the experience of madness, which is an effect of the text as a whole. The author creates a mad textual universe where readers share Laurence's experience, her helplessness and confusion, her distress ('désarroi'). The first part of this chapter focuses on one area of the mad textual universe created in *Les Belles Images* and concentrates on language and meaning. Madness is exemplified at those points in the text when language refuses to signify. The madness in the text is specifically that quality in the writing that unsettles meaning. As Laurence loses faith in language, so, too, readers are forced into a position where their confidence in language and its meaningfulness is undermined. Laurence's struggle to make sense of the world, sense of who she is and what is happening to her, coincides with her struggle with language and is paralleled by readers' efforts to make sense of the text. The particular textual strategies I deal with are the opening up of meaning, the use of irony and enumeration and repetition.

The second part of this chapter examines some of the textual strategies that disrupt and unsettle the narrative of *Les Belles Images*. The disruption and instability in the text which subvert coherence constitute its madness. It is specifically the way in which madness is a quality of the telling of the stories, of the text (the discourse that tells the story), that is my subject here.[1] First, the instability that is inherent in the je/elle split in the narrative voice of the novel is considered. Focus then shifts to textual fragmentation and interruption and multilayering. Finally, disrupted syntax is explored.

For Beauvoir's women protagonists, language is fraught with difficulties. Because they lose faith in language, because they do not use language unequivocally to establish the 'truth,' we are invited to condemn the protagonists in Beauvoir's later texts. She is explicit that in 'La Femme rompue' Monique's guilt is evident in the way her diary contradicts itself.[2] The fact that the woman in 'L'Age de discrétion' is failed by language is a symptom of her breakdown. Murielle's monologue divorces truth from discourse, and Beauvoir can see no outcome for

---

[1]   As before, I am adopting the definitions proposed by Shlomith Rimmon-Kenan. I understand 'story' to be a succession of events. 'Text' refers to the discourse that tells the story. 'Narration' (not treated here) is the process of production of the text. See *Narrative Fiction*, pp. 3–4.

[2]   TCF, p. 175.

her except madness or suicide.[3] In *Les Belles Images*, Laurence's difficulties with language, her struggle to make words signify, is represented as a symptom of her disintegrating personality and mental collapse. However, as Toril Moi has argued in relation to 'La Femme rompue,' the fact that the narrator constantly contradicts herself is not interpreted by modern readers as a sign of her guilt and blindness but rather as demonstration of the inadequacy of language and the unstable nature of meaning. Toril Moi suggests that 'La Femme rompue' 'may paradoxically – and quite unintentionally – come across as a far more "modern" text than any of Beauvoir's other writings.'[4] I believe that the same tension related to language and meaning is to be found in *Les Belles Images*, in the other stories in *La Femme rompue*, and can even be traced in her earlier fiction, too, notably in *L'Invitée*. I have argued elsewhere that to some extent, almost all Beauvoir's texts undermine a patriarchal ideological position on language, refusing to corroborate the view (that she shared to some extent) that language is an unequivocal sign system.[5]

Jacques Derrida's and Julia Kristeva's and, to some extent, Hélène Cixous's writing on language, despite Beauvoir's dismissal of the notion of women's writing, provide a useful theoretical framework for my discussion of the textual strategies that unsettle meaning in *Les Belles Images* and, in part, account for its radical, modern aspect. These are the textual strategies, the qualities that I am reading metaphorically as madness. My intention is to locate points of convergence between their theories about language and meaning and Beauvoir's writing practice.

---

[3]   See TCF, p. 177; ASD, p. 141. In Beauvoir's memoirs, hope is held out for the woman in 'L'Age de discrétion' as, in the end, she is able to talk to André again and as she never at any point loses 'her love for the truth.' Failure is overcome. Remarks to do with *La Femme rompue* are ambiguous at this point in the memoirs. Beauvoir refers to the three stories as the first, second, and third according to the order in which she comments on them in the memoirs ('La Femme rompue,' 'Monologue,' 'L'Age de discrétion'), not according to the order in which they appear in the *La Femme rompue* collection. Fallaize clarified which story Beauvoir's remarks about failure being overcome applied to during the course of an interview (footnote 21, *The Novels*, p. 174). An added confusion is the fact that Beauvoir writes that in choosing to lie to themselves, Laurence and Muriel[le] 'destroy all possibility of communication with others'; this does not make sense as her comments deal exclusively with *La Femme rompue* at this point, and we must assume that she means to write Monique and Murielle. This is especially the case in the light of comments made a few pages earlier, when Beauvoir specifically contrasts the way Laurence and Monique behave: 'Laurence cherche timidement la lumière tandis que tout l'effort de Monique tend à l'oblitérer' (TCF, p. 175); 'Laurence makes timid attempts to reach the truth whereas all Moniques efforts are aimed at obscuring it' (ASD, p. 140, ta). The question of language and meaning in *La Femme rompue* is addressed in detail in the following chapter.

[4]   Moi, 'Intentions and Effects,' p. 78.

[5]   See 'Introduction,' *Simone de Beauvoir's Fiction: Women and Language*, ed. by Alison T. Holland and Louise Renée, New York: Peter Lang, 2005.

For Derrida, meaning is not present in words; rather, meaning is produced through the 'free play of the signifier,' the interplay between present and absent signifiers.[6] His concept of *différance*, translated as both 'difference' and 'deferral' in English, expresses this view of meaning.[7] Meaning is never present; it is the outcome of an endless process of present and absent differences and is endlessly deferred. As meaning cannot be reduced to a single or fixed meaning, there can be no 'transcendental signified' that confers meaning, no transcendental truth beyond language. Derrida rejects as logocentric (from the Greek word *logos* or 'word') philosophies that are based on a transcendental signified, a belief that meaning is fully present in the Word. He argues that written texts in particular can always be read 'other'wise as language constantly evokes meanings that exceed, contradict or disrupt the intended meaning. As Terence Hawkes puts it, because there is a gap between the text and its 'meaning,' 'a text can have no *ultimate*, final meaning.'[8] There can be no comforting closure. Derrida advocates a mode of writing that does not seek to impose a single meaning but incorporates multiple meanings.

Derrida's theories amount to a critique of binary logic, binary oppositions that have shaped Western metaphysics. Cixous argues that the hierarchical binary oppositions that underlie the patriarchal value system can always be traced back to the fundamental male/female opposition where woman systematically incorporates the negative pole. Toril Moi sums up Cixous's theoretical project as 'the effort to undo this logocentric ideology' that silences and oppresses women.[9] For Cixous, the questioning of logocentrism cannot be separated from the questioning of phallocentrism, that is, the system that privileges the phallus as the symbol or source of power.[10] *Écriture féminine* is writing that subverts patriarchal binary schemes and opens up meaning. Cixous, like Derrida, believes that attempts to fix the meaning of a text are not only impossible but also reductive.

The active inclusion of plural meanings within a text, that is, both in the multiplicity of meanings within each word or phrase or other language unit and through intertextuality, the transposition into the text of meanings from other texts, is seen by Kristeva as one of the ways the semiotic disrupts symbolic language.[11]

---

[6]   For my account of Derrida's theories and, indeed, my explanations of Cixous's and Kristeva's analyses, I am indebted to Moi, *Sexual Textual Politics* and to Sellers, *Language and Sexual Difference*.

[7]   Christopher Norris's comments about the term *différance* are interesting: 'Its sense remains suspended between the two French verbs 'to differ' and 'to defer,' both of which contribute to its textual force but neither of which can fully capture its meaning. [...] *Différance* [...] offers in its own unstable meaning a graphic example of the process at work.' *Deconstruction: Theory and Practice*, London: Methuen, 1982, repr. 1986, p. 32.

[8]   Terence Hawkes, *Structuralism and Semiotics*, London: Methuen, 1977, repr. 1986, p. 148.

[9]   Moi, Sexual/Textual Politics, p. 105.

[10]   Hélène Cixous, *Prénoms de personne*, Paris: Seuil, 1974, p. 236.

[11]   For the distinction between the semiotic and the symbolic, see my Introduction. A useful definition of intertextuality is provided by Roudiez, p. 15.

Furthermore, the semiotic energy present in the rhythms and movement of a poetic text can, she argues, return readers to the rhythms, movement, and echolalias of the *chora*, affording readers a total pleasure (*jouissance*) that is 'polymorphic, polyphonic, serene, eternal, unchangeable.'[12] Toril Moi sums up the chora as a rhythmic pulsion perceptible as contradictions, meaninglessness, disruption, silences, and absences in the symbolic language. Deviations from conventional syntax that disrupt the signifying order are characteristic of such writing. In connection with irregularities, modulations, or rhythms that disrupt the anticipated structure of a text, Kristeva mentions the use of exclamation marks, ellipses, and surges in energy, evoking panting, breathlessness, or acceleration.

Kristeva contrasts women's and men's experience of language and the *chora*, suggesting that women's strong links with the pre-Oedipal mother mean that many women are open to allowing the 'spasmodic force' of the unconscious to disrupt their language. However, if women are susceptible to surges of semiotic energy, they also are more vulnerable, more at risk. Susan Sellers provides the following summary of Kristeva's argument:

> Whereas men's return to the semiotic *chora* is brought about through the explosion of rhythms and echolalias we have known as children which act as comforting reminders of early plenitude or, alternatively, give rise to laughter and symbolic play, Kristeva suggests that for women reactivating these rhythms threatens the tenuous nature of our symbolic construction, rendering us 'ecstatic, nostalgic or mad'. (*Language and Sexual Difference*, pp. 104–5)

In short, women who let the semiotic disrupt their language expose themselves to the danger of madness.

A close reading of *Les Belles Images* allows us to pinpoint where the theories of language and meaning I have just outlined intersect with Beauvoir's writing practice. I examine how *différance* operates in the text, to consider how plurality and subversion contribute to madness in the text. Given the fact that the disruption of symbolic language (which I have read metaphorically as madness) poses a (greater) threat to women, it might be expected that semiotic energy will break into the text, that is, into Laurence's voice, at those points where her psychic stability is most at risk. I also look at the extent to which the rhythms, movement, and echolalias of the *chora*, generated by Beauvoir's use of enumeration and repetition, are found at moments when Laurence's lost plenitude is evoked. It may also be possible to identify them at certain points where humour disrupts the narrative.

The text of *Les Belles Images* exposes the problematic nature of meaning, of the relation between signifier and signified, exemplifying a rejection of logocentrism. It embodies/enacts the inadequacy of language that forms an important strand in the narrative. The text of *Les Belles Images* includes a metacommentary on language. Laurence finds herself in a world where meaning, for her, is never fixed,

---

[12]   Quoted in Sellers, p. 103. 'Echolalia' is a term that conveys the ceaseless echoing back and forth between signs. See Jeremy Hawthorn, *A Glossary of Contemporary Literary Theory,* London: Arnold, 1992, p. 72.

always uncertain. Unlike those around her, Laurence cannot take the meaning of words for granted. This is true well before her breakdown. Reflecting that children should be protected from images that might upset them, she distances herself from this idea and makes the comment: 'Réflexion abjecte. Abjecte: un mot de mes quinze ans. Mais que signifie-t-il?'(BI, p. 30); 'An abject thought. Abject: a great word of mine when I was fifteeen. But what does it mean?' (LBI, p. 37). Likewise, when Gilbert informs Laurence that he intends to end his seven year relationship with her mother, '[Laurence] entend des mots qui restent suspendus en l'air, dénués de sens' (BI, p. 46); 'She hears the words that hang in the air, devoid of meaning' (LBI, p. 56, ta). Her attitude toward language contrasts with her father's. When he speaks of love, Laurence affirms: 'Aimer d'amour; vraie valeur. Pour lui ces mots ont un sens' (BI, p. 35); 'To be in love; true worth. for him these words have meaning' (LBI, p.43, ta). By implication, these words lack meaning for Laurence. When she ends her relationship with Lucien, she uses the word 'love' without knowing exactly what she means: 'Mais je ne t'aime plus d'amour. (L'ai-je jamais fait? Ces mots ont-ils un sens?)' (BI, p. 110); But I don't love you any more. (Did I ever? Do those words mean anything?)' (LBI, p. 134), ta). Even when words do mean something, Laurence is aware that meanings are not necessarily shared. Were she to read the books her daughter Catherine reads, she could not know what they mean to her (BI, p. 25); she realises that they do not share a common language (BI, p. 77). The same is true of all signs, not only of language. Laurence compares her own understanding of the poster showing a hungry child with her daughter's and understands they see quite different things (BI, p. 29).

Thus discourse is reduced to words, empty words in which Laurence has no faith. Words refuse to signify for Laurence. When she gets home after the trip to Greece, even apparently straightforward questions are problematic for her. Asked whether she has had a good time, she gives the expected reply, 'terrific!,' but cannot determine whether she is telling the truth: 'Elle ne mentait pas, elle ne disait pas la vérité. Tous ces mots qu'on dit! Des mots ...' (BI, p.170); She was not lying; she was not telling the truth. All these words that are said! Words ...' (LBI, p. 206). She is neither truthful nor lying. The opposition is undermined, and the nature of truth and even its existence are called into question. As Laurence's breakdown reaches its climax, language lets her down: 'Je n'ai pas de mots pour me plaindre ou pour regretter' (BI, p. 153); 'I don't have the words to complain or regret' (LBI, p. 186, ta). She is left without a voice: 'Voici venir ce qu'elle redoute plus que la mort: un de ces moments où tout s'effondre; son corps est de pierre, elle voudrait hurler; mais la pierre n'a pas de voix; ni de larmes' (BI, p. 176); 'Now she is facing what she fears more than death: one of those moments when everything collapses; her body is made of stone, she wants to scream; but the stone has no voice; nor any tears' (LBI, p. 213, ta).[13] Although words may have no stable

---

[13] Laurence's words are reminiscent of what Beauvoir writes in the epilogue to *La Force des choses*: 'il y a des heures si noires qu'il ne reste plus d'autre espoir que ce cri qu'on voudrait pousser' (FCii, p. 498); 'there are hours so black that no other hope is left but the scream you want to let out' (FC, p. 666, ta).

meaning, a subject excluded from language altogether is condemned to mental breakdown and madness.

Interestingly, happiness in *Les Belles Images* is associated with childhood, when Laurence could look to her father to make words/language meaningful. As an adult, she is still willing to accept her father's definitions; during a discussion about art she realises: 'Ce qu'il dit là, elle l'a pensé souvent: enfin je ne le pensais pas avec ces mots; mais maintenant qu'ils sont dits elle les reconnaît pour siens' (BI, p. 150); 'She's often thought what he's saying now; well, I didn't think it in those words; but now they've been spoken she recognises them as her own' (LBI, p. 182, ta). Travelling with her father in Greece, Laurence's regression is exemplified by her dependence on him in relation to language: 'J'aimais retrouver devant cet alphabet le mystère enfantin du langage et que, comme autrefois, le sens des mots et des choses me vînt par lui' (BI, p. 154); 'Through the Greek alphabet I liked rediscovering the childhood mystery of language and was pleased that, as in the past, the meaning of words and things should come to me through him' (LBI, p. 187, ta). This is explicitly the happiest moment in the book. It is no coincidence that happiness is linked with the illusion of transparency in language, with a time when meaning seemed unproblematical. And in the present of the narrative, Laurence comprehends the word 'happiness'; it is as if the word incorporates meaning:

> Papa a commandé pour moi une boisson à la cerise, fraîche, légère, aigrelette, délicieusement puérile. Et j'ai su ce que voulait dire ce mot qu'on lit dans des livres: bonheur. [...] Cet accord d'un ciel bleu et d'un goût fruité, avec le passé et le présent rassemblés dans un visage cher et cette paix en moi, je l'ignorais – sauf à travers de très vieux souvenirs. Le bonheur: comme une raison que la vie se donne à elle-même. Il m'enveloppait [...]. (BI, p. 155)

> Papa ordered me a drink made of cherries, cool, light, slightly sharp, deliciously childish. And I knew the meaning of the word you read in books: happiness. [...] I had known nothing of the harmony between a blue sky and a fruity taste, with the past and present united in a dear face, and the peace within me – except in some very old memories. Happiness: like a justification life provides for itself. It enfolded me [...]. (LBI, pp. 188–89, ta)

In complete contrast, as Laurence experiences mental collapse and is forced to reassess her relationship with her father, language comes to be associated with pain and violence. Laurence is prostrate:

> [...] terrassée par une galopade d'images et de mots qui défilaient dans sa tête, se battant entre eux comme des kriss malais dans un tiroir fermé (si on l'ouvre, tout est en ordre). [...] J'ai été *déçue*. Le mot la poignarde. Elle serre son mouchoir contre ses dents comme pour arrêter le cri qu'elle est incapable de pousser. (BI, pp. 179–80)

> [...] prostrated by a stampede of pictures and words that raced through her head, fighting among themselves like Malay krisses in a closed drawer (if you open it,

everything is in order). [...] I was *disappointed*. The word stabs her. She presses
her handkerchief against her teeth as though to hold back the cry she is incapable
of uttering. I am disappointed. I have cause to be. (LBI, pp. 217–18, ta)

It is by naming her pain that she will recover from it. At the end of the book
Laurence finds her voice.[14] Language is her weapon that she will use to silence
others: 'Malgré elle, la voix de Laurence se monte, elle parle, elle parle, elle ne sait
pas exactement ce qu'elle dit, peu importe, l'important est de crier plus fort que
Jean-Charles et que tous les autres, de les réduire au silence' (BI, p. 182); 'In spite
of herself Laurence's voice is rising, she talks and talks, she's not quite sure what
she's saying, it doesn't matter, what matters is shouting louder than Jean-Charles
and all the others, and reducing them to silence' (LBI, p. 220, ta).

In Beauvoir's textual universe, words and silence are equally meaningful/
less, and both are contingent. The starving little boy in the poster that upsets
her daughter Catherine has his 'mouth closed on a terrible secret' (BI, p. 29;
LBI, p. 36). Laurence anguishes about the effects of words/silence on Catherine:
'Les humeurs quotidiennes, les hasards d'un mot, d'un silence, toutes ces
contingences qui devraient s'effacer derrière moi, ça s'inscrit dans cette enfant
qui rumine et qui se souviendra, comme je me souviens des inflexions de voix de
Dominique' (BI, p. 135); 'Everyday moods, the chance of a word, of a silence,
all the trivial circumstances that should vanish behind me make an impression
on this child who turns things over in her mind and who will remember them,
just as I remember the exact tones of Dominique's voice' (LBI, p. 164, ta). Later
she wonders, with reference to Jean-Charles: 'Est-ce qu'il ne sent pas entre nous
le poids des choses non dites? non pas du silence, mais des phrases vaines [...]'
(BI, p. 140); 'Doesn't he feel the weight of the unsaid things between us? Not the
weight of silence but of the empty phrases [...] (LBI, p. 170). Silence is redefined;
it is not necessarily what is unspoken but can be what is spoken without meaning,
sentences that signify nothing.

The problematic nature of meaning is further underlined as accepted definitions
are called into question; Laurence wonders what being normal means. When
Jean-Charles is advocating consulting a psychologist about Catherine, Laurence
asks him, '– Tourner rond: qu'est-ce que ça veut dire? A mon avis ça ne tourne
pas tellement rond chez les gens que tu juges normaux' (BI, p. 132); 'Running
smoothly – what's that supposed to mean? In my opinion things don't run so very
smoothly with the people you think of as normal' (LBI, p. 160). Being 'normal' is
also something she discusses with her father in Greece:

> – Sans doute à toute époque il est normal d'être effrayé quand on commence à
> découvrir le monde.
> – Alors, si on la rassure, on la rend anormale, ai-je dit.
> C'était une évidence et elle me foudroya. Sous prétexte de guérir Catherine ... on
> allait la mutiler. (BI, p. 159)

---

[14]   Until this point, Laurence has failed to voice the disagreement she feels. See, for
example, BI, pp. 12, 15, 26, 41, 128, 156, 162, 166.

'No doubt in every period it's normal to be frightened when you begin to discover the world.'
'So if they set her mind at rest, they make her abnormal,' I said.
It was patently obvious and it knocked me completely off balance. On the pretext of curing Catherine [...] they were going to maim her. (LBI, p. 193, ta)

This identification of curing with mutilation recalls Laurence's response to the little Greek girl she had watched dancing; life and death are conflated: 'La vie allait l'assassiner' (BI, p. 158); 'Life was going to murder her' (LBI, p. 193).

Laurence's loss of faith in language is, in part, the result of her accurate realisation that language is misused in the circles in which she lives and works, circles where clichés are bandied about as if they represent the truth, where words are consistently used to hide the truth. Laurence acts on her new understanding to a certain extent – language becomes a weapon and a tool of analysis for her – but she is not prepared to take her analysis further and step outside/reject her milieu. Nevertheless, even the limited stand Laurence makes is an important one. For Beauvoir, language, full of traps though it may be, is a vital weapon that women must sieze and use, albeit with caution, for their own ends.[15]

Here, story meets text. So far, I have been discussing mainly language and meaning as theme in *Les Belles Images*. Now, just as the content of the book calls the meaningfulness of language into question, so, too, does the text itself. It repeatedly asserts the equivalence of opposites, thus undermining binary oppositions. Just as lying and truthfulness cancel each other out, so do 'completely different' and 'exactly the same' ('tout à fait différent, exactement pareil', BI, pp. 7, 9, 50) and 'always' and 'never'. Laurence's anxiety is present and not present: 'En réalité, c'est là sans y être, c'est dans la couleur du jour. Elle y pense tout le temps, elle n'y pense jamais' (BI, p. 75); 'In fact it's there without being there, it colours the day. She thinks of it all the time, she never thinks of it' (LBI, p. 91, ta). The distinction between 'full' and 'empty' is subverted: 'Vie trop remplie? trop vide? Remplie de choses vides. Quelle confusion!' (BI, p. 146); 'Too full a life? Too empty? Full of empty things. What confusion!' (LBI, p. 177, ta). The effect is accentuated by repetition. Laurence attempts in vain to make sense of her existence, to impose some order. By asserting the equivalence of opposites in this way, the text can epitomise Laurence's sense of unreality, her sense of existing at a distance. Speaking of the trip to Greece, Laurence can affirm: 'Je mangeais avec appétit et indifférence ...' (BI, p. 156); 'I ate heartily and indifferently ...' (LBI, p. 190, ta). Such contradictory assertions can express a positive moment in the text, as when Laurence has a feeling of wholeness and oneness with the world when the plane takes off for Greece: 'Sous mes pieds s'étalent de blancs paysages qui m'éblouissent et qui n'existent pas. Je suis ailleurs: nulle part et partout' (BI, p. 154); 'Beneath my feet are spread white landscapes which dazzle me and which have no existence. I am elsewhere: nowhere and everywhere'

---

[15]   See Alice Jardine, 'Interview with Simone de Beauvoir,' *Signs*, Winter 1979, 224–36, p. 230.

(LBI, p. 187, ta).[16] Laurence's strange, out-of-body experience is condensed in this undercutting of distinctions. The accumulation of statements of this kind creates an impression of strangeness and alienation for readers. The text is, in a sense, crazy. Placing together as complementary words that are usually defined as contradictory involves redefining both terms and allowing meaning/nonmeaning to emerge from the space between them. Meaning not fully present in words themselves, not expressible by them, emanates from the blank of 'nonmeaning' that exists in the spaces between them. In a sense it is unspoken, unspeakable.

The problematic nature of meaning is further accentuated by the use of irony. *Les Belles Images* is an ironic book.[17] Irony contributes to the creation of a mad textual universe in that it is a source of ambiguity in the text and an embodiment of the 'treacherous,' 'slippery' nature of meaning; at the simplest level, irony is saying one thing whilst meaning is another.[18] It foregrounds the discrepancy that exists between words and meaning and duplicates the gap between appearance and reality. It also involves a certain distancing, which, taken to its extreme, is a form of alienation. Readers, who are invited to collude with Laurence, the narrator, are thus implicated in her alienation from her environment. On another level, irony functions to distance readers from Laurence herself. Does irony suggest a contradiction since it involves control, which is patently not an element of madness? Certainly, irony is a *knowing* form of defence. However, I am suggesting that 'madness' in the text is the outcome of the ambiguity and feelings of alienation created in readers by the use of irony, not an intrinsic quality of the irony itself.

How, then, are these effects of ambiguity and a heightened sense of alienation created? The irony in *Les Belles Images* is multilayered. This layering, which accentuates Laurence's alienation, is rendered even more ambiguous by the je/elle split, which is at the heart of the narrative.[19] Although much of the irony can be attributed to Laurence as narrator, Laurence as character is also ironic and, at times, sarcastic. From the very first page of the novel, irony is directed at Laurence's milieu. As Elizabeth Fallaize says, as the novel opens, readers seek uneasily the source of the malicious remarks that undercut the description of Feuverolles and the guests' conversation.[20] Favourite butts for Laurence's irony are her sister and

---

[16]   This is an echo and revision of Laurence's earlier affirmation that 'le monde est partout ailleurs, et il n'y a pas moyen d'y entrer' (BI, p. 26); 'the world is everywhere somewhere else, and there's no way of getting in' (LBI, p. 32, ta). It is also an appropriation and valorisation of an earlier pejorative statement of Laurence's father about tourists who 'ne sont nulle part, tout en étant partout' (BI, p. 40); 'they're no longer anywhere, even though they're everywhere' (LBI, p. 49, ta).

[17]   The title *Les Belles Images* is, of course, itself ironic and open to a multiplicity of interpretations.

[18]   Irony can also be read as an inscription of hysteria in the text insofar as in hysteria the symptom appears to 'mean' one thing while it actually conceals another 'meaning.'

[19]   The je/elle split is discussed later.

[20]   Fallaize, *The Novels*, p. 119.

brother-in-law, Marthe and Hubert. The tone of Laurence's ironic asides inclines toward the cruel. Her portrait of Hubert is vicious and very funny:

> Hubert allume sa pipe qu'il est bien le dernier homme en France à appeler 'ma vieille bouffarde.' Son sourire de paralytique général, son embonpoint. Quand il voyage il porte des lunettes noires: 'j'adore voyager incognito.' Un excellent dentiste qui pendant ses loisirs étudie consciencieusement le tiercé. (BI, p. 9)

> Hubert lights his pipe: he's certainly the only man left in France who calls it 'my old puffer.' His paralytic smile, his stoutness. When he travels he wears sunglasses: 'I love to travel incognito.' An excellent dentist who conscientiously studies horse racing results in his spare time. (LBI, p. 12, ta)

Her contempt for him even intrudes into Laurence's account of the crucial family meal where Catherine's case is discussed and Laurence realises her complete isolation; she imagines Hubert is eating in silence because 'no doubt he was working out some tortuous exchange of key rings, his latest craze' (BI, p. 174; LBI, p. 211)). As for Marthe, it is her religious faith that is met by Laurence's irony. She puts her sister's conversion down to her being married to Hubert and mocks the poses she adopts, like 'a saint drunk with the joyful love of God' (BI, p. 9; LBI, p. 12). When Marthe drops by to see Laurence unexpectedly, something Laurence has expressly asked her not to do, Laurence imputes this to the fact that she is obeying supernatural impulses and has become very imperious since being inspired 'from on high' (BI, p. 74; LBI, p. 90, ta). Laurence is sarcastic to Marthe's face when she presumes to interfere in the way Laurence brings up Catherine. 'You can always fall back on praying for her,' she tells her, refusing to relent and let Catherine take her first communion (BI, p. 76; LBI, p. 93).

To what extent is it meaningful or possible to separate the two layers of irony, narrator and character? Sometimes Laurence the narrator is clearly directing irony at Laurence the character. However, much of the time the distinction between these two levels of irony is latent rather than actual and is a source of ambiguity, particularly when the utterance in question may be free direct discourse. For example, readers, dependent on Laurence, have no way of knowing the status of the utterance and are left wondering whose anger and bitterness is being expressed, narrator's or character's, when they read: 'Suivre son bonhomme de chemin, sans dévier d'un pouce, défense de regarder à droite ou à gauche, à chaque âge ses tâches, si la colère te prend avale un verre d'eau et fais des mouvements de gymnastique. Ça m'a bien réussi, ça m'a parfaitement réussi [...]' (BI, p. 132); 'Follow your own little road without straying an inch, no looking to the right or the left, to every age its own tasks, if you feel angry swallow a glass of water and do some exercises. It's worked for me, worked perfectly [...]' (LBI, p. 160, ta). Similarly, the status of the bitter irony evinced as the narrative recounts the moment when Laurence is forced to accept Jean-Charles's decision that Catherine should be separated from her friend, Brigitte, is ambiguous: 'Du cheval! ça c'était une idée formidable; même affectivement. Remplacer une amie par un cheval!' (BI, p. 172); 'Horse riding! what a great idea; even from the emotional point of view. Replace a friend by a horse!' (LBI, p. 209, ta). The fact that the interpolation is not in brackets or between dashes increases ambiguity. It suggests that the irony is Laurence the character's. However, a number of lines later, this impression is contradicted to some extent as Laurence appears to have adopted Jean-Charles's point of view that once in Rome, Catherine will hardly think of Brigitte and that if they play things right, she will have completely forgotten her by the following year (BI, p. 173). Here, Laurence the narrator of her story (there is no indication at this point whether the story is being narrated in the first or the third person), may possibly be directing irony/ (self-)criticism at Laurence the character.

The retrospective narration of the final chapter of *Les Belles Images* allows Laurence (narrator) to be ironic at the expense of Laurence (character), exploiting the potential for dramatic irony.[21] Laurence recounts how during a conversation with her father about Dominique, she did not contradict his kindly estimation of the changes in her personality. The irony directed at herself is scathing: 'Je ne voulais pas priver ma pauvre mère des bribes d'amitié qu'il lui accordait' (BI, p. 157); 'I didn't want to deprive my poor mother of the scraps of friendship he afforded her' (LBI, p. 191, ta). Laurence's ironic response to her mother and father's behaviour before she learned of their reconciliation takes on a further level of irony in the context of Laurence's retrospective narration. Laurence, looking back at what has happened, is critical of the blindness and naivety her initial, ironic reaction displayed: '(Maman prenant goût aux réunions de famille! on aura tout vu! et la courtoisie de papa à son égard!)' (BI, p. 173); '(Mummy acquiring a taste for family parties! wonders never cease! and Daddy's gallantry towards her!)' (LBI, p. 210, ta). Such free play with the status of utterances can be read as evidence of the expression of semiotic energy in the text.

At other times these layers of irony, narrator's and character's, are juxtaposed; Laurence as character is ironic; this implies a certain distancing. Then Laurence as narrator distances herself even further and directs irony at Laurence as character, irony at her irony. Thus, when Laurence is unable to concentrate on her work because she is worried about Catherine, we read: '"Voilà bien la condition déchirée de la femme qui travaille," se dit-elle avec ironie. (Elle se sentait bien plus déchirée quand elle ne travaillait pas)' (BI, p. 28); '"There's the tortured state of women who go out to work for you," she said to herself ironically. (She used to feel far more tortured when she didn't work)' (LBI, pp. 34–5, ta). This split and the acute dissociation it reveals are emblematic of the madness of the text.

There is a further level of irony based on complicity between the implied author and readers. Laurence is targetted along with Gilbert and others by the irony generated by the use of the mystifying/distorting language of the technocratic bourgeoisie.[22] One of the most shocking examples is Gilbert's response to the

---

[21]   The narrative is retrospective until BI, p. 179, when storytime and text-time reconverge.

[22]   Beauvoir writes about her intention to evoke technocratic society and to 'faire entendre ce qu'on appelle aujourd'hui son "discours"' ('to make heard what is today referred to as its "discourse"') in TCF, p. 172; ASD, p. 137, ta. There is also a reference to technocratic society in *Que peut la littérature?* where Beauvoir is disparaging about

suicide of a 12-year-old boy in prison that Laurence concurs with: "'Des faux frais." Gilbert expliquait qu'en toute société il y a forcément des faux frais. Oui, forcément' (BI, p. 58); "'Incidental expenses." Gilbert explained that there were necessarily incidental expenses in every society. Yes, necessarily' (LBI, pp. 69–70, ta). In another example, Laurence is sincere in her appraisal of Jean-Charles, yet readers enjoy a wry smile at her expense when they read: "'le côté convulsif des femmes," dit Jean-Charles qui est pourtant féministe' (BI, p. 44); "'the unstable side of women," says Jean-Charles who is nevertheless a feminist' (LBI, p. 54, ta). Again, readers 'know' that Laurence is wrong when she asserts: 'On ne peut pas prendre la responsabilité de tout ce qu'on fait – ne fait pas. "Qu'est-ce que tu fais pour eux?" Ces comptes exigés soudain dans un monde où rien ne compte tellement. C'est comme un abus' (BI, p. 136); 'You can't assume responsibility for everything you do – or don't do. "What do you do for them?" Being suddenly called to account in a world where nothing really counts. It's like an abuse' (LBI, pp. 164–5, ta). We are invited to judge her negatively. The same is true when her *mauvaise foi* is revealed: 'La psychologue dirait qu'elle fait exprès de se rendre malade parce qu'elle ne veut pas emmener Catherine. Absurde. Si *vraiment* elle ne voulait pas, elle refuserait, elle se battrait' (BI, p. 175); 'The psychologist would say she's making herself ill on purpose becuase she doesn't want to take Catherine away on holiday. Ridiculous. If she *really* didn't want to, she'd refuse, she'd fight' (LBI, pp. 212–13, ta, emphasis added). I believe that modern (women) readers tend to resist the invitation to 'condemn' Laurence for her apparent failings and are more likely to sympathise and identify with her, perhaps even considering that the implied author is somehow taking an unfair advantage.

There is a further group of utterances whose status is ambiguous in that it is impossible to know whether the irony, which is clearly intended, is the narrator's or the implied author's. Are we being invited to direct our criticism *with* Laurence (narrator) or *at* her when she refers to books not by their title but by the prize they have won?: 'le Goncourt, le Renaudot' (BI, p. 91). We wonder whether Laurence is sincere when she repeats what 'everyone' knows about the condition of the working class, that it is not what it should be 'bien qu'avec les allocations familiales ils aient presque tous une machine à laver, la télé, et *même* une auto' ('although with family allowances they almost all have a washing machine, television, and *even* a car') (BI, p. 73; LBI, p. 89, ta, emphasis added). Is Laurence aware of the irony when she repeatedly refers to 'le coin "relaxe-silence"' (the quiet space) in her mother's appartment, even as she is describing Dominique's distress?[23] A similar ambiguity adheres to the more playful remark prompted by

---

its optimism 'qui appelle la misère abondance et qui se sert de l'avenir comme d'un alibi' (which calls extreme poverty abundance and uses the future as an alibi) (p. 91, my translation). The transposition of meanings derived from other texts into *Les Belles images*, the process of intertextuality, is, for Kristeva, evidence of semiotic activity.

23   See BI, pp. 49, 50, 58, 100.

Jean-Charles's response to the kaleidoscope, so out of key with Laurence's and the children's, to the effect that it would be an excellent tool for designers of fabrics and wallpaper. The status of the unfinished observation, 'dix idées à la minute ...' ('10 ideas a minute ...') (BI, p. 38; LBI, p. 46) is unclear. If it belongs to Laurence the character, is she being sincere or ironic? Does it express the indulgence or distanced derision of the narrator? Is the irony, then, the implied author's? The cumulative effect of this ambiguity is, yet again, to deprive readers of any firm foothold, a secure place from where they can make judgements.

Enumeration is also related to the questioning of meaning and the undermining of our confidence in language in *Les Belles Images*. The use of lists is one of the most striking features of the text. The text is so dominated by enumeration that this strategy could almost be described as a textual 'tic.' There are examples on virtually every page of the book.[24] This is perhaps quite natural given the premise that a sign never means one thing only. As Laurence reflects when she receives a bouquet from Jean-Charles, 'a bouquet is always something other than flowers; it's friendship, hope, gratitude, cheerfulness' (BI, p. 136; LBI, p. 165, ta). Conversely, given the inadequacies of language, one word is not enough to convey meaning. Interesting theoretical work has been done on enumeration by Béatrice Damamme.[25] She has shown how enumeration can work to create an impression of uncertainty, of groping toward true meaning/the right term. In *Les Belles Images,* adjectives, verbs, and nouns are multiplied. There is an interesting example of this in the final pages of the book; Laurence is depressed and finding it painful to come to terms with her parents' reconciliation and, in particular, to square her mother's present self-satisfaction with the distress she had been feeling. The synonymity of the terms in the two parallel lists is evocative: 'On crie, on pleure, on se convulse comme s'il y avait dans la vie quelque chose digne de ces cris, ces larmes, ces agitations' (BI, p. 177); 'You shout, you cry, you get agitated as though there were something in life worth the shouting, the tears, the agitation (LBI, pp. 214–15, ta). Spaces are created between the different terms, and meaning reverberates there; it is the outcome of the interaction between them, more than the sum of the individual words that are themselves deficient. Enumerations in *Les Belles Images* embody the displacement and deferral of meaning.

An important aspect of Beauvoir's use of lists is rhythm. It is a useful criterion for the selection of quotations to illustrate my contention that enumeration can challenge our confidence in words/language/meaning by the way in which synonymous and antonymous terms are linked. Furthermore, it will be useful to examine these enumerations in the light of the theoretical work done by

---

[24]   Indeed, it is characteristic of much of Beauvoir's writing as a whole. Claire Cayron discusses the pleasure Beauvoir derives from enumeration in *La Nature chez Beauvoir*, Paris: Gallimard, 1973, pp. 163–8.

[25]   Béatrice Damamme, 'Réflexions sur le rôle des démarcateurs de coordination dans les énumérations littéraires,' *Le Français Moderne: Revue de Linguistique Français*, 49(1), January 1981, 20–35.

Madeleine Frédéric.[26] She has shown how enumerations slip almost imperceptibly from highly organised, tightly structured formulations at one end of the spectrum to what she terms 'énumérations chaotiques' at the other. According to her classification, most of the enumerations we are dealing with in *Les Belles Images* vere toward or belong in the disordered category, possessing either a vague synthesizing expression ('formule synthétique') that sums up the terms that make up the enumeration or none at all and frequently linking heterogeneous elements.[27] This is in keeping with the 'madness' of the text. Toward the beginning of *Les Belles Images*, we find the following striking examples of enumeration; describing the early days of her relationship with Jean-Charles, Laurence says:

> Tout était net, frais, parfait: l'eau bleue de la piscine, le bruit luxueux des balles de tennis, les blanches aiguilles de pierre, les nuages roulés en boule dans le ciel lisse, l'odeur des sapins. [...] Dans le parc de l'hôtel, les garçons et les filles en clairs vêtements, la peau hâlée, polis par le soleil comme de beaux galets. Et Laurence et Jean-Charles de clair vêtus, hâlés, polis. Soudain un soir, au retour d'une promenade, dans la voiture arrêtée, sa bouche sur ma bouche, cet embrasement, ce vertige. Alors, pendant des jours et des semaines, je n'ai plus été une image, mais chair et sang, désir, plaisir. (BI, p. 22)

> Everything was neat, fresh, perfect: the blue water in the swimming pool, the opulent sound of the tennis balls, the white mountain peaks, the fluffy white clouds in the clear blue sky, the smell of the pine trees. [...] In the hotel grounds, boys and girls dressed in light colours, tanned, polished by the sun like beautiful pebbles. And Laurence and Jean-Charles dressed in light colours, tanned, polished. Suddenly, one evening, after a drive, in the car, his mouth on my mouth, I was ablaze, reeling. Then, for days and weeks, I was no longer a picture, but flesh and blood, desire, pleasure. (LBI, p. 27, ta)

The quotation begins with an enumeration of three closely related adjectives, none of them alone sufficient to convey the meaning that emerges from the gaps

---

[26]   Madeleine Frédéric, 'Énumération, énumération homologique, énumération chaotique: essai de caractérisation,' in *Styistique, rhétorique et poétique dans les langues romanes*, Actes du XVIIe Congrès international de linguistique et de philologie romanes (Aix-en-Provence, 1983), vol. 8, Aix-en-Provence: Université de Provence, 1986, 104–17.

[27]   Frédéric gives the following definition of 'formule synthétique': 'un terme ou un groupe de termes dont le contenu sémantique recouvre celui de l'ensemble ou d'une partie seulement des termes/des syntagmes constituant la série' (p. 106). Among the examples she gives of vague synthesizing expressions are those that include the word 'chose' ('thing') (see p. 108). A classic example with 'chose' occurs in *Les Belles Images* on p. 81: '[Catherine] apprend des choses qui ne s'enseignent pas en classe: compatir, consoler, recevoir et donner, percevoir sur les visages et dans les voix des nuances qui lui échappaient.' ([Catherine] is learning things that aren't taught at school: to sympathise, to comfort, to give and take, to notice shades of meaning in people's expressions or in their voices that she used to miss' (LBI, pp. 98–9, ta).) 'Tout' (everything) is another such expression. See the following quotation that begins: 'Tout était net, frais parfait [...].'

between them. Then follows a list of objects, of which I say more later. The next enumeration, 'de clair vêtus, hâlés, polis,' made up of three past participles, echoes and condenses the description of the view from Laurence's window. The text reaches a crescendo here as Jean-Charles is about to kiss Laurence for the first time, a kiss expressed by a further enumeration, communicating a sense of urgency. In the final enumeration – 'chair et sang, désir, plaisir' – rhythm underlines the sensuality of their relationship.The rhythm and movement of this passage can be interpreted as a surge of semiotic energy in the text, providing the kind of polymorphic/polyphonic pleasure that Kristeva links to the *chora*. Semiotic energy is apparent later in the text when Laurence's ecstatic, giddy response to the dancing of a Greek child and the intensity of her experience is suggested by a list of past participles: 'Transportée par la musique, éblouie, grisée, transfigurée, éperdue' (BI, p. 158); 'Carried away by the music, dazzled, intoxicated, transfigured, elated' (LBI, p. 192, ta). The effect is reinforced by the way in which these terms echo and reinforce each other. Use of rhythm is also interesting as Laurence seems to reach the lowest point in her breakdown; there are, in fact, five parallel lists here, whose rhythms convey, not only her panic and despair, but also her confusion in the face of such complexity, feelings shared by readers who sink down with Laurence into the seemingly impenetrable/enveloping mass created by the lists before experiencing the dawning of hope as the rhythm of the final list rises up and lifts Laurence and readers to a point beyond despair:

> Ils la forceront à manger, ils lui feront tout avaler; tout quoi? tout ce qu'elle vomit, sa vie, celle des autres avec leurs fausses amours, leurs histoires d'argent, leurs mensonges. Ils la guériront de ses refus, de son désespoir. [...] Qu'a-t-on fait de moi? Cette femme qui n'aime personne, insensible aux beautés du monde, incapable même de pleurer, cette femme que je vomis. Catherine: [...] peut-être elle s'en sortira ... De quoi? De cette nuit. De l'ignorance, de l'indifférence. Catherine ... Elle se redresse soudain. (BI, pp. 180–81)

> They will force her to eat, they'll make her swallow it all; all what? everything she's vomiting, her life, the life the others lead with their bogus love affairs, their preoccupation with money, their lies. They'll cure her of her lack of compliance, of her despair. [...] What have they turned me into? This woman who loves no one, indifferent to the beauties of the world, incapable even of crying, this woman that I'm vomiting. Catherine: [...] perhaps she'll escape ... From what? From darkness. From ignorance, from indifference. Catherine ... She sits up suddenly. (LBI, p. 219, ta)

Reading this, it seems to me that the text also reproduces Laurence's experience of breathlessness for readers. The semiotic energy that Kristeva identifies as erupting in Céline's verse as 'panting,' 'breathlessness' and 'acceleration' of pace, erupts in the text of *Les Belles Images* as Laurence confronts breakdown and madness. Such lists within lists, lists upon lists, are a common feature of *Les Belles Images*. Elsewhere in the text, it is a technique used to portray the advertising industry and the psychological motivations it appeals to. Here, the use of parallel lists suggests not only complexity but also excess and duplicity. Note the series of synonyms that begins the following quotation and the linking of divergent elements in the final list: 'Le lisse, le brillant, le luisant, rêve de glissement, de perfection glacée; valeurs de l'érotisme et valeurs de l'enfance (innocence); vitesse, domination, chaleur, sécurité' (BI, p. 42); 'smoothness, brilliance, shine; the dream of gliding, of icy perfection; erotic values and childhood values (innocence); speed, domination, warmth, security' (LBI, p. 51, ta).

Enumeration is a supple tool that Beauvoir uses skillfully in *Les Belles Images* to communicate Laurence's mood. Compare respectively the joy, determination, wistfulness, and bitterness in the following quotations. Assonance and alliteration reinforce the childlike sense of happiness evoked when Laurence and her daughters look in a kaleidoscope: 'Enchantement des couleurs et des formes qui se font, se défont, papillotent et se multiplient dans la fuyante symétrie d'un octogone' (BI, p. 37); 'A wonderland of colours and shapes that formed, fell apart, quivered with light and multiplied in fleeting symmetry within an octogon' (LBI, p. 46). When Laurence is remembering her first breakdown and trying to convince herself that it will not happen again, a series of verbs together with the repetition of 'je suis' conveys her determination: 'Je ne retomberai pas. Maintenant je suis prévenue, je suis armée, je me tiens en main'(BI, p. 44); 'I won't get ill again. Now I am forewarned, I am armed, I am in control' (LBI, p. 54, ta, and my translation).[28] Repetition combines with enumeration again to express Laurence's wistfulness when she is shopping for Christmas presents: 'Une veste en daim d'une couleur indéfinissable: couleur de brume, couleur du temps, couleur des robes de Peau-d'Ane' (BI, p. 139); 'A suede jacket of a colour without a name – the colour of mist, the colour of the weather, the changeable, magical colour of fairy-tales' (LBI, p. 168, ta). The jacket is at once all and none of these (non)colours. She does not buy the jacket but allows Jean-Charles to choose a necklace for her. Her tone is bitter as she realises what the gift represents: 'C'est une compensation, un symbole, un succédané' (BI, p. 140); 'It's a compensation, a symbol, a substitute' (LBI, p. 170, ta). Here, too, the use of a series of quasi-synonyms reminds us of the inadequacy of words. Alliteration intensifies the effect.

All of the examples I have quoted are what Béatrice Damamme refers to as open enumerations. That is, the final term of the enumeration is not preceded by an 'and,' which would give an impression of finality/completion, of closure. Without an 'and' we feel the list could go on. This openness, this inconclusiveness is characteristic of *Les Belles Images* as a whole and corresponds well with Laurence's frame of mind. It also deprives readers, who are dependent on Laurence's narrative, of any certainty. The lack of closure in Beauvoir's text is an instance of her radical writing practice.

Lists can also create a sense of meaninglessness, deprive reality of its seriousness so that it seems unreal. This is most strikingly the case when it is a matter of lists of catastrophes and the process of detachment is explicated in the text:

---

[28]   The text in the published English translation is cut at this point and simply reads: 'I shall not relapse.'

Les horreurs du monde, on est forcé de s'y habituer, il y en a trop: le gavage des oies, l'excision, les lynchages, les avortements, les suicides, les enfants martyres, les maisons de la mort, les massacres d'otages, les répressions, on voit ça au cinéma, à la télé, on passe. (BI, p. 30)

You're obliged to get used to the horrors of this world, there are too many of them. The force-feeding of geese, excision, lynching, abortions, suicides, brutally ill-treated children, death-camps, the slaughter of hostages, repression: you see it all at the cinema or on television and you ignore it. (LBI, p. 36, ta)

Cadavres sanglants de Blancs, de Noirs, des autocars renversés dans des ravins, vingt-cinq enfants tués, d'autres coupés en deux, des incendies, des carcasses d'avions fracassés, cent dix passagers morts sur le coup, des cyclones, des inondations, des pays entiers dévastés, des villages en flammes, des émeutes raciales, des guerres locales, des défilés de réfugiés hagards. C'était si lugubre qu'à la fin on avait presque envie de rire. [...] On n'aperçoit que des images, proprement encadrées sur le petit écran et qui n'ont pas leur poids de réalité. (BI, p. 147)

Bleeding corpses of Whites, of Blacks, buses overturned in ravines, twenty-five children killed, others cut in half, fires, the smashed wreckage of planes, a hundred and ten passengers killed instantly, cyclones, floods, whole countries laid waste, villages in flames, race riots, local wars, long processions of dazed refugees. It was so dismal that in the end you almost wanted to laugh. [...] All you see are pictures, neatly framed on the small screen and lacking the weight of reality. (LBI, pp.178–9, ta)

Laurence's latent response to the review of the year's events, hysterical laughter, might easily be replicated by readers in response to the transcribed catalogue of disasters. Enumeration is certainly used as a vehicle for humour in *Les Belles Images*.[29] Elizabeth Fallaize has drawn attention to the comic subversion that operates when Jean-Charles conjures up a picture of the future: 'Les déserts se sont couverts de blé, de légumes, de fruits, toute la terre est devenue la terre promise; gavés de lait, de riz, de tomates et d'oranges, tous les enfants souriaient' (BI, pp. 30–31); 'The deserts were covered with wheat, vegetables and fruit, the whole world had turned into the promised land; gorged on milk, rice, tomatoes and oranges, all the children were smiling (LBI, p. 37, ta).[30] Laurence lists the titles of books she sees in a shop window; included in the high-sounding list of 11 titles that could go on (it 'ends' with an ellipsis) we find '*Une nouvelle classe ouvrière, Une classe ouvrière nouvelle*' (BI, p. 73), a comic repetition and reversal. Laurence our narrator detaches herself from her world in order to mock it and,

---

[29]   It has been suggested that from a certain length, all enumerations may be comic, whatever the subject matter. See Barbara C. Bowen's comment during the discussion that follows Francis Bar's paper 'Répétition et énumération chez les auteurs burlesques du XVIIe siècle,' reported in *Actes du colloque organisé par l'Institut d'études romanes et le Centre de civilisation de l'Université de Varsovie*, 1981, pp. 163–86 (p. 186).

[30]   Fallaize, *The Novels*, p. 126.

by extension, herself. Self-parody is characteristic of the text. Can humour be defined as transgressive? To what extent can humour be considered mad? Is there something slightly 'hysterical' in the burlesque description of Laurence's relationship with Lucien, for example? This is what she says:

> Ensuite, que d'agitation! Il me poursuivait, il pleurait, je cédais, il rompait, je souffrais, je cherchais partout la Giulietta rouge, je me pendais au téléphone, il revenait, il suppliait: quitte ton mari, non jamais mais je t'aime, il m'insultait, il repartait, j'attendais, j'espérais, je désespérais, nous nous retrouvions, quel bonheur, j'ai tant souffert sans toi, et moi sans toi: avoue tout à ton mari, jamais. (BI, p. 32)

> Then what turmoil! He pursued me, he cried, I gave way, he broke up with me, I suffered, I looked for the red Alfa Romeo everywhere, I spent all my time on the phone, he came back, he begged: 'leave your husband', no never but I love you, he called me names, he broke off again, I waited, I hoped, I lost hope, we got together again, what happiness, I've suffered so much without you, and I without you, 'tell your husband everything', never ... (LBI, p. 39, ta)

It is revealing to compare this hyperbole used to portray the early days of their relationship once Laurence has become disillusioned, with the language and the use of enumeration to convey her awareness of well-being at that time. We read: 'J'écraserais mes remords, si c'était comme avant; le trouble qui foudroie, la nuit qui flambe, tourbillons et avalanches de désirs et de délices: pour ces métamorphoses on peut trahir, mentir, tout risquer' (BI, p. 63); 'I'd stifle my remorse if things were as they were before – the shattering emotion, the night on fire, whirlwinds and avalanches of longing and delight. For that kind of metamorphosis you can betray, lie, risk everything' (LBI, p. 76). The brittle nature of this hyperbole and Laurence's bitter disappointment are exposed shortly afterwards when she recalls that even last Christmas 'du moins il y avait quelque chose à regretter, quelque chose au monde qui valait son poids de chagrin' ('at least there was something to miss, something in the world that was worth its weight in sorrow'), and she envies Lucien: 'Il connaît encore cette fièvre, et le désespoir, et l'espoir. Il a plus de chance que moi' (BI, p. 65); 'He is still experiencing passion, and despair, and hope. He's luckier than me' (LBI, pp.78–9, ta). It is interesting to note the closure of this list by the use of 'and.' Exceptionally, the impression we have is one of finality. Laurence has not been able to maintain the jolly front behind which she had tried to hide her emptiness from herself.

Her feelings of remoteness become more acute in Greece. Lists of objects in the museum in Athens reproduce in readers the indifference and boredom of Laurence, who remembers that she felt like she was at the bottom of 'a pit if indifference' ('un gouffre d'indifférence') and that her boredom was exacerbated to the point of anguish (BI, p. 167; LBI, p. 203). Her feelings of suffocation are experienced by readers, who can feel smothered by the lists of objects that are so typical of the text and that are sometimes very lengthy indeed: lists of food (BI, p. 8); furniture (BI, p. 45); furniture and clothes (BI, p. 58); books (BI, pp. 72–3); drinks (BI, p. 90); magazines (BI, p. 92); and objects in shop windows, taking up 21 lines (BI, pp. 137–8). These lists convey a sense of over abundance and leave 'no space to breathe.' Clearly, they mirror the world in which Laurence lives and reflect its materialistic values.

A further interesting effect of these lists of objects is to slow down the text. They pin down the text on a temporal level, literally make time stand still. There is something obsessional in Laurence's apparent compulsion to catalogue her environment, perhaps in an attempt to gain some semblance of control over it. The text relentlessly traps readers in the narrator's obsession. Reading long inventories, I am also reminded of Beauvoir's express desire, apparently repudiated when she met Sartre, to 'say/tell it all'; 'je dirais tout' she wrote in *Mémoires d'une jeune fille rangée*.[31]

The feelings of suffocation I have mentioned are effectively reinforced by the use of repetition, an equally striking characteristic of Beauvoir's textual practice in *Les Belles Images*. I have identified 44 words, expressions, sentences, dialogues, and constructions that are repeated throughout the the text, sometimes up to six times. This use of repetition creates a dense web of utterances and duplicates Laurence's feelings of entrapment. Utterances reverberate throughout the narrative like mirror images, *en abyme*, reflections of reflections of reflections. The text structures an obsessive situation. In Freudian terms, the text itself can be described as neurotic as repetition is neurotic or, to be more precise, neurosis is repetition. Freud argued that the neurotic 'repeats instead of remembering.' Therapy involves converting repetition into remembrance.[32] The final chapter of *Les Belles Images* can be read as an attempt to remember. Furthermore, repetition can evoke a sense

---

[31]   See MJF, p. 481. The incident in the Luxembourg Gardens when Sartre 'defeats' Beauvoir, leading her to abandon her project of saying/telling everything, is discussed by Moi in *Simone de Beauvoir*, pp. 15–17. (Note that the use of the conditional tense undercuts the possibility of saying/telling it all.)

[32]   'Remembering, Repeating and Working Through,' *The Complete Psychological Works of Sigmund Freud*, ed. James Strachey, London: The Hogarth Press, 1958, Volume XII (1911–1913), pp. 147–56 (p. 151). My reading accords with Beauvoir's reference to the discoveries of psychoanalysis in 'Existentialisme et la sagesse des nations': 'Il pourrait sembler inutile et même néfaste de révéler à un adolescent qu'il hait son père; mais s'il n'a pas avoué cette haine avec des mots, il ne l'a pas moins affirmée dans ses sentiments, ses conduites, ses rêves, ses angoisses; le psychanalyste ne choisit pas de découvrir gratuitement et brutalement une vérité ignorée; il essaie d'aider son malade à modifier les conduites par lesquelles il réagit à cette réalité; au lieu d'employer ses forces à se dissimuler sa haine, il faut que le sujet s'en libère, non en la niant, mais en l'assumant et en la dépassant; ce qui exige d'abord qu'il la reconnaisse explicitement et la comprenne' (pp. 42–3); 'It may seem useless and even nefarious to reveal to an adolescent that he hates his father, but not admitting this hate with words does not mean he affirms it any less in his feelings, behaviours, dreams, and anxieties. The psychoanalyst is not choosing to brutally and gratuitously uncover an unknown truth; he is trying to help his patient to modify the behaviours by which he reacts to this reality. Instead of using his strength to hide from his hate, the subject must liberate himself of it, not by denying it but by assuming it and surpassing it, which requires that he first recognize it explicitly and understand it' (*Philosophical Writings*, p. 215). This is not to deny, however, that the text of *Les Belles Images* specifically rejects Freud and that in using Freud, I am reading against authorial intention.

of unreality, duplicating Laurence's experience for readers. I suggest that readers who encounter such extensive repetition will inevitably become self-conscious as readers; that is, they will distance themselves from the fictional world of the text and in this way experience Laurence's alienation.

It is useful to quote in full two of the series of repetitions to illustrate just how dense the text can become. Early in the narrative we read:

> (Juste en ce moment, dans un autre jardin, tout à fait différent, exactement pareil, quelqu'un dit ces mots et le même sourire se pose sur un autre visage [...].) (BI, p. 7–8)

> (At this very moment in another garden, completely different, exactly the same, someone is saying these words and the same smile is forming on another face [...].) (LBI, p. 10, ta)

A few pages later we find:

> Dans un autre jardin, tout à fait différent, exactement pareil, quelqu'un dit [...] (BI, p. 9)

> In another garden, completely different, exactly the same, someone is saying [...] (LBI, p. 11, ta)

Again, some 40 pages later we read:

> (Dans un autre salon, tout à fait différent, exactement pareil, avec des vases pleins de fleurs luxueuses, le même cri sort d'une autre bouche: 'Salaud!') (BI, p. 50)

> (In another drawing-room, completely different, exactly the same, with vases full of expensive flowers, the same cry is coming out of another mouth: 'Bastard!') (LBI, p. 61)

This recalls:

> (Est-ce qu'en cet instant, dans un autre coin de la galaxie, un autre Lucien, une autre Laurence disent les mêmes mots? [...]) (BI, p. 32)

> (At this very moment, in another part of the galaxy, are another Lucien, another Laurence saying the same words? [...]) (LBI, p. 40, ta)

which is echoed later in the text:

> Mais la voix nostalgique fait lever en elle comme un écho brouillé de quelque chose vécu jadis, dans une autre vie, ou peut-être en ce moment, sur une autre planète. (BI, p. 60)

> But the nostalgia in his voice arouses something in her mind – a confused echo as it were of something she has known in the past, in another life, or perhaps at this very moment, on another planet. (LBI, pp. 72–3, ta)

All of these quotations are echoed again when Laurence says:

> Juste à cette minute, des tas d'amants sont en train de rompre [...]. (BI, p. 110)

> At this very moment there are masses of lovers breaking up [...]. (LBI, p. 134, ta)

> (Une autre jeune femme, des centaines de jeunes femmes en cette minute se demandent: pourquoi lui plutôt qu'un autre?) (BI, p. 137)

> (Another young woman, hundreds of young women at this very moment are wondering why him rather than someone else?) (LBI, p. 166, ta)

This last quotation links with another series of repetitions:

> 'Pourquoi Jean-Charles plutôt que Lucien?' [...]. [...] (Pourquoi moi plutôt qu'une autre?) (BI, p. 65)

> 'Why Jean-Charles rather than Lucien?' [...]. [...] (Why me rather than someone else?) (LBI, p. 79)

> Pourquoi Jean-Charles plutôt que Lucien? [...] Pourquoi un homme plutôt qu'un autre? (BI, p. 66)

> Why Jean-Charles rather than Lucien? [...] Why one man rather than another? (LBI, p. 80)

> Pourquoi Jean-Charles plutôt qu'un autre? (BI, p. 137)

> Why Jean-Charles rather than someone else? (LBI, p. 166, ta)

Grouping repeated utterances in this way, illustrates just how weighted down the text of *Les Belles Images* is. One series of repetitions is echoed by another. Moreover, the word 'salaud,' which appears in the series just quoted, ricochets through the text, repeated 13 other times on four different occasions. Certain words are concentrated in a particular section of the work; lies and lying ('mensonges,' 'mensonger') are repeated six times in the final third of *Les Belles Images*.[33] As Laurence comes to see more clearly through the glossy veneer of the world in which she lives, her rejection of it becomes more and more vehement and 'no' reverberates throughout the last part of the text, building to a crescendo when Laurence, unable to deny her true feelings any longer, finds her voice and shouts her refusal to comply:

---

[33] See BI, p. 136 'mensonger'; p. 139 'mensonge'; p. 140 'mensonge'; p. 168 'la chaine de mensonges'; p. 180 'il parlerait à cette radio qu'il accusait de mensonge'; p.180 'leurs mensonges.' (Laurence herself lies a number of times in the narrative: to Catherine about Jean-Charles's work BI, p. 29, and to Jean-Charles, not only about Lucien, but also about Goya's Christmas bonus, BI, p. 128; about the number of times Catherine has cried at night, BI, p. 129 (cf. p. 135); about having eaten, BI, p. 137.)

Non. Je ne voulais pas. [...] Je refusais de l'oublier, [...] je refusais qu'un jour elle ressemblât à sa mère [...]. (BI, p. 158)

No. I wouldn't. [...] I refused to forget her, [...] I refused to accept that one day she would be like her mother [...]. (LBI, p. 192, ta)

Non. Non. (BI, p. 179)

No. No. (LBI, p. 217)

'Non, jamais! Je ne me laisserai pas manipuler.' Elle crie: 'Non! Non!' [...] Non. Pourquoi non? [...] 'Non'; elle a crié tout haut. (BI, p. 180)

'No, never! I won't let myself be manipulated.' She shouts: 'No! No!' [...] No. Why no? [...] 'No,' she has shouted out loud. (LBI, pp. 218–19, ta)

Here Beauvoir is also using repetition to make explicit the connections between Laurence, Catherine, and the little Greek girl. Another series of repetitions develops further the identification of Laurence with Catherine:

C'est toi [Laurence] qui la [Catherine] détraque avec tes scrupules, ta sensiblerie. (BI, p. 133)

You're the one [Laurence] who's knocking her [Catherine] off balance with your overscrupulousness, your oversensitivity. (LBI, p. 162)

Sous prétexte de guérir Catherine de cette 'sensiblerie' qui inquiétait Jean-Charles, on allait la mutiler. (BI, p. 159)

On the pretext of curing Catherine of the 'oversensitivity' that worried Jean-Charles, they were going to maim her. (LBI, p. 193, ta)

Donc à Pâques – elle [Laurence] sera guérie [...]. (BI, p. 175)

So at Easter – she [Laurence] will be cured [...]. (LBI, p. 212, ta)

Ils la [Laurence] guériront de ses refus, de son désespoir. (BI, p. 180)

They'll cure her [Laurence] of her lack of compliance, of her despair. (LBI, p. 219, ta)

This repetition and series of identifications reflect Laurence's disintegrating sense of self and accentuate readers' discomfort as regards the narrator's identity. They are placed in the uncomfortable position of depending on a narrator who is not only unreliable but whose personality is disintegrating.

Clearly, each time words reappear, their meaning is transformed, embedded as they are in different contexts.[34] Thus the whole process of undermining our

---

[34]   Kristeva follows Vološinov to argue that all meaning is contextual. Context does not allow us to determine/close the meaning of a text as context itself cannot be fixed.

confidence in fixed meaning is reinforced. When Laurence learns from her mother that her parents intend to live together again, news she finds utterly painful,[35] she recalls the words Gilbert had spoken when he told her that he was about to reject her mother; his words erupt in the text as direct speech having acquired new layers of significance and now refer to both Laurence and her mother with bitter irony:

> On supporte, on supporte, dit Gilbert. (BI, p. 47)

> 'You bear things you know, you bear them,' says Gilbert. (LBI, p. 57, ta)

> 'On supporte, on supporte.' (BI, p. 177)

> 'You bear things you know, you bear them.' (LBI, p. 214)

The text underlines the ambivalence of even apparently straightforward words such as the term that literally means to force-feed that is used to designate four very different situations:

> le gavage des oies (BI, p. 30); the force-feeding of geese (LBI, p. 36, ta)

> gavés de lait, de riz, de tomates et d'oranges (BI, p. 31); gorged on milk, rice, tomatoes and oranges (LBI, p. 37, ta)

> se gavant de glace à l'ananas (BI, p. 38); stuffing themselves with pineapple ice (LBI, p. 47)

> elle se gave de tranquillisants (BI, p. 143); she stuffs herself with tranquillizers (LBI, p. 174)

The horrific present is linked with Jean-Charles's utopic vision of the future, which is linked with an apparently idyllic family meal, which is in turn linked with Dominique's pain and despair. The resonance of this series of repetitions is intensified by the central importance of food and eating in the symbolic landscape in *Les Belles Images*. The term 'se gaver' is remindful of Laurence's plight; or, rather, her words as she lies in bed will recall these earlier instances of force feeding: 'Ils la forceront à manger, ils lui feront tout avaler [...]'(BI, p. 180); 'They will force her to eat, they'll make her swallow it all [...] (LBI, p. 219, ta).

Also in relation to meaning, it is interesting to note how repetition in *Les Belles Images* is used to confer symbolic significance on certain words. Paradoxically, through repetition, words not only can lose their meaning but also come to mean

---

Derrida has shown how every text possesses a number of different contexts. See Moi, *Sexual/Textual Politics*, p. 155.

[35] Repetition of what Dominique said to Laurence underlines the acute pain she feels. This is further reinforced by the use of direct speech. Laurence is 'hearing' her mother's voice in her mind.

'Tu n'imagines pas le plaisir que ça lui a fait.' (Dominique, BI, p. 177)

'Tu n'imagines pas le plaisir que ça lui a fait.' (Laurence, BI, p. 180)

more than themselves. Beauvoir's choice of objects as banal as a safety pin suggests she wished to challenge accepted notions of objects worthy of symbolic status. Through accumulated references the safety pin, rich in childhood and maternal connotations, comes to stand for the true friendship that Laurence has never known and which Jean-Charles believes to be inappropriate for his daughter. When Laurence first meets Catherine's new friend, the the first thing she notices is the large safety pin in the hem of her skirt. Initially, for Laurence it designates Brigitte as a motherless child (and betrays her as an unsuitable friend in terms of the accepted values of her milieu); Laurence is moved to want to do something for her and offers to sew the hem of her skirt. When Brigitte refuses, Laurence nevertheless rearranges the pin in a tender maternal gesture:

> J'ai allumé, Brigitte s'est levée: 'Bonjour, m'dame.' J'ai tout de suite remarqué la grosse épingle de nourrice plantée dans l'ourlet de sa jupe: une enfant sans mère [...]. (BI, p. 53)

> I switched on the light. Brigitte got up.'*Bonjour m'dame.*' Straight away I noticed the the big safety-pin stuck in the hem of her skirt – a child without a mother [...]. (LBI, p. 64)

> – Laissez-moi au moins arranger l'épingle. (BI, p. 55)

> 'At least let me sort out the pin.' (LBI, p. 67, ta)

She feels instinctively protective toward her daughter's friend; she knows she does not want Jean-Charles to meet her but cannot (decides not to) articulate why. In protecting Brigitte, Laurence also protects her daughter by shielding the friendship, the kind of friendship she herself never had as a child. The safety pin rescues yet threatens and betrays, is safe yet a weapon, stands for a mother's absence yet offers maternal tenderness. The safety pin is still in the hem of Brigitte's skirt when Laurence takes the children to the Musée de l'Homme ('l'épingle était encore plantée dans la jupe de Brigitte,' BI, p. 78), and Brigitte is embarrassed when she spots Laurence looking at it. Later, Laurence, now in emotional crisis, remembers the safety pin and the connection with genuine friendship is made explicit: 'Je revois Brigitte, l'épingle fichée dans son ourlet: "Bonjour, m'dame"; et le noeud se reserre dans ma gorge. C'est précieux une amitié' (BI, p. 172); 'I can still see Brigitte, with the pin stuck in her hem – '*Bonjour m'dame.*' And the knot tightens in my throat. It is a precious thing, a friendship' (LBI, p. 209). Friendship, the 'safety pin' that holds together and keeps safe, could have prevented Laurence's breakdown: 'Si j'avais une amie, je lui parlerais au lieu de rester prostrée' (BI, p. 172); 'If I had a friend, I'd talk to her instead of being left prostrate (LBI, p. 209, ta).

Subtle changes, when utterances are echoed rather than repeated, can be extremely eloquent; they are an economical way of marking the progression in Laurence's frame of mind. The nature of her uncertainty changes. On the very first page of the text we read:

Qu'est-ce que les autres ont que je n'ai pas? (BI, p. 7)

What have the others got that I haven't? (LBI, p. 9)

Then a few pages later:

(mais qu'ont-ils que je n'ai pas non plus?) (BI, p. 14)

(but what have they got that I haven't either?) (LBI, p. 18, ta)

And then:

Et de nouveau Laurence se demande: qu'ont-ils que je n'ai pas? (BI, p. 19)

And again Laurence wonders what have the others got that I haven't? (LBI, p. 23, ta)

This becomes:

Il me manque quelque chose que les autres ont ... A moins ... A moins qu'ils ne l'aient pas non plus. (BI, p. 83)

I lack something that other people have ... Unless ... Unless they haven't got it either (LBI, p. 102, ta)

Then, finally:

Est-ce moi qui suis anormale? une anxieuse, une angoissée: qu'est-ce que j'ai qu'ils n'ont pas? (BI, p. 150)

Am I the one who's abnormal? a worrier, over-anxious: what have I got that they haven't? (LBI, p. 182, ta)

Repetition underlines Laurence's revision of her position; she moves from uncertainty through tentative doubt/hope to certainty as she realises that her father is like everyone else:

Ce secret qu'elle se reprochait de n'avoir pas su découvrir, peut-être qu'après tout il n'existait pas. Il n'existait pas: elle le sait depuis la Grèce. (BI, p. 179)

The secret she blamed herself for not being able to find out, perhaps after all it didn't exist. It didn't exist. She has known since the trip to Greece. (LBI, p. 218, ta)

There is a similar progression with regard to her perception of Jean-Charles. It centres around his reaction to the car accident when Laurence swerves to avoid a young cyclist. Words echo in the text as they echo in Laurence's mind, replicating her obsession:

– La voiture est en miettes. (BI, p. 102)

'The car's wrecked.' (LBI, p. 124)

'Je ne trouve vraiment pas ça malin; nous n'avons qu'une assurance tierce-collision.' [...] – Tout le monde aurait témoigné en ta faveur. Il a dit ça sans en penser un mot [...]. (BI, p. 103)

'It really doesn't seem very clever to me. We only have a third-party-collision policy.' [...] Everybody would have given evidence in your favour.' He said that without really believing a word of it [...]. (LBI, p. 125)

'La voiture est en miettes.' (BI, p. 109)

'The car's wrecked.' (LBI, p. 132)

'Je ne trouve ça vraiment pas malin; nous n'avons qu'une assurance tierce-collision ... Tout le monde aurait témoigné en ta faveur.' Et elle réalise en un éclair qu'il ne plaisantait pas. (BI, p. 134)

'It really doesn't seem very clever to me. We only have a third-party-collision policy.' Everybody would have given evidence in your favour.' And in a flash she realised that he was not joking. (LBI, p. 163)

'Jean-Charles ne plaisantait pas.' Combien de fois s'est-elle répété cette phrase pendant cette semaine? Elle se la répète encore. (BI, p. 150)

'Jean-Charles was not joking.' How many times has she repeated that to herself in the course of this week? She's still repeating it. (LBI, p. 182, ta)

As Laurence tells her story her feelings change, and she becomes gradually more aware of her true feelings:

– Mais si, je l'aime bien [Gilbert]. (L'aime-t-elle ou non? elle aime tout le monde.) (BI, p. 18)

'Not at all, I'm fond of him [Gilbert].' (Was she fond of him or not? She was fond of everybody.) (LBI, p. 23, ta)

'J'ai toujours détesté Gilbert.' (BI, p. 48)

'I always loathed Gilbert' (LBI, p. 58)

[Lucien] lui a redit hier avec reproche: 'Tu n'aimes personne!' Est-ce vrai? Mais non. Je l'aime bien. Je vais rompre avec lui, mais je l'aime bien. J'aime bien tout le monde. Sauf Gilbert. (BI, p. 87)

Yesterday [Lucien] had said, with blame in his voice, 'You don't love anyone!' Is that true? Not at all. I'm fond of him. I'm going to break up with him, but I'm fond of him. I'm fond of everyone. Except Gilbert. (LBI, p. 106, ta)

[...] incapable d'aimer. (BI, p. 176)

[...] incapable of loving. (LBI, p. 213, ta)

Qu'a-t-on fait de moi? Cette femme qui n'aime personne [...] incapable même de pleurer [...]. (BI, p. 181)[36]

What have they turned me into? This woman who loves no one [...] incapable even of crying [...]. (LBI, p. 219, ta)

This progression also undermines any notion of truth as an absolute. Just as meanings are never fixed once and for all, truth can never be immutable. It is not so much that Laurence moves from a position of ignorance and error to knowledge and truth but that what is true changes.

At the height of Laurence's crisis, repetition underlines connections between the past and the present. 'J'ai été *déçue*' (I was disappointed) (BI, p. 179) becomes 'Je suis déçue' (I am disappointed) (BI, p. 180). The words in Laurence's head are voiced: 'Je ne permettrai pas qu'on lui fasse ce qu'on m'a fait' (BI, pp. 180–81) becomes her defiant ultimatum to Jean-Charles ' – On ne lui fera pas ce qu'on m'a fait' (BI, p. 181). ('I won't let them them do the same thing to her as they've done to me.' 'They won't do the same thing to her as they've done to me.' LBI, pp. 219, ta)

Repetition exemplifies Laurence's powerlessness, the trap in which she is caught. However profound her disagreements with Jean-Charles, there is no way out: 'Quoi qu'il fasse, ou dise, quoi qu'elle dise ou fasse, il n'y aura pas de sanction' (BI, p. 137); ' Whatever he did or said, whatever she said or did, there would be no penalty' (LBI, p. 166). This repetition combined with reversal suggests the net in which Laurence is caught. The hopelessness of her predicament is evoked by the repetition that occurs when she wonders why she decided to end her relationship with Lucien: 'Pourquoi avait-elle décidé de faire le vide dans sa vie, d'épargner son temps, ses forces, son coeur alors qu'elle ne sait trop quoi faire de son temps, ses forces, son coeur?' (BI, p. 146); 'Why had she decided to make empty space in her life, to economize her time, her energy, her emotions when she is by no means sure what to do with her time, her energy, her emotions? (LBI, p. 177, ta). The repetition of the terms 'trop,' 'vide,' and 'remplie' in apparent disorder in the next sentences exemplifies Laurence's befuddlement: 'Vie trop remplie? trop vide? Remplie de choses vides. Quelle confusion!' (BI, p. 146); 'Too full a life? Too empty? Full of empty things. What confusion!' (LBI, p. 177, ta).

A further, specific use of repetition in *Les Belles Images* occurs particularly in the early part of the book. Laurence, alienated and unsure of herself, echoes those around her, holding onto the language of others in an attempt to anchor herself, to gain some semblance of stability. Sometimes this echoing/imitation is conspicuous:

---

[36]   The reader also recalls what Laurence said earlier: 'Moi aussi, à son âge, je pleurais: comme j'ai pleuré! C'est peut-être pour ça que je ne pleure plus jamais' (BI, p. 25); 'I cried too, at her age: how I cried! Perhaps that's why I never cry any more now' (LBI, p. 31).

– Merveilleuse, dit Marthe avec ferveur.
– Merveilleuse, répète Laurence. (BI, p. 14)

'Wonderful,' said Marthe fervently.
'Wonderful,' repeated Laurence. (LBI, p. 18, ta)

– Un week-end vraiment réussi! dit Jean-Charles.
– Vraiment réussi. (BI, p. 19)

'A thoroughly successful weekend!' said Jean-Charles.
'Thoroughly successful.' (LBI, p. 23)

At other times, echoing is less foregrounded. For example, at Feuverolles, Laurence unwittingly echoes Dominique, though she has just been irritated by her mother's phraseology; 'c'est d'un banal ...' (so banal) (applied by Dominique to Florence and Granada twenty years earlier, and now used in connection with Tahiti which she likens to Saint-Tropez) is echoed by Laurence in her comment on the Paris suburbs, 'c'est d'un déprimant!' (so depressing) (BI, p. 10).[37] When Laurence goes to Dominique, who has been physically maltreated by Gilbert, her words are a direct echo of those used by her colleague, Mona, with regard to aggressive male drivers, 'ce sont des brutes' (they're brutes) (BI, pp. 86 and 124).[38] Once, when speaking to Mona, she becomes aware of what she is doing and stops herself:

> C'est une détente ... Elle allait dire machinalement: indispensable, elle s'est reprise à temps. Elle entend la voix de Gilbert: "Une détente indispensable" [...]. (BI, p. 69)

> It's a way of relaxing ... She was on the point of bringing out an automatic 'that's essential.' She heard Gilbert's voice, 'A way of relaxing that's essential.' (LBI, p. 84, ta)

Laurence's behaviour is especially interesting in the light of the way the text explicitly and insistently associates imitating with Dominique:

> Qui imite-t-elle en ce moment? C'est une scie, entre eux, cette question que posait Freud à propos d'une hystérique. Le fait est que Dominique imite toujours quelqu'un. (BI, p. 34)

> 'Who is she copying at present?' It was an old gag between them, this question of Freud's about an hysteric. The fact was that Dominique was always imitating somebody. (LBI, p. 42)

---

[37]   Fallaize also discusses this example. *The Novels*, pp. 126–7. The echo is missing from the English translation (pp. 12–13).

[38]   This echo is lost in the English translation where 'brute' is rendered as 'sod' (LBI, p. 105) and 'swine' (LBI, p. 151).

(qui imite-t-elle?). (BI, p. 88)

(who was she copying?). (LBI, p. 107)

Imitant toujours quelqu'un faute de savoir inventer des conduites adaptées aux circonstances. (BI, p. 125)

Always copying someone because she couldn't come up with the right behaviour for a particular set of circumstances. (LBI, p. 152, ta)

Qui imitait-elle? la femme qu'elle souhaitait devenir? (BI, p. 176)

Who was she copying? The woman she wanted to become? (LBI, p. 214)

Laurence, like Dominique, lacking any inner conviction about who she is and how she should be, looks to her entourage in search of models. She echoes and imitates others as the text echoes and imitates itself.

Having considered language and meaning in *Les Belles Images*, I now explore disruption and instability in the text of the novel. One of the most unstable and unsettling aspects of *Les Belles Images* is the way the narrative voice shifts from 'je' to 'elle' ('I' to 'she').[39] This split, which is at the heart of the narrative, duplicates, on a textual level, Laurence's loss of psychic unity and feelings of alienation. First-and third-person narratives alternate not only from paragraph to paragraph but also within paragraphs and even within sentences. Let us consider the opening scenes. The novel seems to open in the first person, at least; the only indicators of the origin of narrative voice are in the first person ('Qu'est-ce que les autres ont que je n'ai pas?' 'Pourquoi est-ce que je pense ça?').[40] Then, after the first long, fragmented paragraph, the narrative shifts to the third person ('Laurence a proposé le test du passeur [...]' BI, p. 8),[41] before shifting back to the first person within a sentence: 'Elle s'est beaucoup dépensée, c'est pour ça que maintenant elle se sent déprimée, je suis cyclique' (BI, p. 8); 'She's spent a lot of energy, that's why she feels depressed now, I'm cyclic' (LBI, p. 10, ta). As the narrative continues, mainly in the third person, the first-person narrative interposes a commentary on it. Laurence makes a self-conscious revision of the witty reply she gave to Gilbert: '(Ce n'est pas vrai, en fait. Je dis ça pour être drôle.)' BI, p. 12; '(That is not really true. I'm saying it to be funny)' (LBI, p. 16). Subsequently, her unspoken response to the effusive terms her sister uses to speak of their father breaks up the third-person narrative once more:

---

[39]   Strictly speaking, narration as such does not fall within the terms of reference of this study. Comments on the narrative situation in *Les Belles Images* are restricted to a consideration of how the text is unsettled/disrupted by shifts in narrative voice.

[40]   These might well, of course, be taken for first-person interpolations in a third-person narrative.

[41]   The psychological test, *le test du passeur* (the ferryman's test), is described by Fallaize in *The Novels*, p. 141, footnote 21.

> Laurence se penche sur les dahlias; ce langage la gêne. Bien sûr, il a quelque
> chose que les autres n'ont pas, que je n'ai pas (mais qu'ont-ils que je n'ai pas
> non plus?). Roses, rouges, jaunes, orangés, elle serre dans la main les dahlias
> magnifiques. (BI, p. 14)

> Laurence bends over the dahlias: this kind of talk embarasses her: certainly he
> has something that other people don't possess, that I don't possess (but what
> have they got that I haven't either?). Pink, red, yellow, orange, she grips the
> splendid dahlias in her hand. (LBI, p.18, ta)

Then Laurence's looking out of the window and seeing Jean-Charles flirting with
Gisèle Dufrène seem to be narrated in the first person (BI, p. 17). Here, as in
the first paragraph, this is what the only indicators imply. The narrative shifts to
the first person again as Laurence recalls her breakdown of five years earlier and
tries to convince herself that she is not about to be ill again: 'Maintenant je
n'ai pas de raison de craquer. Toujours du travail devant moi, des gens autour
de moi, je suis contente de ma vie. Non, aucun danger. C'est juste une question
d'humeur' (BI, p. 19); 'Now there's no reason for me to break down. I have as
much work as I can do, people around me, I'm satisfied with my life. No, not
the least danger. It's just a question of mood' (LBI, p. 24, ta). These shifts and
ambiguities present in the opening section of the novel are replicated throughout
the text. However, by the final chapter, the balance has shifted.

Here, the first person narrative is much stronger, more sustained, and it is
the third-person narrative that appears to intrude. Laurence determines: 'Je
récapitulerai ce voyage image par image, mot par mot' (BI, p. 153); 'I'll go back
over the trip picture by picture, word by word' (LBI, p. 186, ta). She engages with
and tells her own story in the first person. The third person breaks into the text in
the present moment when Laurence breaks off her retrospective narrative to drink
the soup Marthe has brought her and to speak to Jean-Charles (BI, pp. 168–70),
and again, very briefly, at the point in the narrative when Laurence gets back from
the trip. Her alienation is perfectly conveyed by the shift as Jean-Charles meets
her at the airport (BI, p. 170). From this point, 'elle' (she) erupts in the the most
painful moments of Laurence's story, when, during the family dinner, Jean-Charles
discusses Catherine (BI, p. 173) and when Laurence becomes aware of her utter
isolation (BI, pp. 175–76). Although Laurence's finding out about her parents'
reconciliation from Dominique is narrated in the first person, her painful meeting
with her father, where he confirms it is true, is narrated in the third person. So, too,
is Laurence's taking to her bed. As Laurence's anguish reaches its climax, and as
text-time and storytime reconverge (storytime and narrative moment coincide),
the narrative voice oscillates between 'elle' and 'je' ('I' and 'she'):

> Je suis jalouse mais surtout, surtout ... Elle respire trop vite, elle halète. [...]
> Ce secret qu'elle se reprochait de n'avoir pas su découvrir, peut-être qu'après
> tout il n'existait pas. Il n'existait pas: elle le sait depuis la Grèce. J'ai été *déçue*.
> Le mot la poignarde. Elle serre le mouchoir contre ses dents comme pour
> arrêter le cri qu'elle est incapable de pousser. Je suis déçue. J'ai raison de l'être.
> (BI, pp. 179–80)

I'm jealous but above all, above all ... She's breathing too fast, she's panting. [...] The secret she blamed herself for not being able to find out, perhaps after all it didn't exist. It didn't exist. She has known since the trip to Greece. I was *disappointed*. The word stabs her. She presses her handkerchief against her teeth as though to hold back the cry she is incapable of uttering. I am disappointed. I have cause to be. (LBI, pp. 217–18 ta)

Laurence's battle to face up to her pain is reproduced in the text as 'je' and 'elle' ('I' and 'she') succeed each other. When the narrative is picked up again as Laurence wakes from exhausted sleep, the first-person voice fades once more and the narrative reverts to 'elle' ('she') for the final three pages that relate Laurence's talk with Jean-Charles. The first person asserts itself only once: 'Il n'a pas envie que je craque de nouveau. Si je tiens bon, je gagne' (BI, p. 182); 'He doesn't want me to crack up again. If I hold out, I'll win' (LBI, p. 221, ta). The intermittency of the first person voice at the end of *Les Belles Images* contributes to readers' lack of confidence in Laurence's stability and sense of self.

The je/elle split that clearly unsettles the text has been addressed and understood differently by a number of critics. It is clear that Laurence is both character in and, at times, first-person narrator of her story. Doubt arises over the user of the third person also present in the text. I believe this, too, can be taken to be Laurence as, alienated from herself, she watches herself act and speak like she watches those around her, 'soudain indifférente, distante, comme si elle n'était pas des leurs' ('suddenly indifferent, remote, as though she didn't belong') (BI, p.19; LBI, pp. 23–24, ta). She is divided against herself and, struggling to hold on to her sense of identity, incapable of sustaining her 'I.'[42] The fact that the first-person voice is more sustained in the early sections of the final chapter, together with the pattern of third-person erruptions into the narrative, add support to this reading as it makes psychological sense. Laurence relives the trip and her homecoming not distanced from herself. As she says of the trip: 'Tout ce qui m'arrivait était vrai' (BI, p. 155); 'Everything that was happening to me was real' (LBI, p. 188). Laurence's 'I' is stifled in moments of overwhelming pain as if she withdraws and has recourse to the third person in order to protect herself. The dominant use of the third person in the narrative present accords with her overriding sense of alienation.

An alternative explanation is that the user of the third person is an external narrative agent. In this version of the narrative situation, we are dealing with two narrative agents, and it is not just Laurence's 'I' that emerges only intermittently; it is her voice too. This is the view of Elizabeth Fallaize, who argues that 'though Laurence's is the *consciousness* which the narrative draws on, her *voice* is intermittent, fading for long stretches of the narrative in which the character apparently retrenches behind her social persona, and reasserting itself at moments where the character seems to approach something resembling self-awareness.'[43]

---

[42]   Jane Heath also argues that Laurence occupies both the first-person and third-person narrative positions. See Heath, p. 128.

[43]   Fallaize, *The Novels*, p. 120.

These different readings are not mutually exclusive. What is of crucial importance is precisely the ambiguity of the narrative situation, the fact that it is fluid, impossible to pin down. The je/elle split unsettles and destabilises the text and enacts its madness.

I now want to address the incoherence that stems from fragmentation and interruption. The first page of the novel introduces readers into a disorienting textual universe. Laurence's monologue is fragmented by dialogue, which is in turn fragmented by Laurence's reflections, thus bringing about what Irène M. Pagès calls a 'desubstantification of the real,' making what is real insubstantial.[44] She shows convincingly how the first paragraph of *Les Belles Images* consists of a monologue interrupted by direct speech and narrative comment.[45] However, there are, I believe, problems with her analysis. It is not clear how 'outside concrete reality can be either negated or confirmed according to the level to which punctuation assigns it within the story' or how Laurence '"empties" the existence of others of all reality' (BI, p. 138) simply by commenting ironically or otherwise on it. Desubstantification cannot be a function of the status of an utterance as indicated by punctuation nor of the purport of a remark. Rather, it comes about as a result of fragmentation and exists on a textual level. It is a function of a textual practice that deprives both descriptive monologue and interpolations of coherence and meaningfulness.[46] This effect is felt in the shocking (from an unprepared reader's point of view) opening paragraph and, subsequently, at different moments throughout the narrative. In the same way that Laurence's personality disintegrates, so, too, does the text. In the same way that her sense of the real becomes more fragile, readers experience the dissolution of the real on a textual level.

Other textual strategies undermine the coherence of the narrative in a similar way. Fragmented/interrupted dialogues are drained of sense. Conversations already under way are picked up and cut off as Laurence's attention wanders. As the narrative recounts one Saturday evening at Feuverolles, an excerpt from a conversation about chic restaurants between Dominique and an anonymous interlocutor (there are no

---

[44]   Irène M. Pagès, 'Beauvoir's *Les Belles images*: "Desubtantification" of Reality Through a Narrative,' *Forum For Modern Language Studies*, 11 (1975), 133–41.

[45]   Pagès, '"Desubtantification" of Reality,' p. 137.

[46]   There are other, more minor, problems with Pagès's argument. Her comments relate to the French text, yet the passage is quoted in her article in an English translation with its different punctuation (p. 138). More seriously, there appears to be some confusion as to whether the different levels of narration she has distinguished are in direct or indirect speech. At first, Pagès suggests that the descriptive part of Laurence's monologue is in direct speech and that the speech of others and Laurence's thoughts are in indirect speech (p. 137). This is not the case; the fact that both levels of narration are in direct speech actually adds to the incoherence of the passage and the disorientation of readers. As Pagès develops her argument, she begins, bafflingly, to refer to the direct speech of the second level of narration. Her assertion that 'in *Les Belles images* the dialogues always take place between Laurence and one of the characters whose existence is part of her own' (p. 135) is simply not true. Laurence repeatedly listens in to the dialogues and conversations of others (see BI, pp. 90–94, 97, 99, 144, 145, 146–7, 149).

reporting clauses) is superseded by a snatch of conversation between Jean-Charles and Dufrène before Laurence's attention is caught once more by Dominique's voice and, midway, her conversation becomes the focus of the narrative again (BI, pp. 92–3). As the guests interrupt one another, the conversation is represented with no typographical clues that it is in fact a dialogue. The distinction between dialogue and narrative is blurred. Two long sentences contain all the contradictory utterances of all of the participants in the conversation. There are, of course, no reporting clauses:

> Avouez qu'il y a des livres qu'on ne peut plus écrire, des films qu'on ne peut plus voir, des musiques qu'on ne peut plus entendre, mais les chefs-d'oeuvre, ça ne date jamais, qu'est-ce qu'un chef d'oeuvre? Il faudrait éliminer les critères subjectifs, c'est impossible, pardon c'est l'effort de toute la critique moderne, et les critères des Goncourt et des Renaudot, je voudrais les connaître, les prix sont encore plus mauvais que l'année dernière, [...] mais non il n'y a pas d'autre critère, de critère objectif. (BI, pp. 94–5)

> You must admit there are books that can no longer be written, films that no one can watch any more, music that can't be listened to, but masterpieces are never dated, what is a masterpiece? Subjective criteria ought to be got rid of, it's impossible, excuse me all modern criticism is tending in that direction, what about the criteria for the Goncourt and the Renaudot, I'd like to know what they are, the winners are even worse than last year, [...] not at all there's no other criterion, no objective criterion. (LBI, pp.114–15, ta)

This irreverent representation of the conversation conveys the jostling of the guests for space to speak. Incoherence is exacerbated as toward the end of the paragraph the conversation seems to split into two parallel conversations happening simultaneously, the final comment apparently a response to an opinion expressed six inputs earlier, or perhaps it is simply the comment of someone unable to force their way into the conversation until now. Unorthodox punctuation (most commas are omitted within what I take to be individual utterances or contributions to the conversation) adds to the impression of speed. The text races on until a fervent remark from Madame Thiron stops everyone in their tracks and the text is brought to an abrupt halt. Not for long, it appears: 'Puis ils repartent ...' ('then they set off again ...') (BI, p. 95; LBI, p. 115, ta); this time, Laurence does not bother even to listen. The representation of dialogue at the New Year's Eve party is equally unsettling/disorienting for readers. Again, dialogue is incorporated into the text with no typological clues: 'Brouhaha, bruit de vaisselle, c'est délicieux, servez-vous mieux' (BI, p. 145); 'Hubbub, clattering crockery, it's delicious, take more than that' (LBI, p. 176, ta). The text makes it clear that there is nothing to choose between dialogue and the clatter of crockery. Once more, readers are dependent on Laurence's attention, and it is not sustained for long. The dialogue that is about wine (BI, p. 145), when Laurence's thoughts drift to last year's party and to Lucien, has shifted to astrology by the time Laurence tunes into the conversation again. In this section of the text, too, dialogue is fragmented. The representation of a snatch of conversation between Laurence's father and Dufrène about literature and art consists of the former's utterance in direct speech, intercalated with Laurence's observations (new paragraph) and then Dufrène's response in elliptical-free direct discourse (new paragraph). His response is not distinguished from the rest of the long paragraph in which it is subsumed: 'L'abstrait ne se vend plus; mais le figuratif non plus, crise de la peinture, que voulez-vous, il y a une telle inflation. Rabâchages. Laurence s'ennuie' (BI, p. 150); 'Abstract art doesn't sell any more; but nor does figurative art, crisis in painting, what do you expect, there's such inflation. The same old thing. Laurence is bored (LBI, p. 182, ta).[47]

Incoherence also derives from the fact that the text is multilayered. Repeatedly, Laurence distances herself to make an observation, then distances herself again to comment on her observation, then again to comment on her comment. This is disconcerting for readers. Encountering such layering in the text, this 'jeu de miroirs,' with its concomitant contradictoriness, readers will share Laurence's uncertainty and, ultimately, her distress. Multilayering is conspicuous in Laurence's reflections on how her mother is perceived. She rejects the view that Dominique owes her successful career to Gilbert and goes on:

> Ils disent aussi, Gisèle Dufrène le pense, que maman a mis le grappin sur Gilbert par intérêt: cette maison, ses voyages, sans lui elle n'aurait pas pu se les offrir, soit; mais c'est autre chose qu'il lui a apporté; elle était tout de même désemparée après avoir quitté papa (il errait dans la maison comme une âme en peine, avec quelle dureté elle est partie aussitôt Marthe mariée); c'est grâce à Gilbert qu'elle est devenue cette femme tellement sûre d'elle. (Évidemment, on pourrait dire ...) (BI, p. 9)

> They say – and Gisèle Dufrène certainly thinks it – that Mama hooked Gilbert with an eye to the main chance: all right, so she could never have afforded this house and her travelling without him; but what he gave her was something quite different. After all she was terribly at a loss after leaving Papa (he wandered about the house like a soul in torment: how callously she walked out the minute Marthe was married), and it was thanks to Gilbert that she became this completely self-assured woman. (Of course, you could say ...) (LBI, pp. 11–12)

In this example, the intrusion of a memory breaks up the text. Inconclusiveness is heightened as Laurence's thoughts are interrupted by the return of Hubert and Marthe from their walk in the forest. Likewise, multilayering characterises the text as Laurence and Jean-Charles drive away from Feuverolles and discuss Gilbert. Laurence's response to Jean-Charles's observation that it is natural she should dislike Gilbert is marked by plurality: ' – Mais si, je l'aime bien. (L'aime-t-elle ou non? elle aime tout le monde.) Gilbert ne pérore pas, c'est vrai, se dit-elle.

---

[47]   The distinction between dialogue and narrative is also blurred on BI, p. 32 (quoted above), where the representation of Laurence's conversations with Lucien has a pantomime quality. See also BI, pp. 66–7, where Jean-Charles's remarks on architecture are interrupted by a whole page of Laurence's reflections on relationships and her marriage before they begin again, only to be interrupted immediately by the doorbell ringing.

Mais personne n'ignore qu'il dirige une des plus grandes sociétés de machines électroniques du monde [...]' (BI, p. 18); '"Not at all, I'm fond of him." (Was she fond of him or not? She was fond of everybody.) Gilbert doesn't hold forth, she said to herself. But everyone knows that he runs one of the biggest electronics companies in the world [...]' (LBI, p. 23, ta). Multilayering can obscure the boundary between the real and the imaginary. An interesting example occurs at the point in the text where Laurence finds Dominique devastated after a violent confrontation with Gilbert:

> Gilbert a sonné à dix heures, elle a cru que c'était le concierge, elle a ouvert. Patricia a tout de suite été pleurer dans les bras de Gilbert, et Lucile criait, il a refermé la porte derrière lui d'un coup de pied, il caressait les cheveux de Patricia, si tendrement, avec une voix apaisante, et là dans l'antichambre il l'avait insultée, giflée, il l'avait saisie par le col du peignoir bleu et traînée dans la chambre. (BI, p. 124)

> Gilbert rang the doorbell at ten o'clock, she thought it was the concierge, she opened the door. Patricia went straight to Gilbert to cry in his arms, and Lucile was shouting, he kicked the door shut behind him, he stroked Patricia's hair, so tenderly, soothed her, and there in the hall he'd shouted at her, slapped her, he'd grabbed her by the collar of her blue dressing-gown and dragged her into the bedroom. (LBI, p. 150, ta)

The text acquires a hallucinatory quality as two narratives are blended in one, the receipt of the letter by Gilbert's new lover and his visit to Dominique. The passage is marked by abrupt shifts in tone, a convulsive rhythm. Reported in the third person, the events are nevertheless implicitly recounted by Dominique herself. (The account is enclosed between '[Dominique] parle d'une voix qui n'appartient à personne' (she speaks in a voice that belongs to no one) and 'la voix de Dominique s'étouffe' (Dominique's voice is stifled).) Thus the narrative situation that prevails in the novel as a whole is paralleled here in this narrative within a narrative.[48]

The passages I have been quoting to illustrate the incoherence that is the product of fragmentation and multilayering make it clear that the use of brackets and dashes and the use of ellipses and silences and breaks in tone have been instrumental in disrupting the text and fostering incoherence in *Les Belles Images*. Moving closer to the text as it were, I now focus specifically on these textual strategies. On a typographical level, the markers, ( ), – , and ... conspicuously fracture the text. Virtually no page of the novel is without them. With regard to meaningfulness and madness, they function in a number of different ways.

The narrative is disrupted by Laurence's observations that are frequently separated from the rest of the narrative by brackets or dashes. However, there is

---

[48]   The real and the imaginary also become conflated as Laurence is at once observer and participant, subject and object, in what might be a scene from an advertisement that is cut through by the advertising text she is thinking up BI, pp. 20–21. See also BI, p. 175, the moment when Laurence is forced to recognise her powerlessness in the face of the united opposition of everyone else.

no consistent pattern. Not all asides are isolated typographically, and comments that appear in brackets at one point in the narrative may appear without brackets at another. On the whole, it appears that asides between dashes are informative; they are often stage directions, or clichéd interjections, whereas brackets tend to contain more emotionally charged memories and intimate thoughts, feelings, and ideas that have no place in Laurence's milieu. A significant proportion of the parentheses are questions, which adds to the tentative tone of the text. However, once more, there is no consistency, and exceptions to the pattern I am suggesting are easily found. Perhaps that is the important point. Readers seek to impose a pattern, to make sense of the text only to be repeatedly thwarted and frustrated as the pattern they expect to find is upset. They encounter a disrupted text, and the disruption itself resists order and logic.

Readers' expectations can be disappointed to dramatic effect. For example, when Jean-Charles is determined to end Catherine's friendship with Brigitte, a comment that we might have anticipated would appear in brackets erupts directly into the text: 'Du cheval! ça c'était une idée formidable; même affectivement. Remplacer une amie par un cheval!' (BI, p. 172); 'Horse riding! what a great idea; even from the emotional point of view. Replace a friend by a horse!' (LBI, p. 209, ta). It is as if Laurence's anger toward Jean-Charles is so intense that it cannot be contained within brackets; it has broken through all Laurence's defences. The exclamation marks (relatively rare in *Les Belles Images*) add to the impression of a surge of powerful emotion.

Notwithstanding the instability of the patterns of parentheses in the text, their use gives rise to a number of interesting conjectures. The use of brackets can be linked with Laurence's sense of alienation. Her apartness is reproduced on a textual level; not all her thoughts can be incorporated in her narrative. I have suggested that the asides in brackets tend to be more emotionally charged, which fits in with Freud's belief that obsessional or unthinkable thoughts can be faced without affect because they are isolated or bracketed off.[49] It may be that, on occasion, Laurence brackets off the painful and unstabilising, that in this way she protects herself. This idea finds some support in the distribution of brackets in the narrative. In the final chapter of *Les Belles Images*, there are significantly fewer parentheses. It is in this chapter that Laurence faces her disappointment and so pain and affect are no longer bracketed off. What was repressed becomes conscious and is therefore included in narrative. As Nicole Ward Jouve said of Hélène Cixous's texts, *Les Belles Images* might be said to display 'the inner logic of a psychoanalytic cure.'[50]

---

[49]   'Inhibitions, Symptoms and Anxiety,' (1926), *The Complete Psychological Works of Sigmund Freud*, Volume XX (1925–1926), pp. 87–175 (pp. 119–21). In his discussion of the technique of isolating, a variation of repression, Freud argues that in obsessional neurosis, a traumatic experience cannot be forgotten as it can be in hysteria. Instead, 'it is deprived of its affect and associative connections are suppressed or interrupted so that it remains as though isolated and is not reproduced in the ordinary processes of thought' (p. 120).

[50]   Nicole Ward Jouve in 'Hélène Cixous: From Inner Theatre to World Theatre' in *White Woman Speaks with Forked tongue: Criticism as Autobiography*, ed. by Nicole Ward

At other times, brackets and dashes are a way of indicating intonation; they introduce voice into the text. It is not only the case that we 'hear' Laurence's voice in the narrative. The intonation of voices she hears is marked in the text, too. The cadence of Thirion's speech, for instance, is patent:

> – Qu'est-ce que je pense de mes consoeurs, petite madame? dit-il à Gisèle. Le plus grand bien; beaucoup sont des femmes charmantes et beaucoup ont du talent (en général ce ne sont pas les mêmes). Mais une chose est sûre: jamais aucune ne sera capable de plaider aux Assises. Elles n'ont pas le coffre, ni l'autorité, ni – je vais vous étonner – le sens théâtral nécessaire. (BI, p. 99)

> 'What do I think of my woman colleagues, my dear lady?' he said to Gisèle. 'I have the highest opinion of them: many are quite charming and many are talented (generally speaking they are not the same ones). But one thing is certain: there is not one of them who will ever be able to argue a case before the assizes. They have not the necessary weight, nor authority, nor – and this will surprise you – the necessary theatrical feeling. (LBI, p. 120)

Ellipsis too, is a disruptive strategy that functions in a number of different ways in the text. In every case, ellipsis disrupts the narrative and creates blanks (empty spaces) in the text, spaces where meaning, unexpressed, can expand. It opens up the text. In some cases, it is a device that enhances the subjective realism of the text. It can simply mark the interruption of Laurence's thoughts by an event in the story. For example, in the opening scenes at Feuverolles: '(Évidemment, on pourrait dire ...)/Hubert et Marthe reviennent de la forêt [...]' (BI, p. 9); '(Of course, you could say ...)/Hubert and Marthe come back from the forest [...]' (LBI, p. 12).[51] Ellipsis repeatedly marks Laurence's or another character's breaking off one train of thought to pursue another. For example, Laurence represents to herself how Dominique might cope with Gilbert's rejection then imagines forewarning her mother: 'Elle se jettera dans le travail, elle prendra un nouvel amant ... Et si j'allais moi-même la prévenir, tout de suite?' (BI, p. 48); 'She will fling herself into work, take a new lover ... Suppose I were to go and warn her, right away?' (LBI, p. 59). Here, Laurence is paralysed by indecision and fear, 'motionless at the wheel of her car' (BI, p. 48; LBI, p. 59). Correspondingly, ellipsis marks a character's breaking off a train of thought to speak as when Laurence leaves off her appraisal of Dominique's character to urge her mother to get ready to go out: 'On la prend pour une femme de tête, maîtresse de soi, efficace .../ – Habille-toi, répète Laurence. Mets des lunettes noires et je t'emmène déjeuner quelque part [...]' (BI, p. 125); 'She's thought to be a capable, self-possessed, efficient woman ... / "Put your clothes on," repeats Laurence. "Wear dark glasses and I'll take you to have lunch somewhere [...]"' (LBI, p. 152, ta). Similarly, ellipsis represents the way in which, in conversation, not all utterances are completed.

Jouve, London: Routledge, 1990, pp. 91–100 (p. 94), quoted in Morag Shiach, *Hélène Cixous: A Politics of Writing*, London: Routledge, 1991.

[51]   For further examples, see BI, pp. 108, 92, and 156. (In this series of quotations, / denotes a line break.)

This occurs for instance when Jean-Charles tells Laurence a story he thinks will appeal to her father. Laurence's reply, ' – Oui, papa aimera ça ...' ('Yes, Papa will like that ...') captures the openness of informal speech (BI, p. 91; LBI, p. 111). Likewise, the way Laurence does not conclude her retort to Gilbert's request that she be there to support Dominique once he has informed her of his plans to marry, accords with Laurence's angrily walking away: '– Pour l'empêcher de se descendre en laissant un mot où elle dirait pourquoi? Ça ferait mauvais effet, du sang sur la robe blanche de Patricia .../ Elle s'éloigne' (BI, p. 97); '"So as to prevent her killing herself and leaving a note to say why? It would look bad, blood on Patricia's white dress ..." She moves away (LBI, pp. 117–18). The way interlocutors constantly interrupt each other is also marked by ellipsis. This is particularly the case when strong convictions and emotions are involved. Marthe desperately wants Laurence to allow Catherine to take her first communion and when Laurence explains that they had Catherine baptised only to please Jean-Charles's mother, who is now dead, Marthe cuts off Laurence: '[...] maintenant qu'elle est morte .../ – Tu prends une grave responsabilité en privant ta fille de toute instruction religieuse' (BI, p. 75); '"[...] but now she's dead ..."/ "You are taking a grave responsibility on yourself by depriving your daughter of any religious instruction"' (LBI, p. 92). When Laurence's father fails to support her view that it is normal to be 'tourneboulé' (upset) at Catherine's age and that she should be allowed to remain friends with Brigitte, Laurence's dismay and anger lead her to interrupt his pronouncements: 'Si la psychologue la trouve désaxée .../ – Mais tu ne crois pas aux psychologues!' (BI, p. 174); '"If the psychologist thinks her disturbed ..."/ "But you don't believe in psychologists!"' (LBI, p. 212). The final way in which ellipsis promotes subjective realism is by marking a pause, as when Jean-Charles asks Laurence if she is ready, '"Tu es prête? ..." demande Jean-Charles' (BI, p. 85); '"Are you ready? ..." asks Jean-Charles' (LBI, p. 104, ta). In all these cases, ellipsis creates space for the unspoken in the text.

At other comic moments in the narrative, ellipsis is used to cut off potentially endless repetition, more of the same. This is the case at the point where Laurence remembers the early days of her relationship with Lucien: 'Tous ces aller et retour et toujours retomber au même point ...' (BI, p. 32); 'All these comings and goings and always back at the same place ...' (LBI, p. 39). The suggestion is that, were it not broken off in this way, the parodic representation of Laurence's affair with Lucien might continue. In the same way, ellipsis implies the endlessness and also the predictability of the Feuverolles guests' conversation: 'Puis ils repartent ...' (BI, p. 95); 'Then they set off again ...' (LBI, p. 115, ta). It is as if the text is turning its back on what they are saying. Once more, ellipsis opens up a space in the narrative.

Ellipsis leaves room for the unexpressed and inexpressible. Thoughts may not be completed because they are too emotionally charged. About the early days in her relationship with Jean-Charles, Laurence says: 'J'ai retrouvé aussi cette douceur plus secrète que j'avais connue jadis, assise aux pieds de mon père ou tenant sa main dans la mienne ...' (BI, p. 22); 'And I also rediscovered that more secret happiness which I had known long before, sitting at my father's feet or holding his hand in mine ...' (LBI, p. 27). Or thoughts may not be completed because they are too frightening or threatening; Laurence struggles to name her disappointment, 'Je suis jalouse mais surtout, surtout ...' (BI, p. 179); 'I am jealous but above all, above all ...' (LBI, p. 217). Ellipsis repeatedly introduces ambiguity and uncertainty into the narrative. Ellipsis also translates Laurence's own uncertainty on a textual level. What, she wonders, should she do to preserve precious moments for her children? – 'Les empêcher de grandir. Ou alors ... quoi?' (BI, p. 57); 'Stop them growing up. Or else ... what?' (LBI, p. 68).[52] Ellipsis suggests the tentativeness of Laurence's steps toward understanding: 'Il me manque quelque chose que les autres ont ... A moins ... A moins qu'ils ne l'aient pas non plus' (I lack something that other people have ... Unless ... Unless they haven't got it either) (BI, p. 83; LBI, p. 102, ta); 'Ce soupçon qui lui est venu l'autre jour ... il était peut-être fondé' (The suspicion that had come into her mind the other day ... perhaps it was well-based) (BI, p. 91; LBI, p. 110). As she lies in bed trying to determine how she should go on, ellipses leave spaces in the text for a wealth of associations and meaning to expand in and fill: 'Catherine: [...] peut-être elle s'en sortira ... De quoi? De cette nuit. De l'ignorance, de l'indifférence. Catherine ...' (BI, p. 181); Catherine: [...] perhaps she'll escape ... From what? From darkness. From ignorance, from indifference. Catherine ... (LBI, p. 219, ta).

Not all breaks and silences in the text are marked by ellipses. Often signalled by an abrupt shift in tone, typographically unmarked breaks and ruptures in the text are unsettling and destabilising. This is the case in the following example that occurs early in the text. Laurence is at work thinking about how she is going to visit her father and about her relationship with her parents when the narrative thread is broken and readers are disoriented by the exclamation that begins the following paragraph. It takes them some time to realise that the narrative has moved on and that Laurence is trying to park:

> C'est son père qu'elle aime le plus – le plus au monde – et elle voit Dominique bien davantage. Toute ma vie ainsi: c'est mon père que j'aimais et ma mère qui m'a faite.
> 'Espèce de mufle!' Elle a hésité une demi-seconde de trop [...]. (BI, p. 33)

> It was her father she loved – best in the world – and she saw much more of Dominique. my whole life has been like that: it was my father I loved and my mother who formed me.

---

[52]   There is a similar example on BI, p. 167: 'Cette pensée que je retenais depuis ... quand? m'a soudain transpercée.' (The thought that I'd been holding back since ... when? suddenly pierced through me (LBI, p.203, ta).) In an interview with Jacqueline Piatier in *Le Monde*, Beauvoir draws attention to the fact that Laurence, 'un être de fuite' (a being in flight), often does not finish her sentences, that 'ses conclusions restent en suspens' (her conclusions remain unfinished). 'Beauvoir Présente *Les Belles Images*,' *Le Monde*, 23 December 1966, p. 17.

'You lout!' She hesitated half a second too long [...]. (LBI, p. 41, ta)

Ruptures in the text also signal Laurence's anxiety at the gulf she sees opening up between herself and her father. During the trip to Greece, she cannot agree with him but does not voice her disagreement about the poverty she sees ('je passais outre' BI, p. 162). When she sees no sign of the 'austere happiness' that her father is convinced rewards the poor (BI, pp. 84 and 162; LBI, pp. 102 and 196–97), her doubts are made explicit in the text: 'Mais j'aurais tout de même bien voulu que papa me dise où exactement il avait rencontré des gens que leur dénuement comblait' (But still I should have liked Papa to tell me exactly where he had met people whose destitution made them so happy) (BI, p. 162; LBI, p. 197); '"Un austère bonheur": ce n'est pas du tout ce que je lisais sur ces visages rougis par le froid' ('"An austere happiness": it was not that at all which I read on those faces reddened with the cold') (BI, p. 165). Laurence tries to explain to herself how her father could be so mistaken and supposes he has known Greece in the summer months when it must be 'plus gai.' However, when she holds out this possible mitigation to her father he rejects it: ' – La Grèce n'est pas gaie, m'a dit papa avec un soupçon de reproche; elle est belle' (BI, p. 167); '"Greece isn't cheerful," said Papa, with a hint of reproof. "It's beautiful"' (LBI, p. 202). Laurence's disillusionment is not expressed. There is a sharp break in the text. The narrative shifts abruptly to the visit to the museum. A similar rupture occurs earlier when Laurence does not challenge her father's unconvincing reasons for not signing petitions. At this point her disagreement and disappointment are implicit in her silence that is reproduced on a textual level as the narrative unexpectedly moves to Athens (BI, p. 166).

Moving on from how brackets, dashes, ellipses, ruptures, and silences fragment, disrupt, and destabilise the text of *Les Belles Images*, I now examine how the text of this novel is disrupted at a syntactical level. Syntax and punctuation, which establishes syntax, are important because, as Roger Fowler points out, 'syntax exercises a continuous and inexorable control over our apprehension of literary meaning and structure.'[53] I construe transgressive (disordered and fragmented) syntax as a symptom of madness in the text. For, as Alice Jardine puts it, 'disturbances in the syntactic chain – the insurgence of rhythm and intonation into the ranks of grammatical categories for example – may be seen as an attack against the ultimate guarantor of our identity.'[54]

Les Belles Images is characterised by contorted, transgressive syntax. Broken and disarticulated syntax often conveys pain and the pangs of Laurence's anguish.[55]

---

[53]   Roger Fowler, *A Dictionary of Modern Critical Terms*, London: Routledge, 1987, p. 243.

[54]   Jardine, *Pre-Texts*, p. 234.

[55]   This is reminiscent of what Julia Kristeva says about Marguerite Duras in an interview with Susan Sellers: 'It's through being imperfect that Duras's sentences translate suffering rather than in the fireworks of musical and vocal pleasure we find in Joyce. For Duras, the expression of pain is painful.' *Women's Review*, Number 12, 19–21, p. 21.

One of the most striking examples occurs at the point in the text where Laurence realises the enormous responsibility she bears as a parent: 'Pointe de feu à travers le coeur. Anxiété, remords' (BI, p. 135); 'A burning stab through the heart. Anxiety, remorse' (LBI, p. 164, ta).[56] Contorted syntax recurs when Laurence remembers her depression five years earlier: 'Il me semblait n'avoir plus d'avenir: Jean-Charles, les petites en avaient un; moi pas; alors à quoi bon me cultiver?' (BI, p. 43); 'It seemed to me that I had no future anymore: Jean-Charles, the children had one; not me; so what was the point in improving my culture?' (LBI, p. 53, ta). And spasmodic syntax translates the intense emotion that destabilises Laurence as she watches the little Greek girl dance:

> Une charmante fillette qui deviendrait cette matronne. Non. Je ne voulais pas. Avais-je bu trop d'ouzo? Moi aussi j'étais possédée par cette enfant que la musique possédait. Cet instant passionné n'aurait pas de fin. La petite danseuse ne grandirait pas; pendant l'éternité elle tournerait sur elle-même et je la regarderais. Je refusais de l'oublier, de redevenir une jeune femme qui voyage avec son père; je refusais qu'un jour elle ressemblât à sa mère, ne se rappelant même pas avoir été cette adorable ménade. Petite condamnée à mort, affreuse mort sans cadavre. La vie allait l'assassiner. Je pensais à Catherine qu'on était en train d'assassiner. (BI, p. 158)

> A charming little girl who would turn into that matronly woman. No. I wouldn't have it. Had I drunk too much ouzo? I too was possessed, possessed by the child who was possessed by the music. This impassioned moment would never end. The little dancer would never grow up: she would spin throughout eternity and I would watch her. I refused to forget her, to turn back into a young woman travelling with her father; I refused to accept that one day she would be like her mother, not even remembering that she had ever been this enchanting maenad. Child condemned to death, to an appalling death with no corpse. Life was going to murder her. I thought of Catherine whom they were murdering right then. (LBI, p. 192, ta)

Disarticulation is especially marked during the culmination of Laurence's breakdown that has been building up throughout the novel. Laurence considers and rejects the idea that jealousy is at the root of her collapse: 'Oedipe mal liquidé, ma mère demeurant ma rivale. Électre, Agamemnon. Est-ce pour cela que Mycènes m'a tant émue? Non. Non. Billevesées' (BI, p. 179); 'Oedipus not properly dealt with, my mother still my rival. Electra, Agamemnon. Was that why Mycenae moved me so much? No. No. Nonsense' (LBI, p. 217, ta). The repressed emotion

---

[56] An alternative analysis of such syntax is to read it as sentences that are fragmented and the fragments separated by full stops. See Lisa Dahl's discussion of James Joyce's expressionistic sentences in 'The Attributive Sentence Structure in the Stream of Consciousness Technique with Special Reference to the Interior Monologue used by Virginia Woolf, Joyce and O'Neill,' *Neuphilologische Mitteilungen*, 68, 1967, 440–54, pp. 449–50.

that is giving rise to her inner conflict ('Le tiroir est refermé, les kriss se battent.' The drawer is closed again, the krisses are fighting.) is her disappointment with her father. Laurence's pain at recognising and naming her disappointment is conveyed by broken syntax, duplicating her breathlessness that is denoted in the text: 'Je suis jalouse mais surtout, surtout ...' (BI, p. 179); I'm jealous but above all, above all ... (LBI, p. 217, ta). Laurence dozes off, exhausted after confronting her pain and wakes to find Jean-Charles there. Her refusal to see the doctor is expressed in disarticulated syntax: ' – Non jamais! Je ne me laisserai pas manipuler. Elle crie: – Non! Non!' (BI, p. 180); '"No, never! I won't let myself be manipulated." She shouts: "No! No!"' (LBI, p. 218, ta). Laurence's struggle to find a way forward is related in fractured, convulsive syntax:

> Elle retombe sur son oreiller. Ils la forceront à manger, ils lui feront tout avaler; tout quoi? tout ce qu'elle vomit, sa vie, celle des autres avec leurs fausses amours, leurs histoires d'argent, leurs mensonges. Ils la guériront de son refus, de son désespoir. Non. Pourquoi non? Cette taupe qui ouvre les yeux et voit qu'il fait noir, à quoi ça l'avance-t-il? Refermer les yeux. Et Catherine? lui clouer les paupières? 'Non'; elle a crié tout haut. Pas Catherine. Je ne permettrai pas qu'on lui fasse ce qu'on m'a fait. Qu'a-t-on fait de moi? Cette femme qui n'aime personne, insensible aux beautés du monde, incapable même de pleurer, cette femme que je vomis. Catherine: au contraire lui ouvrir les yeux tout de suite et peut-être un rayon de lumière filtrera jusqu'à elle, peut-être elle s'en sortira ... De quoi? De cette nuit. De l'ignorance, de l'indifférence. Catherine ... Elle se redresse soudain. (BI, pp. 180–81)

> She falls back on her pillow. They'll force her to eat, they'll make her swallow it all; all what? everything she's vomiting, her life, the life the others lead with their bogus love affairs, their preoccupation with money, their lies. They'll cure her of her lack of compliance, of her despair. No. Why no? The mole that opens its eyes and sees that it's dark, where does that get it? Close them again. And what about Catherine? should her eyelids be nailed shut? 'No': she's shouted out loud. Not Catherine. I won't let them them do the same thing to her as they did to me. What have they turned me into? This woman who loves no one, indifferent to the beauties of the world, incapable even of crying, this woman that I'm vomiting. Catherine: not like me, open her eyes at once and perhaps a gleam of light will reach her, perhaps she'll escape ... From what? From darkness. From ignorance, from indifference. Catherine ... She sits up suddenly. (LBI, p. 219, ta)

This paragraph, quoted in full because it exemplifies Beauvoir's use of fragmented, disrupted syntax, begins with Laurence falling back on her pillow and ends with her sitting up, a reversal that marks a critical moment, a turning point for her. Laurence has found in herself the strength to challenge Jean-Charles and fight for her daughter. The intense emotions that are destabilising Laurence are parallelled in the unsettled, disrupted syntax of the passage.

In conclusion, I have shown how language in *Les Belles Images* is used to reproduce Laurence's breakdown. Enumeration and repetition mediate her feelings of alienation, strangeness, indifference, boredom, and suffocation. They mirror

Laurence's uncertainty and her disintegrating sense of identity. The text duplicates her obsession and is, itself, neurotic. And above all, the text epitomises her loss of faith in language. In Laurence's universe the meaningfulness of language cannot be taken for granted. Readers who are invited to interpret a loss of confidence in language as a symptom of breakdown and madness, a sign of failure and guilt, find themselves placed in this same position. In the mad textual universe created by Beauvoir, readers are trapped in an uncomfortable place where they share Laurence's distress. I have also shown how Beauvoir's textual strategies undermine the stability and coherence of the text of *Les Belles Images* and located the madness of the text metaphorically in instability and incoherence. Shifts in narrative voice, fragmentation, interruption, and multilayering all contribute to the creation of a mad textual universe. Madness is replicated at a syntactical level, too.

Beauvoir is generally perceived to produce texts that are *lisible/readerly*. Yet a close reading of her texts does not corroborate this view. *Les Belles Images* demonstrates the intrinsic inadequacy of language. Language will not submit to control, and meaning remains fluid. Beauvoir's texts have much in common with texts that are *scriptible/writerly*. Indeed, her texts undermine the *lisible/scriptible* opposition. Beauvoir crosses the *écrivain/écrivant* boundary.

Chapter 4
La Femme rompue

Beauvoir's writing practice in *La Femme rompue* is similar in many ways to her writing practice in *Les Belles Images*. In her memoirs, Beauvoir tells us that she made the decision to adopt the same technique, asking her readers to read between the lines.[1] Like Laurence, the three women protagonists in *La Femme rompue* experience a loss of sense of self and are threatened with breakdown and even madness. This chapter explores the ways in which Beauvoir's writing practice reproduces, metaphorically, this madness in the text. Rather than analysing each story in turn, I adopt a thematic approach. This highlights the differences and similarities between the stories that are marked to differing degrees by textual excess and transgression.

I begin my reading with an examination of the relationship between language and truth, focusing on 'La Femme rompue' and arguing that Beauvoir's textual strategies call into question the nature of truth and the possibility of objective meaning. Next, I consider the ways Beauvoir's writing practice puts the meaningfulness of language itself into question in 'L'Age de discrétion' and 'La Femme rompue.' The particular textual strategies I analyse are the opening up of meaning and the use of irony, repetition, and inconclusiveness. 'Monologue' stands out from the other two stories, indeed from Beauvoir's work as a whole, and my reading of this story focuses on how madness is exemplified in the excess and violence of its language. I go on to consider the treatment of identity in *La Femme rompue* as unfixed and unstable. The final part of this chapter explores how the text duplicates the disintegration of the sense of self experienced by characters on the brink of madness. I identify the disruption and instability in the text which subvert coherence and constitute its madness.

I adopt the same theoretical framework as for my analysis of *Les Belles Images*. The work of Derrida, Cixous, and Kristeva on opening up meaning/the inclusion of plural meanings is very relevant here. Also, as we have seen, Julia Kristeva has identified a number of features that disrupt and destabilise the text under the influence of semiotic drives, arguing that semiotic energy is expressed in a variety of ways affecting rhythm, language, and meaning. A number of the 'mad' textual strategies I am concerned with in this chapter coincide with these features. To recap, deviations from conventional syntax that disrupt the signifying order are characteristic of such writing. Ruptures, absences, and breaks in symbolic language reveal semiotic tension in a text. Likewise, any irregularity, modulation, or rhythm that disrupts the anticipated structure of the text is evidence of semiotic activity. In addition, an apparent lack of logical construction is, as Toril Moi

---

[1]   TCF, p. 175.

points out, evidence that the semiotic has broken through 'the strict rational defences of conventional social meaning.'[2]

Notwithstanding Beauvoir's rejection of her ideas, Hélène Cixous's theories on *écriture féminine* intersect with Beauvoir's writing practice. A number of the textual strategies that constitute the madness in Beauvoir's fiction correspond to aspects of feminine writing. It is possible to read her texts as a challenge to the 'rules of (linear) logic, objective meaning, and the single, self-referential viewpoint decreed by masculine law.' Beauvoir's writing can be described as 'feminine' to the extent that it 'deconstructs the 'all-powerful, all-knowing "I"' and calls into question conventional notions of character as a stable, unified construct.[3]

My starting point, then, is to examine the relationship between language and truth and the way objective meaning is put in question by Beauvoir's writing practice. For Elizabeth Fallaize, the stories collected in *La Femme rompue* are narratives of bad faith, and the women narrating their own stories are deceiving themselves, using discourses to conceal their situation from themselves.[4] This reading is in line with the authorial reading of *La Femme rompue* found in Beauvoir's memoirs.[5] It is based on the premise that there exists an objectively true and correct version of their stories that they are too blind or perhaps too wilful to see. Elizabeth Fallaize adopts the 'detective stance' advocated by Beauvoir and, reducing the texts to a coherent narrative, tells us what really happened. This is an extremely convincing reading, especially of 'L'Age de discrétion' and 'Monologue.' In both these stories, a 'concealed' version of events emerges from the spoken and the unspoken in the text. It seems to me the case of 'La Femme rompue' is more complex.

I want to explore the extent to which a quite different reading is also possible, one that sees Monique in the process of constructing reality. Far from positing a true version of events against which to measure the bad faith of the narrator, the text can be shown to question the very notions of truth and reality. According to Elizabeth Fallaize, Monique 'weaves a web of specious interpretations and mystifications in an attemp to protect herself from an unpalatable truth.'[6] There is ample textual evidence to support this interpretation. However, I believe an equally convincing possibility is that the process of writing allows Monique to construct a coherent narrative that corresponds with the new circumstances in which she now finds herself. Her original narrative was not 'wrong'; it simply no longer makes sense of her experience.

The diary performs two main roles. On the one hand, Monique uses the diary to construct the narrative of Maurice's infidelity. She, too, adopts the detective stance. It is no wonder that this narrative is faulty, as Maurice continues to manipulate her and lie to her even after he has admitted he is having an affair. She is forced to

---

[2]   Moi, *Sexual/Textual Politics*, p. 11.
[3]   Sellers, *Language and Sexual Difference*, p. 145.
[4]   Fallaize, *The Novels*, pp. 154–5.
[5]   TCF, pp. 175–6.
[6]   Fallaize, *The Novels*, p. 165.

revise her hypotheses as she discovers more facts about Maurice's behaviour.[7] On the other hand, Monique also uses her diary to review her life with Maurice and the way she has brought up her daughters. This narrative too is subject to multiple revisions. However, the text does not posit a shift from error to understanding. If Monique has not been a perfect wife and mother after all, nor can she be held entirely responsible for the failure of her marriage or the way her daughters choose to live their lives. The text demonstrates how discourse is not merely a true or false reflection of reality but actually constructs reality and that this construction is necessarily a process involving constant revisions.

In her diary entry of 15 January, Monique recounts the experience of re-reading her diary. The reasons she has stopped writing her diary for the past two weeks are complex. It is not only, as Elizabeth Fallaize puts it, that she is 'stunned by the evidence of the flagrant self-deception of her narrated self.'[8] It is also that words are inadequate:

> Les mots ne disent rien. Les rages, les cauchemars, l'horreur, ça échappe aux mots. Je mets des choses sur le papier quand je reprends des forces, dans le désespoir ou l'espoir. Mais la déconfiture, l'abrutissement, la décomposition, ce n'est pas marqué sur ces pages. Et puis elles mentent tant, elles se trompent tant. (LFR, p. 222)[9]

> Words say nothing. Rages, nightmares, horror – words cannot encompass them. I set things down on paper when I feel strong enough, either in despair or in hope. But the feeling of total bewilderment, of stunned stupidity, of falling to pieces – these pages do not contain them. And then these pages lie so – they get things so wrong. (TWD, p. 194, ta)

Monique feels that language is failing her. Also, as reader of the narrative, as opposed to the writer of it, Monique is shocked by the realisation that Maurice has been manipulating her. As reader, she becomes aware of a narrative thread she has previously missed, that we as readers have seen. Every line of the diary may call for a correction or a denial as Monique claims, but this is not due to Monique's dishonesty but to the nature of language and meaning. It is only through the process of writing that Monique comes to realise why she started writing the diary at all – not, as she first thinks, because her new-found freedom made her feel young again (LFR, p. 122), nor because she was unused to being alone (LFR, p. 139).

---

[7] When Monique learns from Luce Couturier that Maurice has been seeing Noëllie for far longer than he has admitted, she writes: 'Toute cette année, il faut que je la revoie à la lumière de cette découverte. [...] Quand je pense que j'en suis réduite à des hypothèses!' (LFR, p. 171); 'I must look back over the whole of this year again in the light of this discovery. [...] When I think that I have to fall back on conjectures!' (TWD, p. 149).

[8] Fallaize, *The Novels*, p. 166.

[9] I argue below that although words cannot fully encapsulate what Monique is feeling and experiencing (the signified is never fully present in the signifier), in fact, the text does communicate her pain and distress.

Writing has brought Monique to an awareness of the anxiety she had been feeling the day of her first diary entry, an anxiety that without the narrative process may well have remained for her, 'cachée au fond du silence et de la chaleur de cet inquiétant après-midi' (LFR, p. 222); 'hidden deep under the silence and the warmth of that disturbing afternoon' (TWD, p. 194).[10] (I say, for her. I believe that for readers of her diary, her anxiety is not completely hidden even in the first entry.)

It is not the case that Monique has been deliberately writing untruths. The situation is far more complicated than that. She writes: 'Oui, tout au long de ces pages je pensais ce que j'écrivais et je pensais le contraire' (LFR, pp. 222–3); 'Yes: throughout these pages I meant what I was writing and I meant the opposite' (TWD, p. 194). Monique uses both the terms mistaken (se gourer) and lying: 'Je me mentais. Comme je me suis menti!' (LFR, p. 223); 'I was lying to myself. How I lied to myself!' (TWD, p. 194). These terms appear synonymous.

Monique asks if everyone is as blind as she is or is she a half-wit. In fact, everyone is in the same predicament as far as language and the inadequacy of words are concerned. Monique claims in this diary entry that although she had been telling herself that Noëllie was unimportant and that Maurice preferred her, in fact, she had known that this was not true. Can this be right? Maurice had not given her the information she would have needed to realise this was the case; the experience of her friend, Isabelle, went against this verdict (LFR, pp. 134–5); Maurice's friend and colleague, Couturier, reassured Monique that Maurice still loved her (LFR, p. 199). For me, the writing of the diary is not Monique's desperate attempt to convince herself that truth is indestructible and that time changes nothing;[11] rather, the diary plots in detail the process of her painful realisation that this is not the case. I believe that evidence that Monique uses her diary to weave myths is far outweighed by evidence of her growing self-awareness and willingness to question her beliefs and attitudes. I am constantly struck by Monique's honesty and her willingness to face painful truths.[12] I reject the authorial reading in *Tout Compte fait* as the only possible reading of 'La Femme rompue' and take the text to be transgressive to the extent that it undermines the notion of objective truth.

Having considered language and truth, I now turn to language and the ways in which Beauvoir's writing practice opens up meaning. I define the slipping of language into meaninglessness and the inclusion of plural meanings as transgressive and read this metaphorically as madness in the text. As in *Les Belles Images*, though to a much lesser extent, 'L'Age de discrétion' contains

---

[10]   When Monique discovers that Maurice had met Noëllie in Rome in October, she reinterprets the moment when they parted at Nice airport. Interestingly, we read: 'On passe sous silence des gênes, des malaises pour lesquels on ne trouve pas de mots, mais qui existent' (LFR, p. 171); 'One never mentions the disagreeable feelings and the uneasiness that one cannot give a name to, but that exist nevertheless' (TWD, p. 148).

[11]   Suggested by Fallaize, *The Novels*, p. 169.

[12]   For example, the diary entry written in the evening on Wednesday 16 December, LFR, pp. 211–14.

a metacommentary on language. The woman refuses to discuss things with André; her anger and pain are such that language is powerless: 'les mots s'y briseraient' (AD, p. 42); 'words would shatter against [them]' (TAD, p. 35). Her loss of faith in language worsens to a point where she writes: 'Les mots se décomposaient dans ma tête: amour, entente, désaccord, c'étaient des bruits, dénués de sens' (AD, p. 66); 'The words came to pieces in my mind: love, understanding, disagreement – they were noises, devoid of meaning' (TAD, p. 55). For the woman, this painful loss of faith in language is temporary. At the end of the narrative, she reasserts the value of language and words, and the couple are able to communicate with each other again: 'De nouveau nous pouvions nous parler' (AD, p. 79). She is moved to quote the words of the thirteenth-century poem *Aucassin et Nicolette* and comments: 'Je retrouvais les vieux mots dans ma gorge, tels qu'ils avaient été écrits. [...] "Voilà le privilège de la littérature," ai-je dit. "Les images se déforment, elles pâlissent. Les mots, on les emporte avec soi"' (AD, p. 80); 'The old words, just as they were first written, were there on my lips. [...] "That's the great thing about writing," I said. "Pictures lose their shape; their colours fade. But words you carry away with you"' (TAD, pp. 67–8).

It is in keeping with this muted questioning of the meaningfulness of language on the thematic level that the loss of meaning of language is enacted in the text of 'L'Age de discrétion' in a muted way, too. Significantly, the meaning of lying is questioned; the woman clearly remembers André's inviting her to go early with him to Villeneuve 'du bout des lèvres' (half-heartedly), and yet she is sure he is not lying when he denies this (AD, p. 81). The text underlines the paradox that time passes both very slowly and extremely fast. This is encapsulated in the contradiction that makes fast and slow synonomous: 'Et maintenant, ce serait très rapide et très lent: nous allions devenir de grands vieillards' (AD, pp. 71–2); 'And now it would be very fast and very slow: we were going to turn into really old people' (TAD, p. 60).

In the previous chapter, repetition in *Les Belles Images* was read as a sign of madness in the text. I argued that repetition (neurosis on a textual level) can duplicate obsession and undermine readers' confidence in fixed meaning and the immutability of truth. Repetition works in a comparable way in *La Femme rompue*, too. In addition, repetition in 'L'Age de discrétion' mirrors on a textual level the woman's belief that time may pass but that she will be largely unaffected by change as she lives in an eternal present.[13] From the balcony of her flat, the woman repeatedly sees the same things: cranes (AD, pp. 11, 17), the new block of flats described as a high wall with lots of holes in it, like so many eyes ('une haute muraille percée de petits trous' (AD, p. 11); 'les yeux de la grande muraille' (AD, p. 30)). However, echoes, can and do serve to undermine this point of view. For example, the description of the couple's breakfast tea is repeated in a pleasing symmetrical way at the beginning of the narrative:

---

[13] See below.

J'ai versé dans les tasses du thé de Chine très chaud, très noir. [...] Combien de fois nous étions-nous assis face à face à cette petite table, devant des tasses de thé très noir, très chaud? Et de nouveau demain, dans un an, dans dix ans ... (AD, pp. 9–10)

I poured out the China tea, piping hot and very strong. [...] How many times had we sat there opposite one another at that little table with piping hot, very strong cups of tea in front of us? And we should do so again tomorrow, and in a year's time, and in ten years' time ... (TAD, p.7)

The rhythm is gentle and rocking and this combined with ellipsis reinforces the suggestion that this will go on recurring unchanged. The next day, a discordance in the echo underlines the woman's realisation that 'this morning is not like yesterday' and suggests she has been knocked off balance: 'nous boirons du thé de Chine très noir, très fort' (AD, p. 31); 'we will drink very black, very strong China tea' (TAD, p. 26, ta). A further example is the description of André sleeping. Once again, the textual echo recalls the original position and underlines how it is different, undermining the notion that the woman's world is preserved from change. Compare: 'Attendrissement du réveil. André était recroquevillé sur le lit, les yeux bandés, la main appuyé contre le mur, dans un geste enfantin [...]' (AD, p. 9) to: 'Quand je me suis réveillée le matin, il dormait recroquevillé, la main appuyée contre le mur. J'ai détourné les yeux' (AD, p. 42). ('Tender awakening. André was curled up in bed, wearing an eye mask, one hand pressed against the wall in a childlike gesture' (TAD, p. 7, ta) compared with: 'When I woke up in the morning he was curled up in bed sleeping, with his hand pressed against the wall. I looked away' (TAD, p. 35, ta).) The change is made explicit in the text. The woman who was moved to tears the previous evening by the sight of objects associated closely with André (AD, p. 41) remains unmoved by his slippers and pipe because of her anger the following morning (AD, p. 42).

Other examples of repetition in 'L'Age de discrétion' both pick up on the central theme of time and emphasise the intensity of the woman's feelings. Utterances in the present (or future) tense in direct speech are repeated in the imperfect (or conditional) in narrative comments. The woman's dismay and incredulity at Philippe's decision are underlined: '"C'est impossible. Philippe!" C'était impossible' (AD, p. 33); '"It's impossible. Philippe!" It was impossible' (TAD, pp. 27–8, ta). The text conveys how the woman is consumed by anger: '"Je ne te reverrai pas de ma vie!" [...] Je ne le reverrais plus' ('"I shall never see you again as long as I live." [...] I should never see him again') (AD, p. 35; TAD, p. 29). Her words are then repeated to André: 'Je ne le reverrai jamais et je ne veux pas que tu le revoies' ('I shall never see him again and I don't want you to see him again either') (AD, p. 35; TAD, p. 29). 'Je ne le reverrai pas. Je ne veux pas que tu le revoies' is repeated again towards the end of the dialogue (AD, p. 36; TAD, p. 30). Yet once more, after their quarrel, the woman reassures André 'C'est fini, fini' ('It's over, over'), and the narrative continues 'C'était fini' ('It was over') (AD, p. 46; TAD, p. 39, ta). This pattern – this seesawing from present to past and future to conditional – carries the narrative forward.

Repetition is also clearly linked to obsession in 'L'Age de discretion.' Snatches of the woman's dialogues with Philippe and André that affect her deeply are repeated, reappearing as direct speech in the text: 'Nous avons sûrement notre part de responsabilité' ('We certainly have our share of responsibility') (AD, pp. 36–7; TAD, pp. 30–31); and 'vos entêtements séniles' ('your senile obstinacy') (AD, pp. 35 (twice), 37; TAD, pp. 29, 31). André's words to his mother about the contrast between the history of humanity and the history of men resonate with the woman and are repeated, acquiring a new significance, encapsulating the profound bond between them: 'C'est dommage que [l'histoire] des hommes soit si triste' (AD, pp. 77–8); 'It's a pity that [the history] of men should be so sad' (TAD, pp. 65–6).[14]

Inconclusiveness is a symptom of madness in the text insofar as it challenges the notion of objective meaning, introduces plural meanings, and is a source of instability in the text. In 'L'Age de discretion,' from the point in the narrative where the woman shuts herself away in her flat for three days until it is time for her to join André in Villeneuve and as she is overwhelmed by self-doubt, questions become far more predominant. At times, the text is weighted down with questions to an astonishing degree; the woman's insecurity centres on her relationship with André, in which she invests all her hope:

> Mais pourrait-il combler ce vide en moi? Où en étions-nous? Et d'abord, qu'avions-nous été l'un pour l'autre [...]? [...] M'a-t-il aimée comme je l'aimais? [...] S'est-il avisé que notre amour ne lui suffisait pas? En a-t-il été déçu? [...] Une autre femme réussirait-elle à lui donner davantage? La barrière entre nous, qui l'avait élevée? Lui, moi, nous deux? Y avait-il une chance de l'abbattre? (AD, pp. 65–6)

> But could he fill this emptiness within me? Where did our relationship stand? And in the first place what had we been for one another [...]? [...] Had he loved me as I loved him? [...] Did he come to the conclusion that our love was not enough for him? Did it disappoint him? [...] Would another woman have succeeded in giving him more? Who had set up the barrier between us? Had he? had I? Both of us? Was there any possibility of doing away with it? (TAD, p. 55)

Even when she is with André again, the woman's doubts persist: 'Etait-il vraiment content de me revoir?' she asks (AD, p. 66); 'Was he really pleased to see me again?' (TAD, p. 56). The couple are reconciled, but the predominance of questions in the final paragraph of the story (eight questions in 21 lines) indicates just how uncertain the future is (AD, pp. 83–4).

One interesting aspect of the block of retrospective narrative that forms the second half of 'L'Age de discrétion' is the intermittent appearance of the present

---

[14] In a much lower key, repetition in the text reveals how each individual has a repertoire of ready-made ideas. The woman repeats verbatim that she finds the collegiate church at Champeaux no less beautiful for having visited the Acropolis (AD, pp. 15–16, 50–51). Could this be another sign of age?

tense when the narrating character comments in the narrative present on the experiencing character's situation. These shifts in focalisation open up meaning and contribute to inconclusiveness, introducing some instability in the text. For example, when André suggests leaving for Villeneuve immediately, the experiencing character's response, reported in the past tense, is that André is running away instead of looking for a way to get close again (AD, p. 52). The narrating character comments in the present tense that André frequently spends a few days with his mother without her, before focalisation immediately shifts back to the experiencing character whose conclusion, reported in the past tense, is that André is avoiding intimacy. Of course, the narrating character at the point of narration is by now aware that she had misinterpreted André's suggestion and knows that he was sincere when he asked her to go with him.[15] Likewise, when the woman describes her first night in Villeneuve, focalisation shifts rapidly between the experiencing character and the narrating character, indicated by shifts in tense:

> Il me semblait avoir quitté [ma chambre] la veille. Un an déjà! chaque année passe plus vite que la précédente. Je n'aurais pas tellement à attendre avant de m'endormir à jamais. Cependant je savais combien les heures peuvent lentement se traîner. Et j'aime encore trop la vie pour que l'idée de la mort me console. (AD, p. 68)

> It seemed to me that I had left [my room] just the day before. A year already! Each year goes by more quicky than the last. I wouldn't have to wait so very long before going to sleep for ever. Yet I knew how slowly the hours can drag by. And I still love life too much for the idea of death to be a consolation. (TAD, p. 58, ta)

Ambiguity and instability are heightened. Interjections in the narrative present/ present tense reveal the extent to which the woman's views remain constant. This is true of her views on time for instance:

> C'est terrible – j'ai envie de dire c'est injuste – que [le temps] puisse passer à la fois si vite et si lentement. [...] Tragiquement ma vie se précipite. Et cependant elle s'égoutte en ce moment avec quelle lenteur – heure par heure, minute par minute. Il faut toujours attendre que le sucre fonde, que le souvenir s'efface, que la blessure se cicatrise, que le soleil se couche, que l'ennui se dissipe. Etrange coupure entre ces deux rhythmes. Au galop mes jours m'échappent et en chacun d'eux je languis. (AD, pp. 64–5)

> It's dreadful – I feel like saying it's unfair – that [time] can go by both so quickly and so slowly. [...] My life is rushing tragically by. And yet how very slowly it's dripping away at the moment, hour by hour, minute by minute. You always have to wait until the sugar melts, the memory dies, the wound scars over, the sun sets, the boredom wears off. Strange rift between these two rhythms. My days fly galloping from me and I languish in each and every one of them. (TAD, p. 54, ta)

---

[15]   The misunderstanding (noncommunication) is resolved: AD, pp. 80–82.

These comments – in the narrative present – are prompted by the woman's experience of time dragging as she waits to be able to rejoin André. The crisis she has been through has certainly brought about a shift in her views of time from benign to malign, and it is these extreme views that she continues to hold after the narrated events; she appears no less reconciled to her fate now harmony has been restored between her and André. In this passage, the repetition, hour by hour, minute by minute, enacts in a simple way the drip drip of time.

Shifting focalisation also reveals the complexities of her feelings for André. After their quarrel over Philippe, the woman spends the day thinking about André and what he has done. Her thoughts are reported in the imperfect and conditional perfect in free indirect discourse. There is a shift into the perfect and present tense and a shift in focalisation from the experiencing character to the narrating character. In spite of the reconciliation that has intervened, the narrating woman's judgements remain severe:

> Sa sensibilité, sa moralité se sont émoussées. Va-t-il continuer sur cette pente? De plus en plus indifférent ... Je ne veux pas. Ils appellent indulgence, sagesse, cette inertie du coeur; c'est la mort qui s'installe en vous. Pas encore, pas maintenant. (AD, p. 43)

> His sensibility, his moral standards have become dulled. Is he going to carry on down that path? More and more indifferent ... I can't bear it. They call this apathy of the heart indulgence, wisdom; it's death getting established in you. Not yet, not now. (TAD, p. 36, ta)

Admittedly, there is the possibility that these comments are also free indirect discourse focalised through the experiencing character, but the shift from the conditional perfect tense to the present and the break between the last word of the interjection in the present tense 'maintenant' (now) and the following words, 'ce jour-là' (that day) appear to preclude this. Inconclusiveness is heightened here by ellipsis which marks the unspeakable in the text.[16]

I now turn to language and meaning in 'La Femme rompue.' The metacommentary on language is more prominent in this story. Early in her diary, Monique questions the power of words; she recognises she will not die of a broken heart, that 'the words we uttered were merely words' (LFR, p. 132; TWD, p. 114). She is aware that accepted definitions cannot be relied upon and asks: 'Mais que signifie le mot "exigeance" après toute une vie d'amour et d'entente?' (LFR, p. 133); 'But what does the word insist mean after a whole life of love and understanding?' (TWD, p. 115). She struggles to apply a definition to her response to Maurice's unfaithfulness: 'Et tantôt je me trouve sage, et tantôt je m'accuse de lâcheté' (LFR, p. 149); 'And sometimes I think myself sensible, and sometimes

---

[16] Further examples of interjections in the narrative present/the present tense include the following: on the woman's reluctance to admit she is wrong, p. 44; on retirement, p. 58; on memory, p. 65; on the woman's relationship with André and also with Manette, p. 66; on the ritual of looking at old photos, p. 72.

I accuse myself of cowardice' (TWD, p. 130). Monique does not know if she is making a mountain out of a molehill or a molehill out of a mountain (LFR, p. 151). After a quarrel with Maurice, Monique calls Colette, who stays with her mother until midnight. Monique can no longer distinguish what is good and bad for her: 'Elle m'a fait du bien, m'a fait du mal, je ne sais plus où est mon bien ni mon mal' (LFR, p. 188); 'She was good for me, was bad for me, I no longer know what's good or bad for me' (TWD, p. 164, ta). (And yet, in New York, Monique will ask her daughter Lucienne if she is happy and will disregard her response that happiness is one of her mother's words that holds no meaning for her, concluding that Lucienne must not be happy (LFR, p. 249).)

As she is affected by a sense of unreality, things in Monique's flat come to seem like imitations to her. This is enacted in the text as mutually exclusive terms become synonymous: 'La lourde table du living-room: elle est creuse' (LFR, p. 152); 'The massive table in the sitting-room – it is hollow' (TWD, p. 132). Following a 'friendly' discussion with Maurice (that she nevertheless describes as 'disappointing'), Monique denies that defining things differently has any impact on reality: 'En fait, ce bavardage n'a rien changé à rien. On a donné d'autres noms aux choses: elles n'ont pas bougé' (LFR, pp. 207–208); 'Things have been given other names: they have not altered in any way' (TWD, p. 181). She has a Gothic sense of hidden meanings lying behind her every word: 'Désormais, toujours, partout, derrière mes paroles et mes actes il y a un envers qui m'échappe' (LFR, p. 218); 'From now on, always, everywhere, there is a reverse side to my words and my actions that escapes me' (TWD, p. 190). She is painfully aware of the slippery nature of meaning: '"Rien n'est changé entre nous!" Quelles illusions je me suis faites sur cette phrase. Voulait-il dire que rien n'était changé puisqu'il me trompait déjà depuis un an? Ou ne voulait-il rien dire du tout?' (LFR, p. 172); '"Nothing has changed between us!" What illusions I built up for myself upon those words. Did he mean to say that nothing had changed because he had already been deceiving me for the past year? Or did he really mean nothing at all?' (TWD, p. 149). Monique accuses Maurice of playing with words when he denies that moving out of their flat comes down to leaving her (LFR, p. 243).

The lack of secure knowledge is intolerable to Monique. 'L'ignorance me ronge' ('My ignorance is eating away at me'), she says (LFR, p. 175; TWD, p. 152, ta). When Maurice finally tells Monique that he has been unfaithful for the past eight years, she loses any basis on which to form a judgment as to what is true and what is fiction: 'Faut-il le croire? je ne me suis pas aveuglée pendant huit ans. Il m'a dit ensuite que c'était faux. Ou est-ce à ce moment-là qu'il mentait? Où est la vérité? existe-t-elle encore?' (LFR, p. 184); 'Should I believe him? I didn't hide the truth from myself for eight years. Then he told me it wasn't true. Or was it then that he was lying? Where is the truth? Does it still exist?' (TWD, p. 160, ta). There is a hall of mirrors effect. The boundary between what is true and what is fiction is blurred. When Maurice finds Monique listening to Stockhausen, she admits that she cannot understand it. What Maurice takes to be her frankness (honesty) is actually calculated; Monique has understood that Maurice has understood why she is listening to that music and knows he would not believe her if she claimed to be enjoying it (LFR, p. 181). Again, during the (verbally) violent quarrel when Monique asks Maurice to choose between her and Noëllie, Monique takes his suitcase out of the wardrobe and starts throwing his clothes in it. The meaning of the words *truth* and *sincere* are subverted/undermined: 'Je voulais qu'il parte; je le voulais vraiment, j'étais sincère. Sincère parce que je n'y croyais pas. C'était comme un affreux psychodrame où on joue à la vérité. C'est la vérité, mais on la joue' (LFR, p. 185); 'I wanted him to go; I really wanted it – it was sincere. Sincere because I did not believe in it. It was like a dreadful psychodrama where they play at truth. It is the truth, but it is being acted' (TWD, p. 161).

Monique can no longer distinguish the true and the false (LFR, p. 187). She wants to get to the truth of her life but begins to question how accurate memory is: 'Mais peut-on se fier à sa mémoire? J'ai beaucoup oublié, et il semble que parfois même j'ai déformé les faits ('But can one trust one's memory? I have forgotten a great deal, and it seems that sometimes I have even distorted the facts') (LFR, p. 213; TWD, p. 185, ta); 'J'ai oublié beaucoup de choses. [...] Je m'imaginais avoir toujours été de bonne foi. C'est horrible de penser que ma propre histoire n'est plus derrière moi que ténèbres' ('I have forgotten a great deal. [...] I always imagined myself to be honest. It's dreadful to think that behind me my own past is no longer anything but shifting darkness') (LFR, pp. 224–5; TWD, p. 196). Monique's conviction that the truth exists to be uncovered (LFR, p. 236) is replaced by her acceptance that she will never know what the truth is (LFR, p. 244). The text underlines the paradoxical nature of existence: 'Curieux qu'on ne puisse comprendre sa propre histoire qu'en s'aidant de l'expérience des autres – qui n'est pas la mienne, qui n'aide pas' (LFR, p. 194); 'Strange that one can only understand one's own case by the help of other people's experience – experience that is not the same as mine, and that doesn't help' (TWD, p. 169). The only help is no help.

Irony adds to the inconclusiveness of 'La Femme rompue.' The status of some of Monique's comments at the beginning of the narrative is ambiguous. It is not at all clear that irony is intended when we read: 'Il aurait pu continuer [à mentir] au lieu de me parler. Même tardive, je dois lui savoir gré de sa franchise' (LFR, p. 130); 'He might have gone on [lying] instead of telling me. However belated, I must be grateful to him for his candour (TWD, pp. 112–13, ta). This comment appears at a point when Monique is extremely angry having just discovered Maurice's infidelity. Is this free indirect discourse, relating what Maurice said to Monique when he woke her at three o'clock on Sunday morning, sentiments that infuriate Monique? Or is it possible that this is what Monique actually believes? Perhaps, although this is hard, for modern readers at least, to credit. Likewise, in the same diary entry, at the point in the narrative where Monique questions Maurice about how long he has been lying to her, readers are likely to perceive irony in 'il a *à peine* hésité'('he *scarcely* hesitated') although none may be intended (LFR, p. 132; TWD, p. 114, emphasis added). After Monique's initial shock and anger, it is only in the final quarter of the story that irony reappears. Here any irony is sarcastic and bitter. But there is almost always a doubt as to whether the text is ironic and it is quite possible to read the following examples as sincere:

Il me regardait de cet air sincère qui lui coûte si peu. (LFR, p. 220)

He gazed at me with that sincere look that comes so easily to him. (TWD, p. 191)

Il ne prend que quinze jours de vacances au lieu de trois semaines (ce qui est un sacrifice, m'a-t-il fait remarquer, étant donné sa passion pour le ski). (LFR, p. 220)

He is only taking a fortnight's holiday instead of three weeks (which is a sacrifice, he pointed out to me, seeing how passionately he loves ski-ing). (TWD, p. 192)

C'est ce que j'ai choisi, n'est-ce pas? (LFR, p. 221)

That's what I chose, isn't it? (TWD, p. 193)

J'avais pris l'habitude de téléphoner à Isabelle trois fois par jour, à Colette au milieu de la nuit. Alors maintenant je paie quelqu'un pour m'écouter, c'est tordant. (LFR, pp. 238–9)

I had taken to phoning Isabelle three times a day and Colette in the middle of the night. And now I'm paying someone to listen to me, it's hilarious. (TWD, p. 208, ta)

Monique accuses Maurice of torturing her like a Nazi:

Il avait l'air accablé. Vraiment c'était lui la victime. Il a été jusqu'à me dire: 'Monique! aie un peu pitié de moi!' (LFR, p. 241).

He looked devastated. really he was the victim. He went so far as to say to me: 'Monique! Have some pity for me!' (TWD, p. 210, ta)

Repetition is a striking characteristic of the text of 'La Femme rompue.' Monique's obsessions and obsessiveness that are made explicit on a thematic level are reproduced on a textual level through repetition.[17] The unrelenting nature of Monique's fears and anxieties is on occasion accentuated by repetition in the imperfect and present tenses. The narrative pivots on these repetitions: 'De nouveau je pensais à Colette et je m'inquiétais. Et je m'inquiète' ('I was thinking of Colette again, and I was worried. And I am worried now') (LFR, p. 126; TWD, p. 109); 'Comme l'appartement était vide! Comme il est vide!' ('How empty the flat was! How empty it is!') (LFR, p. 127; TWD, p. 110). Monique's fear builds up as she writes her diary; fear for her daughter Colette's health develops into fear of being

---

[17]   See LFR, pp. 141, 183, 236, 239, 247. Monique writes: 'Et puis ça se répète, ça piétine, ça devient assommant; c'est tellement assommant, même pour moi' (LFR, p. 238); 'And then it gets repetitive, it doesn't advance, it grows dreadfully boring: it is so very boring, even for me' (TWD, p. 207).

alone, fear of the silence in her flat, and fear as a result of her constant bleeding, to become a dread of the future – 'j'ai peur' ('I am afraid') is the final, one sentence paragraph of the story.[18] The future is encapsulated in the dark window of the flat which acquires symbolic significance through repetition: 'La fenêtre était noire' ('The window was dark') (fifth diary entry, 25 September, LFR, p. 127; TWD, p. 110, ta); 'La fenêtre était noire; elle sera toujours noire' ('The window was dark, it will always be dark') (last diary entry, 24 March, LFR, p. 252; TWD, p. 220, ta). The dark window frames the story.

Repetition translates the intensity of Monique's emotions that at times threaten to overwhelm her. It conveys Monique's shock and disbelief when she learns that Maurice has been unfaithful. The only entry in her diary the following morning is: 'Ainsi c'est arrivé. Ça m'est arrivé' (LFR, p. 130); 'So it's happened. It's happened to me' (TWD, p. 12). The next day again she writes: 'Eh bien, oui! Ça m'est arrivé' (LFR, p. 130); 'Yes, here I am! It's happened to me' (TWD, p. 112). Similarly, Monique repeats over and over that Maurice has lied to her; the words 'il m'a menti' echo in the text.[19]

Certain fragments of hurtful conversations recur again and again: 'Il n'y a rien de changé entre nous' (nothing has changed between us);[20] 'les femmes qui ne font rien' (women who don't do anything).[21] As Monique becomes aware of the extent of Maurice's unfaithfulness, her willingness to give up her spring holiday comes to represent her naive (and misplaced) trust in Maurice: 'La guérison de la leucémie mérite bien quelques sacrifices!' ('A cure for leukaemia is certainly worth a few sacrifices!') (LFR, p. 128; TWD, p. 111); 'Je me sacrifie à la guérison de la leucémie. Pauvre idiote!' ('"I will sacrifice myself to the cure of leukaemia." Poor fool!'(LFR, p. 171). Monique is tortured by the idea that she may not have been a good mother and rehearses Maurice's accusations that she is responsible for Colette's 'stupid' marriage and for driving Lucienne to leave home.[22] The word 'castratrice' (castrating woman) resonates in the text.[23] She is entirely preoccupied by the situation in which she finds herself. She returns obsessively to the strategy she should adopt and the need to be patient.[24]

Monique relives over and over again certain moments of her past. The memory of the moment when she and Maurice swore to be faithful to each other is in sharp, painful contrast to what is happening now.[25] The colour blue that infuses this moment is echoed in a disconnected account of a dream Monique has as her crisis reaches its climax: 'L'autre nuit, en rêve, j'avais une robe bleu ciel et le

---

[18] 'J'ai peur' is repeated on pp. 127, 129, 236, 237, 238, and on p. 252 twice.

[19] Noted for the first time on p. 130 and repeated three times on p. 133.

[20] LFR, pp. 136, 137, 172, 208.

[21] LFR, pp. 155 (twice), 157, 158.

[22] LFR, pp. 186, 188.

[23] LFR, pp. 186, 192.

[24] LFR, pp. 134, 135, 140, 149, 157, 159.

[25] LFR, pp. 131, 132, 133.

ciel était bleu' (LFR, p. 237); 'In a dream the other night I had on a sky-blue dress and the sky was blue' (TWD, p. 207). The motif of the blue sky, associated with moments of well-being and plenitude, is also connected with the Egyptian statuette that symbolises for Monique the loving relationship she has lost (LFR, p. 232).[26] It figures, too, in the memory of a weekend in Nancy in the early days of her relationship with Maurice when he had been madly in love with her ('éperdu d'amour,' TWD, p. 162). The allusion to the sky and autumn leaves as Monique watches Maurice leave to join Noëllie for the weekend – 'un tendre ciel d'été' ('a soft summer sky') – prompts the memory, painful because it highlights what she has lost, of driving back from Nancy with Maurice (LFR, p. 150; TWD, p. 130).

Diary entries between 6th and 20th February are undated. Monique's crisis appears to reach a climax as she stops eating and dressing and is terrified because she is still menstruating after almost three weeks. Seemingly random diary entries during this time underline the fragility of Monique's mental health. Disconnected repetition accentuates this effect further. During her time alone in the flat in January, Monique had re-read Maurice's old letters to discover that the memory of their love has replaced the real thing for the past ten years, although Maurice has smiled at her and looked at her in the same way (LFR, p. 224; TWD, p. 195): '(Oh! si seulement je retrouvais ces regards et ces sourires!)' ('(Oh, if only I could get back those looks and those smiles!)', ta), she lamented at the time. Now, in her delirium, Monique imagines she hears Maurice's words and that his looks and smiles are floating around her:

> Ces sourires, ces regards, ces mots, ils ne peuvent pas avoir disparu. Ils flottent dans l'appartement. Les mots souvent je les entends. Une voix dit à mon oreille, très distinctement: "Ma petite, ma chérie, mon chéri ..." Les regards, les sourires, il faudrait les attraper au vol, les poser par surprise sur le visage de Maurice, et alors tout serait comme avant. (LFR, p. 237)

> Those smiles, looks, words can't have vanished. They're floating around here in the flat. I often hear the words. A voice says in my ear, very distinctly, 'Poppet, sweetheart, darling ...' I ought to catch the looks and smiles in mid-air and pop them by surprise on Maurice's face, then everything would be the same as before. (TWD, p. 207, ta)

Repetition can stop time. In January, while Maurice and Noëllie are away skiing in Courchevel, Monique recalls the painful memory of watching Maurice leave (for the first time with Monique's knowledge) to spend the weekend with Noëllie in mid-October. In the diary entry in October, details of cleaning the car, getting in, switching on the engine, and pulling out, slow down the text and accentuate Monique's pain. She watches him drive away: 'Il filait très vite, il a disparu. Pour toujours. Il ne reviendra jamais. Ça ne sera pas lui qui reviendra' (LFR, p. 150);

---

[26]   The statuette is literally broken by Quillan. Monique sticks it back together again but it is no longer full of tenderness and blue sky but is naked and desolate (LFR, p. 232).

'He drove off very fast; he disappeared. For ever. He will never come back. it will not be he who comes back' (TWD, p. 130). In the diary entry in January, it is repetition that slows down the text: 'Je me disais "Il ne reviendra pas." [...] Il n'est pas revenu. Pas lui [...]. Il est parti. Il sera parti pour toujours' (LFR, p. 223); 'I said to myself then, "He will not come back," [...] He has not come back. Not him [...]. He is gone. For ever he will be gone' (TWD, pp. 194–5). The same words are repeated again at the end of the narrative in the last but one diary entry: 'Il sera parti. Je rentre et il sera parti' (LFR, p. 252); 'He will be gone. I'm going back and he will be gone' (TWD, p. 219).

I have been considering examples of textual echoes and repetition at different points in the text. There are numerous examples, too, of repetition that occurs at a particular point in the text. At times, this simply translates intensity or reproduces the repetition that characterises everyday speech.[27] Elsewhere, this repetition reflects Monique's compulsion and can seem to trap readers and make time stand still. These moments are a textual duplication of those times when Monique finds the effort of doing anything at all insurmountable, as in New York: 'Quand je suis seule, je reste immobile pendant des minutes sur le bord du trottoir, entièrement paralysée' (LFR, p. 252); 'When I am by myself I stand there motionless for minutes on end at the edge of the pavement, utterly paralysed' (TWD, p. 219). One such moment occurs when she watches Maurice and Noëllie leave the cinema: 'Ils marchaient bras dessus, bras dessous, vite et en riant. J'aurais pu cent fois les imaginer marchant bras dessus, bras dessous, en riant' (LFR, p. 175); 'They went arm in arm, walking fast and laughing. I might have pictured them walking arm in arm and laughing a hundred times' (TWD, p. 152). The same effect is found at the point where Monique remembers a time in the past when she came home unexpectedly and found Maurice talking on the phone. For a moment Monique was overcome by a sense of unreality, profoundly shocked that Maurice might have been unfaithful: 'Il riait au téléphone: ce rire tendre et complice que je connais bien. Je n'ai pas entendu les mots: seulement cette tendresse complice dans sa voix' (LFR, p. 187); 'He was laughing on the telephone – that laugh of tenderness and complicity that I know so well. I didn't hear the words just the tender complicity in his voice' (TWD, p. 163, ta). In January, while Maurice is spending a fortnight skiing with Noëllie, Monique shuts herself away in her flat. After a break of 12 days,[28] she picks up her diary again:

---

[27] For example, Monique screams three times at Maurice to go away – 'va-t-en' (LFR, p. 185). And when Maurice sends Monique flowers on her birthday we read: 'Ce rappel des douceurs perdues, irrémédiablement perdues, abbattaient toutes mes défenses' (LFR, p. 204); 'This reminder of lost, hopelessly lost happiness, knocked all my defences to the ground' (TWD, p. 177). I also like the examples, 'On peut toujours descendre plus bas, et plus bas encore, et encore plus bas. C'est sans fond' ('You can always go lower, and lower still, and still lower. There is no bottom') (LFR, p. 238; TWD, p. 207) (which echoes 'je tombe plus bas, toujours plus bas' ('I am falling lower, lower all the time'), LFR, p. 232; TWD, p. 203) and 'il a insisté, insisté' ('He pressed me and pressed me') (LFR, p. 237; TWD, p. 206) where the meaning of the words is captured exactly in the repetition.

[28] Monique says two weeks (LFR, p. 222).

> Je devrais ouvrir une boîte de conserves. Ou me faire couler un bain. Mais
> alors je continuerais à tourner en rond dans mes pensées. Si me faire couler un
> bain. Mais alors je continuerais à tourner en rond dans mes pensées. Si j'écris,
> ça m'occupe, ça me permet de fuir. (LFR, pp. 220–21)

> I should open some canned food. Or run myself a bath. But then I'd go on
> pursuing my thoughts round and round. Yes run myself a bath. But then I'd go
> on pursuing my thoughts round and round. If I write it keeps me busy, it lets me
> escape. (TWD, p.192, ta)

The text reproduces Monique's experience of time and the obsessive nature of
her thoughts. In the same entry we read: 'Je suis sale, les draps sont sales, le ciel
est sale derrière les vitres sales, cette saleté est une coquille qui me protège, je
n'en sortirai plus jamais' (LFR, p. 222); 'I am filthy, the sheets are filthy, the sky
is filthy behind the filthy windows, the filth is a shell that protects me, I'll never
leave it again' (TWD, p. 193, ta). Again repetition of the word 'dirty' slows down
the text. Monique considers suicide but rejects the idea: 'Mais je ne veux pas, je ne
veux pas! J'ai quarante-quatre ans, c'est trop tôt pour mourir, c'est injuste! Je ne
peux plus vivre. Je ne veux pas mourir' (LFR, p. 222); 'But I don't want to, I don't
want to! I'm forty-four, it's too soon to die, it's not fair! I can't live any longer. I
don't want to die (TWD, p. 193, ta). Repetition combined with exclamation marks
evoke Monique's desperation.[29]

Inconclusiveness contributes to the undermining of readers' confidence in the
meaningfulness of language. One way inconclusiveness is heightened in 'La Femme
rompue' is by ellipsis. At times, ellipsis is linked to the pain of not knowing.[30]
Elsewhere, ellipsis accentuates the tenuous nature of Monique's 'knowledge,' her
sense of reality. In a long diary entry on her birthday, Monique describes how she
felt after a long, friendly conversation with her husband: 'Je finissais par croire
que Noëllie n'existait pas ... Illusion, prestidigitation' (LFR, p. 207); 'I ended up
believing that Noëllie did not exist ... Illusion, sleight of hand (TWD, p. 180).
Silence is made explicit in this example (a colleague Maurice is supposed to be
working with at the laboratory has just phoned him at home):

> – ... C'est-à-dire ... Je devais y aller, mais je suis grippé. [...]
> Je n'entendais que ce silence: '... C'est-à-dire.' Et encore un silence après. Je
> suis restée immobile, le regard rivé sur le téléphone. J'ai répété dix fois les deux
> répliques, comme un vieux disque fatigué: 'Que vous y étiez aussi – ... C'est-à-
> dire ...' Et implacablement, chaque fois, ce silence. (LFR, p. 145)

> '... What I mean is ... I was supposed to go, but I have a cold.' [...]

---

[29]   There are distinct echoes here of Murielle's monologue. Note the emphasis on dirt
(albeit that the two women's views are diametrically opposed) and the repetition of 'je ne
veux pas.'

[30]   Ellipsis also functions to disrupt/ interrupt the text, creating gaps where thoughts
and feelings are too painful for Monique to articulate. See below.

I heard only the silence – '... What I mean is.' And another silence afterwards. I stayed there motionless, my eyes fixed on the telephone. Ten times over I repeated the two phrases, like an old, worn-out record: 'That you were there too – ... What I mean is ...' And mercilessly, each time, the silence. (TWD, p. 126, ta)

Ellipsis at the beginning of a paragraph marks a gap in Monique's writing. It marks time passing and Monique's being lost in thought as she sits writing her diary. It can also signal suppressed thoughts. It is a quite exceptional technique, which effectively opens up meaning: '... J'ai arrosé les plantes vertes' ('... I watered the pot-plants') (LFR, p. 127; TWD, p. 110); '... J'ai cherché un refuge dans notre passé' ('... I sought refuge in our past') (LFR, p. 151; TWD, p. 131, ta).

Questions promote inconclusiveness in 'La Femme rompue' too. Given Monique's lack of secure knowledge and the fact that the narrative is her attempt to understand and make sense of her experience, the high number of questions in the text is unsurprising. In a sense, the text reproduces Monique's weariness at asking questions and not knowing any answers (LFR, p. 152). Monique questions Maurice, Isabelle, Colette, Lucienne, in fact, everyone around her. In particular, the question 'why?' reverberates throughout the text: why has Maurice stopped loving her?;[31] why has he rejected her physically? (LFR, p. 164); why did he lie? (LFR, p. 172); why Noëllie? (LFR, p. 196); why now? (LFR, pp. 172, 197). Monique's obsessions are duplicated in the scores of questions she asks over and over again. She is tormented by questions about Maurice and whether or not he has changed;[32] questions about Maurice's relationship with Noëllie;[33] questions about the strategy she should adopt;[34] questions about her self and who she is;[35] and as she gets braver, questions about how she has suceeded as a mother.[36] And the questions Monique asks are not generally isolated in the text; they tend to appear in series, literally weighing down the text and trapping readers in Monique's obsessions and anguish. For example, when Monique learns from Luce Couturier that Maurice is still lying to her and in fact his relationship with Noëllie has been going on for over a year: 'Pourquoi m'a-t-il menti? Il me croyait incapable de supporter la vérité? ou il avait honte? Alors pourquoi m'a-t-il parlé? Sans doute parce que Noëllie était fatiguée de la clandestinité?' (LFR, p. 172); 'Why did he lie to me? Did he think I couldn't cope with the truth? or was he ashamed? In that case why did he tell me? Probably because Noëllie was tired of concealment?' (TWD, p. 149, ta).

Inconclusiveness also results from multilayering. The text reproduces the effect of Monique's dreaming. The boundary between the real and the imaginary is undermined. Beauvoir's skillful use of tense contibutes to the disorientation

---

[31]   See LFR, pp. 194, 223, 239, 247.
[32]   See LFR, pp. 144, 151 188, 192, 196, 199.
[33]   See LFR, pp. 141, 161, 165, 172, 173, 197, 199.
[34]   See LFR, pp. 144, 148, 149,194, 202, 214, 226.
[35]   See LFR, pp. 201, 226, 237, 238, 239, 240, 250.
[36]   See LFR, pp. 190, 200, 213, 216, 219, 248–9.

of readers. In Monique's dream, recounted in the present tense, she faints from sheer unhappiness and waits, paralysed, for Maurice to come to her. He merely glances at her and walks away. We read, 'je me suis réveillée, c'était encore la nuit' ('I woke up and it was still night'), but it becomes apparent that Monique is in fact still dreaming. This time the account is in the past continuous tense: Monique was entering a corridor that was becoming narrower and narrower, making it difficult for her to breathe. Soon she would have to crawl and would die, trapped. At this point, it is not clear whether/at what point the narrative refers to Monique's dream or reality: 'J'ai hurlé. Et je me suis mise à l'appeler plus doucement, dans les larmes. Toutes les nuits je l'appelle [...]' (LFR, p. 193); 'I screamed. And I began calling to him more gently through my tears. Every night I call to him [...]' (TWD, p. 168, ta). Does she wake up once she shouts out? Does she really call Maurice's name? The text makes it impossible to answer these questions.

Having examined language in 'L'Age de discrétion' and 'La Femme rompue,' I now look at 'Monologue.' 'Monologue' contains no metacommentary on language, but at times the text itself puts the meaningfulness of language in question. Paradox is one way it does this. Murielle uses her last two earplugs to stop the telephone ringing because she cannot bear to hear that it is not ringing ('entendre que le téléphone ne sonne pas'), to hear the silence (MO, p. 87). Noise and silence are conflated: 'Arrêter ce vacarme ce silence: dormir' (MO, p. 87); 'Stop the din the silence: sleep' TMO, p. 75, ta). It is the silence of her family as much as the noise of her neighbours that threatens to stop Murielle sleeping. It is as if Murielle is accusing her family of keeping her awake (by not contacting her/their silence) in the same active sense that her neighbours are (by having a party) and of doing so deliberately, as if to torture her. The meaning of the word 'truth' appears to be opened up: 'on devient bon pour le cabanon on avoue tout le vrai et le faux' (MO, p. 88); 'you get so you are fit for the loony bin you confess everything what's true what's false (TMO, p. 76, ta). This is reinforced when Murielle imagines the book she will write, which will tell 'la vérité la vraie' ('the real genuine truth') (MO, p. 90; TMO, p. 77).

Madness is exemplified in the excess and violence of language in 'Monologue.' Indeed, 'Monologue' is shocking for the obscenity and violence of its language. The whole text is hyperbolic, excessive. This is epitomised in relation to sexuality and the body. In 'Monologue,' the body is an expression of Murielle's hurt, the site where she projects her anger and disappointment. And for Murielle, the body equates with perverted sexuality. Murielle's monologue returns obsessively to images of sex which is consistently associated with dirt and disgust. The text is as much an instance of coprophilia (morbid pleasure in dung and filth), as a case of coprolalia (obsessive use of obscene language). One of her earliest childhood memories is filtered through the sordid lens that distorts all Murielle's perceptions; she remembers one 14th July when her father had lifted Bernard (Nanard), her brother, onto his shoulders to see the fireworks while she had remained on the ground, trapped in the crowd that was like an animal on heat, with people's groins pressing into her face. Murielle is deprived of the light, joy, and excitement that her brother is lifted up to see.

Throughout the text, Murielle's disgust is focused on her mother whom she accuses of incest with Nanard. Murielle is also convinced that her mother seduced her, Murielle's first husband and manipulated her into marrying him to guarantee her own pleasure and Murielle's unhappiness. She visualizes the sex act in violent terms and is preoccupied by animality and filth:

C'est elle qui l'a harponné au cours de gymnastique et se l'est envoyé crado comme elle était ça n'avait rien de ragoûtant de se la farcir mais avec les hommes qui lui étaient passés sur le corps elle devait en connaître des trucs et des machins c'était le genre à se mettre à cheval sur le mec je la vois d'ici c'est tellement dégueux la façon dont les bonnes femmes baisent. (MO, p. 105.)

It was she who hooked him at the gym and she had it off with him filthy as she was it can't have been very inviting to stuff her but with all the men she'd had before she must have known a thing or two she was the type who'd get astride the bloke I can just imagine her it's so disgusting the way women fuck. (TMO, pp. 90–91, ta)

Murielle is reluctant to name the female genitalia, although she might have chosen from an available repertoire of obscene terms. Instead, they figure as an empty space, a filthy gap: 'Cette momie ça donne le frisson d'imaginer son entrejambes elle dégouline de parfums mais par en dessous elle sent [...] elle ne se lavait pas [...]' (MO, pp. 105–6); 'That old bag it makes you shudder to think of between her legs she drips with perfume but underneath she stinks [...] she didn't wash [...]' (TMO, p. 91, ta). The term 'momie' (mummy) in the original French adds overtones of putrefaction. The same emphasis on animality and filth recurs in Murielle's recollection of Albert's infidelity with Nina, who had been her 'very dear friend.' In Murielle's delusion, her daughter Sylvie's suicide must also be linked in some way to what she defines as perverted sex. Murielle's need to sleep and the fact that she must take her sleeping drug in suppository form make up a constant refrain in the story. The images used to express this are sexual and obscene. She accuses the doctor of sadism and, appropriating and reversing a phallic image, complains: 'je ne peux pas me bourrer comme un canon' (MO, p. 88); 'I can't stuff myself like a cannon' (TMO, p. 75, ta).

Obscene and offensive language is found not only in relation to sex and the body. Examples of such language can be found on virtually every page. Murielle's pain permeates the vitriol that characterises her monologue. She directs her rage and spite at everyone: her family; her 'friend' Dédé; her housekeeper, Mariette; her neighbours; indeed, the whole of humanity. She prides herself on 'telling it straight':

Je ne suis pas raciste mais je m'en branle des Bicots des Juifs des Nègres juste comme je m'en branle des Chinetoques des Russes des Amerlos des Français. Je m'en branle de l'humanité qu'est-ce qu'elle a fait pour moi je me le demande. S'ils sont assez cons pour s'égorger se bombarder se napalmiser s'exterminer je n'userai pas mes yeux à pleurer. Un million d'enfants massacrés et après? les

enfants ce n'est jamais que de la graine de salauds ça désencombre un peu la
planète ils reconnaissent qu'elle est surpeuplée alors quoi? Si j'étais la terre ça
me dégoûterait toute cette vermine sur le dos je la secouerais. (MO, pp. 102–3)

I'm not a racist but I don't give a fuck about Wogs Jews Niggers just like I
don't give a fuck about Chinkies Russians Yanks the French. I don't give a fuck
about humanity what has it ever done for me I wonder. If they are bloody stupid
enough to murder one another bomb one another plaster one another with napalm
wipe one another out I'm not going to cry my eyes out. A million children have
been massacred so what? children are never anything but the seed of bastards
it unclutters the planet a little they all admit it's overpopulated so what? If I
were the earth it would disgust me all this vermin on my back I'd shake it off.
(TMO, p. 88, ta)

The repetition of 'je m'en branle' (I don't give a fuck), the use of offensive, racist
terms – 'Bicots,' 'Nègres,''Chinetoques,' 'Amerlos' (Wogs, Niggers, Chinkies,
Yanks) – the defiant tone exemplified by the rhetorical questions, the enumeration
– 's'égorger se bombarder se napalmiser s'exterminer' – that hammers home the
violence that leaves Murielle indifferent, the outrageous sentiments expressed, all
contribute to the shocking effect of this passage. Murielle's egocentricity and lack
of empathy are astounding. Typically, this rant against humanity ends in self-pity
– 'ma fille à moi est morte et on m'a volé mon fils' ('My own daughter's dead and
they've stolen my son from me') – but Murielle's pain has little impact on readers
left feeling appalled and battered by her vituperative monologue. The same is true
at the point where Murielle rounds on her 'friend' Dédé:

On a assez profité de moi Dédé la première. Elle buvait mon whisky elle se
pavanait dans mon cabriolet. Maintenant, elle joue l'amie au grand coeur. Mais
elle n'a pas même été foutue de m'appeler de Courcheval cette nuit. Quand son
cocu voyage et qu'elle s'emmerde alors oui elle ramène son gros cul même si
je n'en ai aucune envie. Mais c'est le jour de l'an je suis seule je me ronge. Elle
danse elle rigole pas une minute elle n'a pensé à moi. Personne jamais ne pense
à moi. (MO, p. 111)

I've had enough of people taking advantage of me Dédé worst of all. She drank
my whisky showed off in my convertible. Now she's playing the big-hearted
friend. But she couldn't even be fucked to ring me from Courcheval tonight.
When her cuckold of a husband is away and she's bored stiff then she brings
her fat arse here even when I don't want her to. But it's New Year's Eve I'm
alone I'm eating my heart out. She's dancing she's laughing she hasn't thought
of me for a single minute. Nobody ever thinks of me. (TMO, p. 95, ta)

The vulgarity of the language used is extremely shocking. Once more, Murielle's
pain, the pain of abandonment, carries little weight.

In summary, my analysis of language in *La Femme rompue* has shown the
different ways in which the meaningfulness of language is called into question.[37]

---

[37]   If space had allowed, this chapter might also have examined the use of enumeration
in *La Femme rompue*. Enumeration characterises the texts of 'L'Age de discrétion' and

At times, the text enacts this through questioning existing definitions. Paradox, contradiction, and irony also play a part. Repetition both reproduces the protagonists' obsessions and undermines confidence in fixed meanings.[38] Madness is also exemplified in the inconclusiveness that results from ellipsis, an overabundance of questions and shifting, unstable focalisation. It is through violence and excess that the language of 'Monologue' consitutes a discourse of madness.

Leaving the question of language, I now turn to the treatment of identity in *La Femme rompue*. Conventional definitions of identity as fixed and stable are called into question. Characters who find themselves at the limits of sanity are threatened by a loss of identity as their personalities disintegrate. The threat to the sense of self of the woman in 'L'Age de discrétion' is far more muted than in the other stories. Alone in her flat, the woman does confront and question her notions of who she is and how she has lived her life. To some extent. It is painful for her to examine her views on time and memory, her work, her relationships with her son and husband. Yet she emerges fundamentally unchanged from her self-examination. Her self-awareness remains limited. For instance, she never questions the way she has related to her son Philippe, taking over his life and using him to fill a vacuum in her own life. She does not take Philippe's accusations seriously enough to address them and is now on the verge of using André, her husband, to fill the gap in her life: 'Il ne me restait qu'un espoir: André' (AD, p. 65).

In 'Monologue' we find no direct questioning of identity on the part of Murielle. She appears sure of who she is. Her monologue is intended to construct an image of her as an extremely attractive, perfect wife and mother of the utmost integrity. The image she constructs is for others' consumption; the monologue is both her rehearsal of the arguments she will use with Tristan the following day and a rebuttal of the accusations that obsess her. Indeed, Murielle wants the whole world to 'see her as she really is'; she imagines her photograph in *Vogue* (MO, p. 97) and her autobiography in every bookshop window (MO, p. 90). In this story the breakdown in identity consists in the gap between Murielle's self-image and reality and in her frantic, desperate, obsessional attempts to protect her hyperbolic self-image.

In 'La Femme rompue,' as Monique's crisis deepens, she experiences a loss of sense of self and faces breakdown and madness.[39] Her self-definition has

---

'La Femme rompue' to the extent that there is at least one example – and usually several – on virtually every page. Enumeration translates intensity whilst also opening up meaning. As in *Les Belles Images*, meaning reverberates in the gaps between the terms in the enumeration. As I have argued, Beauvoir's frequent recourse to enumeration encapsulates the inadequacy of words – one word alone – to fully convey meaning. There are relatively fewer examples of enumeration in 'Monologue.' Generally speaking, those that are found relate to Murielle, such as 'propre pure intransigeante' ('decent pure uncompromising') (MO, p. 89; TMO, p. 77, ta), for example.

[38] Repetition in 'Monologue' will be treated as an aspect of textual disruption. See below.

[39] Toward the end of the story, Monique writes: 'Devenir folle: ça serait une bonne manière de me défiler' (LFR, p. 239); 'going mad: that would be a good way out' (TWD, p. 209, ta). However, her psychiatrist, Doctor Marquet, tells Monique that even with the

depended on Maurice, seeing herself through his eyes (LFR, p. 180). She no longer recognises herself or Maurice: 'Je croyais savoir qui j'étais, qui il était: et soudain je ne nous reconnais plus, ni lui ni moi (LFR, p. 192); 'I thought I knew what kind of person I was: what kind of person he was. And all at once I no longer recognize us, neither him nor me' (TWD, p. 167). She feels that at least if Maurice were dead she would know whom she has lost and who she is. As it is, she no longer knows anything: 'Je ne sais plus rien' (LFR, p. 193). When Maurice accuses her of trying to blackmail him with her misery, she asks 'Est-ce que je sais qui je suis?' (LFR, p. 237); 'Do I know who I am?' (TWD, p. 207, ta). She loses her sense of self: 'Moi, qu'est-ce que c'est? Je ne m'en suis jamais souciée. J'étais garantie puisqu'il m'aimait' (LFR, p. 239); 'Me, what's that? I've never bothered about it. I was guaranteed because he loved me' (TWD, p.208, ta). Along with her sense of self, Monique loses her image:

> Un homme avait perdu son ombre. [...] Moi j'ai perdu mon image. Je ne la regardais pas souvent; mais à l'arrière plan elle était là, telle que Maurice l'avait peinte pour moi. [...] Il fait noir, je ne me vois plus. Et que voient les autres? Peut-être quelque chose de hideux. (LFR, p.238)

> A man had lost his shadow. [...] As for me, I've lost my image. I didn't look at it often; but it was there, in the background, just as Maurice had painted it for me. [...] It's dark, I can't see myself any more. And what do others see? Maybe something hideous. (TWD, pp. 207–8, ta)

For Monique, by betraying the values they have shared (authenticity, honesty, and sincerity), Maurice has murdered all the words that she might have used to define herself:

> Je ne sais plus rien. Non seulement qui je suis mais comment il faudrait être. Le noir et le blanc se confondent, le monde est un magma et je n'ai plus de contours. Comment vivre sans croire à rien ni à moi-même? (LFR, p. 251)

> I don't know anything anymore. Not only who I am but how I ought to be. Black and white merge into one another, the world is an inextricable muddle and I no longer have any clear outlines. How is it possible to live without believing in anything or in myself? (TWD, p. 219, ta)

If Monique's loss of identity coincides with her loss of faith in language, then it is also important to note that language and writing also play a part in her recovery.

---

abuse of alcohol and drugs, she has never been in real danger of becoming mad. Monique concludes: 'C'est une issue qui m'est fermée'; 'It's a way out that is closed to me.' Nevertheless there are a number of examples in the diary of Monique's paranoia (including LFR, pp. 238, 242, and 244) and there is a distinct echo of Murielle's insane delusions in Monique's desire to see Maurice's friends and colleagues die in order to wipe out their negative images of her (LFR, p. 166). (This also recalls *L'Invitée* and Françoise's desire to kill Xavière and so wipe out her version of Françoise's behaviour.)

Monique uses her diary to (re)construct her identity, to discover who she is.[40] Aware that her diary is not a repository of absolute truth, she continues to keep it all the same: 'J'ai repris mon stylo non pour revenir en arrière mais parce que le vide était si immense en moi, autour de moi, qu'il fallait ce geste de ma main pour m'assurer que j'étais encore vivante' (LFR, p. 223); 'I picked up my pen again not to go back over old ground but because the emptiness within me, around me was so vast that I needed this movement of my hand to make sure that I was still alive' (TWD, p. 194, ta). The process of character construction is referred to explicitly in the text. Monique's psychiatrist insists that she write her diary and she is in no doubt as to his reasoning: 'Il essaie de me rendre de l'intérêt pour moi-même, de me restituer mon identité' (LFR, p. 239); 'He is trying to give me back an interest in myself, to restore my identity' (TWD, p. 208, ta).

We have seen that the undermining of conventional definitions of identity as fixed and stable (reliable) is an important aspect of madness in the text. In La Femme rompue, the women protagonists' loss of sense of self (or in Murielle's case, her mistaken sense of self) is duplicated on a textual level. I now look at textual strategies that introduce instability into the narrative and unsettle meaning. I read the incoherence in Beauvoir's fictional texts as madness. For, as Peter Brooks has argued, 'mental health is a coherent life story, neurosis is a faulty narrative.'[41] Nothing is meaningful in itself. We create meaning by organising our experience. Now, insofar as the text resists order and logic, insofar as it tends toward meaninglessness (which is the meaning of the text), then the text is mad. In the mad textual universe Beauvoir creates, readers are disorientated and share the helplessness of characters trying to make sense of their lives. First, temporal incoherence and the distortion of time are considered. Focus then shifts to textual fragmentation and interruption and incoherence. Finally, I treat disrupted syntax.

'Monologue' refuses to convey a sense of chronology, a sense of linear logic. Readers have to work to impose a sequential pattern on events. In 'Monologue,' readers are drawn into Murielle's madness and obsession as they attempt to make sense of her monologue at the same time as they are repelled by the vulgarity and sordidness of her delusion. They are confused by the nonlinear structure of the story. No concessions are made; readers piece together Murielle's history, learning a little of the puzzle at a time. Readers look in vain for linear logic in the text; incidents are related in disorder, prompted by seemingly inconsequential details. An associative logic carries the narrative forward. The past intrudes in the present and the present disrupts the narration of past events. Quoting a fairly lengthy passage in full will allow me to demonstrate this. It occurs toward the beginning of the narrative:

---

[40]   This point is made by Fallaize, The Novels, pp. 167 and 171.

[41]   Peter Brooks, 'Psychoanalytic Constructions and Narrative Meanings,' Paragraph, 7, 1986, 53–76 (pp. 53–4).

Ça devait arriver ils dansent au-dessus de ma tête. Alors là ma nuit est foutue demain je serai en morceaux je devrai me doper pour voir Tristan et ça foirera. Il ne faut pas! Salauds! Je n'ai que ça dans la vie le sommeil. Salauds. Ils ont le droit de me piétiner ils en profitent. «L'emmerdeuse d'en dessous elle ne peut pas gueuler c'est le jour de l'an.» Rigolez je trouverai un moyen de vous avoir elle vous emmerdera l'emmerdeuse jamais je ne me suis laissé piétiner. Albert était furax: «Pas besoin de faire un éclat!» bien si justement! Il dansait avec Nina sexe à sexe elle étalait ses gros seins elle puait le parfum mais on sentait en dessous une odeur de bidet et lui qui se trémoussait il bandait comme un cerf. [...]

Ils vont crever le plafond et me dégringoler sur la gueule. Je les vois d'ici c'est trop dégueux ils se frottent l'un contre l'autre sexe à sexe ça les fait mouiller les bonnes femmes elles se rengorgent parce que le type a la queue en l'air. Et chacun se prépare à cocufier son meilleur ami sa très chère amie ils le feront cette nuit même dans la salle de bains même pas allongés la robe retroussée sur les fesses suantes quand on ira pisser on marchera dans le foutre comme chez Rose la nuit de mon éclat. (MO, pp. 90–91)

It was bound to happen they're dancing right over my head. Now my night is fucked tomorrow I'll be in pieces I'll have to dope myself to see Tristan and it will be a balls-up. You mustn't! Bastards! It's all I have in life sleep. Bastards. They're allowed to trample on me and they're making the most of it. 'The pain in the arse downstairs can't kick up a fuss it's New Year's Eve.' Laugh away I'll find a way to get you back she'll be a pain in your arse the pain in the arse I've never let anyone trample on me. Albert was livid: 'No need to make a scene!'oh yes indeed there was! he was dancing with Nina crotch to crotch she was sticking out her big tits she stank of perfume but underneath there was a whiff of bidet and he was wiggling about he had a hard-on like a stag. [...]

They're going to break through the ceiling and come down on my head. I can imagine what they're doing its too disgusting they're rubbing against each other sex to sex it makes the slags cream they're proud as punch because the bloke's got his prick in the air. And all of them are getting ready to cuckold their best friend their very dear friend they'll do it tonight even in the bathroom not even lying down dresses hitched up on their sweating arses when you go and piss you'll tread in the come like at Rose's the night I made a scene. (TMO, p. 78, ta)

In terms of events that make up the story, it emerges only gradually that Murielle's ex-husband, Albert, was unfaithful to her, with her best friend, Nina, at a party given by Rose and that Murielle, when she found out, made a scene. She is reliving those events in the present, imagining the same event taking place again (only this time multiplied, as every guest, 'chacun' is about to betray their partner), at her upstairs neighbour's where there is a noisy party going on. (If this sequence of events can be worked out, it is nevertheless virtually impossible to distinguish fantasy and reality. Was Albert only dancing with Nina?). The text presents readers with a baffling, disordered series of statements, an extremely convoluted narrative. The dancing in the present gives rise to Murielle's insistence that she will not allow herself to be trampled on ('piétiner'), which prompts the memory of an incident in the past when Albert might have thought he could trample on her but when she refused to acquiesce. This memory in turn moves Murielle to imagine the present scene upstairs until her lurid, delusional vision of the present gives way once more to the painful recollection of the incident in the past. The past and present coalesce. A succession of textual echoes serves as a narrative thread providing hinges on which it pivots:

'ils dansent au-dessus de ma tête' – 'Il dansait avec Nina' – 'Ils vont crever le plafond';

'Ils ont le droit de me piétiner' – 'jamais je ne me suis laissé piétiner';

'Il dansait avec Nina sexe à sexe' – 'ils se frottent l'un contre l'autre sexe à sexe';

'elle étalait ses gros seins' – 'elles se rengorgent';

'il bandait comme un cerf' – 'le type a la queue en l'air';

'une odeur de bidet' – 'dans la salle de bains' – 'les fesses suantes';

'"Pas besoin de faire un éclat!"' – 'on marchera dans le foutre comme chez Rose la nuit de mon éclat'.

It is according to this associative logic that the narrative progresses.

Disrupted chronology is characteristic of the text as a whole. Present, past and future jostle in the text, within the same paragraph and even within the same sentence: 'Si je pouvais dormir je n'ai pas sommeil l'aube est encore loin c'est une heure lugubre et Sylvie est morte sans m'avoir comprise je ne m'en guérirai pas' (MO, p. 104); 'If only I could sleep I'm wide awake dawn is far away still it's a ghastly hour of the night and Sylvie died without understanding me I'll never get over it' (TMO, p. 89).

Before concluding my examination of temporal incoherence in 'Monologue,' I would like to address briefly the experience of time that is conveyed. It is typified by distortion and reification. Actual time is marked in the text, time moves on, and yet the narrative seems to trap readers in the eternal present of an unchanging obsession. Words, motifs, and images are repeated and echoed in the text, Murielle does not move on. Repetition can literally stop time in the text. 'J'en ai marre, j'en ai marre marre marre marre [...]' ('I'm sick of it I'm sick of it sick sick sick [...]') takes up 12 lines of text, making (story) time stand still (MO, p. 96; TMO, p. 83). Readers are held fast, unable to move/read on.[42] Likewise, 'Je veux gagner.

---

[42]   Fallaize makes the following point: 'The reader is left embarassed, bewildered, confronted with the responsibility as reader and uncertain whether to conscientiously read the words, contemplate them on the page or fall back on counting them (a surprisingly frequent reaction). *The Novels*, p. 161. (The word 'marre' is repeated 81 times all together.)

Je veux je veux je veux je veux je veux' ('I must win. I must I must I must I must I must') (MO, p. 109; TMO, p. 93) traps readers in the text. In a way, by making time stand still, the text exemplifies Murielle's own words: 'Toute ma vie il sera deux heures de l'après-midi un mardi de juin' (MO, p. 111); 'All my life it will be two o'clock in the afternoon one Tuesday in June' (TMO, p. 96).

Although it is far from being as disrupted as 'Monologue,' 'La Femme rompue' is not a simple linear/chronological narrative either. The past disrupts the present to a lesser, though nonetheless real, degree as memories involuntarily erupt into Monique's thoughts.[43]

The first words of 'L'Age de discrétion' – 'Ma montre est-elle arrêtée? Non. Mais les aiguilles 'n'ont pas l'air de tourner.' ('Has my watch stopped? No. But its hands do not seem to be going round.') (AD, p. 9; TAD, p. 7) – place time at the centre of the narrative. It is the main preoccupation of the woman. This story comes at the opposite end of the spectrum to 'Monologue.' The use of tense and temporal organisation (as opposed to temporal disruption) reflect the self-conscious narration which is in keeping with the fact that the woman, the intradiegetic narrator, is a writer. In 'L'Age de discretion,' generally speaking, we find control and containment not transgression. The imperfect tense predominates, revealing the extent to which the woman is attached to the past, the way things used to be. The first half of the text literally seesaws between 'autrefois' and 'maintenant,' in the past and now.[44] The text captures the paradox that we grow old in a world that is forever young and that continually changes in an eternal present (AD, p. 11). The story is divided into five parts. The narrative moment in the first two parts is the present. In the first, the woman recounts her day as she waits for her son, Philippe to arrive. The echo/repetition of the opening words at the end of the first part – 'Et me voilà en train de regarder ma montre dont les aiguilles n'ont pas l'air de tourner.' ('And here I am, looking at my watch, whose hands don't seem to be going round.') (AD, p. 21; TAD, p. 18, ta) – encapsulates the paradoxical power of time to pass slowly as well as rapidly that the woman is so conscious of. In the second part, the woman recounts the previous evening as she waits for her husband, André, to waken. Embedded in these narratives within narratives are other, earlier narratives: a visit to the butcher's (AD, p. 12), a walk along Boulevard Raspail at sunset the previous evening (AD, p. 17), the start of Philippe's relationship and marriage with Irène (AD, p. 23); in this way, the text enacts the woman's perception that the past is made of 'reflets, échos, se renvoyant à l'infini' ('reflections, echoes, reverberating back and back to infinity') (AD, p. 17; TAD, p. 14). In the second half of the text, the woman's conviction that she lives in an eternal present and that growing old will not represent a loss for her falters, and the narrative moment shifts; a retrospective narrative replaces the reflection on recent events in the present.

---

[43]   See LFR, pp. 131, 141, 150. These examples are discussed in relation to textual disruption later in this chapter.

[44]   See AD, pp. 12, 15, 17, 20, 21, 28, 32, 43, 48, 51.

The final three parts of the story form one narrative block, which is narrated from the same point, a point shortly after the narrated events. The chronology is made explicit – time is 'counted out,' contained and controled: three days later (AD, p. 32), two days after that (AD, p. 37), two days later (AD, p. 38), and so on. At the point where the woman decides to tell the story of her life with André, there is even a brief (three lines), self-conscious shift into the past-historic, the tense that signals mastery over events (AD, p. 65). The woman's attempt to recapture the past fails. Toward the end of the narrative when the woman and André are reconciled, she experiences a moment out of time. There are distinct textual echoes of the early pages of the narrative. Compare: 'La jeunesse de ce paysage me saute aux yeux [...]. Le monde se crée sous mes yeux dans un éternel présent [...].' ('The youthfulness of the landscape leaps out at me [...]. The world brings itself into being before my eyes in an everlasting present [...].') (AD, p. 11; TAD, pp. 8–9, ta) with: 'Et cette renaissance et cette permanence me donnaient une impression d'éternité. La terre me semblait fraîche comme aux premiers âges et cet instant se suffisait.' ('And this rebirth and this permanence gave me a feeling of eternity. The earth seemed to me as fresh and new as it had been in the first ages and this moment sufficed to itself.' (AD, p. 80; TAD, pp. 67–8).[45] The difference is that the woman now recognises that time does not stand still – her impression is just that, an impression – time must always pass. As narrative time and story time reconverge at the end of the narrative, the woman is filled with apprehension at the prospect of old age: 'Au loin c'étaient les horreurs de la mort et des adieux; c'étaient les râteliers, les sciatiques, les infirmités, la stérilité mentale, la solitude dans un monde étranger que nous ne comprendrons plus et qui continuera sa course sans nous' (AD, p. 83); 'Far ahead there were the horrors of death and farewells: it was false teeth, sciatica, infirmity, intellectual barrenness, loneliness in a strange world that we would no longer understand and that would continue on its way without us' (TAD, pp. 70–71, ta). In terms of the treatment of time, 'L'Age de discrétion' stands apart from 'Monologue' and 'La Femme rompue.' Whereas it is characterised by control and containment of time, the other two stories are marked by temporal disruption and incoherence. In a sense, the whole of the woman's narrative is an attempt to keep time at bay and deny its potentially disruptive force. Temporal incoherence is one source of disruption and instability in the text. Fragmentation and interrruption are another, and it is this aspect of Beauvoir's writing practice that I now address.

The narrative of 'La Femme rompue' is fractured and interrupted. This is frequently marked typographically – generally by brackets but also by dashes – but other asides that are not indicated typographically interrupt the narrative, too. Yet other breaks in the narrative are marked by ellipses. The diary entry written one week after Maurice's return from Rome is a good illustration of the way the text is disrupted. Monique is feeling let down by Maurice and senses something is not right; but whatever it is, it is not within her consciousness. An aside between dashes suggests Monique is attempting to formulate an idea or articulate a feeling

---

[45] See also AD, p. 17: 'La perpetuelle jeunesse du monde me tient en haleine.' ('The perpetual youthfulness of the world holds me spellbound' (TAD, p. 14, ta).)

that is unfamiliar: 'Avant – avant quoi? – quand par extraordinaire je sortais sans Maurice [...]' (LFR, p. 127); 'Before – before what? – when exceptionally I went out without Maurice [...]' (TWD, p. 110, ta). An ellipsis indicates a break in the narrative as Monique is unable or unwilling to pursue the idea that before, Maurice was always there when she needed him (LFR, p. 127). Her recollection of how they used to listen to music together, enclosed in parentheses, interrupts her account of how their lives are different now. Writing of Maurice's decision to abandon his medical practice, against her wishes, to devote himself to research, Monique notes, between dashes, how – exactly as she feared – he has become stale (LFR, p. 128). Here, dashes reproduce a familiar, conversational tone. Later on the same page, one parenthesis contains Monique's comment on the fact that what is left unsaid is as important as what is actually said in a diary and another her memory of meeting Maurice for the first time and falling in love at first sight. A few lines later, an ellipsis interrupts the narrative; Monique is reflecting on how Maurice has changed but does not follow through her train of thought – the memory is too painful. She simply concludes after the break that something has changed as, before, she would never have written about him behind his back.[46]

Parentheses break into the text and interrupt the narrative throughout Monique's diary. Very often, they contain memories that have become a source of pain. The account in the past tense of the early hours of the morning when Maurice wakes her and provokes Monique to ask if there is another woman in his life is interrupted by a memory in the present tense – Monique relives a precious experience from her past: '(J'aime m'endormir avant lui pendant qu'il travaille dans son cabinet)' (LFR, p. 130); '(I like going to sleep before him when he's working in his consulting-room)' (TWD, p. 113). The ensuing painful dialogue with Maurice is interrupted by the vivid memory of the moment they promised each other always to be faithful:

> (Tout était bleu au-dessus de notre tête et sous nos peids; on apercevait à travers le détroit la côte africaine. Il me serrait contre lui. 'Si tu me trompais, je me tuerais. – Si tu me trompais, je n'aurais pas besoin de me tuer. Je mourrais de chagrin.' Il y a quinze ans. Déjà? Qu'est-ce que quinze ans? Deux et deux font quatre. Je t'aime, je n'aime que toi. La vérité est indestructible, le temps n'y change rien.) (LFR, p. 131)

> (Everything was blue above our heads and beneath our feet; on the other side of the strait we could see the coast of of Africa. He held me against him. 'If you deceived me I'd kill myself.' 'If you deceived me I wouldn't need to kill myself. I'd die of a broken heart.' Fifteen years ago. Already? What's fifteen years? Two and two make four. I love you, I love you alone. Truth can't be destroyed, time doesn't affect it.) (TWD, pp. 113–14, ta)

---

[46] Keeping a diary is held by certain analysts of real diaries to be incompatible with satisfactory intimate relationships. See Valerie Raoul, *The French Fictional Journal: Fictional Narcissism/ Narcissistic Fiction*, Toronto: University of Toronto Press, 1980, p. 29. According to Moi, 'in Simone de Beauvoir's works the very appearance of the form or genre of the diary signifies emotional anguish.' *Simone de Beauvoir*, p. 245.

Here, the series of short sentences and the stacatto rhythm suggest Monique's rising panic. The direct speech – 'je t'aime, je n'aime que toi' – is not enclosed in speech marks, it breaks into the text and heightens instability. When the dialogue continues immediately after the parenthesis, it is as if Monique has held two thoughts in her mind simultaneously. The text reproduces the way shock can make us experience in slow motion – an instant lasts an age, or at least the length of a nine-line parenthesis.

As Monique's struggle intensifies, interjections become less connected with the narrative they interrupt/fragment. It is hard for Monique when Maurice decides that in future he will spend the night with Noëllie rather than coming home after spending the evening with her. The painful image of Maurice and Noëllie together in the morning is interrupted by a memory of a precious moment in their shared past:

> Il se rase, il lui sourit, les yeux plus sombres et plus brillants, la bouche plus nue sous le masque de mousse blanche. Il apparaissait dans l'embrassure de la porte, avec dans les bras, enveloppé de cellophane, un grand bouquet de roses rouges: est-ce qu'il lui apporte des fleurs? (LFR, p. 141)[47]

> He is shaving, smiling at her, with his eyes darker and brighter, his mouth more naked under the mask of white foam. He appeared in the doorway holding an enormous bunch of red roses wrapped in cellophane: does he take her flowers? (TWD, p. 123, ta)

In this example, without any typographical indication, the memory of the past erupts in the text; present and past collide. This is disorientating and momentarily confusing. At this point in the text, the detail slows the pace of the narrative to such an extent that it almost stops, as if Monique were paralysed by this vivid, painful memory. Again, when Maurice leaves early one morning to join Noëllie for the weekend, Monique watches him from the window. The present moment is interrupted by a flashback: 'Il faisait un tendre ciel d'été, au-dessus des derniers feuillages d'automne. (La pluie d'or des feuilles d'acacia sur une route rose et grise, en revenant de Nancy.) Il est monté dans la voiture [...]' (LFR, p. 150); 'Above the last autumn leaves there was a soft summer sky. (The golden rain of the acacia leaves on a pink and grey road, as we came back from Nancy.) He got into the car [...]' (TWD, p. 130). The insistent memory of a time when she and Maurice had been madly in love intrudes. Such interpositions unsettle the narrative and disorient readers.

As well as holding memories, brackets also contain painful thoughts – literally and typographically. For example, Monique hears Maurice's key turning in the the lock on her birthday and she recognises the taste in her mouth as the taste of fear: '(le même exactement que lorsque j'allais voir à la clinique mon père agonisant)' (LFR, p. 204); '(the same, exactly, as when I used to go to see my father

---

47   The red roses are mentioned again on p. 144.

dying in hospital)' (TWD, p. 177, ta). Several entries later, Monique refers to her father's death again, linking it to her giving up on keeping well informed and maintaining an interest in the world around her: '(Quelque chose s'est brisé. J'ai arrêté le temps à partir de ce moment-là)' (LFR, p. 211); '(Something snapped. I stopped time from that moment on)' (TWD, p. 184).

Ideas that preoccupy or obsess Monique break into the text in parentheses. Monique had been so sure that it was Maurice who had said to her at *Club 46* that nothing had changed between them until Maurice denied it (LFR, p. 208); she cannot let the idea go: '(Qui a dit: "Il n'y a rien de changé"? Maurice ou moi? Sur ce journal j'ai écrit que c'était lui. Peut-être parce que je souhaitais le croire ...)' (LFR, p.213); '(Who was it who said "Nothing has changed"? Maurice or me? In this diary I wrote that it was him. Perhaps because that's what I wanted to believe ...)' (TWD, p. 185, ta). Maurice is more and more a stranger to Monique and her constant questioning of his looks and words is duplicated in the text. We read: 'Il me semble parfois lire dans son regard ... pas exactement de la pitié; dirai-je: une légère dérision? (Ce drôle de coup d'oeil qu'il m'a jeté, quand je lui ai raconté ma sortie avec Quillan)' (LFR, p. 181); 'And sometimes I think I read in his eyes ... not exactly pity. Shall I say a very faint mockery? (That odd look he gave me when I told him about going out with Quillan)' (TWD, p. 157). The inconclusiveness of the text as Monique wonders what Maurice is thinking of her is further heightened by the yet unasked/unanswered question in parentheses as to the meaning of his response to her seeing Quillan.

Parentheses also contain narrative comment. Multilayering can introduce instability in the text as when Monique distances herself from her narrative to anticipate the comment of her (nonexistent) narratee/her critical self to the effect that her reaction is banal, then distances herself again to acknowledge that she has also thought the opposite with equal conviction (LFR, p. 202). The account of the cocktail party is fragmented by Monique's narrative comments and questions. '(Il a beau dire, je persiste à penser qu'il aurait dû l'empêcher de venir)' ('(Whatever he may say I still think he should have prevented her from coming)') (LFR, p. 164; TWD, p. 143); '(Est-ce que l'an dernier Maurice était déjà attiré par Noëllie? est-ce que ça se voyait? [...])' ('(Could it be that Maurice was already attracted by Noëllie last year? [...])') (LFR, p. 165; TWD, p. 144). Later, the free indirect discourse relating Diana's account of her conversation with Noëllie is interrupted by narrative comment: 'Elle ne renoncera jamais à lui, ni lui à elle. Moi, je suis une femme très bien (elle tient à ce formule, semble-t-il) mais je n'apprécie pas Maurice à sa vraie valeur' (LFR, p. 199); 'She will never give him up, nor he her. As for me, I am an admirable woman (she is fond of that formula it seems), but I do not value Maurice at his true worth' (TWD, p. 173). Similarly, Monique distances herself from the account she is giving of her evening with Isabelle to comment, in parentheses, that Isabelle is right. Again, at this point, multilayering contributes to inconclusiveness. Monique picks up the term that Isabelle uses 'se détraquer' and possibly uses it in a broader sense; whereas Isabelle is worried that Monique is ruining her health through misuse of stimulants and tranquillisers, Monique appears to believe she is having a breakdown: '(C'est vrai que je me détraque. [...])' (LFR, p. 233; TWD, p. 203).[48] It is at this point that she notes for the first time that she has started menstruating two weeks early; the bleeding will continue for the next 23 days.

Monique's snide remarks about Noëllie also interrupt the text in parentheses, remarks such as '(Elle aurait des goûts?)' (LFR, p. 152); '(So she possesses taste, does she?)' (TWD, p. 132). Or interruptions such as: 'Il a vu le dernier Bergman avec elle au mois d'août, en projection privée (Noëllie ne va qu'à des projections privées ou à des galas) et il ne l'a pas trouvé bon' (LFR, p. 153); 'He saw the latest Bergman with her in August, at a private showing (Noëllie only goes to private showings or galas), and he did not think much of it' (TWD, p. 133). The diary entry where Monique reports her conversation with Diana about Noëllie is characterised by asides between dashes or in parentheses. These suggest a conversational, familar tone. Separated off from the narrative proper are Monique's strategic decisions that she chooses not to share with her 'friend.' At one point, Diana tells Monique that Noëllie will leave Maurice if she gets a better offer, and Monique's response is enclosed in brackets: '(Je préférerais qu'il prenne l'initiative)' (LFR, p. 155); '(I should rather he took the initiative)' (TWD, p. 134). When Monique learns from Diana that Noëllie has lied about winning a case, she decides to expose her dishonesty: '(Il y a une chose que je lui dirai: ce n'est pas elle qui a plaidé l'affaire Rampal)' (LFR, p. 155); '(There is one thing that I shall tell him though – it was not she who argued the Rampal case at all)' (TWD, p. 134). The ensuing dialogue with Maurice is interrupted by Monique's hurt reaction to his comments about women without careers: '(Les femmes qui ne font rien: le mot m'est resté sur le coeur. Ce n'est pas un mot de Maurice)' (LFR, pp. 155–6); '(Women who do nothing: the expression stuck in my throat. It was not one of Maurice's expressions)' (TWD, p. 135). At this stage, Monique is still defending the Maurice she knew in the past.

In 'La Femme rompue,' ellipses disrupt the text as well as contribute to the undermining of the meaningfulness of language. There are many examples where ellipsis simply represents the hesitations, false starts, unfinished ideas, and interruptions that generally characterise conversation.[49] In places, ideas are unfinished because they are unthinkable, intolerable. Pain makes Monique break off: 'Ils sont en pyjama, ils boivent du café, ils sourient ...' ('They are in their pyjamas; they are drinking coffee, smiling at one another ...') (LFR, p. 140; TWD, p. 122); 'Ce lit vide à côté du mien, ce drap plat et froid ...' ('The empty bed next to mine, the flat, cold sheets ...') (LFR, p. 192; TWD, p. 167). The recollection of the last time she and Maurice made love, is too difficult to pursue and the narrative

---

48   This is not conveyed by the English translation.
49   For example:
'Tu sais bien que je travaille ...' (LFR, p. 132).
'Tu disais que tu mourrais de chagrin ...' (LFR, p. 132).
'— Tu as raison. Mais je n'ai pas osé ... [...] — Pas osé?' (LFR, p. 146).
'Je me disais: j'exigerai qu'il rompe, tout de suite ...' (LFR, p. 133).

is interrupted: 'Nous n'avons pas fait l'amour depuis Mougins; et encore, si on appelle ça faire l'amour ...' (LFR, p. 163); 'We haven't made love since Mougins; if then, if you can call that making love ...' (TWD, p. 142, ta). Correspondingly, Monique recognises that her sense of self has depended on Maurice and is brought up against the idea the he may no longer love her. Ellipsis ruptures the text. The idea is unspeakable: 'S'il ne m'aime plus ...' (LFR, p. 239); 'If he does not love me any more ...' (TWD, p. 208).

On the whole, dashes are used to convey the familiar tone of conversation. One example is where Monique writes about the lack of physical intimacy between herself and Maurice. She does so in the third person by alienating that aspect of her relationship in her body, writing that their bodies come together with pleasure but without passion ('fièvre'). 'Rarely, to be honest,' she admits in an aside between dashes (LFR, p. 138). Dashes indicate the intonation of speakers in a dialogue. This is striking at the point where Maurice moots for the first time the idea of living apart from Monique. It is possible to hear the exact tone and intonation of his voice: ' – Ce dont j'aurais envie – je ne lui en ai pas parlé, c'est toi que ça concerne – c'est de vivre seul pendant quelque temps. Il y a une tension entre nous qui disparaîtrait si nous cessions – oh! provisoirement – d'habiter ensemble' (LFR, p. 234); 'What I'd like – I haven't spoken to her about it, you 're the one it concerns – is to live by myself for a certain time. There's a tension between us that would vanish if we stopped – just provisionally! – living together' (TWD, p. 204, ta). The very tentativeness of his suggestion, his long-winded exposition, and his exclamation are immediately undercut by Monique's direct question: 'Tu veux me quitter?' (LFR, p. 235); 'You want to leave me?' (TWD, p. 204). I am tempted to see this exchange as a source of subversive humour in the text. It is not at all certain that it is intended.

There is no room in Murielle's monologue for parentheses, and ellipsis is used relatively rarely.[50] That is not to say that the narrative flows smoothly. It is clear from all the quotations already given that the text of 'Monologue' is extremely fragmented. Murielle's monologue is repeatedly interrupted. Interrupted by events in the story – by her upstairs neighbours starting to dance (MO, p. 90), for example, or by the wind (MO, p. 100) or by Murielle herself breaking off to light some incense (MO, p.104) – or interrupted by ideas or memories that erupt in Murielle's mind. The monologue pivots on these moments and changes direction.

---

[50]   Most commonly, ellipsis is used to indicate the absence from Murielle's monologue of the words of those she is speaking with, that is, ellipses stand for the missing parts of these implied dialogues. For example, Murielle has a 'conversation' with her mother (MO, p. 105) and with Tristan (MO, pp. 115–17). Elsewhere, there are also three examples of ellipsis rupturing the text: one when Murielle breaks down after a desperate appeal not to be left alone (MO, p. 104); one when she bangs her head against the wall (MO, p. 118); and another as she calms down before making her 'prayer' to God (MO, p. 118). At one point, ellipsis signifies the unspeakable in the text; Murielle cannot bring herself to say the words of her mother (MO, p. 104), words that are finally spoken on p. 112: 'Tu l'as tuée!' ('You've killed her!' (TMO, p. 96).)

Frequently, it is interrupted by particular phrases or expressions that recur throughout the monologue or in certain sections of it. Repetition duplicates on a textual level the obsessions that trap Murielle. Ideas and memories echo in the text. I should like to illustrate this by quoting one series of interrelated repetitions. Murielle is haunted by the memory of the words of her father, whom she believes to be the only person who ever loved her and her first loss: 'Sacrée petite bonne femme' (MO, p. 88); 'Hell of a little wench' (TMO, p. 76, ta). This memory is linked to her self-image as someone who is frank and truthful, 'propre pure intransigeante' ('decent pure uncompromising') (MO, p. 89; TMO, p. 77, ta), someone who is incapable of cheating: 'Dès l'enfance j'ai eu ça dans le sang: ne pas tricher' (MO, p. 89); 'No cheating: I've had that in my bones since I was a child' (TMO, p. 77). The idea recurs, breaking into the narrative: 'Pas de concession pas de comédie: je me retrouve dans cette petite bonne femme. Je suis vraie je suis propre je ne joue pas le jeu' (MO, p. 90); 'No compromise no play-acting: that hell of a little wench was me all right. I'm true I'm decent I don't play the game' (TMO, p. 77, ta). One childhood memory epitomises for Murielle these qualities she so admires in herself, the time she admitted that she did not love her new baby brother: 'La dadame qui susurre: "Alors, on l'aime son petit frère?" Et j'ai répondu posément: "Je le déteste"' (MO, p. 89); 'The kind lady whispering "So we love our little brother, do we?" And I answered calmly, "I hate him"' (TMO, p. 77, ta). It is a moment she relives again and again: 'Je suis resté cette petite bonne femme qui avait répondu: "Je le déteste" franche intrépide intègre' ('I've stayed that hell of a little wench who answered "I hate him" frank bold honest') (MO, p.91; TMO, p.78, ta); 'Moi je suis lucide je suis franche j'arrache les masques. La dadame qui susurre: "Alors, on l'aime bien son petit frère?" Et moi d'une petite voix posée: "Je le déteste." Je suis resté cette petite bonne femme qui dit ce qu'elle pense qui ne triche pas' ('Me I'm clear sighted I'm frank I tear masks off. The kind lady whispering "So we love our little brother, do we?" And my calm little voice: "I hate him." I'm still that hell of a little wench who says what she thinks and doesn't cheat' (MO, p.102; TMO, p.88, ta).[51] Murielle is driven to self-justification. Over and over again, she repeats the notion that she has been rejected by others because of her honesty: 'Ça les fait gueuler ils n'aiment pas qu'on voie clair en eux ils veulent qu'on croie leurs belles paroles ou du moins qu'on fasse semblant' ('It makes them mad they don't like being seen through they want you to believe their fine words or at least to pretend to') (MO, p. 90; TMO, p.77, ta); 'Lucide trop lucide. Ils n'aiment pas qu'on voie clair en eux; moi je suis vraie je ne joue pas le jeu j'arrache les masques' ('Clear sighted too clear sighted. They don't like being seen through; me I'm true I don't play the game I tear masks off') (MO, p. 97; TMO, p. 83, ta); 'Les gens n'acceptent pas qu'on leur dise leurs vérités. Ils veulent qu'on croie leurs belles paroles ou du moins

---

[51]   The only place Murielle admits to cheating/play-acting is in bed: 'pas de comédie – sauf un peu au lit il faut ce qu'il faut' (MO, p. 96); 'no play-acting – except a little in bed needs must' (TMO, p. 82, ta).

qu'on fasse semblant' ('People can't bear being told the truth about themselves. They want you to believe their fine words or at least to pretend to') (MO, p. 102; TMO, p. 88, ta). This is just one of numerous series of repetitions and echoes that weigh down the text. Such obsessive thoughts continually break into the narrative, contributing to the fragmentation of the text and reproducing the trap in which Murielle finds herself.

The text of 'L'Age de discrétion'is fragmented and interrupted to a far, far lesser degree than the texts of 'La Femme rompue' and 'Monologue.' The few examples there are, support the argument that fragmentation and interruption are related to pain. For instance, in the following example, ellipsis marks a break in the narrative, revealing the woman's pain at the idea that one day Philippe would form an intimate relationship with another woman: 'Il ne s'attachait pas à elles. Je pensais que s'il s'attachait ... Je pensais qu'il ne s'attacherait pas [...]' (AD, p. 23); 'He was not fond of them. I used to think that if he fell in love ... I used to think he would not fall in love [...]' (TAD, pp. 18–19). The idea is unspeakable/unthinkable; she is unable to formulate her original hypothesis. The gap is left, and the woman's second hypothesis, now proved wrong, follows.[52] Parentheses contain painful thoughts. When André comes home late for lunch having seen Philippe and tells the woman that he has some news from him, the narrative is interrupted by the woman's worst fears: '(Il partait pour l'étranger, très loin, pour des années?)' (AD, p. 33); '(Was he leaving for abroad, a great way off, for years and years?)' (TAD, p. 27). Cruel parodic humour at Irene's expense also breaks into the narrative. Brackets enclose the woman's clever mimicry of Irene's unspoken words that interrupts her account of the conversation they have together about Philippe's change of heart about his career (AD, p. 25).

To sum up, in different ways and to varying degrees, the narratives of the three stories in *La Femme rompue* are fragmented and interrupted. I am suggesting that fragmentation and interruption are sources of incoherence and instability in the text and thus constitute key elements of the discourse of madness.

I now examine how Beauvoir's texts are disrupted at a syntactical level. As in Chapter 3, I read transgressive syntax, that is, syntax that is disordered and fragmented, metaphorically as a duplication of madness in the text. 'Monologue' is Beauvoir's most transgressive text and her most 'crazy'. That it is perceived as such is, to a considerable extent, owing to its eccentric syntax. It is in this text that her (mis)use of punctuation is flagrant. The text is not without punctuation, but conventional rules of punctuation are flouted. A sense of disarray is generated as readers, largely deprived of boundaries normally marked by punctuation, attempt to make sense of the text. Sometimes, sentence-internal punctuation is missing. At other times, confusion arises because utterances that might normally be divided into two sentences or more are amalgamated, as when Murielle goes over Sylvie's suicide, seeking to disculpate herself: 'Oui, si j'étais de ces mères qui se lèvent

---

[52]   It is interesting to note that the biggest gap of all in the narrative is, in fact, the story of Philippe's wedding day; not a single word is uttered about it.

à sept heures du matin on l'aurait sauveé moi je vis sur un autre rythme ce n'est pas criminel comment aurais-je deviné?' (MO, p. 112); 'Yes, if I were one of those mothers who get up at seven in the morning she would have been saved I live according to another rhythm there's nothing criminal about that how could I have guessed?' (TMO, p. 96). Whole sections of text lack punctuation. Readers encountering series of undifferentiated clauses must themselves impose order on the text. Disorientation is increased when clauses they might differentiate appear jumbled. This is the case, for instance, early in the text where Murielle imagines her family celebrating the New Year without her. Noisy, festive people in the street – 'Salauds! ils me déchirent les tympans [...]' ('Bastards! they're shattering my eardrums [...]') (MO, p. 87; TMO, p. 75, ta) – become conflated with Murielle's family – 'Salauds! Ils me cavalent dans la tête je les vois je les entends' ('Bastards! They go round and round in my head I can hear them I can see them') (MO, p. 88; TMO, p. 75, ta) – and we read:

> Je n'ai rien à foutre d'eux seulement qu'ils ne m'empêchent pas de dormir; on devient bon pour le cabanon on avoue tout le vrai et le faux qu'ils ne comptent pas là-dessus je suis une forte nature ils ne m'auront pas. (MO, p. 88)

> I don't give a fuck about them only they mustn't stop me from sleeping; it makes you fit for the loony bin you admit everything what's true what's false they needn't count on that though I'm strong by nature they won't get me. (TMO, p. 76, ta)

I believe few readers are not forced to re-read such utterances a number of times in order to make sense of them. In so doing, in repeating a fragment of text over and over, they replicate the obsessions that grip Murielle.

Elsewhere, disarticulated, disjointed syntax translates Murielle's distress. When she burns some incense because she imagines she smells vomit, she is reminded of Sylvie's funeral: 'Cette odeur d'encens c'est celle du service funèbre; les cierges les fleurs le catafalque: mon désespoir. Morte; c'était impossible!' (MO, p. 104); 'This smell of incense is the same as at the funeral service; the candles the flowers the catafalque: my despair. Dead; it was impossible!' (TMO, pp. 89–90, ta). The convulsive rhythms of this jerky syntax are unmistakable. In addition, series of short, asyntactic and disarticulated sentences suggest breathlessness, duplicating a rapid intake of breath. This can suggest Murielle's being rocked by powerful emotions. For instance when she remembers her father: 'Mon père m'aimait. Personne d'autre. Tout est venu de là' (MO, p. 90); 'My father loved me. No one else. It all stems from that' (TMO, p. 78, ta). Or when she relives the pain of Sylvie's death: 'Sylvie est morte. Cinq ans déjà. Elle est morte. Pour toujours. Je ne le supporte pas' (MO, p. 104); 'Sylvie died. Five years ago already. She's dead. For ever. I can't bear it' (TMO, p. 90, ta). This example occurs just after the example of convulsive syntax quoted above and is immediately followed by Murielle's breaking down and uttering desperate pleas: 'Au secours j'ai mal j'ai trop mal qu'on me sorte de là je ne veux pas que ça recommence la dégringolade non aidez-moi je n'en peux plus ne me laissez pas seule ...' (MO, p. 104); 'Help I'm hurting

I'm hurting too much someone get me out of this I don't want to collapse again no help me I can't stand it anymore don't leave me by myself' (TMO, p. 90, ta).

Together, the lack of sentence-internal punctuation in much of the text and series of short, asytactic utterances have the effect of hurrying readers along.[53] Murielle's racing thoughts and rapid speech are mirrored in the text. The representation of Murielle's telephone call to Tristan is exemplary. Murielle's voice leaves no room for Tristan's. Long, unpunctuated sentences reproduce her relentless onslaught. This is how Murielle puts her case to Tristan early in the call:

> Toute la nuit j'ai réfléchi je n'avais rien d'autre à faire et vraiment je t'assure c'est anormal cette situation on ne va pas continuer comme ça enfin nous sommes toujours mariés quel gaspillage ces deux appartements tu revendrais le tien pour au moins vingt millions et je ne te dérangerais pas n'aie pas peur pas question de reprendre la vie conjugale on ne s'aime plus d'amour je m'enfermerais dans la chambre du fond ne m'interromps pas tu pourrais avoir toutes les nanas que tu voudrais je m'en torche mais puisqu'on est restés amis il n'y a pas de raison pour qu'on ne vive pas sous le même toit. (MO, p. 115)

> I've been thinking it over all night I had nothing else to do and I assure you this is an absurd position it can't go on like this after all we are married what a waste these two flats you could sell yours for at least twenty million and I'd not get in your way never fear no question of taking up married life again we're no longer in love I'd shut myself up in the room at the back don't interrupt you could have all the Fanny Hills you like I don't give a hoot but since we're still friends there's no reason why we shouldn't live under the same roof. (TMO, p. 99)

These 13 lines of print without a pause appear in more than three pages of text without a paragraph break. Tristan's brief utterances appear in the text only as blanks (ellipses), and their import is gathered only from Murielle's response: 'Tu n'as pas le droit de priver [Francis] d'un vrai foyer ... Mais si revenons là-dessus' ('You have no right to deprive [Francis] of a real home ... Yes yes we do have to go over all this again') (MO, p. 115; TMO, p. 99); 'Quelquefois je me demande si ce n'était pas un coup monté ... Oui un coup monté: c'est tellement incroyable ce grand amour et puis ce lâchage ... Tu ne t'étais pas rendu compte? de quoi?' ('Sometimes I wonder whether it wasn't a put-up job ... Yes a put-up job – it's so unbelievable that terrific passion and now this dropping me ... You hadn't realised? Hadn't realised what?') (MO, pp. 116–17).[54] Readers, like Tristan, can experience Murielle's monologue, her only weapon, as an assault.[55] It seems to pin us down.

---

[53]   Readers attempting to read unpunctuated sections of text aloud can actually experience breathlessness as they are deprived of the breathing space punctuation provides.

[54]   See also MO, pp. 114, 117.

[55]   The story's epigraph is from Flaubert: 'Elle se venge par le monologue.' ('The monologue is her form of revenge.')

Beauvoir's use of syntax in 'L'Age de discrétion' is very different. The woman's narrative is self-consciously, carefully constructed. Elizabeth Fallaize refers to the literarity of the text and shows the way in which the woman constructs 'highly polished mythical moments.'[56] One of the most striking examples of self-consciously literary writing occurs in the passage describing when the woman goes to meet her friend, Martine in the park:

> En entrant dans le jardin, l'odeur m'a prise au coeur: odeur des alpages où je marchais sac au dos, avec André, si émouvante d'être l'odeur des prairies de mon enfance. Reflets, échos, se renvoyant à l'infini: j'ai découvert la douceur d'avoir derrière moi un long passé. (AD, p. 17)

> As I came into the gardens I was moved by the smell of cut grass – the smell of the high Alpine pastures where I used to walk with André with a rucksack on my back, a smell so moving for being the smell of the meadows of my childhood. Reflections, echoes, reverberating back and back to infinity: I have discovered the pleasure of having a long past behind me. (TAD, p. 14, ta)

Syntax duplicates the ricochet effect of memories prompting memories. Phrases and nouns are placed next to each other without conjunctions – the smell of the mountain pastures where she walked with André and the smell of the meadows of her childhood; reflections and echoes. The effect is reinforced by use of the present participle. The self-conscious, agrammatical construction suggests the emotional response of the woman.

According to Elizabeth Fallaize's reading, the woman uses these highly literary constructions to protect herself from the truth of her situation. I would also argue that the text reveals how the woman's perception of her situation changes – indeed, has to change because the positive outlook she had in the past no longer corresponds to circumstances, to lived reality. However, as Elizabeth Fallaize points out, the text does not posit a shift from error to understanding; the woman's negative view of old age at the end of the story is as extreme as the rosy picture she holds at the beginning and is undercut by the example of André's mother, Manette.[57]

Highly polished passages stand out in a much less literary narrative that imitates the rhythms and cadences of spoken language. One word sentences – the names of people and places – punctuate the early part of the text: 'Irène' (AD, p. 22; TAD, p. 18)[58]; 'André' (AD, p. 32; TAD, p. 27); 'Philippe' (AD, p. 45; TAD, p. 37); Milly (AD, p. 48; TAD, p. 40). Appearing relatively early in the story, these names seem to call up untold memories, to stand for what is unspoken. As the woman

---

[56]   Fallaize, *The Novels*, pp. 158–9.

[57]   Fallaize, *The Novels*, p. 157. The woman is just as extreme with regard to Philippe. From being everything to her – she actually thinks of him as belonging to her (AD, p. 11) – he becomes nothing.

[58]   This is followed immediately by a second one word sentence: 'Pourquoi?' ('Why?'), which suggests all the woman's objections to her son's choice of partner.

loses confidence in the power of memory to keep time at bay, this construction disappears. At other points in the narrative, single-word sentences carry the force of a verdict. Verdicts about André: 'Vieilli' ('Aged') (AD, p. 43; TAD, p. 36); about her book: 'Inutile; A jeter au feu. [...] Inutile' ('Useless. Only fit for burning. [...] Useless') (AD, p.63; TAD, p.53); about remembering her past: 'Non' ('No') (AD, p.65; TAD, p.55). The final words of the story include such a single-word sentence that suggests the woman's grim determination: 'Espérons. Nous n'avons pas le choix' ('Let's hope so. We have no choice in the matter') (AD, p. 84; TAD, p. 71). This construction produces an impression of the woman as someone who is at best decisive but possibly also peremptory and rigid.

The literary passages are also in contrast to series of simple sentences that create a sense of immediacy, the sense that the woman is thinking through difficult ideas. The rhythm of these series of simple sentences is jerky. One example is related to André's response to growing old: 'Tout le monde l'ennuyait. Et moi? Il m'avait dit, voilà très longtemps: "Du moment que je t'ai, je ne pourrai jamais être malheureux." Et il n'avait pas l'air heureux. Il ne m'aimait plus comme autrefois' (AD, p. 32); 'Everyone bores him. And what about me? A great while ago now he said to me, "So long as I have you I can never be unhappy." And he does not look happy. He no longer loves me as he did' (TAD, p. 27). Similarly, following the woman's conversation with Irène when she suspects that André has continued to see Philippe against her wishes: 'Je l'ai raccompagnée jusqu'à la porte. J'ai repassé dans ma tête nos dernières répliques. S'était-elle coupée par perfidie ou par maladresse? En tout cas ma conviction était faite. Presque faite' (AD, p. 39); 'I saw her as far as the door. I went over our last exchanges in my mind. Had she given herself away out of treachery or clumsiness? At any rate my mind was made up. Almost made up' (TAD, p. 33, ta). Series of short sentences in dialogues and the jerky rhythm that results communicates the woman's anger. To Irène she says about Philippe: 'Je ne veux pas le revoir. Point. Point final' (AD, p. 38); 'I don't want to see him again. Full stop. The end' (TAD, p. 32). She is angry with André when he denies that it is he who has persuaded Philippe to write to her: 'Bien sûr que si. Tu t'es bien foutu de moi. "Tu sais comme ça lui en coûte de faire les premiers pas." Et tu les avais faits! En cachette' (AD, p. 40); 'It certainly was. You really took the piss out of me. "You know how hard it is for him to make the first move." And you'd made it! In secret' (TAD, p. 33, ta). The woman repeats André's words – with no reporting clause – and her astonishment and anger are palpable.

At times the style becomes elliptical and asyntactic translating the woman's emotional and physical pain. When she finds André waiting for her to waken after their quarrel we read: 'Mais il restait cette barre de fer dans ma poitrine. Mes lèvres tremblaient. Me raidir davantage, couler à pic, me noyer dans les épaisseurs de solitude et de nuit. Ou essayer d'attraper cette main qui se tendait' (AD, p. 45); 'But there was still that iron bar in my chest. My lips trembled. Harden myself even more, sink to the bottom, drown in the depths of loneliness and the night. Or try to catch his outstretched hand' (TAD, p. 38, ta). In the same way, when she is in crisis the woman recalls what her friend said to comfort her and is desolate: 'Ne pas préjuger de l'avenir. Facile à dire. Je le voyais. Il s'étendait devant moi à perte de vue, plat, nu. Pas un projet, pas un désir. Je n'écrirais plus. Alors que ferais-je? Quel vide en moi, autour de moi. Inutile' (AD, p. 63); 'Don't make your mind up about the future in advance. Easy enough to say. I could see the future. It stretched away in front of me as far as the eye could see, flat, bare. No plan, no desire. I wouldn't write any more. So what would I do? What emptiness in me, around me. Useless (TAD, p. 53, ta). Here we have a series of short asyntactic sentences. Martine's words are repeated without introduction, echoing in the text as they echo in the woman's mind (AD, p. 61). The verdict on herself is delivered in a one word sentence: she is useless, just like her book (five lines earlier). Elliptical summaries also evoke the woman's pain and distress: 'Etrange coupure entre ces deux rhythmes. Au galop mes jours m'échappent et en chacun d'eux je languis' (AD, pp. 64–5); 'Strange rift between these two rhythms. My days fly galloping from me and I languish in each and every one of them' (TAD, p. 54, ta).

Examples of disrupted, fragmented syntax are quite rare in 'L'Age de discretion.' They are found when the woman is affected by powerful emotions. Early in the text, this is excitement at being with Philippe again. The past erupts in the present, disrupting the narrative:

> Pendant que nous dînions à cette table où si souvent j'ai fait manger Philippe (allons, finis ta soupe; reprends un peu de boeuf; avale quelque chose avant de partir faire ton cours), nous avons parlé de leur voyage – beau cadeau de noces offert par les parents d'Irène, ils en ont les moyens. (AD, p. 23)

> While we were having dinner at the table where I had so often given Philippe his meals (come on, finish your soup; help yourself to more beef; get something down you before you set off for your lecture), we talked about their trip – a handsome wedding present from Irène's parents, they can afford that sort of thing. (TAD, p. 19, ta)

When the woman is feeling devastated after her quarrel with André, we read: 'Le visage d'André, sa voix; le même, un autre, aimé, haï, cette contradiction descendait dans mon corps; mes nerfs, mes muscles se contractaient dans une espèce de tétanos' (AD, p. 44); 'André's face, André's voice; the same man, another, loved, hated, this contradiction penetrated my body; my nerves, my muscles contracted in a kind of paralysis' (TAD, p. 37, ta). The convulsive rhythm here contrasts with the easy, flowing rhythm of the passage describing their reconciliation:'C'était lui, au passé, au présent, le même, je le reconnaissais' ('It was him, the past, the present, the same, I recognised him') (AD, p. 45; TAD, p. 38, ta); 'J'ai souri faiblement, il s'est approché, il a passé un bras autour de mes épaules, je me suis agrippée à lui, et j'ai pleuré doucement. Chaude volupté des larmes glissant sur la joue. Quelle détente! C'est si fatiguant de détester quelqu'un qu'on aime' ('I gave a weak smile, he came close and put an arm round my shoulders, I clung to him and cried quietly. The warm voluptuousness of tears runing down my cheek. What a relief! It's so tiring to hate someone you love') (AD, p. 46; TAD, pp. 38–9). In these examples, the text seems to build up to a crescendo. This is particularly true of the second, where short sentences flow one into another then tension is released as the woman cries. Poetic diction, combined with an asyntactic construction, suggests powerful emotion. However, even once they have made up, disrupted syntax contributes to the impression that all is not yet well: 'C'était fini; nous étions réconciliés. [...] Cet orage avait été trop bref pour rien changer entre nous: mais n'était-il pas le signe que depuis quelque temps – quand? – imperceptiblement quelque chose avait changé?' (AD, p. 47); 'It was over; we'd made up. [...] The storm had been too short to change anything between us: but wasn't it a sign that for some time – since when? – imperceptibly something had changed? (TAD, p. 39, ta).

Powerful emotions and pain also mark the syntax of 'La Femme rompue'. The syntax of the story is characterised by short sentences. Even before Maurice tells her about his affair with Noëllie, a series of short sentences is suggestive of the effort Monique is making to control her anger: 'C'est de l'indifférence. C'est de la dureté. Inutile de rager. Assez' (LFR, p. 129); 'It's indifference. It's hardness of heart. No point in losing one's temper. Stop it' (TWD, p. 112). In the following example, short sentences suggest finality. The rhythm is the rhythm of a bell tolling: 'Il filait très vite, il a disparu. Pour toujours. Il ne reviendra jamais. Ça ne sera pas lui qui reviendra' (LFR, p. 150); 'He drove off very fast; he disappeared. For ever. He will never come back. It will not be he who comes back' (TWD, p. 130). Elsewhere a series of short sentences suggests frantic anxiety:

> Etais-je devenue moche? vraiment trop moche? En ce moment je le suis, oui: décharnée, des cheveux morts, le teint brouillé. Mais il y a huit ans? Ça je n'ose pas lui demander. Ou suis-je sotte? ou du moins pas assez brillante pour Maurice? (LFR, pp. 225–6)

> Had I become ugly? really too ugly? Just now I am, yes: too thin, lifeless hair, sallow complexion. But eight years ago? That I daren't ask her. Or am I stupid? or at least not brilliant enough for Maurice? (TWD, p. 197, ta)

Short, asyntactic paragraph leaders (sometimes forming self-contained paragraphs) convey the almost overwhelming impact on Monique of ideas and images and emotions. They have the force of hammer blows in the text: 'Des souvenirs implacables' ('Pitiless memories') (LFR, p. 190; TWD, p. 166); 'Des fantasmes idiots' ('Stupid fantasies') (LFR, p. 194; TWD, p. 169, ta); 'L'affreuse descente au fond de la tristesse' ('The hideous fall into the abyss of sadness') (LFR, p. 203; TWD, p. 177); 'Ce lourd silence' ('This heavy silence') (LFR, p. 213; TWD, p. 185, ta).

Syntax communicates Monique's depression. Note the falling rhythm of this series of short sentences: 'Où serai-je? dans la tombe? dans un asile? Ça m'est égal. Tout m'est égal ...' (LFR, p. 244) 'Where shall I be? in my grave?, in an asylum? I don't care. I don't care about anything ...' (TWD, p. 213, ta). Intermittently, Monique's depression is such that she resorts to writing her diary in note form. For example: 'Vu Marguerite. Passé un grand moment avec Colette. Mais rien à en dire' (LFR, p. 176); 'Saw Marguerite. Spent a good deal of time with Colette. But nothing worth recording' (TWD, p. 153).

As in the other stories in the collection, fragmented syntax translates pain. It is the spasmodic rhythm of the text that has an impact on readers. For example, the very first entry, where Monique admits she is hurting: 'Avec une semaine de retard, je commence à souffrir. Avant, j'étais plutôt éberluée. Je ratioicinais, j'écartais cette douleur qui fond sur moi ce matin: les images' (LFR, p.141); 'Now with a week's delay, I'm beginning to suffer. Before, I was more shocked. I rationalised, I pushed aside the pain that is overwhelming me this morning: the images (TWD, p. 122, ta). Monique is bereft: 'Toutes les nuits je l'appelle; pas lui: l'autre, celui qui m'aimait' (LFR, p. 193); 'Every night I call to him; not him: the other one, the one who loved me' (TWD, p. 168, ta). Along with Maurice she has lost everything: 'Je n'ai rien d'autre que mon passé. Mais il n'est plus bonheur ni fierté: une énigme, une angoisse' (p. 213); 'I possess nothing other than my past. But it is no longer pride nor happiness: an enigma, anxiety' (TWD, p. 185, ta). As her distress reaches its climax, Monique cannot see a way forward: 'Il n'est pas revenu. Pas lui: et un jour il n'y aura même plus son simulacre à mes côtés. [...] Il est parti. Il sera parti pour toujours. Je ne vivrai pas sans lui. Mais je ne veux pas me tuer. Alors?' (LFR, p. 223); 'He has not come back. Not him: and one day there won't even be this semblance of him at my side any more. [...] He's gone. He'll be gone forever. I won't live without him. But I don't want to kill myself. What then?' (TWD, p. 194, ta). Her pain and self disgust are expressed in convulsive syntax: 'Tout entière truquée, pourrie jusqu'à l'os, jouant des comédies, exploitant sa pitié' (LFR, p. 237); 'Phoney through and through, completely rotten, play-acting, exploiting his pity' (TWD, p. 207, ta). The final diary entry distils the excruciating pain of abandonment and loss:

> Je me suis assise devant la table. J'y suis assise. Et je regarde ces deux portes: le bureau de Maurice; notre chambre. Fermées. Une porte fermé, quelque chose qui guette derrière. Elle ne s'ouvrira pas si je ne bouge pas. Ne pas bouger; jamais. Arrêter le temps et la vie.
>
> Mais je sais que je bougerai. La porte s'ouvrira lentement et je verrai ce qu'il y a derrière la porte. C'est l'avenir. La porte de l'avenir va s'ouvrir. Lentement. Implacablement. Je suis sur le seuil. Il n'y a que cette porte et ce qui guette derrière. J'ai peur. Et je ne peux appeler personne au secours. J'ai peur. (LFR, p. 252)
>
> I sat down at the table. I'm sitting there now. And I look at the two doors: Maurice's study, our bedroom. Closed. A closed door, something that is lying in wait behind it. It won't open if I don't move. Don't move; ever. Stop time and life.
>
> But I know I'll move. The door will open slowly and I'll see what's behind the door. It's the future. The door to the future is going to open. Slowly. Relentlessly. I am on the threshold. There is only the door and what is lying in wait behind it. I'm afraid. And I can't call to anyone for help. I'm afraid. (TWD, p. 220, ta)

The initial repetition – I sat down, I am sitting – suggests inertia. Asyntactic, fractured syntax is redolent of pain. The series of short sentences suggests inevitability. Monique's fear and rising panic are palpable as the passage builds to a crescendo. Repetition adds to the intensity of the text.

In conclusion, my reading of the relationship between language and truth in 'La Femme rompue' leads me to argue that Monique constructs a narrative that makes sense of her changing experience rather than attempts to conceal the truth from herself; the text calls into question the nature of truth and reality and the possibility of objective meaning. I have shown how Beauvoir's writing practice in *La Femme rompue* throws the meaningfulness of language itself into question and defined this, metaphorically, as madness in the text. I have argued that madness is exemplified too in the violence and excess of the language in 'Monologue.' The rejection of a conception of identity as fixed and stable in this collection of stories is in keeping with the idea that meaning is fluid and not to be enclosed. I have also demonstrated how stability and coherence are undermined by Beauvoir's textual strategies and located the madness of the text precisely in instability and incoherence. Beauvoir's writing practice maintains readers in a state of tension and confusion and the text of *La Femme rompue* is often demanding and uncomfortable.

Postscript

My ambition in writing this book has been to make it more difficult to speak of Beauvoir's indifference to style, to ignore the way she has written her novels and short stories. I wanted to bring out the writerly nature of her fiction.

It has clearly emerged that far from being flat, detached, and controlled, Beauvoir's writing is frequently inflected by forceful emotions and disrupted.[1] Madness is enacted in the text of her fiction, duplicated by textual strategies. It is inherent in the text in those qualities that destabilise meaning and identity, that represent chaos. Marks of excess, plurality, disruption, and transgression are an inscription of madness at a discursive level. In Simone de Beauvoir's fiction, symbolic language is disrupted by the semiotic.

The closer one gets to Simone de Beauvoir's writing, the more conspicuous its rich complexity becomes. Such writing resists closure. *L'Invitée*, *Les Mandarins*, *Les Belles Images*, and *La Femme rompue* correspond to Simone de Beauvoir's definition of true fiction:

> Un vrai roman ne se laisse donc ni réduire en formules, ni même raconter; on ne peut pas plus en détacher le sens qu'on ne détache un sourire d'un visage. Quoique fait des mots, il existe comme les objets du monde qui débordent tout ce qu'on peut en dire avec des mots. ('Littérature et métaphysique,' p. 90)

> A true novel, therefore, allows itself neither to be reduced to formulas nor even to be retold; one can no more detach its meaning from it than one can detach the smile from a face. Although made of words, it exists as objects in the world do, which exceed anything that can be said about them in words. ('Literature and Metaphysics,' p. 270)

---

[1]   It is true that in her oeuvre as a whole, variations in tone are considerable. *Moi* argues convincingly that the range in tone of Simone de Beauvoir's writings (vital to lifeless) is related to the 'degree of disavowal she engages in'. *Simone de Beauvoir*, pp. 249–52. My readings of *L'Invitée*, *Les Mandarins*, *Les Belles images* and *La Femme rompue* are in complete opposition to those such as Susan Marie Loffredo's. She contends that 'Beauvoir's fiction is written unambiguously, both in terms of action and chronology' and that 'her skillfully and coolly controlled prose' does not fit situations where emotional control is lost. See 'A Portrait of the Sexes: The Masculine and the Feminine in the Novels of Simone de Beauvoir, Marguerite Duras and Christiane Rochefort', unpublished doctoral dissertation, Princeton University, 1978, pp. 280–81. See also Evans, *Masks of Tradition*, p. 92 where she refers to the 'flatness' of Simone de Beauvoir's prose and pp. 99–100 where she discusses the 'no-frills quality' of her style. She quotes approvingly, Jacques Ehrmann's view that Simone de Beauvoir always maintains 'her distance, her self-control and an entire lucidity'. In 'Simone de Beauvoir and the related destinies of woman and intellectual', *Yale French Studies*, 27, 1961, 26–32 (p. 29). As I recorded in my Introduction, Brosman defines the tone of *Les Belles images* as 'detached,' p. 86.

Far from being definitive, my readings of madness in the text open up meaning. Reading madness in the text is to perceive the ambiguities and contradictions of existence operating there. The insistent voice of madness breaks into the text, disrupting order and logic, demanding to be heard.

Bibliography

Works by Simone de Beauvoir

Books

L'Invitée, coll. folio, Paris: Gallimard, 1943; *She Came to Stay*, trans. Yvonne Moyse and Roger Senhouse, London: Fontana, 1982.

Le Sang des autres, coll. folio, Paris: Gallimard, 1945; *The Blood of Others*, trans. Yvonne Moyse and Roger Senhouse, Harmondsworth: Penguin, 1986.

Tous les Hommes sont mortels, coll. folio, Paris: Gallimard, 1946; *All Men are Mortal*, trans. Leonard M. Friedman, Cleveland, Ohio: World Publishing, 1955.

Pour une Morale de l'ambiguïté, coll. idées, Paris: Gallimard, 1947; *The Ethics of Ambiguity*, trans. Bernard Fretchman, New York: Citadel Press, 1976.

L'Existentialisme et la sagesse des nations, including 'L'Existentialisme et la sagesse des nations,' 'Idéalisme moral et réalisme politique,' 'Littérature et métaphysique' and 'Oeil pour oeil', coll. Pensées, Paris: Nagel, 1948; Translations: 'Existentialism and Popular Wisdom,' 'Moral Idealism and Political Realism,' 'Literature and Metaphysics' and 'Eye for an Eye' in *Simone de Beauvoir: Philosophiocal Writings*, ed. Margaret A. Simons, Urbana and Chicago: University of Illinois Press, 2004.

Le Deuxième Sexe, 2 vols, coll. folio, Paris: Gallimard, 1949; *The Second Sex*, trans. H.M. Parshley, Harmondsworth: Penguin, 1975.

Les Mandarins, coll. folio, Paris: Gallimard, 1954; *The Mandarins*, trans. Leonard M. Friedman, London: Fontana, 1977.

Mémoires d'une jeune fille rangée, coll. folio, Paris: Gallimard, 1958; *Memoirs of a Dutiful Daughter*, trans. James Kirkup, Harmondsworth: Penguin, 1965.

La Force de l'âge, coll. folio, Paris: Gallimard, 1960; *The Prime of Life*, trans. Peter Green, Harmondsworth: Penguin, 1988.

La Force des choses, 2 vols, coll. folio, Paris: Gallimard, 1963; *Force of Circumstance*, trans. Richard Howard, Harmondsworth: Penguin, 1981.

Une Mort très douce, coll. folio, Paris: Gallimard, 1964; *A Very Easy Death*, trans. Patrick O'Brian, Harmondsworth: Penguin, 1983.

Les Belles Images, coll. folio, Paris: Gallimard, 1966; *Les Belles Images*, trans. Patrick O'Brian, London: Fontana, 1985.

La Femme rompue, coll. folio, Paris: Gallimard, 1968; *The Woman Destroyed*, trans. Patrick O'Brian, London: Fontana, 1982.

La Vieillesse, coll. folio, Paris: Gallimard, 1970; *Old Age*, trans. Patrick O'Brian, Harmondsworth: Penguin, 1986.

Tout Compte fait, coll. folio, Paris: Gallimard, 1972; *All Said and Done*, trans. Patrick O'Brian, New York: Paragon, 1993.

Quand Prime le Spirituel, Paris: Gallimard, 1979; *When Things of the Spirit Come First*, trans. Patrick O'Brian, London: Fontana, 1986.

La Cérémonie des adieux and *Entretiens avec Jean-Paul Sartre*, coll. folio, Paris: Gallimard, 1981; *Adieux: A Farewell to Sartre*, trans. Patrick O'Brian, Harmondsworth: Penguin, 1990.

Lettres à Sartre, 2 vols, Paris: Gallimard, 1990; *Letters to Sartre*, trans. and ed. Quintin Hoare, London: Vintage, 1993.

Interviews, Lectures, and Prefaces

Preface to Leduc, Violette, *La Bâtarde*, Paris: Gallimard, 1964.

Contribution to a 1964 debate on literature published in *Que peut la littérature?*, ed. Yves Buin, Paris: Union Générale d'Éditions, 1965, pp. 73–92.

Interview in Jeanson, Francis, *Simone de Beauvoir ou l'entreprise de vivre*, Paris: Seuil, 1966. Summary in Francis and Gontier, *Les Écrits*, pp. 220–21.

'Mon expérience d'écrivain,' Lecture given in Japan, October 1966, published in Francis and Gontier, *Les Écrits*, pp. 439–57.

'Simone de Beauvoir Présente *Les Belles images*,' Interview with Jacqueline Piatier, *Le Monde*, 23 December 1966, p. 17.

'Prière d'insérer,' *La Femme rompue*, reproduced in Francis and Gontier, *Les Écrits*, pp. 231–2.

'Interview with Simone de Beauvoir,' Ved Solverg Saetre, *Vinduet*, 3, 1968, 196–201. Summary and extracts in Francis and Gontier, *Les Écrits*, pp. 233–4.

'Sartre and *The Second Sex*,' Inteview with Nina Sutton, *Guardian*, 19 February 1970, p.11.

Preface to Ophir, Anne, *Regards féminins: condition féminine et création littéraire*, Paris: Denoël/ Gontier, 1976, reprinted in Francis and Gontier, *Les Écrits*, pp. 577–9.

'Beauvoir elle-même,' Interview with Catherine David, *Le Nouvel Observateur*, 22 January 1979, pp 82–90.

'Interview with Simone de Beauvoir,' Alice Jardine, *Signs*, Winter, 1979, 224–36.

'Interview with Simone de Beauvoir: Paris, 6 July 1985,' Elizabeth Fallaize and Jill M. Wharfe, in Wharfe, Jill. M., 'Perfect Interlocutors: Intertextuality and Divergence in the Fiction of Simone de Beauvoir and Sartre,' unpublished doctoral thesis, University of Birmingham, 1988, Appendix 1.

Secondary Sources

Abel, Elizabeth, ed., *Writing and Sexual Difference,* Brighton: Harvester, 1982.

Aranda, Francisco, *Luis Buñuel: A Critical Biography*, trans. and ed. David Robinson, New York: Da Capo Press, 1976.

Arp, Kristana, *The Bonds of Freedom: Simone de Beauvoir's Existentialist Ethics*, Chicago: Open Court, 2001.

Artaud, Antonin, *"Le Moine" de Lewis raconté par Antonin Artaud* (first published in 1931), in *Oeuvres complètes*, vol. VI, Paris: Gallimard, 1966.

Ascher, Carol, *Simone de Beauvoir: A Life of Freedom*, Boston: Beacon Press, 1981.

Atack, Margaret and Phil Powrie, eds, *Contemporary French Fiction by Women: Feminist Perspectives*, Manchester: Manchester University Press, 1990.

Audet, Jean-Raymond, *Simone de Beauvoir face à la mort*, Paris: L'Age d'homme, 1979.

Badiou, Alain, *Almagestes*, Paris: Seuil, 1964.

Bainbrigge, Susan, 'The Case of Henri Perron: Writing and Language in Crisis' in in Holland and Renée, pp. 97–112.

Bair, Deidre, 'Simone de Beauvoir: Politics, Language and Feminist Identity,' *Yale French Studies*, 72, 1986, 149–62.

Banfield, Anne, *Unspeakable Sentences: Narration and Representation in the Language of Fiction*, London: Routledge and Kegan Paul, 1982.

Bar, Francis, 'Répétition et énumération chez les auteurs burlesques du XVIIe siècle,' in *Actes du colloque organisé par l'Institut d'études romanes et le Centre de civilisation de l'Université de Varsovie*, 1981, pp. 163–86.

Barthes, Roland, *S/Z*, Paris: Seuil, 1970.

Belsay, Catherine, *Critical Practice*, London: Methuen, 1980.

Bennett, Jay, *Simone de Beauvoir: An Annotated Bibliography*, New York/London: Garland, 1988.

Bernheimer, Charles and Claire Kahane, eds, *In Dora's Case: Freud-Hysteria-Feminism*, London: Virago, 1985.

Botting, Fred, *Gothic*, London: Routledge, 1996.

Brooks, Peter, 'Psychoanalytic Constructions and Narrative Meanings,' *Paragraph*, 7, 1986, 53–76.

Brosman, Catherine Savage, *Simone de Beauvoir Revisited*, Twayne's World Authors Series 820, Boston: Twayne, 1991.

Butler, Judith, 'Sex and Gender in Simone de Beauvoir's Second Sex,' *Yale French Studies*, 72, 1986, 35–49.

Cameron, Deborah, *Feminism and Linguistic Theory*, New York: St. Martin's Press, 1985.

Card, Claudia, ed., *The Cambridge Companion to Simone de Beauvoir*, Cambridge: Cambridge University Press, 2003.

Cardinal, Marie, *Les Mots pour le dire*, Paris: Grasset, 1975.

Cayron, Claire, *La Nature chez Simone de Beauvoir*, Paris: Gallimard, 1973.

Celeux, Anne-Marie, *Jean-Paul Sartre, Simone de Beauvoir: Une expérience commune, deux écritures*, Paris: Librairie Nizet, 1976.

Chesler, Phyllis, *Women and Madness*, New York: Avon, 1972.

Cixous, Hélène, *Entre L'Ecriture*, Paris: Editions des Femmes, 1986.

———, *Prénoms de personne*, Paris: Seuil, 1974.

———, 'Le Rire de la Méduse,' *L'Arc 61*, 1975, 39–54.

———, 'Sorties,' in Clément, Catherine and Hélène Cixous, *La Jeune Née*, Paris: Union Générale d'Editions 10/18, 1975, pp. 115–246.

Clément, Catherine and Hélène Cixous, *La Jeune Née*, Paris: Union Générale d'Editions 10/18, 1975.

The Complete Psychological Works of Sigmund Freud, ed. James Strachey, London: The Hogarth Press, 1958, 'Remembering, Repeating and Working Through,' vol. XII (1911–1913) pp. 147–56; 1955, 'The Uncanny,' vol. XVII (1917–1919), pp. 218–52; 1959, 'Inhibitions, Symptoms and Anxiety,' vol. XX (1925–1926) pp. 87–175.

Corbin, Laurie, *The Mother Mirror: Self-Representation and the Mother-Daughter Relation in Colette, Simone de Beauvoir, and Marguerite Duras*, New York: Peter Lang, 1996.

Dahl, Liisa, 'The Attributive Sentence Structure in the Stream of Consciousness Technique with Special Reference to the Interior Monologue used by Virginia Woolf, Joyce and O'Neill', *Neuphilogische Mitteilungen*, 68, 1967, 440–54.

Damamme, Béatrice, 'Réflexions sur le rôle des démarcateurs de coordination dans les énumérations littéraires', *Le Français Moderne: Revue de Linguistique Français*, 49 (1), January 1981, 20–35.

Derrida, Jacques, *L'Écriture et la différance*, Paris: Seuil, 1967.

Diagnostic and Statistical Manual of Mental Disorders, 4th ed., Washington, DC: American Psychiatric Association, 1994.

Donovan, Josephine, ed., *Feminist Literary Criticism: Explorations in Theory*, Lexington: University Press of Kentucky, 1975.

Eagleton, Mary, ed., *Feminist Literary Theory: A Reader*, Oxford: Basil Blackwell, 1986.

Eagleton, Terry, *Literary Theory: An Introduction*, Oxford: Basil Blackwell, 1983.

Ehrmann, Jacques, 'Simone de Beauvoir and the Related Destinies of Woman and Intellectual,' *Yale French Studies*, 27, 1961, 26–32.

Evans, Martha Noel, *Fits and Starts: A Genealogy of Hysteria in Modern France*, New York: Cornell University Press, 1991.

——, *Masks of Tradition: Women and the Politics of Writing in Twentieth-Century France*, Ithaca: Cornell University Press, 1987.

Evans, Mary, *Simone de Beauvoir: A Feminist Mandarin*, London: Tavistock, 1985.

——, 'Views of Women and Men in the Work of Simone de Beauvoir,' *Women's Studies International Quarterly*, 4, 1980, 395–404.

Everley, Christine, 'War and Alterity in *L'Invitée*,' *Simone de Beauvoir Studies*, 13, 1996, 137–50.

Fallaize, Elizabeth, 'Folie, monologue et nouvelle: "Monologue" de Simone de Beauvoir,' in *La Nouvelle hier et aujourd'hui*, eds. Johnnie Gratton and Jean-Philippe Imbert, Paris: L'Harmattan, 1997, pp. 107–14.

——, 'Narrative Structure in *Les Mandarins*,' in *Literature and Society: Studies in Nineteenth and Twentieth Century French Literature*, ed. C.A. Burns, Birmingham: Goodman, 1980, pp. 221–32.

——, *The Novels of Simone de Beauvoir*, London: Routledge, 1988.

——, 'Resisting Romance: Simone de Beauvoir, "The Woman Destroyed" and the Romance Script,' in *Contemporary French Fiction by Women:*

Feminist Perspectives, eds Atack, Margaret and Phil Powrie, Manchester: Manchester University Press, 1990, pp. 15–25.

Felman, Shoshana, *La Folie et la Chose Littéraire*, Paris: Seuil, 1978; *Writing and Madness (Literature/ Philosophy/Psychoanalysis)*, trans. Martha Noel Evans and the author, with the assistance of Brian Massumi, Palo Alto, California: Stanford University Press, 2003.

———, *La «Folie» dans l'oeuvre romanesque de Stendhal*, Paris: Librairie José Corti, 1971.

Ferguson, Ann, 'Lesbian Identity: De Beauvoir and History,' *Women's Studies International Forum*, 8 (3), 1985, 203–8.

Fishwick, Sarah, *The Body in the Work of Simone de Beauvoir*, Oxford: Peter Lang, 2002.

Foucault, *Histoire de la folie à l'âge classique*, coll. tel, Paris: Gallimard, 1972; *Madness and Civilisation*, trans. Richard Howard, London and New York: Routledge, 1989.

Fowler, Roger, *A Dictionary of Modern Critical Terms*, London: Routledge, 1987.

Francis, Claude and Fernande Gontier, *Les Écrits de Simone de Beauvoir: La vie – L'écriture*, Paris: Gallimard, 1979.

Frédéric, Madeleine, 'Énumération, énumération homologique, énumération chaotique: essai de caractérisation,' in *Styistique, rhétorique et poétique dans les langues romanes*, Actes du XVIIe Congrès international de linguistique et de philologie romanes, (Aix-en-Provence, 1983), vol. 8, Aix-en-Provence: Université de Provence, 1986, 104–17.

Fullbrook, Edward and Kate Fullbrook, *Simone de Beauvoir: A Critical Introduction*, Cambridge: Polity, 1998.

Gallop, Jane, *Feminism and Psychoanalysis: the Daughter's Seduction*, London: Macmillan, 1982.

Gardiner, Judith Kegan, 'On Female Identity and Writing by Women,' in *Writing and Sexual Difference*, ed. Abel, Elizabeth, Brighton: Harvester, 1982, pp. 177–92.

Genette, Gérard, *Figures III*, Paris: Seuil, 1972.

Gilbert, Sandra M. and Susan Gubar, *The Madwoman in the Attic: The Woman Writer and the Nineteenth-Century Literary Imagination*, New Haven: Yale University Press, 1979.

Girard, René, 'Memoirs of a Dutiful Existentialist,' in *Critical Essays on Simone de Beauvoir*, ed. Elaine Marks, Boston: Hall, 1987, pp. 84–8.

Godard, Linda, 'Pour une nouvelle lecture de la question de la "femme": Essai à partir de la pensée de Jacques Derrida,' *Philosophiques*, 12 (1), 1985, 147–64.

Hawkes, Terence, *Structuralism and Semiotics*, London: Methuen, 1977, repr. 1986.

Hawthorn, Jeremy, *A Glossary of Contemporary Literary Theory*, London: Arnold, 1992.

Heath, Jane, *Simone de Beauvoir*, London: Harvester Wheatsheaf, 1989.

Hewitt, Leah D., *Autobiographical Tightropes: Simone de Beauvoir, Nathalie Sarraute, Marguerite Duras, Monique Wittig, and Maryse Condé*, Lincoln: University of Nebraska Press, 1990.

Hibbs, Françoise Arnaud, *L'Espace dans les romans de Simone de Beauvoir: son expression et sa fonction*, Stanford French and Italian Studies 59, Saratoga, California: Anma Libri, 1989.

Holland, Alison T. and Louise Renée, eds., *Simone de Beauvoir's Fiction: Women and Language*, New York: Peter Lang, 2005.

Holly, Marcia, 'Consciousness and Authenticity: Toward a Feminist Aesthetic,' in *Feminist Literary Criticism: Explorations in Theory*, ed. Josephine Donovan, Lexington: University Press of Kentucky, 1975, pp. 38–47.

Holveck, Eleanore, *Simone de Beauvoir's Philosophy of Lived Experience*, Oxford: Rowman & Littlefield, 2002.

Hunter, Diane, 'Hysteria, Psychoanalysis and Feminism: The Case of Anna O,' *Feminist Studies*, 9, 1983, 465–88.

Jardine, Alice, 'Pre-texts for the Transatlantic Feminist', *Yale French Studies*, 62, 1981, 220–36.

Jeanson, Francis, *Simone de Beauvoir ou l'entreprise de vivre*, Paris: Seuil, 1966.

Jung, Carl G., 'Approaching the Unconscious,' in *Man and His Symbols* by Carl G. Jung and M.-L. von Franz, Joseph L. Henderson et al., New York: Dell Publishing, repr. 1979.

Kauffmann, Dorothy, 'Simone de Beauvoir: Questions of Difference and Generation,' *Yale French Studies*, 72, 1986, 121–31.

Keefe, Terry, 'Psychiatry in the Post-War Fiction of Simone de Beauvoir', *Literature and Psychology*, 29 (3), 1979, 123–33 (Reprinted in Elaine Marks, ed., *Critical Essays on Simone de Beauvoir*, Boston: Hall, 1987, pp. 131–43).

———, *Simone de Beauvoir*, Basingstoke: Macmillan, 1998.

———, *Simone de Beauvoir: Les Belles Images*, *La Femme rompue*, Glasgow Introductory Guides to French Literature 12, Glasgow: University of Glasgow French and German Publications, 1991

———, *Simone de Beauvoir: A Study of her Writings*, London: Harrap, 1983.

Kilgour, Maggie, *The Rise of the Gothic Novel*, London: Routledge, 1995.

Kristeva, Julia, *Desire in Language: A Semiotic Approach to Literature and Art*, ed. Leon S. Roudiez, New York: Columbia University Press, 1980.

———, 'A Question of Subjectivity,' An Interview with Susan Sellers, *Women's Review*, Number 12, 19–21.

———, *La Révolution du langage poétique*, Paris: Seuil, 1974.

———, 'Talking about *Polylogue*' in *French Feminist Thought*, ed. Toril Moi, Oxford: Blackwell, 1987, pp. 110–17.

Kruks, Sonia, 'Living on Rails: freedom, Constraint, and Political Judgement in Beauvoir's "Moral" Essays and *Les Mandarins*' in Scholz and Mussett, pp. 67–86.

Langer, Monika, 'Beauvoir and Merleau-Ponty on Ambiguity' in *The Cambridge Companion to Simone de Beauvoir*, ed. Claudia Card, Cambridge: Cambridge University Press, 2003, pp. 87–106.

Lasocki, Anne-Marie, *Simone de Beauvoir ou l'entreprise d'écrire: Essai de commentaire par les textes*, La Haye: Martinus Nijhoff, 1971.

Le Doeuff, Michèle, 'Simone de Beauvoir and Existentialism,' *Feminist Studies*, 6, 1980, 277–89.

Lewis, Matthew G., *The Monk*, (first published in 1795), Oxford: Oxford University Press, 1995.

Loffredo, Susan Marie, 'A Portrait of the Sexes: The Masculine and the Feminine in the Novels of Simone de Beauvoir, Marguerite Duras and Christiane Rochefort,' unpublished doctoral dissertation, Princeton University, 1978.

MacAndrew, Elizabeth, *The Gothic Tradition in Fiction*, New York: Columbia University Press, 1979.

Marks, Elaine, ed., *Critical Essays on Simone de Beauvoir*, Boston: Hall, 1987.

————, 'Introduction', in *Critical Essays on Simone de Beauvoir*, ed. Elaine Marks, Boston: Hall, 1987.

————, *Simone de Beauvoir: Encounters with Death*, New Brunswick, New Jersey: Rutgers University Press, 1973.

————, 'Transgressing the (In)cont(in)ent Boundaries: The Body in Decline,' *Yale French Studies*, 72, 1986, 181–200.

Marks, Elaine and Isabelle de Courtivron, eds, *New French Feminisms: An Anthology*, Brighton: Harvester, 1981.

Marlowe, Christopher. *The Tragical History of Dr. Faustus*. ed. R.G. Lunt. London: Blackie & Son, [n.d.].

McNay, Lois, *Foucault and Feminism: Power, Gender and the Self*, Cambridge: Polity, 1992.

Merleau-Ponty, Maurice, 'Metaphysics and the Novel,' in *Critical Essays on Simone de Beauvoir*, ed. Elaine Marks, Boston: Hall, 1987, pp. 31–44.

Merquoir, J.G., *Foucault*, London: Fontana, 1985.

Miller, Nancy K., *Subject to Change*, New York: Columbia University Press, 1988.

Mitchell, Juliet, 'Femininity, Narrative and Psychoanalysis: Women: The Longest Revolution,' in *Feminist Literary Theory: A Reader*, ed. Mary Eagleton, Oxford: Basil Blackwell, 1986, pp. 100–103.

————, *Psychoanalysis and Feminism: A Radical Reassessment of Freudian Psychoanalysis*, Harmondsworth: Penguin, 1975.

————, 'Simone de Beauvoir, Freud and The Second Sex,' in *Critical Essays on Simone de Beauvoir*, ed. by Elaine Marks, Boston: Hall, 1987, pp. 121–30.

Moers, Ellen, *Literary Women*, London: W.H. Allen, 1977.

Moi, Toril, *Feminist Theory and Simone de Beauvoir*, Oxford: Basil Blackwell, 1990.

————, ed., *French Feminist Thought*, Oxford: Blackwell, 1987.

————, 'Intentions and Effects: Rhetoric and Identification in Simone de Beauvoir's 'The Woman Destroyed,' in Toril Moi, *Feminist Theory and Simone de Beauvoir*, Oxford: Blackwell, 1990.

————, 'Introduction,' in *French Feminist Thought*, ed. Toril Moi, Oxford: Blackwell, 1987, pp. 1–13.

————, ed., *The Kristeva Reader*, Oxford: Blackwell, 1986.

————, *Sexual Textual Politics: Feminist Literary Theory*, London: Methuen, 1985.

————, *Simone de Beauvoir: The Making of an Intellectual Woman*, Oxford: Blackwell, 1994.

Mussett, Shannon M., 'Personal Choice and the Seduction of the Absolute' in Scholz and Mussett, pp. 135–56.

Norris, Christopher, *Deconstruction: Theory and Practice*, London: Methuen, 1982, repr. 1986.

Okely, Judith, *Simone de Beauvoir*, London: Virago, 1986.

Ophir, Anne, *Regards féminins: condition féminine et création littéraire*, Paris: Denoël/ Gontier, 1976.

Pagès, Irène, 'Simone de Beauvoir's *Les Belles Images*: Desubstantification of Reality Through a Narrative', *Forum for Modern Language Studies*, 11, 1975, 133–41.

————, 'Simone de Beauvoir and the New French Feminisms,' *Canadian Woman Studies: Les Cahiers de la Femme*, 6 (1), 1984, 60–62.

Penfold, P.S., 'Women and Depression', *Canadian Journal of Psychiatry*, 26 (1), 1981, 24–31.

Poe, Edgar Allen, 'The Pit and the Pendulum', (first published in 'The Gift,' 1843), in *Tales of Mystery and Imagination*, new edn, London: Dent, 1993, pp. 239–53.

Powrie, Phil, 'Rereading Between The Lines: A Postscript on *La Femme rompue*,' *Modern Language Review*, 87, 1992, 320–29.

Ramazanolu, Caroline, ed., *Up Against Foucault: Exploration of Some Tensions between Foucault and Feminism*, London: Routledge, 1993.

Raoul, Valerie, *The French Fictional Journal: Fictional Narcissism/ Narcissistic Fiction*, Toronto: University of Toronto Press, 1980.

Rigney, Barbara H., *Madness and Sexual Politics in the Feminist Novel: Studies in Brontë, Woolf, Lessing and Atwood*, Madison: University of Wisconsin Press, 1978.

Rimmon-Kenan, Shlomith, *Narrative Fiction: Contemporary Poetics*, London: Methuen, 1983.

Roudiez, Leon S., 'Introduction' in Julia Kristeva, *Desire in Language: A Semiotic Approach to Literature and Art*, ed. Leon S. Roudiez, New York: Columbia University Press, 1980.

Sage, Lorna, *Women in the House of Fiction: Post-War Women Novelists*, London: Macmillan, 1992.

Sankovitch, Tilde, A., *French Women Writers and the Book: Myths of Access and Desire*, Syracuse, New York: Syracuse University Press, 1988.

Sartre, Jean-Paul, Contribution to a 1964 debate on literature published in *Que peut la littérature?*, ed. Yves Buin, Paris: Union Générale d'Éditions, 1965, pp. 107–27.

Scholz, Sally J. and Shannon M. Mussett, eds, *The Contradictions of Freedom: Philosophical Essays on Simone de Beauvoir's 'Les Mandarins'*, New York: State University of New York Press, 2005.

Sedgwick, Eve Kosofsky, *The Coherence of Gothic Conventions*, London: Methuen, 1976.

Sellers, Susan, *Language and Sexual Difference: Feminist Writing in France*, London: Macmillan, 1991.

Shiach, Morag, *Hélène Cixous: A Politics of Writing*, London: Routledge, 1991.

Showalter, Elaine, *The Female Malady: Women, Madness and English Culture 1830–1980*, London: Virago, 1987.

————, ed., *The New Feminist Criticism*, London: Virago, 1986.

Simons, Margaret A., ed., *Feminist Interpretations of Simone de Beauvoir*, Pennsylvania: The Pennsylvania State University Press, 1995.

Squier, Susan, 'Mirroring and Mothering: Reflections on the Mirror Encounter Metaphor in Virginia Woolf's Work,' *Twentieth Century Literature*, 27, 1981, 272–88.

Suleiman, Susan Rubin, 'Simone de Beauvoir and the Writing Self', *L'Esprit créateur*, 29 (4), 1989, 42–51.

Tidd, Ursula, *Simone de Beauvoir: Gender and Testimony*, Cambridge: Cambridge University Press, 1999.

Vintges, Karen, *Philosophy as Passion: The Thinking of Simone de Beauvoir*, Bloomington and Indiapolis: Indiana University Press, 1996.

Viti, Elizabeth, 'A Questionnable Balance: Anne Dubreuilh and the Language of Identity Crisis' in Holland and Renée, pp. 113–35.

Ward Jouve, Nicole, 'Hélène Cixous: From Inner Theatre to World Theatre' in *White Woman Speaks with Forked tongue: Criticism as Autobiography*, ed. Nicole Ward Jouve, London: Routledge, 1990, pp. 91–100.

Wardman, Harold, 'Self-Coincidence and Narrative in *L'Invitée*', *Essays In French Literature*, 19, 1982, 87–103.

Weedon, Chris, *Feminist Practice and Poststructuralist Theory*, Oxford: Basil Blackwell, 1987.

Wharfe, Jill. M., 'Perfect Interlocutors: Intertextuality and Divergence in the Fiction of Simone de Beauvoir and Sartre,' unpublished doctoral thesis, University of Birmingham, 1988.

Winegarten, Renée, *Simone de Beauvoir: A Critical View*, Oxford: Berg, 1988.

Wollheim, Richard, *Freud*, Glasgow: Fontana, 1971.

Index